Transitions in Regional Economic Development

T0271961

At a time of extraordinary challenges confronting the world, this book analyses some of the profound changes occurring in the development of cities and regions. It discusses the uncertainties associated with the stalling of hyper-globalization and asks whether this creates opportunities for resurgent regional economies driven by local capabilities, resource efficiencies and domestic production. Theory and evidence on socio-economic and environmental transitions underway in many regions are brought together. Implications of the shifting balance of global power towards emerging economies in the East are explored, along with the consequences of urbanization in the global South for politics and democracy. Dilemmas surrounding migration are also discussed, including whether incomers displace local workers and depress wages, or bring benefits in the form of know-how, new technology and investment. More integrative concepts of the region and theories of regional development are analysed, recognising the role of human capital, knowledge, innovation, finance, infrastructure and institutions.

This was originally published as a special issue of *Regional Studies.*

Ivan Turok is Executive Director of the Economic Performance and Development Unit, Human Sciences Research Council, South Africa. He is also Honorary Professor at the Universities of Cape Town, South Africa, and Glasgow, UK.

David Bailey is Professor of Industrial Strategy, Economics & Strategy Group, Aston University, UK.

Jennifer Clark is an Associate Professor of Public Policy, Georgia Institute of Technology, USA.

Jun Du is Professor of Economics, Economics & Strategy Group, Aston Business School, Aston University, UK.

Ugo Fratesi is Associate Professor of Regional Economics, Department of Architecture, Built Environment and Construction Engineering, Politecnico di Milano, Italy.

Michael Fritsch is Professor of Economics, Friedrich Schiller University Jena, Germany.

John Harrison is Reader in Human Geography, Department of Geography, Loughborough University, UK.

Tom Kemeny is Lecturer in Human Geography, University of Southampton, UK.

Dieter Kogler is Lecturer in Economic Geography, University College Dublin, Ireland.

Arnoud Lagendijk is Professor of Economic Geography, Radboud University Nijmegen, The Netherlands.

Tomasz Mickiewicz is Professor of Economics, Aston University, Birmingham, UK.

Ernest Miguelez is Junior Researcher, CNRS, GREThA-University of Bordeaux, France.

Stefano Usai is Director of the Centre for North South Economic Research (CRENoS), University of Cagliari, Italy.

Fiona Wishlade is Director of the European Policies Research Centre, University of Strathclyde, Scotland.

Regions and Cities
Series Editor in Chief
Joan Fitzgerald, *Northeastern University, USA*

Editors
Maryann Feldman, *University of North Carolina, USA*
Gernot Grabher, *HafenCity University Hamburg, Germany*
Ron Martin, *University of Cambridge, UK*
Kieran P. Donaghy, *Cornell University, USA*

In today's globalised, knowledge-driven and networked world, regions and cities have assumed heightened significance as the interconnected nodes of economic, social and cultural production, and as sites of new modes of economic and territorial governance and policy experimentation. This book series brings together incisive and critically engaged international and interdisciplinary research on this resurgence of regions and cities, and should be of interest to geographers, economists, sociologists, political scientists and cultural scholars, as well as to policy-makers involved in regional and urban development.

For more information on the Regional Studies Association visit www.regional studies.org

There is a **30% discount** available to RSA members on books in the *Regions and Cities* series, and other subject related Taylor and Francis books and e-books including Routledge titles. To order just e-mail Joanna Swieczkowska, Joanna. Swieczkowska@tandf.co.uk, or phone on +44 (0)20 3377 3369 and declare your RSA membership. You can also visit the series page at www.routledge.com/ Regions-and-Cities/book-series/RSA and use the discount code: **RSA0901**

Transitions in Regional Economic Development

Edited by
**Ivan Turok, David Bailey,
Jennifer Clark, Jun Du, Ugo Fratesi,
Michael Fritsch, John Harrison,
Tom Kemeny, Dieter Kogler,
Arnoud Lagendijk, Tomasz Mickiewicz,
Ernest Miguelez, Stefano Usai and
Fiona Wishlade**

Routledge
Taylor & Francis Group

LONDON AND NEW YORK

First published 2018 by Routledge

2 Park Square, Milton Park, Abingdon, Oxfordshire OX14 4RN
52 Vanderbilt Avenue, New York, NY 10017

Routledge is an imprint of the Taylor & Francis Group, an informa business

First issued in paperback 2019

British Library Cataloguing in Publication Data
A catalogue record for this book is available from the British Library

ISBN 13: 978-1-138-31043-8 (hbk)
ISBN 13: 978-0-367-89170-1 (pbk)

Typeset in Times New Roman
by RefineCatch Limited, Bungay, Suffolk

Publisher's Note
The publisher accepts responsibility for any inconsistencies that may have
arisen during the conversion of this book from journal articles to book chapters,
namely the possible inclusion of journal terminology.

Disclaimer
Every effort has been made to contact copyright holders for their permission to
reprint material in this book. The publishers would be grateful to hear from any
copyright holder who is not here acknowledged and will undertake to rectify
any errors or omissions in future editions of this book.

Contents

Citation Information

The chapters in this book were originally published in *Regional Studies*, volume 51, issue 1 (January 2017). When citing this material, please use the original page numbering for each article, as follows:

Chapter 1
Global reversal, regional revival?
Ivan Turok, David Bailey, Jennifer Clark, Jun Du, Ugo Fratesi, Michael Fritsch, John Harrison, Tom Kemeny, Dieter Kogler, Arnoud Lagendijk, Tomasz Mickiewicz, Ernest Miguelez, Stefano Usai and Fiona Wishlade
Regional Studies, volume 51, issue 1 (January 2017) pp. 1–8

Chapter 2
Contesting European regions
Michael Keating
Regional Studies, volume 51, issue 1 (January 2017) pp. 9–18

Chapter 3
Foregrounding the region
Anssi Paasi and Jonathan Metzger
Regional Studies, volume 51, issue 1 (January 2017) pp. 19–30

Chapter 4
Towards a theory of regional diversification: combining insights from Evolutionary Economic Geography and Transition Studies
Ron Boschma, Lars Coenen, Koen Frenken and Bernhard Truffer
Regional Studies, volume 51, issue 1 (January 2017) pp. 31–45

Chapter 5
Shifting horizons in local and regional development
Andy Pike, Andrés Rodríguez-Pose and John Tomaney
Regional Studies, volume 51, issue 1 (January 2017) pp. 46–57

Chapter 14

Analysing the regional geography of poverty, austerity and inequality in Europe: a human cartographic perspective
Dimitris Ballas, Danny Dorling and Benjamin Hennig
Regional Studies, volume 51, issue 1 (January 2017) pp. 174–185

For any permission-related enquiries please visit:
http://www.tandfonline.com/page/help/permissions

Notes on Contributors

Patrick Adler is a PhD Candidate at the Department of Urban Planning, University of California, Los Angeles, USA.

David Bailey is Professor of Industrial Strategy, Economics & Strategy Group, Aston University, UK.

Dimitris Ballas is Senior Lecturer at the Department of Geography, University of Sheffield, UK.

Ron Boschma is Professor in Regional Economics at the Section of Economic Geography, Urban and Regional Research Centre Utrecht (URU), Faculty of Geosciences, Utrecht University, The Netherlands.

Chia-Lin Chen is based at the Department of Urban Planning and Design, Xi'an Jiaotong-Liverpool University, Jiangsu Province, China.

Jennifer Clark is Associate Professor of Public Policy, Georgia Institute of Technology, USA.

Lars Coenen is a Professor at the Centre for Innovation, Research and Competence in the Learning Economy (CIRCLE), Lund University, Sweden.

Riccardo Crescenzi is a Professor at the Department of Geography and Environment, London School of Economics, UK.

Danny Dorling is a Professor at the School of Geography and the Environment, University of Oxford, UK.

Kathryn R. Dotzel is a PhD Candidate at the Department of Agricultural, Environmental, and Development Economics, The Ohio State University, USA.

Jun Du is Professor of Economics, Economics & Strategy Group, Aston Business School, Aston University, UK.

Michael Dunford is Emeritus Professor of Geography at the University of Sussex, Brighton, UK and Full Professor at Chinese Academy of Sciences, Institute of Geographical Sciences and Natural Resources Research, Beijing, China.

Alessandra Faggian is Associate Professor at the Department of Agricultural, Environmental, and Development Economics, The Ohio State University, USA.

Richard Florida is Director of the Martin Prosperity Institute, and Professor of Business and Creativity at the Rotman School of Management, Martin Prosperity Institute, University of Toronto, Canada.

Ugo Fratesi is Associate Professor of Regional Economics, Department of Architecture, Built Environment and Construction Engineering, Politecnico di Milano, Italy.

Koen Frenken is Professor of Innovation Studies, Copernicus Institute of Sustainable Development, Faculty of Geosciences, Utrecht University, The Netherlands.

Michael Fritsch is Professor of Economics, Friedrich Schiller University Jena, Germany.

David Gibbs is Professor of Human Geography, School of Environmental Sciences, University of Hull, UK.

Edward L. Glaeser is Fred and Eleanor Glimp Professor of Economics at the Department of Economics, Harvard University, Cambridge, USA.

John Harrison is Reader in Human Geography, Department of Geography, Loughborough University, UK.

Benjamin Hennig is Senior Lecturer at the Faculty of Life and Environmental Sciences, School of Engineering and Natural Sciences, University of Iceland.

Simona Iammarino is Professor of Economic Geography and Head of Department at the Department of Geography and Environment, London School of Economics, UK.

Michael Keating is Chair in Scottish Politics at the School of Social Science, University of Aberdeen, UK.

Tom Kemeny is Lecturer in Human Geography, University of Southampton, UK.

Eric Knight is Associate Professor at the University of Sydney Business School, The University of Sydney, Australia.

Dieter Kogler is Lecturer in Economic Geography, University College Dublin, Ireland.

Arnoud Lagendijk is Professor of Economic Geography, Radboud University Nijmegen, The Netherlands.

Weidong Liu is Professor in Economic Geography at the Chinese Academy of Sciences, Institute of Geographical Sciences and Natural Resources Research, China.

Charlotta Mellander is a Professor of Economics, and Director of the Prosperity Institute, at the Department of Economics, Jönköping International Business School, Sweden.

Jonathan Metzger is a Lecturer at the Division of Urban and Regional Studies, School of Architecture and the Built Environment, KTH – Royal Institute of Technology, Sweden.

Tomasz Mickiewicz is Professor of Economics, Aston University, Birmingham, UK.

Ernest Miguelez is Junior Researcher, CNRS, GREThA-University of Bordeaux, France.

Kirstie O'Neill is LSE Fellow in Environment at the Department of Geography and Environment, London School of Economics, UK.

Anssi Paasi is Professor in Geography at the Department of Geography, University of Oulu, Finland.

Andy Pike is Professor of Local and Regional Development, and Director of the Centre for Urban and Regional Development Studies (CURDS) at Newcastle University, UK.

Isha Rajbhandari is a PhD Candidate at the Department of Agricultural, Environmental, and Development Economics, The Ohio State University, USA.

Andrés Rodríguez-Pose is a Professor of Economic Geography at the Department of Geography & Environment, London School of Economics, UK.

Bryce Millett Steinberg is Postdoctoral Fellow in International and Public Affairs, Watson Institute for International and Public Affairs, Brown University, USA.

John Tomaney is Professor of Urban and Regional Planning at the UCL Faculty of the Built Environment, Bartlett School of Planning, UK.

Bernhard Truffer is Department Head at Eawag (Swiss Federal Institute of Aquatic Science and Technology), Department of Environmental Social Science, Switzerland.

Ivan Turok is Executive Director, Economic Performance and Development Unit, Human Sciences Research Council, South Africa, and Honorary Professor, Universities of Cape Town, South Africa, and Glasgow, UK.

Stefano Usai is Director at the Centre for North South Economic Research (CRENoS), University of Cagliari, Italy.

Roger Vickerman is Professor of European Economics at the School of Economics; he is also Dean for Europe, both at the University of Kent, UK.

Fiona Wishlade is Director of the European Policies Research Centre, University of Strathclyde, UK.

Dariusz Wójcik is Professor of Economic Geography and Director of Graduate Studies (Research) at the School of Geography and the Environment, Oxford University Centre for the Environment, University of Oxford, UK.

Global reversal, regional revival?

Ivan Turok, David Bailey, Jennifer Clark, Jun Du, Ugo Fratesi, Michael Fritsch, John Harrison, Tom Kemeny, Dieter Kogler, Arnoud Lagendijk, Tomasz Mickiewicz, Ernest Miguelez, Stefano Usai and Fiona Wishlade

Regional Studies celebrates its 50th anniversary with this special issue. This introductory article reflects back on developments since the journal was started and offers signposts for urban and regional research looking ahead. It outlines the changing global context for regional studies and identifies some of the ways in which the need for regional research is enhanced by the extraordinary challenges currently confronting the world. It also introduces important themes from the recent history of the journal that are likely to feature in future. This is obviously a highly selective exercise, given the considerable breadth and depth of regional research over the years.

Regional Studies was launched into a very different environment where regions and nations were more self-contained and there was little dispute that space, place and proximity really mattered. There were no personal computers and no containerized transport, let alone the internet and digital devices enabling instantaneous sharing of information around the world. In the global North this was an optimistic era of full employment, rising prosperity, and diminishing social and spatial inequalities. It was also a period of relative political stability and ignorance of global warming, although the Cold War and nuclear threats loomed large, and there was growing unrest in many countries in the global South. In the North, capital and labour markets were closely regulated, and social protection systems were extensive. Regional studies was a new academic field, with very few journals focused on the development of sub-national territories.

Circumstances have changed radically since then. 'Globalization' sums up many influential trends, typified by the interconnection of regions and nations through cross-border flows of trade, capital, labour, technology and information. The increasing openness of territorial boundaries and the integration of world markets have rewarded highly skilled groups, well-positioned city-regions and selected emerging economies, illustrated by the burgeoning of manufacturing in the Asian Tigers and China. However, freer trade and financial deregulation have also been accompanied by economic volatility and financial instability. Deindustrialization, privatization and welfare reductions in many advanced economies have enlarged social and spatial inequalities and left low- and middle-income groups worse off than before.

Falling transport costs, heightened human mobility and new communications technologies have prompted many economists to predict the death of distance and the demise of cities and regions. Geographers have recognized that conditions have changed by proposing a more permeable, fluid concept of the region, and focusing more on the shifting flows, movements and relationships between regions. Intensified competition for trade, talent and multinational investment has amplified regional disparities by raising the stakes for winning, and leaving less-favoured people and places further behind, bearing the costs of adjustment in lower wages and lost jobs, and fuelling a sense of injustice (Ballas, Dorling, & Hennig, 2017, in this issue). Regional research has become a broader, multidimensional endeavour, combining knowledge and insights from a range of disciplines beyond economic geography.

Since the financial crisis of 2008 and the protracted period of sluggish and unequal growth, the impetus to hyper-globalization has stalled. The frailty of most advanced economies, financial austerity and a shift in the balance of global power towards emerging economies in the East have provoked anxiety and frustration in the West (Dunford & Liu, 2016, in this issue). People have felt buffeted by forces beyond their control and questioned the benefits of intertwined world markets. Resentment towards new waves of immigration and international institutions has risen, epitomized by Britain's vote to exit Europe, despite the broad economic consensus that this is not in the national interest. Global trade and capital flows have been pushed into reverse by rising protectionism and the dismantling of free-trade agreements. Tough patriotic sentiments are partly responsible for large financial penalties imposed on foreign multinationals such as Apple, Google, Deutsche Bank, Volkswagen and BP. At the very time when international cooperation is required to mitigate the risks of climate change, illicit financial flows, escalating refugee crises and mounting threats to security and peace, popular opinion seems to favour going it alone. Enlightened thinking also risks being crowded out by uncompromising – even chauvinistic – reactions to unfolding events.

The implications for cities and regions of the fracturing of the international order are highly uncertain. Resurgent popular nationalism would have profound consequences for all territories by inhibiting foreign direct investment (FDI), external trade and access to scarce skills, and forcing more reliance on local capabilities and domestic production. Some argue that a reversal of globalization would dampen economic progress and suppress opportunities for the world's poorest places and populations. Alternatively, patriotic impulses that challenge ossified structures and global cartels could provoke a resurgence of regional enterprise and organic growth. Well-conceived policy reforms that disrupt business inertia could engender another Schumpeterian wave of innovation and creativity based on smaller-scale production. Dynamic regional multipliers might be spurred by efforts to localize resource flows so as to secure the supply of food and scarce materials, to cut energy consumption and to regenerate degraded ecosystems. Enhanced democratic constraints on business short-termism may also curb financial speculation and encourage longer-term investment in the real economy.

Furthermore, international disengagement might serve to bolster local and regional identities and renew a sense of place and belonging. This could elevate the obligations on civic leaders and rebuild confidence in the role of city and regional institutions. Against this, heightened perceptions of fear and insecurity could foster a 'new tribalism' through separatist movements, ethnic tensions, insurgent splinter groups and other inward-looking forces that escalate conflict and pull countries and regions apart. Much depends on whether democratic institutions are capable of responding to the genuine concerns of citizens and can meld different interests and values together in pursuit of shared agendas and collective solutions. Meanwhile, if the Paris climate deal leads to restrictions on fossil fuel extraction in favour of clean energy, this could make many regions reliant on oil, gas and coal reserves vulnerable to stranded assets and obsolete power generation systems. The case for regional studies is accentuated rather than diminished in all these scenarios. Systematic analyses of how different territories are adapting to the unravelling of globalization and introducing more holistic and resilient strategies to cope with the turbulence are urgently needed.

Over the last three decades, global integration has favoured selected metropolitan regions as strategic nodes in international networks of financial, trade and information flows. Dense agglomerations have functioned as knowledge hubs and magnets of entrepreneurial dynamism, thereby spurring wider productivity improvements and prosperity (Florida, Adler & Mellander, 2016, in this issue). Major city-regions with far-sighted leadership challenge nations as economic entities and demand enhanced powers and resources to lead the recovery and promote more robust growth. The new conventional wisdom suggests that compact and connected cities drive competitiveness, cohesion and sustainable development (Buck, Gordon, Harding, & Turok, 2005). Yet this is far from straightforward or inevitable. Addressing urban infrastructure deficits, integrating migrant populations through affordable housing, and mitigating spiralling carbon emissions presents a formidable policy agenda for which most city governments are ill-prepared. Traditional bureaucracies also lack the agility and capacity for cooperation and learning required to meet complex contemporary challenges. Taking a fashionable example, driverless cars could reduce congestion, improve efficiency, transform the urban environment and save many lives. Yet introducing this technology requires many subtle policy changes which depend on city and national authorities working hand in hand with car-makers and other interests to agree new safety standards, liability issues and more responsive regulatory procedures.

Meanwhile, the rural–urban transition in the global South has emerged as an exceptional opportunity to transform the structure of economies based on agriculture and mineral resources, and to raise living standards across the board. Yet, the scale and rate of urbanization in Africa and Asia are daunting challenges to avoid dysfunction and disaster if population growth in sprawling mega-cities continues to outstrip industrialization and local government's capacity to manage the process through coordinated investments in land, infrastructure and housing (Turok, 2016). Concentrated populations can spur economic progress and political reform through the pressure for change and necessity-driven innovation (Glaeser & Steinberg, 2017, in this issue). Yet overcrowded human settlements can also foment social conflict over competition for scarce resources and vulnerability to flooding, fire, disease and other environmental hazards. There is a sizeable research agenda to understand the physical and institutional conditions required to ensure that urbanization fosters broad-based development, while avoiding the degradation and exploitation experienced historically in the North.

These socio-economic, spatial and environmental trajectories and transitions provide fertile terrain for theoretical development and empirical research. The character and determinants of lasting prosperity are bound to vary in different contexts, but not enough is known about how and why. Theories of economic development have variously and separately emphasized the importance of resource endowments, physical infrastructure, finance and productive investment, skills and human capital, advanced knowledge and innovation, and the quality of public institutions and leadership. The synergies between them are clearer and more concrete at the city and regional levels than at the national level. The respective roles of the state and market are also likely to vary in different circumstances, but in ways that are poorly understood and articulated at present. Neither exists in a vacuum or in an abstract 'national' space. A more balanced and interactive relationship between government, private sector and civil society may be important to come to terms with the wicked problems outlined above.

What follows is a selection of key themes that have featured prominently in *Regional Studies* in recent years and that are likely to be influential in future. The editors' choice of topics is reflected in the papers selected for publication in this special issue.

THE CONCEPT AND POLITICS OF THE REGION

Despite sustained interrogation, the region remains an elusive concept with multiple meanings (Keating, 2016, in this issue). The debates over regions surround what and where they are; why and how they are there; and what they do and for whom they do it. These questions occupy academics and policy-makers like never before, in places and settings that demonstrate the growing significance of the region in many different realms (Paasi & Metzger, 2016, in this issue). Basic concerns relating to how we interrogate regions and regional development remain central. Emergent thinking challenges any notion that there is a singular logic for regions. It is vital for researchers to explore the raison d'être and diverse forms of such places and social constructs (Agnew, 2013).

This is apparent in the twin drivers of territorial change – economic and political – which remain at the heart of advancing regional studies. Over the last decade there has been significant effort to go beyond the classic territorial–relational divide, such that regions are seen as the outcome of both external relationships and internal territorial processes. The geographical extension and internationalization of regional studies are also noteworthy in bringing forward new knowledge and challenging established ideas. Accounts of Southern urbanism have done much to enliven recent debates (e.g., Lawhon, Silver, Ernstson, & Pierce, 2016; Roy, 2011); their new insights provoking researchers to reflect on how theories and concepts are shaped by geographical and political contexts (Peck, 2015).

Paasi and Metzger (2016, in this issue) take up the challenge of conceptualizing the region. All new approaches tend to criticize previous ideas for reducing or reifying the region in some way. Drawing on a Latourian reading of actor–network theory (ANT), they ask searching questions about who or what is ascribing region-ality to an entity, how and why they are doing this, and what this concept actually does, or means, as a result? The implications are threefold: (1) it is a timely reminder that it is never the spatial form that acts, but rather social actors embedded in particular spatial forms who act; (2) emphasizing the role of agency and interests in regionalization processes reinforces the need for accounts grounded in everyday social practices; and (3) the regional studies community should enact and perform regional studies in such a way that its own research practices are open to scrutiny.

Keating (2016, in this issue) deepens the idea of construction in how regions are conceptualized and operationalized. Six frames are presented as drivers of polit-ical and institutional change, and keys for analysing the main dimensions of regionalism. Each frame is underpinned by different logics which, because they point in different directions, provide divergent outlooks on how regionalism should be practised. Often at work in the same places, this paper acts as a timely intervention demonstrating how conflicts are worked out in the realm of politics, which remains an important focus for regional studies.

The rapid pace of internationalization means that local and regional develop-ment is now recognized as a global concern. Pike, Rodríguez-Pose, & Tomaney (2016, in this issue) trace the evolution of thinking about territorial development over the last 50 years. They note that practices vary greatly, despite globalizing trends. More importantly, the experience of regionalism and the impacts of devel-opment are increasingly uneven too. Researchers retain an important role in improving the evidence base to inform more progressive, spatially balanced outcomes for localities and regions.

ENTREPRENEURSHIP IN A REGIONAL CONTEXT

Regional Studies has been a vital forum for debates about regional entrepreneur-ship, with special issues published in 1984, 1994, 2004 and 2014 (Fritsch & Storey, 2014). Efforts to understand the determinants of regional entrepreneurship have benefited from positioning the spatial context alongside the personality traits of business founders, their social relations and the degree of acceptance of self-employment within their regions (Kibler, Kautonen, & Fink, 2014; Westlund, Larsson, & Olsson, 2014). Important research has also been undertaken on entre-preneurship as a route out of poverty (Frankish, Roberts, Coad, & Storey, 2014), and the role of new business formation in stimulating regional competition, productivity and innovation (e.g., Berlemann & Jahn, 2015; Brixy, 2014).

An unresolved issue that warrants further research is to distinguish between different types of new business, and to identify innovative and knowledge-inten-sive start-ups that play a distinctive role in regional growth. Florida et al. (2016, in this issue) propose this line of investigation by bringing together city context, radical innovation and the formation of impactful new firms. They situate Jane Jacobs alongside Joseph Schumpeter at origins of entrepreneurship theory. A systemic analysis of the performance of different types of start-ups could usefully incorporate a region's historical development, industrial structure, ownership structure and availability of resources (Szerb, Acs, Autio, Ortega-Argilés, & Komlósi, 2013). Multilevel analyses linking individual attributes – family background, education, employment history, personality etc. – to their regional context would be invaluable for improved academic understanding and policy purposes.

Another promising avenue for research involves combining entrepreneurship with emerging analysis of the quality of institutions (Rodríguez-Pose & Garcilazo, 2015). Multiple attributes need to be incorporated, including formal institutions, social capital, culture and traditions. Since formal systems such as tax laws and labour market regulations tend to be uniform across each country, the informal institutions are particularly relevant. Recent analyses have revealed a surprising persistence of entrepreneurship levels over long periods (Fritsch & Wyrwich, 2014). This seems to be conducive to resilience against external shocks and to promote regional growth (Glaeser, Kerr, & Kerr, 2015). The regional culture of entrepreneurship seems important, but poorly understood. Sizeable variations also exist in countries with dispersed spatial structures and federal political systems. This is even more pronounced in emerging economies, where regional entrepreneurship research remains undeveloped.

THE GEOGRAPHY OF INNOVATION

Entrepreneurship is often associated with innovation, and recent literature on the sources of economic growth leaves little doubt that this is a key driver of national and regional prosperity. *Regional Studies* has published many papers on regional innovation activity and technological change. Policies to stimulate development often assume that highly ranked regions offer templates that can be applied elsewhere. There are many fallacies in such an approach, including disregarding the unique conditions in each region which generate distinctive capacities and patterns of specialization over time. A best-practice approach also neglects how actors involved in creating new ideas are embedded in complex regional and international networks of production and value creation. These are not easily reproduced or transferred elsewhere.

Theories of economic development would benefit from shifting away from a top-down perspective towards more of a bottom-up approach where knowledge production, creativity and entrepreneurship are the starting points and prosperity is the outcome. Recent research in Evolutionary Economic Geography offers fresh insights in this regard by examining how knowledge production is translated into regional economic fortunes (Kogler, 2015). It starts with regional scientific and technological competencies that develop into place-specific development trajectories (Boschma & Martin, 2010; Kogler, Rigby, & Tucker, 2013). The emphasis is on understanding the factors leading to knowledge production and then analysing the dynamics leading to the introduction and diffusion of novel products and processes.

Many studies in the field of regional innovation currently focus on large cities, especially those considered to be exemplars of strong performance. Although cities may be 'innovation machines' (Florida et al., 2016, in this issue) that drive the development of nations, other locations may also generate new knowledge with the potential to initiate technological change (Glückler, 2014). Moreover, some cities are more innovative than others, and this varies between countries and continents. It may be that development theories need more careful adaptation to different contexts (Roy, 2011; Scott & Storper, 2015). An important avenue for future research pertains to the role of networks in fostering innovation. The contribution of public entities to initiating and supporting innovation is also frequently underestimated.

Universities have always been important sites for knowledge production, traditionally focused on basic research and educating graduates. Contemporary universities are also expected to engage in entrepreneurial activities, but can get caught between supply-push and demand-pull approaches to innovation. Spin-off and start-up activities are popular areas of research, yet lacking an understanding of the transfer mechanisms between basic science and applied research (Feldman & Kogler, 2010). The role of entrepreneurs is particularly important – the interplay between individuals, institutions and local knowledge potential offers fresh insights into innovation processes at large.

GLOBAL NETWORKS

Debates about the relative importance of economic relationships within and between regions date back to the seminal contribution of Alfred Marshall. Recent research has emphasized the need to locate regions in their wider context and to recognize forms of proximity other than geographical. Linkages and networks that channel knowledge across space through cognitive, organizational and social dimensions play crucial roles as complements to, or substitutes for, physical proximity. The extent to which economic trajectories are shaped by local interactions ('buzz') or global connections ('pipelines') will vary between different types of locality, activity and actors involved.

Multinationals may be uniquely placed to influence both local and global scenarios. Their relationship to regions has been mostly studied through the lens of global production networks (Coe & Yeung, 2015), where global value chains and connectivity chains are understood in relation to the loci of value creation. This is a crucial issue with the extension of FDI from manufacturing to services, which now represent the majority of total flows. Emerging economies also play an increasingly important role in FDI. They tend to concentrate on neighbouring countries, which gives rise to complex spatial structures. South–South linkages are also growing, exemplified by China's expanding investments in agriculture, mining and industrial production in Africa.

Regional development is shaped by increasingly complex flows of different forms, strengths and directions (Crescenzi & Iammarino, 2017, in this issue). The connectivity networks of regions allow economic agents to gain access to knowledge diffused from elsewhere, and thereby capture some of the benefits of knowledge creation processes, which tend to be more highly concentrated. Such insights represent advances on the traditional FDI literature, which has tended to focus on the factors that make regions attractive to external investment.

The role of finance in regional development has been neglected compared with manufacturing and services. Research has focused on locational decisions without interrogating the peculiarities of this sector, such as the uncertainty and imperfect information characterizing financial procedures. Understanding the geography of finance requires knowledge of the internal mechanisms of such organizations, as well as the traditional tools of regional analysis. Knight and Wojcik (2016, in this issue) extend the concept of financial information beyond the usual transactions between firms to include more strategic information in relation to resource allocation and product and process innovation. This provides a finer-grained and more dynamic perspective on the activities of financial institutions. Their decisions about whether to invest or disinvest, and where to locate their headquarters and other operations, have major impacts at the regional scale and are based on a combination of the external environment and internal strategies.

MIGRATION AND MOBILITY

Record inflows of asylum-seekers and economic migrants to Europe and elsewhere in recent years have pushed migration to the forefront of many political agendas. The sensitivity of large-scale migration makes it imperative to strengthen the evidence base in the face of prejudice and misinformation. A better understanding might assist policy-makers to move beyond a reactive approach and towards strategies that promote integration. Key themes for research include the root causes, mechanisms and consequences of migration for sending and receiving regions, the diverse social composition of migration flows and the role of temporary migration. *Regional Studies* has a strong track record of publishing work on regional migration, including the implications for territorial development. Lack of reliable, comparable migration data has been a perennial constraint.

The migration of highly skilled and qualified people, such as graduates, scientists, engineers, senior managers and entrepreneurs, has been of particular interest in recent years because of their disproportionate economic impact (Kubis & Schneider, 2015). Research has explored the determinants of their geographical mobility and the consequences for the flow of expertise and ideas between regions (Iammarino & Marinelli, 2015; Krabel & Flöther, 2014; Nifo & Vecchione, 2014). A longstanding question has been whether human capital is attracted more by the quality of local amenities or the availability of jobs. Another major debate has concerned the impact of migration on the regional economy, including whether incomers displace local workers and depress wages, or bring benefits in the form of know-how, new technology and investment (Faggian, Rajbhandari, & Dotzel, 2017, in this issue).

Despite the improved understanding of human capital mobility, many issues require further research. Outstanding questions surround the principal sources of attraction of those who generate knowledge and ideas, and the processes by which they migrate. Temporary migration is a neglected topic, enabling the circulation of information and expertise, and the building of relationships between regions. It can take many forms, including research visits by scientists to other laboratories, exchange programmes by professionals and academics, expatriate workers sent to foreign subsidiaries, and short-term migration to acquire skills and work experience. More research is also needed on the consequences of mobility for the regions left behind, including the long-term effects of a brain drain and loss of economic dynamism. The tendency to devolve powers over education and training policy to regional and local governments could discourage investment in people if they simply migrate elsewhere afterwards. Yet skilled migration can also benefit the sending region through the return flows of ideas, skills and techniques, and the potential to establish economic linkages across regions (Faggian et al., 2017, in this issue). The shifting trajectories of migration movements and the socio-economic and political barriers to refugee integration are other themes for investigation.

INFRASTRUCTURE AND REGIONAL DEVELOPMENT

Infrastructure has long been a focus of policies to bolster regional development. These investments are often highly visible and politically attractive, but because of their large-scale character, they pose risks of major cost overruns, environmental damage and overstated developmental effects. Public procurement provides an economic stimulus generating many jobs and other spinoffs during their construction. The completed projects are intended to produce more efficient, liveable and safer cities and regions that encourage private investment, as long as the costs are not prohibitive and the infrastructure is maintained and renewed before it decays. Many of these schemes are transport related. Chen and Vickerman (2016, in this issue) focus on a comparison of high-speed rail (HSR) projects in China and the UK. They identify methodological challenges in evaluating such projects, highlighting how methods have evolved from simple cost–benefit analyses to more sophisticated efforts to distinguish different scales of economic impact (local, regional, national) and incorporate enhancements in economic performance achieved through efficiencies, accessibility and agglomeration.

Regional Studies has a particular interest in the spatial distribution of the beneficiaries of infrastructure investments. Chen and Vickerman demonstrate that HSR often makes core areas more accessible at the expense of peripheral regions, which remain passed over (or passed through) places. The development promised by advocates of HSR accrues to advanced regions with the capacity to absorb the accessibility advantages. More widespread benefits would require additional investments in connectivity to local networks and careful integration of HSR stations into local land-use plans to ensure coherent urban development. This echoes the message of urban planning that investment in subways, light rail, trams and bus rapid transport systems need to be aligned with other sectoral and spatial plans. It is apparent in the burgeoning interest in higher density, mixed-use transit-oriented development.

The role of infrastructure in regional development also covers information and communications technologies (ICTs). These are vital to regional competitiveness, including globally connected cities as well as peripheral regions. The role of the public sector is more ambiguous in ICT investments than in transport or utilities such as water and sanitation, where the state is often the only actor with the authority and resources to deliver the required facilities at scale. The 'smart cities' discourse merges ICT and urban infrastructure, and reflects the transition to thinking about accessibility and efficiency as a matter of mitigating the costs of movement of people and goods, including the environmental damage. The state performs a sophisticated and dynamic role as a regulator, funder and user of these schemes. Research can make an important contribution in establishing appropriate evaluation criteria, in analysing the consequences of smart city investments for urban productivity, liveability and sustainability, and in providing feedback to promote policy learning and improvement over time.

THE TRANSITION TO A GREEN ECONOMY

Environmental research and policy has mirrored the trajectory of *Regional Studies* in shifting from a local to a global orientation. It is no longer sufficient to analyse and manage the use of natural resources and consequential environmental degradation at the local and regional scales. Globalization has been accompanied by a rapid increase in the extraction and consumption of fossil fuels, minerals, biomass, water, agricultural land, forests and biodiversity (Bringezu et al., 2016). The new sustainable development goals require all countries to measure progress towards more efficient and enduring use of these resources, which will in turn require ambitious efforts to drive more responsible behaviour by firms, industries, households and governments (Graute, 2016). Stronger global conventions and governance arrangements may be needed to monitor and regulate the production and consumption of natural resources in order to mitigate the harm for local communities, ecosystems, economies and the planet as a whole. Without this broader perspective, the environmental burdens could easily be displaced from wealthy regions onto weaker and poorer places.

The coincidence of looming environmental threats with the global economic slowdown and rising social inequality has prompted a search for broad-based and mutually beneficial policy responses. The green economy is one of the umbrella concepts (along with the circular economy or low-carbon economy) that could draw together diverse sectoral, economic and territorial interests around a shared agenda (Borel-Saladin & Turok, 2013). It offers a positive vision of the future, in contrast to the apocalyptic perspective common in the environmental literature. It promises a targeted economic stimulus to launch the transition to a low-carbon, more equitable economy, and to spur long-term prosperity based on new technologies and improvements in resource efficiency. This recognizes that things can be done to reverse the destruction of ecosystems while simultaneously improving human well-being. The emphasis is on pursuing the combined benefits of interactions between the economy and the environment, rather than accepting trade-offs and compromises. A good example is the idea of shifting from the current system of production and consumption, which is based on a linear process from natural resource extraction to waste, towards a more circular economy encompassing repair, reassembly, refurbishment and recycling.

Gibbs and O'Neill (2016, in this issue) confirm the significance of the green economy for regional development, but with an important caveat. When environmental concerns are addressed, this often takes the form of 'green-washing', i.e., thinly veiled versions of business as usual. Rather than launching a process of social and environmental transformation, the priorities of green economy initiatives may be much more limited in practice and remain locked into established techniques and paradigms. To induce genuine change, green economy schemes need to be grounded within a broader transition framework (Boschma, Coenen, Frenken, & Truffer, 2017, in this issue). Cities and regions can play prominent roles by promoting innovative niches oriented to alternative forms of production and consumption. They may prompt important changes in the regime level of rules and institutions by experimenting with different regulations. This may alter the various relationships that enable and accelerate the transition. Local niches can thereby foster shifts in the paradigm and establish important milestones in progressing towards more resilient and sustainable futures (Boschma et al., 2017, in this issue).

This seems some way off at present. Gibbs and O'Neill (2016, in this issue) provide telling examples of how radical initiatives concerned with slow food and de-growth can move beyond local niches and act as symbols of broader change. Yet, can such practices really have wider, paradigmatic consequences? Multiple local practices may be able to bind many different places together in a shared transition trend, thereby extending niches from the local to global level. However, moving beyond such niches to influence broader systems is extremely challenging. Deeper transitions may require political advocacy going beyond green initiatives and transitions research. *Regional Studies* may have a valuable role to play in exploring the interaction between economic, technological, institutional and political systems at different scales to yield novel insights which facilitate real progress in moving towards more sustainable and inclusive economies.

CONCLUSIONS

A 50th anniversary is a significant landmark in the development of any institution. This special issue is an opportunity to review how *Regional Studies* has developed over time and where it is heading. It deliberately sets out to reflect on what can and should be learnt from past urban and regional research, and to be agenda-setting by including ideas at the forefront of regional thinking. It outlines the changing global context of regional studies and some of the factors that are bound to influence the journal's development. A novel feature is the collaboration between many established academics and emerging scholars from across the world to share knowledge and incorporate different perspectives. Above all, the special issue calls for a greater awareness of the shifting international environment for regional studies and identifies some of the key strategic concerns facing regional development theory and policy.

DISCLOSURE STATEMENT

No potential conflict of interest was reported by the authors.

REFERENCES

Agnew, J. A. (2013). Arguing with regions. *Regional Studies*, *47*(1), 6–17. doi:10.1080/00 343404.2012.676738

Ballas, D., Dorling, D., & Hennig, B. (2017) Analysing the regional geography of poverty, austerity and inequality in Europe: A human cartographic perspective, *Regional Studies*. doi:10.1080/00343404.2016.1262019

Berlemann, M., & Jahn, V. (2015). Regional importance of Mittelstand firms and innovation performance. *Regional Studies*, *49*, 1819–1833.

Borel-Saladin, J., & Turok, I. (2013). The Green economy: Incremental change or transformation? *Environmental Policy and Governance*, *23*, 209–220. doi:10.1002/eet.1614

Boschma, R., Coenen, L., Frenken, K., & Truffer, B. (2017). Towards a theory of regional diversification: combining insights from Evolutionary Economic Geography and Transition Studies. *Regional Studies*. doi:10.1080/00343404.2016.1258460

Boschma, R. A., & Martin, R. L. (Eds.). (2010). *Handbook of evolutionary economic geography*. Chichester: Edward Elgar.

Bringezu, S., Potocnik, J., Schandl, H., Lu, Y., Ramaswami, A., Swilling, M., & Suh, S. (2016). Multi-scale governance of sustainable natural resource use – challenges and opportunities for monitoring and institutional development at national and global level. *Sustainability*, *8*, 778–803. doi:10.3390/su8080778

Brixy, U. (2014). The significance of entry and exit for regional productivity growth. *Regional Studies*, *48*, 1051–1070. doi:10.1080/00343404.2014.895804

Buck, I., Gordon, I., Harding, A., & Turok, I. (Eds.). (2005). *Changing cities: Rethinking urban competitiveness, cohesion and governance*. London: Palgrave.

Chen, C., & Vickerman, R. (2016). Can transport infrastructure change regions' economic fortunes?: Some evidence from Europe and China. *Regional Studies*. doi:10.1080/0034 3404.2016.1262017

Coe, N. M., & Yeung, H. W. (2015). *Global production networks: Theorizing economic development in an interconnected world*. http://doi.org/10.1093/acprof :oso/9780198703907.001.0001

Crescenzi, R., & Iammarino, S. (2017). Global investments and regional development trajectories: The missing links. *Regional Studies*. doi:10.1080/00343404.2016.1262016

Dunford, M., & Liu, W. (2016). Uneven and combined development. *Regional Studies*. doi:10.1080/00343404.2016.1262946

Faggian, A., Rajbhandari, I., & Dotzel, K. R. (2017). The interregional migration of human capital and its regional consequences: a review. *Regional Studies*. doi:10.1080/0034340 4.2016.1263388

Feldman, M. P., & Kogler, D. F. (2010). Stylized facts in the geography of innovation. In B. Hall, & N. Rosenberg (Eds.), *Handbook of the economics of innovation* (pp. 381–410). Oxford: Elsevier.

Florida, R., Adler, P., & Mellander, C. (2016). The city as innovation machine. *Regional Studies*. doi:10.1080/00343404.2016.1255324

Frankish, J. S., Roberts, R. G., Coad, A., & Storey, D. J. (2014). Is entrepreneurship a route out of deprivation? *Regional Studies*, 48, 1090–1107. doi:10.1080/00343404.2013.871384

Fritsch, M., & Storey, D. J. (2014). Entrepreneurship in a regional context: Historical roots, recent developments and future challenges. *Regional Studies*, 48, 939–954. doi:10.1080 /00343404.2014.892574

Fritsch, M., & Wyrwich, M. (2014). The long persistence of regional levels of entrepreneurship: Germany, 1925–2005. *Regional Studies*, 48, 955–973. doi:10.1080/00343404 .2013.816414

Gibbs, D., & O'Neill, K. (2016). Future green economies and regional development: A research agenda. *Regional Studies*. doi:10.1080/00343404.2016.1255719

Glaeser, E., & Steinberg, B. (2017). Transforming cities: does urbanization promote democratic change?. *Regional Studies*. doi:10.1080/00343404.2016.1262020

Glaeser, E. L., Kerr, S. K., & Kerr, W. K. (2015). Entrepreneurship and urban growth: An empirical assessment with historical mines. *Review of Economics and Statistics*, 97, 498–520. doi:10.1162/REST_a_00456

Glückler, J. (2014). How controversial innovation succeeds in the periphery? A network perspective of BASF Argentina. *Journal of Economic Geography*, 14(5), 903–927. doi:10.1093/jeg/lbu016

Graute, U. (2016). Local authorities acting globally for sustainable development. *Regional Studies*, 50(11), 1931–1942. doi:10. 1080/00343404.2016.1161740

Iammarino, S., & Marinelli, E. (2015). Education–job (mis)match and interregional migration: Italian university graduates' transition to work. *Regional Studies*, 49, 866–882. doi: 10.1080/00343404.2014.965135

Keating, M. (2016). Contesting European regions. *Regional Studies*. doi:10.1080/0034340 4.2016.1227777

Kibler, E., Kautonen, T., & Fink, M. (2014). Regional social legitimacy of entrepreneurship: Implications for entrepreneurial intention and start-up behaviour. *Regional Studies*, 48, 995–1015. doi:10.1080/00343404.2013.851373

Knight, E., & Wojcik, D. (2016). Geographical linkages in the financial services industry: a dialogue with organizational studies. *Regional Studies*. doi:10.1080/00343404.2016.125 4768

Kogler, D. F. (2015). Editorial: Evolutionary Economic Geography – Theoretical and empirical progress. *Regional Studies*, 49(5), 705–711. doi:10.1080/00343404.2015.1033178

Kogler, D. F., Rigby, D. L., & Tucker, I. (2013). Mapping knowledge space and technological relatedness in U.S. cities. *European Planning Studies*, 21(9), 1374–1391. doi:10 .1080/09654313.2012.755832

Krabel, S., & Flöther, C. (2014). Here today, gone tomorrow? Regional labour mobility of German university graduates. *Regional Studies*, 48, 1609–1627. doi:10.1080/00343404. 2012.739282

Kubis, A., & Schneider, L. (2015). Regional migration, growth and convergence – A spatial dynamic panel model of Germany. *Regional Studies*, 0, 1–15.

Lawhon, M., Silver, J., Ernstson, H., & Pierce, J. (2016). Unlearning (un)located ideas in the provincialization of urban theory. *Regional Studies*, *50*(9), 1611–1622. doi:10.1080/00343404.2016.1162288

Nifo, A., & Vecchione, G. (2014). Do institutions play a role in skilled migration? The case of Italy. *Regional Studies*, *48*, 1628–1649. doi:10.1080/00343404.2013.835799

Paasi, A., & Metzger, J. (2016). Foregrounding the region. *Regional Studies*. doi:10.1080/00343404.2016.1239818

Peck, J. (2015). Cities beyond compare? *Regional Studies*, *49*(1), 160–182. doi:10.1080/00343404.2014.980801

Pike, A., Rodríguez-Pose, A., & Tomaney, J. (2016). Shifting horizons in local and regional development. *Regional Studies*. doi:10. 1080/00343404.2016.1158802

Rodríguez-Pose, A., & Garcilazo, E. (2015). Quality of government and the returns of investment: Examining the impact of cohesion expenditure in European regions. *Regional Studies*, *49*, 1274–1290. doi:10.1080/00343404.2015.1007933

Roy, A. (2011). Slumdog cities: Rethinking subaltern urbanism. *International Journal of Urban and Regional Research*, *35*(2), 223–238. doi:10.1111/j.1468-2427.2011.01051.x

Scott, A. J., & Storper, M. (2015). The nature of cities: The scope and limits of urban theory. *International Journal of Urban and Regional Research*, *39*(1), 1–15. doi:10.1111/1468-2427.12134

Szerb, L., Acs, Z. J., Autio, E., Ortega-Argilés, R., & Komlósi, E. (2013). *REDI: The regional entrepreneurship and development index – measuring regional entrepreneurship, final report*. Brussels: European Commission, Directorate-General for Regional and Urban policy. doi:10.2776/79241

Turok, I. (2016). Getting urbanisation to work in Africa: The role of the urban land–infrastructure–finance nexus. *Area Development and Policy*, *1*(1), 30–47. doi:10.1080/23792949.2016.1166444

Westlund, H., Larsson, J. P., & Olsson, A. R. (2014). Start-ups and local entrepreneurial social capital in the municipalities of Sweden. *Regional Studies*, *48*, 974–994. doi:10.1080/00343404.2013.865836

Contesting European regions

Michael Keating

ABSTRACT

Contesting European regions. *Regional Studies*. A regional or 'meso'-level of regulation and policy-making has emerged in Europe. This cannot adequately be explained by functional imperatives or drivers. A constructivist perspective sees the region as the outcome of political contestation over the definition and meaning of territory. Six competing conceptual frames for regionalism are proposed: integrative; competitive; welfare; identity; government; and the region as a refraction of social and economic interests. Any given case will reflect a balance among these conceptions. Such an understanding permits a combination of comparative analysis with an understanding of individual cases and avoids both dismissal of territory and territorial determinism.

摘要

争夺欧洲区域。区域研究。在欧洲已浮现区域或 "中" 层级的规范与政策制定。而此一现象无法由功能规律或驱力充分解释之。建构论的观点，将区域视为对领土的定义与意义进行政治争夺的结果。本文提出六个区域主义的竞争概念架构：整合、竞争、福祉、认同、政府，以及区域作为社会和经济利益的折射。任何给定的案例皆反映出这些概念之间的平衡。此般理解容许结合比较分析和对于个别案例的理解，并同时避免忽视领域以及领域决定论。

RÉSUMÉ

Contestation de régions européennes. *Regional Studies*. Un niveau régional, ou «méso»-niveau, de réglementation et d'élaboration de politiques a vu le jour en Europe. Il ne s'explique pas de façon adéquate par des impératifs fonctionnels ou des facteurs-clé. Une perspective constructiviste considère la région comme la conséquence d'une contestation politique concernant la définition et la signification

15

du mot territoire. Six cadres conceptuels rivaux pour le régionalisme sont proposés, à savoir: intégratif; compétitif; aide sociale; identité; gouvernement; et la région, en tant que réfraction d'intérêts sociaux et économiques. Toute affaire donnée reflètera un équilibre entre ces conceptions. Une telle interprétation permet une analyse comparée au meme temps que une connaissance de cas individuels, et évite à la fois la révocation du territoire et un déterminisme territorial.

ZUSAMMENFASSUNG

Auseinandersetzung über europäische Regionen. *Regional Studies*. In Europa ist eine regionale bzw. 'mittlere' Ebene der Regulierung und Politik entstanden. Dies lässt sich durch funktionale Imperative oder Faktoren nicht ausreichend erklären. In einer konstruktivistischen Perspektive wird die Region als Ergebnis einer politischen Auseinandersetzung über die Definition und Bedeutung von Gebiet aufgefasst. Vorgeschlagen werden sechs miteinander konkurrierende konzeptuelle Rahmen des Regionalismus: integrativ, wettbewerbsorientiert, sozial, Identität, Regierung und die Region als Brechung von sozialen und wirtschaftlichen Interessen. In jedem gegebenen Fall spiegelt sich ein Gleichgewicht zwischen diesen Konzeptionen wider. Ein solches Verständnis ermöglicht die Kombination einer vergleichenden Analyse mit einem Verständnis von Einzelfällen und vermeidet sowohl eine Ablehnung des Gebiets als auch einen territorialen Determinismus.

RESUMEN

Confrontación sobre las regiones europeas. *Regional Studies*. En Europa ha surgido un nivel regional o 'meso' de la regulación y formulación de políticas. Esto no puede explicarse adecuadamente mediante imperativos o factores funcionales. En una perspectiva constructivista se considera que la región es el resultado de una controversia política sobre la definición y el significado de territorio. Se proponen seis marcos contrapuestos para el regionalismo: integrador; competitivo; social; identidad; gobierno; y la región como una refracción de los intereses sociales y económicos. Cualquier caso determinado reflejará un equilibrio entre estos conceptos. Comprender esto nos permite un análisis comparativo y un entendimiento los casos individuales y evitando tanto el rechazo del territorio como el determinismo territorial.

CONCEPTUALIZING REGIONS

This article is a reflection on the constitution of the region in the 50 years since *Regional Studies* was founded. The term 'region' is used in multiple ways in the social sciences. In international relations, it refers to the supranational level. In other disciplines, the focus is on the sub-state level, at a number of different scales. Regions can also be conceptualized as inter-state spaces, crossing state boundaries. Of interest in this article is the rise of the intermediate or 'meso' (Sharpe, 1992) region, between the state and the local level.

The rise of the region has often been explained by reference to functional imperatives or drivers. Some emphasize economic globalization, which is eroding the capacity of the nation-state and enhancing the efficacy of smaller units in facing the challenges of competition and meeting citizen preferences (Ohmae, 1995). Others put forward arguments about efficiency and the optimal level for service delivery and regulation (Hooghe & Marks, 2009). Some point to the tendency of government to respond to underlying patterns of social identity (Erk, 2007; Kymlicka, 2007). Functional arguments, however, are teleological, explaining change by reference to its effects. At best, functional arguments present reasons for changing the spatial scale of government, but reasons are not the same as causes. Reasons are, moreover, normatively contested as they rely on some transcendent objective. For example, arguments about large or small units of government have shifted over recent decades, from consolidation in the interests of planning and economies of scale to fragmentation (under the influence of public choice theory) in the interest of competition and variation. Regions are too different in their geographical scale and institutional realization to be explained by a single set of drivers. Determinist theories also underplay the role of agents and political competition.

Instead, a constructivist approach sees regions as the outcome of contestation among social and political actors in specific conditions. It does not take the ontology of regions for granted but sees them as potential spaces to be filled in with social and economic content, and often contested. This is consistent with modern theories of territory which have moved away from a rigid definition of boundaries and emphasized flexibility and multiple meanings. Territory is not just a topological concept but a sociological one, which is socially constructed (Lefebvre, 1974) and constituted by its social and economic content and its utility in explanation of social processes and outcomes. Territory is constructed in two senses: its definition and meaning are a matter for interpretation by social, political and economic actors and by citizens; and actors themselves seek to construct systems at particular spatial scales and give them particular meanings. Such an approach also meets the demand for conceptually consistent but contextualized understanding (Rutten & Boekma, 2012; Storper, 2011a); but this makes it difficult to do comparative analysis. Finally, territory is contested in that its definition, significance and uses have important outcomes for the distribution of power and resources. There is no 'objective' or purely technical definition of the region or the 'right' spatial level at which to conduct particular policies or regulate economic, social and environmental systems. Instead, different conceptualizations of the region have developed across time and in different places, and have competed with each other.

Spatial rescaling is currently transforming the nation-state as economic, social and political systems that previously were largely contained within its boundaries migrate to new levels (Brenner, 2009; Brenner, Jessop, Jones, & MacLeod, 2003; Keating, 2013). The outcome is not a single territorial grid but a multiplicity of possible spaces and constructions (Goodwin, Jones, & Jones, 2012; Paasi, 2009; Pike, 2007; Varró & Lagendijk, 2013). None of this means that the region should be dismissed as a category of analysis or as not 'real', but rather that it is a conceptual rather than a reified phenomenon. So this produces multiple regionalisms, which may or may not coincide. This article does not seek to create taxonomy of regionalisms in which each case belongs in a given category since that would simplify matters and not aid understanding. Instead, six conceptual or interpretive frames are proposed which explore diverse ways of constructing the region as an economic, social and political project. The frames refer to the key dimensions in the social construction of territory and are: integrative regionalism; competitive regionalism; welfare regionalism; identity regionalism; regions as government; and regionalism as a refraction of social and economic interests.[1] Any given case will probably be open to more than one interpretation and it is the contest among these that produces the outcome.

INTEGRATIVE REGIONALISM

Mainstream social science was long wedded to a vision of modernization that saw it as a process of territorial integration and functional differentiation (Finer, 1997; Parsons, 1971); Emile Durkheim (Durkheim, 1964, p. 187) declared that 'we can almost say that a people is as much advanced as territorial divisions are more superficial'. This perspective was influenced by the advance of industrial production with its distinct rationality, the breakdown of traditional and peripheral societies in the late 19th century, the creation of unified markets, cultural integration, and the institutional incorporation of territories. Territorial integration occurred largely within the rigid territorial parameters of the nation-state but, within these, students of state- and nation-building emphasized deterritorialization (Deutsch, 1972; Giddens, 1985; Lipset & Rokkan, 1967).

By the 1970s there was more appreciation that national integration was not always complete and that significant regional economic, social and political cleavages remained within nation-states (Rokkan, 1980, 1999). Then came a recognition that regional differentiation was not just the legacy of older, pre-industrial society, but was reproduced under conditions of modernity (Tarrow, 1978). Focus then moved towards territorial management, the strategies that states use to integrate peripheral territories into national political and economic systems (Keating, 1988; Rokkan & Urwin, 1983).

From the 1960s, the region became a key unit for policy design and modernization. The context was the 'Keynesian welfare state' resting on the twin pillars of national economic regulation and national welfare standards. The territorial counterpart was 'spatial Keynesianism' (Brenner, 2004) in the form of regional policy designed to overcome market imperfections and integrate lagging regions into national economic space. Regions, and local governments, were used to extend public services and welfare provision.

Post-Second World War regional policies tended to be depoliticized and integrative, focusing on technical logic. Regional policy was essentially positive-sum, offering declining regions help to develop, boosting the national economy by mobilizing idle resources, and helping wealthy regions by relieving congestion and providing markets for their goods. Preferred institutional mechanisms were development agencies and centralized allocation of resources.

Starting in the 1970s and 1980s, the European Union (as it now is) pursued essentially similar strategies. The European Regional Development Fund (later Structural and Cohesion Policy) sought a spatial dimension to the single market by overcoming structural obstacles and facilitating an optimal spatial division of labour. Once again, the reasoning was integrative and technical and the European Commission has consistently presented an economic, rather than a redistributive, justification for the policy (Begg, 2010; Keating, Hooghe, & Tatham, 2015). Its own spatial map of NUTS (Nomenclature des unités territoriales statistiques) reflected a purely technical logic.

In practice, depoliticized and integrative regionalism proved difficult to sustain. Both states and the European Commission have had to institutionalize the policy and provide for delivery mechanisms. They have sought to engage local economic, social and political actors in development policy, sometimes seeking to marginalize existing local elites in the name of modernization and sometimes co-opting them. There were regional development commissions, public–private partnerships and mechanisms for citizen input. The European Union shied away from interfering with structures of territorial government, which are the prerogative of the member states. It did, however, insist on the principles of subsidiarity, taking issues to the local level, and of partnership, including local civil society. The whole process inevitably raised questions about development priorities and whether state visions of the spatial division of labour corresponded to local priorities. Development based on a technical, economic logic was challenged by opposition groups and social movements concerned with the social implications of change (Keating, 1988). The result was a politicization of regional development and a contest for the definition of the region, its economic and social meaning, and its institutionalization by states, the European Union and regional actors.

COMPETITIVE REGIONALISM

Since the 1980s, there has been an important reconceptualization of regional economic development. The region is seen less as an object of state and European policy and more as an economic unit in its own right. One factor has been the decline of national regional policies, only partly compensated by European regional policy. The opening of national economic borders through global and European free trade and capital mobility has hampered inter-regional redistribution and diversionary policies. The old logic, by which transfers to poor regions came back to the wealthy regions as orders for their goods, no longer holds as consumers can spend their money on imports. Regional policy is expensive and less effective and is restricted by European competition policies.

Both national and European regional policies have been affected by new thinking about spatial economic development captured by the term 'new regionalism'

(Keating, 1998), which stresses the importance of the local and regional scale to the understanding and steering of economic development (Cooke & Morgan, 1998; Scott, 1998; European Commission, 2013; European Commission Directorate-General for Regional and Urban Policy, 2014). New Economic Geography (Krugman, 2011) stays close to classical economics in emphasizing how the proximity of producers can lower transaction costs and exploit economies of agglomeration in supply chains or 'clusters' (Porter, 2001). Other accounts (Gertler, 2010; North, 2005) focus on the role of institutions in promoting that balance of competition and cooperation in which markets thrive. Attention has moved from the traded dependencies of transaction costs models to 'untraded interdependencies' in the form of tacit knowledge and face-to-face exchange, an idea dating back to Alfred Marshall (Marshall, 1920). Institutional accounts fade into sociological accounts, focusing on the characteristics of local societies, including social structures and mechanisms for sharing knowledge and fostering collaboration. These, in turn, fade into cultural explanations, focusing on the characteristics of the population, including social capital and trust (Malecki, 2012; Putnam, 1993).

Regions and localities are portrayed as more than mere locations of productions but rather as production systems, with their own internal logic and interdependencies but linked into global trading systems and supply chains (Crouch, Le Galès, Trigilia, & Voelzkow, 2001). In this way, regions are constructed on the basis of economic factors, but using economic sociology rather than neo-classical principles.

A further move has been to portray these local and regional production systems as being in competition as Ricardian comparative advantage (in which each territory has an optimal role in the spatial division of labour) gives way to absolute, or competitive, advantage in which some territories can gain an unassailable lead (Kitson, Martin, & Tyler, 2004; Scott, 1998). This goes against a principle of neo-classical economics that only firms compete. The concept of regional competition and competitiveness has been strongly criticized as incoherent (Bristow, 2005, 2010). It reifies regions as the appropriate unit of analysis; even if territory is relevant, it does not necessarily correspond to regions in other senses. Yet this is precisely the way in which the theme is used to construct the region. Ohmae (2001) is impatient with political concepts, insisting that regions emerge from market order; Alesina and Spolaore's (2003) theories about the 'size of nations' (by which they mean states and regions) do the same. Regional politicians can use the theme of competitive growth to construct a shared regional interest, expanding their home electoral and social support base. States and the European Union can use it to step back from diversionary regional policy and equalization, putting the responsibility back to regions. Competition also rests upon a dominant form of justification in the modern world by evoking the market.

The notion of the competitive region potentially narrows the agenda for regional policies to a concern with productivity and market advantage (Bristow, 2005). It is true that policy-makers have sought to rebut criticisms that this amounts to entrenched neo-liberalism by extending the definition beyond the narrow criterion of production costs. The European regional competitiveness index (Annoni & Dijkstra, 2013) combines disparate factors and refers to matters that are assumed to enhance productivity. Others open up beyond considerations of firm productivity to include social and environmental factors (Aiginger, Bärenthaler, & Sieber, 2013; Aiginger & Firgo, 2015; Organisation for Economic Co-operation and Development (OECD), 2014). These might be relevant to a discussion about regional productivity and welfare, but they do not address the central issue about competiveness: that it is inherently relational and a zero-sum game. This puts competitive regionalism at odds with other concepts of the region, such as welfare.

WELFARE REGIONALISM

If regions are in competition for absolute advantage, it follows that there will be an increase in inter-regional disparities. The economic marginalization of regions in the global division of labour and the territorial impact of plant closures in turn promotes the idea of the region as a defensive space and a 'revolt of the poor'. There is also a 'revolt of the rich' as politicians in prosperous regions cite the need to compete in European and international markets to complain about the burden of transfers to poorer compatriots. Such transfers, whether explicitly through fiscal equalization and regional policy or implicitly through national welfare programmes, have become increasingly salient as the region has become a recognizable unit and regional accounts are available. So demands to limit transfers have become a major political issue in Germany, Italy, Spain, Belgium and the UK. On the other hand, systems of fiscal transfer have proved quite resilient. They are institutionally embedded in national political systems and survey evidence suggests that public support for inter-regional transfers remains rather high. Inter-regional solidarity is weaker, however, in wealthy regions and those with a strong sense of distinct identity (Henderson, Jeffery, & Wincott, 2013). This raises normative issues about inter-regional equity and the idea of territorial justice (Storper, 2011b).

Rescaling also presents questions about intra-regional equity. Competitive development is presented as in the interests of all within the region. Yet any given development strategy will produce winners and losers, whether these be defined by class, gender, age or location. Another possible consequence of inter-regional competition is that of a 'race to the bottom' as regions, needing to attract investment and wealthy taxpayers, cut public expenditures, especially on welfare, along with taxes. It is for this reason that theories of fiscal federalism have traditionally advocated that redistributive policies should be located at the higher, federal level, where externalities can be taken into account (Oates, 1999). It is also why for most of the 20th century the social democratic left tended to favour centralization while those on the market right favoured decentralization.

This can no longer be taken for granted. In some cases, regions have been constructed as sites of opposition to austerity policy and locations of social solidarity. This is clearly visible in Scotland, where support for devolution and independence are linked to themes of welfare, but is also visible in cities and regions elsewhere. Offsetting the race to the bottom, there are also signs of a 'race to the top' in the provision of public services as regional parties and leaders compete to innovate and impress their electorates (Costa-Font & Rico, 2006; Gallego & Subirats, 2011) or to the middle as regions converge (Dupuy, 2012). In regions with a strong identity, the affective solidarity that underlies welfare states may play at that level, so creating alternative communities for sharing (Béland & Lecours, 2008; McEwen & Moreno, 2005).

The welfare state has been both restructuring and rescaling spatially (Ferrera, 2005; Hemerijck, 2013; Kazepov & Barberis, 2008). There is a move away from passive social assistance towards active labour market policy, aimed at getting people into work. The older pattern of need based upon low incomes or periodic unemployment has been supplemented by new social risks linked to precarious employment, disability and other forms of disadvantage. Activation policies are increasing linked to local and regional labour markets and to other spatial policy instruments, notably economic development. In many European countries, they are managed by partnerships of business and labour, often with a European input via the social funds. This has strengthened the region as a space for social compromise and negotiation and for policy delivery.

Governments and the European Commission seek to reconcile competitive and welfare regionalism with successive formulas like socially inclusive growth, but the dilemmas remain. The 'place-based' approach (Barca, 2009) yet again rehearsed the need to promote both growth and social inclusion, but also recognized that they are distinct. When policies are put into practice the conflicts between the economic and the social often re-emerge. Economic and social issues are thus increasingly presented in a territorial framework, but this does not mean that there is really as shared regional interest, that regionalism is caused by economic or social grievance. In order to express such grievances territorially, there has to be a territorial framework, identity or repertoire of symbols to map onto. These are provided by territorial identities, government, and the territorialization of economic and social interests themselves.

IDENTITY REGIONALISM

Regions are sites of social identity formation, which can be integrative or autonomist. Integrative regionalism goes back to the late 19th century, seeking to sustain historic identities and loyalties, but within a national political modernizing project (Applegate, 1990; Núñez Seixas, 2001). It competed with autonomist regionalism, which re-emerged in the 1970s in the form of the demand for recognition of national diversity. It is tempting to make a distinction between regionalisms and minority nationalisms, the latter being committed to separatism, but this is too simple. Since the late 19th century, the term 'nation' has carried with it the connotation of a right to self-determination, so movements asserting the existence of a distinct people with the right to set their own constitutional future have adopted the term, putting them on the same normative plane as states themselves. In the modern world, however, the nature of statehood has been changed by transformation of the state and the emergence of new conceptions of sovereignty. The degree of self-government desired is an empirical question to be examined in context, not a defining feature.

Some observers have used the terms 'ethnoregionalist' (Newman, 1996) or 'ethnonationalist' (Connor, 1994) to denote the new movements, but that is to introduce the difficult, contested and normative language of ethnicity. Sub-state nationalist movements in Catalonia and Scotland have taken pains to disavow ethnic particularism in favour of a 'civic nationalism' that is inclusive of the whole population, including incomers (Keating, 2001a, 2001b). Basque national-ists have abandoned the ethnic exclusivism of Sabino Arana, who founded the Basque Nationalist Party at the end of the 19th century. Some movements in the Balkans have sought to distance themselves from the prevailing ethnic nation-alism by stressing a consciously multi-ethnic regionalism (Stjepanovic, 2012). The term 'regional nationalist' (Keating, 1988) is less prejudicial although not uncontested.

Regional nationalism in the 1970s was widely attributed to retarded moderniza-tion or a 'revolt against modernity' (Lipset, 1975) in line with contemporary modernization theories, but has since been subject to a theoretical reappraisal as part of the latest phase of modernity (Olsson, 2009). While all nationalisms look both back and forward, the new regional nationalisms are characterized by their relationship to the new opportunities created by rescaling.

A key element in this is the use of Europe as a new framework for the discur-sive projection of the political community and for new forms of autonomy (Duerr, 2015). For some, like the Scottish National Party (SNP), the European Union lowers the cost of independence, since it guarantees market access and limits the power of large states by pooling authority. Others have gone further, seizing on the pooling of sovereignty in Europe to make a 'post-sovereign' argument for autonomy within a multilevel system of Europe, states and regions (Keating, 2004). This was long the position of mainstream Catalan nationalism and is now the dominant strand in the Basque Nationalist Party. Europe thus provides a discursive space in which to articulate demands for recognition as something more than a region defined by the state constitution. There were also hopes that Europe could provide more concrete opportunities for regions to act in transna-tional space and exercise real power, focused on the movement for a Europe of the Regions. The Maastricht Treaty established the Committee of the Regions (CoR) (Piattoni & Schonlau, 2015) and gave regions access to the Council of the European Union, but as part of national delegations. The CoR never gained substantial power, one reason being that regions are defined very differently in different member states and the European Union has not cultivated regions as rivals to the states but rather uses them as objects of policy and territorial integra-tion. Its key term is not autonomy but territorial cohesion.

Justifications by those claiming self-determination have moved away from primordial conceptions of the nation towards democratic principles, based on the right of people to decide their own fate. Yet, as Jennings (1956) argued, the prin-ciple of self-determination of peoples makes little sense unless someone can first define the people. Contemporary regional nationalists construct their political community in a variety of ways. One is by historical interpretation and revision, to establish the ontological reality of the political community as something constructed through time, if not primordial. This provides a counter-narrative to state-based histories founded upon a teleology of integration and unity. It is linked to arguments about the foundations of political authority and sovereignty (Keating, 2001b). Basque nationalists insist on the primacy of their historic rights (*fueros*) as pre-constitutional, while Spanish nationalists claim that all political rights derive from the 1978 Constitution (Herrero de Miñon, 1998). Scottish nationalists reject the absolute sovereignty of the Westminster Parliament and argue that Scottish conceptions of sovereignty are distinct and pluralist (MacCormick, 1999). Catalan nationalists take as a reference point Catalonia before 1714 as an autonomous trading nation within a federal Crown of Aragon, itself nested in a Spanish confederation and with links across Europe and the Mediterranean. Flemish nationalists point to the glorious era of Flanders as a cultural centre and trading nation in the early modern period. Of course, these accounts have varying degrees of plausibility both in the units to which they refer and in the historical experience. Flanders as a historical reference point is rather different from the modern region, both in geographical scope and social and political meaning. Padania (northern Italy) is a modern invention in spite of efforts by Northern League propagandists to present it as 'the oldest community in Europe' (Oneto, 1997). Yet such historical narratives are not mere nostalgia but, as often happens with history, project contemporary debates into the past, while giving their own nation a modernist, progressive and democratic teleology to match that of the states themselves. Normative assessments, however, have varied from seeing them as forms of emancipatory democracy (Gagnon, 2014; Guibernau, 2013) to condemning them as unfit to join the community of European nations (Weiler, 2014).

Regional nationalist movements have adopted the themes of the new regionalism to construct both their political communities and their policy prospectuses. So in some wealthy regions, the region/nation is discursively constructed as a space of economic dynamism, endowed with competitive capacity. Tradition is linked to modernity, as in the Bavarian slogan *laptop und lederhosen* and, far from being an obstacle to modernization, is seen as a source of social capital as the region is credited with just those virtues that underpin new regionalism (Keating, Loughlin, & Deschouwer, 2003). Social solidarity is also pressed into service, so that the region/nation is seen as essentially cohesive, albeit in different ways. Scotland and Wales have been constructed as bastions of social democracy, while Flanders is presented as more individualistic and less welfare-dependent than Wallonia; northern Italy is portrayed as being less dependent than the south.

It is very difficult to measure how far popular identities have shifted in the direction of sub-state regions since identity is a multidimensional concept and national surveys use different meanings and questions. On the rare occasions when the same question has been used cross-nationally, its meaning is different in different places. The Linz/Moreno Question (Guinjoan & Rodon, 2016), asking people on a five-point scale whether they identify with the state or the sub-state nation, has been asked regularly in Spain, the UK and Belgium (but in Belgium Europe and the local level are also included). The main finding is that even in places with strong regional nationalist movements, most citizens have developed dual identities rather than identifying exclusively with one level or another. Identity is thus not a given but another field by which regions can be constructed and given meaning.

REGIONS AS GOVERNMENT

These multiple meanings of region do not produce a definitive political outcome or institutional response. Some conceptions point to regions as arms of the central state; others to regions as self-regulating economic systems; others again raise the issue of political autonomy and citizen representation. The combination of these conceptions has, however, encouraged moves towards elected regional government. States have sought mechanisms to recapture functional systems that have escaped their purview through rescaling, and also to incorporate territorial social and political actors. They, and the European Union, seek legitimacy for their new modes of intervention, territorial administration and regulation. Opposition movements, challenging economically driven or technocratic regionalism in the name of social considerations, seek to broaden the agenda of regional policy and expand the range of stakeholders. Regional nationalists seek autonomy as a first-order objective. These competing visions have led to the politicization of the regional question. The institutional response has been the establishment of representative and accountable government as the only way to broker and compromise the divergent meanings of regionalism and to provide legitimate outcomes. There has been a rise in regional government (Hooghe, Marks, & Schakel, 2010), but the response is far from uniform, and some states have been reluctant to establish territorial government that might correspond with political identities. This was long the case in France and remains so in Central and Eastern Europe (Yoder, 2012).

Much has been written about a move from government to governance (Bellamy & Palumbo, 2010). The latter term is notoriously elastic but usually refers to a mode of regulation based on networks rather than hierarchy. Multilevel governance in turn refers to networks spanning spatial levels and the public and private sectors (Bache & Flinders, 2004; Hooghe & Marks, 2001; Piattoni, 2010). As a general comment on the state of the world this might be unexceptional, as any social system can be analyzed by territory and function. The claim that the world is moving from government to multilevel governance, however, suggests that there is a shift from the multipurpose, centralized, hierarchical state to a looser order of networks. The term 'governance' (and its multilevel variant) is applied with particular frequency to the European and regional levels, probably because of the lack of strongly integrated governmental institutions. Yet, in so far as governance refers to networks and loose constellations of institutions, the trend is away from this, to elected, multipurpose regional government. Governance may be no more than a transitional stage towards government as new scales are institutionalized (Goetz, 2008).

Elected regional government has the effect of fixing the territorial scale and boundaries of regional systems, much as the nation-state 'caged' social and economic systems (Mann, 1993). Regions, however, are less tightly bounded than states, given the competing territorial imaginations and the ease of functional systems in economy and society to escape their borders. These borders in themselves have little that is natural about them but reflect historical patterns and the balance of political forces. Having been established, however, they show great resilience as parties and leaders use them to establish power bases and institutional resources. Even the most apparently arbitrary boundaries then become entrenched, as in the German *Länder*. The French regional reform of 2015, merging regions into larger units, is an exception, and these were among the least socially embedded regions in Europe.

The rise of the meso has created an effective system of multilevel federalism, even if the term 'federalism' is not always used. Students of federal government make a distinction between coordinate and cooperative federalism. In the coordinate ideal type, each level of government has its own competences, which it exercises independently. In the cooperative mode, competences are shared and the emphasis is on joint policy-making, within vertical policy communities spanning the two levels. During the Keynesian welfare era, the emphasis was on cooperation. There is now a growing interest in a third variety, competitive federalism (Dente, 1997). Regions compete for investment, technology and markets, as in the competitive regionalism discussed above. They also compete over policy innovation and service provision. Governments in stronger regions have called for more autonomy and disentanglement of central and regional competences. This is visible in Germany, Belgium, Italy and Spain, where regions have complained about the centre using framework laws to restrict regional autonomy. There has also been pressure from richer regions to devolve tax power; poorer regions have been much less keen on the idea. Poorer German *Länder* have slowed down federal reforms and Wallonia is less enthusiastic about further federalism than Flanders. So the tension between integrative regionalism and regionalism as differentiation has increased.

REGIONS AND THE REFRACTION OF INTERESTS

Modernization and integration theory tended to assume that the growth of class and sectoral alignments would efface territorial differences within the nation-state. Even after the emergence of regional government, Pastori (1980) could write of 'regions without regionalism' and Trigilia (1991) and Le Galès (1997) of the 'paradox of the regions'. The idea was that regional governments had been set up, but the articulation of social and economic interests continued to be on a national scale. Regions were, in other words, not constructed around substantive interests, which left regional arenas rather hollow. Experience in recent years, however, shows a more complex picture. Class and sector do not displace territory but are refracted by it in distinct ways at different territorial levels under the twin influences of rescaling of functional systems in economy and society, and the emergence of regional government, which encourages an institutional isomorphism in which interest articulation reflects government structures. The differential territorialization of sectoral and class interests thus becomes a key factor in the construction of the region. This process has not been fully explored in the literature, apart from the work of Keating and Wilson (2014), which explores the organization and territorial orientation of representative groups and the horizontal and vertical relations among them and with government.

Business groups are aware of the importance of territory to economic development and how context affects the success of investment. Large firms take great care in choosing investment locations and assuring the supply of infrastructure, labour and technological innovation. Large business, however, is wary of capture by territorial political systems, especially where left-wing or environmentalist forces are strong. They tend, therefore, to favour functional regionalism, depoliticization of development policy and agencies dominated by business interests. Small businesses are less mobile and more dependent on local public goods and support, on local markets and, in some places, protectionist networks to defend local traders. They are often closer to local political concerns as their owners and managers are local citizens and may share local identities. This makes them more supportive of regional structures and government, sometimes combining free-market rhetoric with practical protectionism and dependence on territorial government.

Trade unions are in principle based on class and have historically expanded across national territories, overcoming local particularisms. They favour national welfare standards and in some states have been incorporated into state-level forms of social partnership and social compromise. Increasingly, however, they have been drawn into local and regional alliances in defence of threatened sectors, which have taken on a territorial as well as a sectoral focus. They have adopted new regionalist themes of economic development, emphasizing human capital, labour market policies and activation. They seek at regional level to recover positions they lost with the demise of national-level corporatist structures and collective bargaining. Consequently, they have moved away from their previous emphasis on the central level to embrace regional arenas and decentralization. As mass organizations (albeit declining in numbers) they are also open to popular forms of identity and must take account of new regionalist and minority nationalist politics in places like Spain, Belgium or the UK. So they are cross-pressured, which generates internal tensions.

Environmentalist groups often have local origins and the impact of environmental change is first experienced locally; but regulation is at a wider level. Environmental groups remain locally rooted and are often in alliance with groups defending local traditions. At the same time, they are connected to the European level, which is more accessible and capable of making rules binding all the way down the spatial scales.

Social and economic interests are thus refracted by territory, with the emergence of a territorial-level interest articulation. This may take the form of the construction of a common territorial interest, underpinned by the rhetoric of territorial competition. Alternatively, the region may become an arena for interest intermediation and compromise. Regional policy communities may emerge within or across sectors. There may be new social alliances and oppositions; at the regional level there is often a productivist alliance of business and trade unions against environmentalists.

The rescaling of policy communities thus serves also to construct the region as a space of social compromise, facilitated by regional governments, which seek to incorporate interests as a means for strengthening regional capacity and by the preference of the European Union for the incorporation of civil society in the delivery of its own development programmes.

CONCLUSIONS: CONTESTED REGIONS

Regions have been studied from a variety of disciplinary perspectives: economic, legal, geographical, sociological, historical, cultural and political. None is determinant but an interdisciplinary approach enables a richer understanding of the phenomenon. The constructivist approach allows one to see territory as a field in flux, with multiple influences at work and no definitive outcome. As the state's monopoly on the definition of territory is weakened, the field is more open and contested. In some places the very foundations of sovereignty are challenged, while in others there are territorialized struggles over resources. There is competition between states and the European Union over the definition of regions for spatial policy interventions. The drawing of regional boundaries influences patterns of inclusion and exclusion and the balance of political and social forces. The same is true of the internal constitution of regions. Elected regional government has often been in tension with corporatist forms of representation. Regions as vehicles for state policy are in tension with regions as a form of territorial autonomy. Regions are arenas for playing out some of the most important political issues such as the balance between economic competition and social solidarity.

Yet regionalism is not a one-way project leading to a 'regional world' or Europe of the Regions. States remain important actors in shaping space and, at a time of austerity, have sought to reinforce their control. European requirements on debts and deficits have led the Eurozone states to introduce constitutional limits applicable to all levels. In Spain, austerity has had asymmetrical effects, with Catalonia pushing towards independence while other regions, unable to take the burden, have asked the state to take competences back. France has imposed mergers of regions in the name of economy, while Italy has rolled back promises of federal reform and extensive devolution. The European order is characterized by both centrifugal and centripetal tendencies.

The six conceptualizations proposed here provide frames of analysis for understanding the complexities of rescaling and the rise of the region. This is not an exhaustive taxonomy, nor is it an empirical finding based on hard facts, but a means of identifying key aspects of the social reality and interpreting cases. It is offered not as a conclusive way of understanding regions but as a means of capturing the fluidity of relationships while not destroying the basic object of study. In this way, it contributes to understanding how social, political and economic relationships are refracted by territory, while avoiding territorial determinism.

DISCLOSURE STATEMENT

No potential conflict of interest was reported by the author.

FUNDING

The research on which this paper is based was conducted under an Economic and Social Research Council (ESRC) Professorial Fellowship [grant number RES-051-27-0302].

NOTE

1. It is of the essence of the constructivist approach that this schema is not the product of inductive reasoning or empirical generalization. It is, rather, a scheme of interpretation whose test is not a comparison with a hard empirical reality but rather its utility in explanation and understanding (Hacking, 1992; Kratochwil, 2008). It is to be judged not by whether it is right or wrong but according to whether it is useful. By the same token, it is not claimed that other conceptualizations are wrong but merely that they should be judged in the same way.

REFERENCES

Aiginger, K., Bärenthaler, S., & Sieber, S. (2013). *Competitiveness under new perspectives* (WWW for Europe Working Paper No. 44).

Aiginger, K., & Firgo, M. (2015). *Regional competitiveness under new perspectives* (Online Policy Paper No. 26 (WIFO)). WWW for Europe. http://www.wifo.ac.at/

Alesina, A., & Spolaore, E. (2003). *The size of nations.* Cambridge, MA: MIT Press.

Annoni, P., & Dijkstra, L. (2013). *EU regional competitiveness index.* Brussels: European Commission Joint Research Centre.

Applegate, C. (1990). *A nation of provincials: The German idea of Heimat.* Berkeley: University of California Press.

Bache, I., & Flinders, M. (2004). *Multi-level governance.* Oxford: Oxford University Press.

Barca, F. (2009). *An agenda for a reformed cohesion policy. A place-based approach to meeting European Union challenges and expectations* (Independent Report prepared at the request of Danuta Hübner, Commissioner for Regional Policy). Brussels European Commission.

Begg, I. (2010). Cohesion or confusion: A policy searching for objectives. *Journal of European Integration, 32*(1), 77–96. doi:10.1080/07036330903375115

Béland, D., & Lecours, A. (2008). *Nationalism and social policy. The politics of territorial solidarity.* Oxford: Oxford University Press.

Bellamy, R., & Palumbo, A. (2010). *From government to governance.* London: Ashgate.

Brenner, N. (2004). *New state spaces. Urban governance and the rescaling of statehood.* Oxford: Oxford University Press.

Brenner, N. (2009). Open questions on state rescaling. *Cambridge Journal of Regions, Economy and Society, 2*(1), 123–139. doi:10.1093/cjres/rsp002

Brenner, N., Jessop, B., Jones, M., & MacLeod, G. (2003). Introduction: State space in question. In N. Brenner, B. Jessop, M. Jones, & G. MacLeod (Eds.), *State/space. A reader* (pp. 1–26). Oxford: Blackwell.
Bristow, G. (2005). Everyone's a 'winner=': Problematising the discourse of regional competitiveness. *Journal of Economic Geography, 5*(3), 285–304. doi:10.1093/jeg/lbh063
Bristow, G. (2010). *Critical reflections on regional competitiveness.* London: Routledge.
Connor, W. (1994). *Ethnonationalism. The quest for understanding.* Princeton: Princeton University Press.
Cooke, P., & Morgan, K. (1998). *The associational economy. Firms, regions, and innovation.* Oxford: Oxford University Press.
Costa-Font, J., & Rico, A. (2006). Vertical competition in the Spanish National Health System (NHS). *Public Choice, 128*, 477–498. doi:10.1007/s11127-005-9011-y
Crouch, C., Le Galès, P., Trigilia, C., & Voelzkow, H. (2001). *Local production systems in Europe. Rise or Demise?* Oxford: Oxford University Press.
Dente, B. (1997). Federalismo e politiche pubbliche. In A. Martelli (Ed.), *Quale federalismo per l'Italia? Terzo rapporto sulle priorità nazionali* (pp. 189–208). Milan: Mondadori.
Deutsch, K. W. (1972). *Nationalism and social communication: An inquiry into the foundations of nationality.* Cambridge,MA: MIT Press.
Duerr, G. M. E. (2015). *Secessionism and the European Union. The future of Flanders, Scotland, and Catalonia.* Lanham: Rowman & Littlefield.
Dupuy, C. (2012). La course vers le milieu des régions. Compétition et politiques régionales d'éducation en France et en Allemagne. *Canadian Journal of Political Science/ Revue canadienne de science politique,45*(4),881–907.doi:10.1017/S0008423912001072
Durkheim, E. (1964). *The division of labour in society.* New York: Free Press.
Erk, J. (2007). *Explaining federalism: State, society and congruence in Austria, Belgium, Canada, Germany and Switzerland.* London: Routledge.
European Commission. (2013). *EU cohesion policy contributing to employment and growth in Europe* (Joint paper from the Directorates-General for Regional & Urban Policy and Employment, Social Affairs & Inclusion).
European Commission Directorate-General for Regional and Urban Policy. (2014). *Investment for jobs and growth. Promoting development and good governance in EU regions and cities. Sixth Report on Economic, Social and Territorial Cohesion.*
Ferrera, M. (2005). *The new boundaries of welfare.* Oxford: Oxford University Press.
Finer, S. E. (1997). *The history of government, III. Empires, monarchies and the modern state.* Oxford: Oxford University Press.
Gagnon, A. (2014). *Minority nations in the age of uncertainty.* Toronto: University of Toronto Press.
Gallego, R., & Subirats, J. (2011). Comporta el desplegament autonòmic un augment de les desigualtats a Espanya? Descentralització, polítiques de benestar i justicia social. In R. Gallego, & J. Subirats (Eds.), *Autonomies i desigualtats a Espanya: Perceptions, evolució social i polítiques de benestar* (pp. 23–31). Barcelona: Institut d'Estudis Autonómics.
Gertler, M. (2010). Rules of the game: The place of institutions in regional economic change. *Regional Studies, 44*(1), 1–15. doi:10.1080/00343400903389979
Giddens, A. (1985). *The nation state and violence.* Cambridge: Polity.
Goetz, K. H. (2008). Governance as a path to government. *West European Politics, 31*(1–2), 258–279. doi:10.1080/01402380701835066
Goodwin, M., Jones, M., & Jones, R. (2012). *Rescaling the state. Devolution and the geographies of economic governance.* Manchester: Manchester University Press.

Guibernau, M. (2013). Secessionism in Catalonia: After democracy. *Ethnopolitics*, *12*(4), 368–393. doi:10.1080/17449057.2013. 843245

Guinjoan, M., & Rodon, T. (2016). A scrutiny of the Linz–Moreno question. *Publius: Journal of Federalism*, *46*(1), 128–14. doi:10.1093/publius/pjv031

Hacking, I. (1992). *The social construction of what?* Cambridge, MA: Harvard University Press.

Hemerijck, A. (2013). *Changing welfare states*. Oxford: Oxford University Press.

Henderson, A., Jeffery, C., & Wincott, D. (2013). *Citizenship after the nation-state*. Basingstoke: Macmillan.

Herrero de Miñon, M. (1998). *Derechos históricos y constitución*. Madrid: Tecnos.

Hooghe, L., & Marks, G. (2001). *Multilevel governance and European integration*. Lanham: Rowman & Littlefield.

Hooghe, L., & Marks, G. (2009). Does efficiency shape the territorial structure of government? *Annual Review of Political Science*, *12*, 225–241. doi:10.1146/annurev. polisci.12.041107.102315

Hooghe, L., Marks, G., & Schakel, A. (2010). *The rise of regional authority. A comparative study of 42 democracies*. London: Routledge.

Jennings, I. (1956). *The approach to self-government*. Cambridge: Cambridge University Press.

Kazepov, Y., & Barberis, E. (2008). La dimensione territoriale delle politiche sociali in Europa: alcune riflessioni sui processi di rescaling e governance. *Revista delle Politiche Sociali*, *3*, 51–78.

Keating, M. (1988). *State and regional nationalism. Territorial politics and the European state*. Brighton: Wheatsheaf.

Keating, M. (1998). *The new regionalism in Western Europe. Territorial restructuring and political change*. Cheltenham: Edward Elgar.

Keating, M. (2001a). *Plurinational democracy. Stateless nations in a post-sovereignty era*. Oxford: Oxford University Press.

Keating, M. (2001b). *Nations against the state. The new politics of nationalism in Quebec, Catalonia and Scotland* (2nd ed.). Basingstoke: Palgrave.

Keating, M. (2004). European integration and the nationalities question. *Politics and Society*, *31*(1), 1–22.

Keating, M. (2013). *Rescaling the European state. The making of territory and the rise of the meso*. Oxford: Oxford University Press.

Keating, M., Hooghe, L., & Tatham, M. (2015). Bypassing the nation-state?: Regions and the EU policy process. In J. Richardson & S. Maizey (Eds.), *European Union: Power and policy-making* (4th ed.). Abingdon: Routledge.

Keating, M., Loughlin, J., & Deschouwer, J. (2003). *Culture, institutions and economic development. A study of Eight European regions*. Cheltenham: Edward Elgar.

Keating, M., & Wilson, A. (2014). Regions with regionalism? The rescaling of interest groups in six European States. *European Journal of Political Research*, *53*(4), 840–857.

Kitson, M., Martin, R., & Tyler, P. (2004). Regional competitiveness: An elusive yet key concept? *Regional Studies*, *38*(9), 991–999. doi:10.1080/0034340042000320816

Kratochwil, F. (2008). Constructivism: What it is (not) and how it matters. In D. della Porta & M. Keating (Eds.), *Approaches and methodologies in the social sciences. A pluralist perspective* (pp. 80–99). Cambridge: Cambridge University Press.

Krugman, P. (2011). The New Economic Geography, now middle-aged. *Regional Studies*, *45*(1), 1–7. doi:10.1080/00343404.2011. 537127

Kymlicka, W. (2007). *Multicultural odysseys. Navigating the new international politics of diversity*. Oxford: Oxford University Press.

Lefebvre, H. (1974). *La production de l'espace*. Paris: Anthropos.

Le Galès, P. (1997). Gouvernement et gouvernance des regions: faiblesses structurelles et nouvelles mobilisations. In P. Le Galès & P. Lequesne (Eds.), *Les paradoxes des regions en Europe* (pp. 237–264). Paris: La Découverte.

Lipset, S. M. (1975) The revolt against modernity. In *Consensus and conflict. Essays in political sociology* (pp. 68–81). New Brunswick: Transaction.

Lipset, S. M., & Rokkan, S. (1967). *Party systems and voter alignments*. New York: Free Press.

MacCormick, N. (1999). *Questioning sovereignty*. Oxford: Oxford University Press.

McEwen, N., & Moreno, L. (2005). *The territorial politics of welfare*. London: Routledge.

Malecki, E. J. (2012). Regional social capital: Why it matters. *Regional Studies*, *46*(8), 1023–1039. doi:10.1080/00343404.2011.607806

Mann, M. (1993). *The sources of social power*, Vol. II: *The rise of classes and nation-states, 1760–1914*. Cambridge: Cambridge University Press.

Marshall, A. (1920). *Principles of economics*. London: Macmillan.

Newman, S. (1996). *Ethnoregional conflict in democracies*. London: Greenwood.

North, D. C. (2005). *Understanding the process of economic change*. Princeton: Princeton University Press.

Núñez Seixas, X.-M. (2001). The region as essence of the fatherland: Regionalist variants of Spanish nationalism (1849–1936). *European History Quarterly*, *31*(4), 486–518.

Oates, W. E. (1999). An essay on fiscal federalism. *Journal of Economic Literature*, *37*(3), 1120–1149. doi:10.1257/jel.37.3.1120

Ohmae, K. (1995). *The end of the nation state: The rise of regional economies*. New York: Free Press.

Ohmae, K. (2001). How to invite prosperity from the global economy into a region. In A. J. Scott (Ed.), *Global city regions. Trends, theory, policy*. Oxford: Oxford University Press.

Olsson, A. (2009). Theorizing regional minority nationalism. In I. Karolewski & A. Suszycki (Eds.), *Multiplicity of nationalisms in contemporary Europe* (pp. 108–130). Lanham: Rowman & Littlefield.

Oneto, G. (1997). *L'invenzione della Padania. La rinascità della communità più antica d'Europa*. Ceresola: Foedus.

Organisation for Economic Co-operation and Development (OECD). (2014). *How's life in your region? Measuring regional and local well-being for policy making*. Paris: OECD.

Paasi, A. (2009). The resurgence of the 'region' and 'regional identity': Theoretical perspectives and empirical observations on regional dynamics in Europe. *Review of International Studies*, *35*, 121–146. doi:10.1017/S0260210509008456

Parsons, T. (1971). *The systems of modern societies*. Englewood Cliffs: Prentice-Hall.

Pastori, G. (1980). Le regioni senza regionalismo. *Il Mulino*, *10*(2), 268–283.

Piattoni, S. (2010). *The theory of multi-level governance. Conceptual, empirical, and normative challenges*. Oxford: Oxford University Press.

Piattoni, S., & Schonlau, J. (2015). *Shaping EU policy from below: EU democracy and the committee of the regions*. Cheltenham: Edward Elgar.

Pike, A. (2007). Editorial: Whither regional studies? *Regional Studies*, *41*(9), 1143–1148. doi:10.1080/00343400701675587

Porter, M. (2001). Regions and the new economics of competition. In A. J. Scott (Ed.), *Global city regions. Trends, theory, policy* (pp. 139–157). Oxford: Oxford University Press.

Putnam, R. (1993). *Making democracy work. Civic traditions in modern Italy*. Princeton: Princeton University Press.

Rokkan, S. (1980). Territories, centres, and peripheries: Toward a geoethnic–geoeconomic–geopolitical model of differentiation within Western Europe. In J. Gottman (Ed.), *Centre and periphery. Spatial variations in politics* (pp. 63–81). Beverly Hills: Sage.

Rokkan, S. (1999). *State formation, nation-building and Mass politics in Europe. The theory of Stein Rokkan* (ed. P. Flora, S. Kuhnle, & D. Urwin). Oxford: Oxford University Press.

Rokkan, S., & Urwin, D. (1983). *Economy, territory, identity. Politics of West European peripheries*. London: Sage.

Rutten, R., & Boekma, F. (2012). From learning region to learning in a socio-spatial context. *Regional Studies, 46*(8), 981–992. doi:10.1080/00343404.2012.712679

Scott, A. (1998). *Regions and the world economy. The coming shape of global production, competition, and political order*. Oxford: Oxford University Press.

Sharpe, L. J. (1992). The European meso: An appraisal. In L. J. Sharpe (Ed.), *The rise of meso government in Europe* (pp. 1–39). London: Sage.

Stjepanovic, D. (2012). *Contesting territories in Southeastern Europe: The politics of regionalism in Dalmatia, Istria, Sandzak and Vojvodina* (doctoral thesis). Florence: European University Institute.

Storper, M. (2011a). From retro to avant-garde: A commentary on Paul Krugman's 'The New Economic Geography, now middle-aged'. *Regional Studies, 45*(1), 9–15. doi:10.1080/00343404. 2011.537130

Storper, M. (2011b). Justice efficiency and economic geography: Should places help one another to develop? *European Urban and Regional Studies, 18*(1), 3–21. doi:10.1177/0969776410394553

Tarrow, S. (1978). Regional policy, ideology and peripheral defense: The case of Fos-sur-Mer. In S. Tarrow, P. J. Katzenstein, & L. Graziani (Eds.), *Territorial politics in industrial nations* (pp. 42–61). New York: Praeger.

Trigilia, C. (1991). The paradox of the region: Economic regulation and the representation of interests. *Economy and Society, 20*(3), 306–327. doi:10.1080/03085149100000015

Varró, K., & Lagendijk, A. (2013). Conceptualizing the region – In what sense relational? *Regional Studies, 47*(1), 18–28. doi:10.1080/00343404.2011.602334

Weiler, J. (2014). *Scotland and the EU: A comment* (Online). UK Constitutional Law Association,https://ukconstitutionallaw.org/2014/09/10/debate-j-h-h-weiler-scotland-and-the-eu-acomment/

Yoder, J. (2012). *Crafting democracy: Regional politics in post-communist Europe*. Lanham: Rowman & Littlefield.

Foregrounding the region

Anssi Paasi and Jonathan Metzger

ABSTRACT

Foregrounding the region. *Regional Studies*. This paper scrutinizes the everlasting but transforming significance of the concept of region for regional studies and social practice. After tracing the changing meanings of this category, it highlights one characteristic aspect of the progress of the academic conceptualizations of the region: recurrent iterations of critiques regarding various forms of essentialism and fetishism. The main focus then moves to the conceptualization of the region and the articulation of ideas about what regions substantially 'are' and 'do', and what makes the region a worthy object of attention (scholarly or otherwise). The paper concludes with a discussion about the implications of the perspective on regions developed in the article for the future of regional studies.

摘要

突显区域。区域研究。本文探究区域概念之于区域研究和社会实践的持续存在但改变中的显着性。透过追溯此一范畴意义的改变，本文强调学术对区域的概念化进程中的一个特微面向：有关各种形式的本质主义和拜物教的重复批评。本文主要的焦点接着移至区域的概念化，以及有关区域实际上"是什麼"与"做什麼"，以及什麼让区域成为值得关注的对象（学术或非学术）的概念阐述。本文于结论中，探讨文中所发展的区域视角对未来区域研究的意涵。

RÉSUMÉ

Mise en valeur de la région. *Regional Studies*. La présente communication examine de près la signification perpétuelle, mais en évolution, du concept de la région pour les études régionales et les pratiques sociales. Après avoir relevé les significations changeantes de cette catégorie, elle met en lumière un aspect caractéristique de l'évolution de la conceptualisation académique de la région: des itérations récurrentes de critiques concernant différentes formes d'essentialisme et de fétichisme. La communication se concentre ensuite principalement sur la conceptualisation de la région et l'articulation d'idées sur ce que «asont» et ce que «afont» substantiellement les régions, et ce qui fait de la région un sujet digne de cette attention (académique ou autre). La communication se termine par une discussion sur les implications de la perspective sur des régions développées dans l'article sur l'avenir des études régionales.

ZUSAMMENFASSUNG
Thematisierung der Region. *Regional Studies*. In diesem Beitrag untersuchen wir die unvergängliche, aber veränderliche Bedeutung des Konzepts der Region für die Regionalwissenschaft und soziale Praxis. Nach einer Nachverfolgung der veränderten Bedeutungen dieser Kategorie wird ein charakteristischer Aspekt des Fortschritts der akademischen Konzeptualisierungen der Region hervorgehoben: wiederkehrende Iterationen von Kritiken verschiedener Formen des Essentialismus und Fetischismus. Anschließend verlagert sich der Hauptschwerpunkt auf die Konzeptualisierung der Region und die Äußerung von Ideen zum Thema, was Regionen im Wesentlichen 'sind' und 'tun' und was die Region zu einem lohnenswerten Gegenstand der (wissenschaftlichen oder anderweitigen) Betrachtung macht. Der Beitrag endet mit einer Erörterung der Implikationen der im Artikel entwickelten Perspektive der Regionen für die Zukunft der Regionalwissenschaft.

RESUMEN
La región en primer plano. *Regional Studies*. En este artículo realizamos un escrutinio del significado sempiterno pero en transformación del concepto de la región para los estudios regionales y la práctica social. Después de hacer un seguimiento de los significados cambiantes de esta categoría, destacamos un aspecto característico del progreso de las conceptualizaciones académicas de la región: iteraciones recurrentes de críticas con respecto a las diferentes formas de esencialismo y fetichismo. Después trasladamos el principal enfoque a la conceptualización de la región y la articulación de ideas sobre qué 'son' y 'hacen' básicamente las regiones, y lo que hace que la región sea digna de atención especial (académica o cualquier otra). Concluimos el artículo con un debate sobre las repercusiones de la perspectiva de las regiones desarrollada en el artículo para el futuro de los estudios regionales.

INTRODUCTION

It has become practically axiomatic in the social science literature to note how 'the region is back' in both academia and wider societal life – in spite of contrasting tendencies related to globalization and all kinds of flows and networks (Entrikin, 2008; Fawn, 2009; Harrison, 2008; Keating, 2004). Debates on the differences between specific regions and the justification of regional divisions have not been merely academic exercises. Countless governmental bodies, committees and planning offices in dramatically variegated political and geographical settings around the world have been involved in such deliberations, with or without academic support, as state and quasi-state governance arrangements continuously remain the major context for both sub- and supra-state regionalization and region-building efforts (Moisio & Paasi, 2013).

As part of the evolution of this wider political landscape, academic scholars have contributed to guiding debates and shaping new rationalities by launching newfangled terms into discussions on regions and regionalism. Categories such as city-region, mega-region, learning region, creative region, competitive region, resilient region or bioregion, for example, have attached new meanings to the abstract idea of region. The burgeoning plethora of such widely circulated regional–conceptual hybrids in both academic literature and in the language of regional development think-tanks and planning organizations further attests to how academic debates about the nature and characteristics of regions are rooted in complex and contestable social, economic and political dynamics (Barnes, 2011; Bristow, 2010; Paasi, 2010, 2011).

For decades, *Regional Studies* has functioned as a medium for a critical discussion around such terms (e.g., Crawshaw, 2013; Jones & Paasi, 2013; Pike, 2007). Linking in with this tradition of critical enquiry concerning the labelling of particular aspects of the world as 'regions' and the backgrounds and consequences of such practice, the key task of this paper is to discuss various ways of *foregrounding the region*. In linguistics 'foregrounding' refers to the practice of distinguishing a concept from the surrounding words or images. The main discursive vehicle for achieving this effect with regards to discussions about regions is naturally through the deployment of the 'keyword' *par excellence* of such debates: the concept of region itself (cf. Williams, 1983). The present paper takes a manifest interest in how this concept has evolved and been mobilized over the past decades by scrutinizing the variegated meanings that have been attached to it in academic research. Thus, its main focus is to trace and review *conceptualizations* of the 'region', that is, how scholars have articulated and justified ideas about what regions substantially 'are' and 'do', activities that have continually enacted the region as a worthy object of attention (scholarly or otherwise).

The paper particularly focuses on the *metageography* or *spatial imaginary* of the research field (e.g., Haughton & Allmendinger, 2015; Murphy, 2008). As argued by Murphy (2008, p. 9), metageographical conceptions are important because they play a powerful role in organizing and shaping understandings of the world, and therefore, by extension, also influence action (cf. Faludi, 2012). Our approach to the topic is guided by a broadly defined pragmatist sensibility. Partly following Barnes (2008), a pragmatist approach to concepts is understood here as calling for an attentiveness to the situated definition of terms within partially connecting (or not) communities of practice and epistemic communities, and to investigate the drivers and outcomes of conceptual innovations. Further, it implores the researcher never to assume that there is one 'correct' way of defining a concept, which would somehow capture the essence of its supposed object. In line with such a sensibility, within the context of the paper, the conceptual history of the region is understood not as a step-wise progression towards some form of essential truth about what the region 'really is', but rather as attempts at grappling with spatiotemporally located intellectual, political and social challenges.[1]

Consequently, the arguments put forth in the paper rest upon a conviction that it is impossible to understand academic struggles between competing conceptualizations of the region in a productive way if one treats them as somehow separate from the wider political and social 'career' of the region–concept and without recognizing that academics are by no means the only ones who sometimes creatively, sometimes unreflexively (re)conceptualize regions. Undoubtedly, spatial concepts such as 'region' to some degree function as contestable totems for academic fields and other spheres of professional and political practice, and the act of their perpetual redefinition is simultaneously an illustration of academic struggle over symbolic capital/prestige and a powerful mirror of wider societal, often state-related developments and concerns (Paasi, 2011). Such power struggles recurrently involve the caricaturing and denouncement of one's predecessors or contestants competing conceptualizations as problematic, naïve or unscientific. In recent decades this has in the academic debate over the nature of regions often played out as consecutive series of accusations of *essentialism* or *fetishism* between various schools/traditions of regional studies. From the heat of such denunciations, it becomes apparent that contrasting conceptualizations make a difference through producing diverging *ontological politics* (Mol, 1999).[2] In relation to this, it is particularly noteworthy that contemporary understandings of the 'regional world' to some degree universalize the notion of the region and blur the conceptualization of regions with that of basically all other key spatial categories such as territory, place, scale or network. This 'ontological slipperiness' of the concept of region within contemporary geography and regional studies is further evinced by how it is excluded from Jessop, Brenner, and Jones's (2008) elaboration of a possible framework for defining the relations between these other key concepts of geography. As a consequence, there appears to emerge a need to ask – perhaps provocatively – if regional studies as a discipline becomes less relevant in a world in which 'regions', as they are currently understood at the research front of regional studies specifically and social theory generally, on the one hand appear to be everywhere, but on the other hand appear to lack any form of attention-grabbing specificity. The question arises: what difference does it make, in such a world, to insist on defining certain relational entities as 'regions' – and why is this important?

In order to fulfil the ambitions set forth in this introduction, the paper proceeds in two steps. The first part of the paper provides an – inevitably brief – investigation into the *conceptual history* of the academic understanding of the idea of *region*, which must also be understood as part of a wider social history (Koselleck, 2002). The historical exposition serves to demonstrate that the transformation (or rather, the perpetual rethinking) of the concept of region is by no means a new tendency, but how the pace of invention and reproduction of spatial keywords nonetheless seems to be accelerating (Agnew, 1989; Barnes, 2011; Harrison, 2008; Paasi, 2011). After this the modus of enquiry is shifted to a manner more akin to *conceptual pedagogy* (Deleuze & Guattari, 1994) to discuss the implications of one specific aspect of the evolution of academic conceptualizations of the region, namely, the recurrent waves of criticism regarding various forms of essentialism and fetishism, that is, the supposedly erroneous assignment of coherence and agency to things such as regions. This debate is then turned somewhat on its head through the posing of the question if, in a relationally complex world, there is any way to conceptualize anything without risking falling prey to some variant of this critique. Perhaps conceptualization always entails a form of fetishism, and the interesting questions to ask rather come to concern the situated consequences of adopting specific ways of 'carving up' and putting labels on various aspects of the (regional) world. The paper then wraps up with a discussion of some of the implications of the perspective put forth in the paper for the future of regional studies as an academic discipline.

WHAT REGIONS ARE AND DO: CONCEPTUALIZING 'THE REGION'

It was for a long time typical in the practice of the newly institutionalized regional geography to search for formal regions (labelled as natural and later geographical regions) on various grounds (nature, culture, coexistence of various elements) and ultimately put them onto maps.[3] Distinguishing and isolating such regions from each other was a crucial part of this activity. Regions were understood to be products of research process whether they were seen as 'really existing entities' or 'mental devices' (cf. Blaut, 1962; Minshull, 1967), and the purpose of studying them was generally conceived to be the production of maps that gave a specific territorial shape and name to a region in the wider regional matrix. In practice, both approaches depended upon a 'bordering' process carried out by the researcher, but there nonetheless existed a deep ontological division between the two approaches that has stayed with regional studies ever since. This chasm runs between basically a naturalist–realist ontology, on the one hand, and a more pragmatist sensibility, on the other. The first of these considers there to be an underlying 'natural' or at least 'real' object, the region, which can be uncovered through analysis, i.e., correctly picked out and 'traced'. From this angle the interesting question is, 'are we getting it right or wrong?', and the answer will be ultimately decided by the quality of the analysis. The other proceeds from a completely different implicit question: is there some utility and relevance to labelling and treating certain aspects of the world as 'regions'? Kimble's (1951) answer was critical: regional geographers may be trying to put boundaries that do not exist around regions that do not matter! For many other representatives of regional geography the answer was much more positive, while being typically contestable (Agnew, 1989; Harrison, 2008).

After the Second World War a new ambition to control, manage and plan regional systems emerged. Capitalist urbanization and industrialization and the related concentration of population and the economy created uneven development and urban problems. Systematic approaches to economic, urban and transport issues accentuated functional/nodal regions, relative location and interaction – an idea that had been emergent in geography already before the war (e.g., Walter Christaller in Germany) (cf. Barnes, 2011; Paasi, 2011). The rise of regional science and the quantitative revolution entailed a search for abstract spatial patterns/forms, which were treated as logical, geometric realities, underlying and to some degree separate from the contextual meanings of social life. The traditional regional geographic inwards-oriented language of unity/particularity (manifesting in such terms as synthesis, uniqueness, holism, whole, totality, organism, personality, etc.) was rejected by regional scientists. Spatial–analytical approaches instead purposely distanced their network-based kinetic functional conceptualization of the region from any form of inwards oriented, holistic regional thinking (Haggett, 1965).

The rise of critical regional studies soon led to responses against the objectivist and often strongly positivistic character of quantitative regional science: on the one hand, it was seen to be blind to power dynamics and, on the other, to fail properly to take into account the subjective nature of human experience. Based on these two different points of critique, the proponents of Marxist and humanistic approaches revitalized the studies of regions, the former problematizing regions in relation to uneven development (Massey, 1978), the latter highlighting the significance of regional identities and spatial experiences (Buttimer, 1979). The key agency in the making of regions in Marxist accounts is the accumulation of capital, which is related to uneven capitalist development. Massey (1978), for example, suggested that the analysis of uneven development should not start from any prespecified, fixed regionalization of space but rather investigate the patterns of capital accumulation, from which geographical analysis must then produce the concepts in the terms of the spatial divisions of labour. Massey's sensitiveness to history led her to develop the famous 'geological metaphor': the development of spatial structures can be viewed as a product of the combination of 'layers' of the successive activity (Massey, 1984, p. 118). Hudson (2002, 2007) in particular has developed Marxist political economy approaches further in the analysis of the production of places/regions.

Regions as social constructs

Marxists and humanistic views provided a critical stepping stone towards so-called 'new regional geography'. This was a heterogeneous set of theoretical approaches where *social practice* was seen as the key 'source' of regions, in contrast to the preceding 'discipline-centric' perspective in which geographers produced definitions of regions and regional divisions as a result of their research process. By bringing together various strands of critique against quantitative regional science, and further adding influences from simultaneous developments in social theory and philosophy, scholars accentuating the structuration of practice and power relations in space–time advanced new views on regions and moved attention to individual and institutional practices/discourses that mediated agency and social structures. A region was now seen as an 'actively passive meeting place of social structures and human agency', which is 'lived through, not in' (Thrift, 1983, p. 38), a historically contingent process (Pred, 1984), or a process of institutionalization where certain territorial, symbolic and institutional shapes emerge as part of the transforming spatial division of labour (Paasi, 1986). For some scholars the effort to advance regional geographies inescapably claimed new philosophical/ methodological solutions to the problems of context, causation, ethnography and narrative. They saw realist philosophy particularly useful for developing new critical regional geographies (Sayer, 1989; cf. Agnew, 1989).

Geographers increasingly regarded regions as *social constructs* that were produced/reproduced by social actors in and through variegated social practices and discourses. The region is thus not thought to be 'constructed' or 'discovered' by scholars, but is rather apprehended as the outcome of contestable 'region-building' or regionalization processes. Rather than just geographers themselves, actors such as politicians, entrepreneurs, journalists, teachers or voluntary associations were thought to assume key positions as activists and advocates in the process of articulating the meanings and functions attached to regions. In relation to these, the role of the scholar becomes that of tracing and documenting the unfolding of such processes and the roles of actors/social relations through which regions become, transform, achieve meanings and may ultimately become deinstitutionalized. Within this 'New Regional Geography' literature, agency and power relations involved in the construction of a region are generally considered to extend both inside and outside of such regions as processes, constituting and opening the region towards a wider institutional matrix of economic, political and cultural relations. However, important questions, such as who or what it is that 'constructs' a region or what this construction means in terms of social practice or power relations, often remained unanswered or were answered in partial, contradictory ways (Paasi, 2010).

Relational/poststructuralist conceptions of region

One highly significant methodological (and ontological) question that arises in the wake of previous developments is whether 'social construction' denotes the *process* of constructing regions or some ready-made *products* of such construction (cf. Hacking, 1999). This issue is crucial for regional studies since it raises a critical methodological question regarding the relation between *history* and the region, i.e., whether the region is understood in terms of 'being', that is, a fixed entity or neutral background/medium for social processes, or something that is perpetually 'becoming' as part of these social processes, i.e., is itself a process.

Echoing Pred's (1984) and Paasi's (1986, 1991) early works, several scholars now conceptualize regions as historically contingent processes that are 'becoming' rather than just 'being', and thereby querying the relevance of ever painting a synchronic 'still life' of a regional configuration, without taking into regard the wider relational arrangements in time and space as well as the power relations that uphold, perpetuate or transform this pattern. They further argue the need for considering the potential (or rather, highly likely) prospect that the present configuration may just be but a snapshot, a temporary stabilization (of lesser or greater duration), of one specific moment in a 'coming together' of heterogeneous trajectories of change (Massey, 2005). Contemporary academic interest in regions, following this kind of rationality, can be labelled as a relational–topological approach that is often nourished by post-structuralist thinking which has inspired much of the regional research agenda since the late 1990s. Some scholars have been keen advocates of relational approaches (Allen, Cochrane, & Massey, 1998) and understand regions as entities shaped by social relations and networks made up of complex linkages and flows with a specific territorial reach. From this viewpoint also boundaries are results of networking and connections (Murdoch, 2006; Painter, 2010). Rather than being a neat fixed level in a nested scalar hierarchy, the relations sustaining the region are understood to stretch far beyond its imagined territorial and scalar borders in Euclidean space. Other scholars have offered often sympathetic critiques of straightforward one-sidedly relational views (Harrison, 2008, 2013; Jones, 2009; Metzger, 2013; Metzger & Schmitt, 2012; Varró & Lagendijk, 2013).

To many commentators, the pertinence and relevance of regions and regional geography has been fundamentally challenged as a consequence of transforming socio-spatial and power relations and the ongoing, sometimes radical, reorganization of social, political and cultural spatialities around the world – sometimes collectively referred to as 'globalization' (cf. Scott & Storper, 2007). In response, some scholars have sought to rethink, for example, the global regional geographies of the world system of production (Taylor, 1988), while others accentuate the need to trace the changing regional worlds of distribution, often in the context of the new geopolitics of city-regionalism (Jonas, 2012). Another group has taken a more overtly politically engaged position and suggests that the opening of borders is a major challenge for a progressive (social) science and politics (Massey, 2005): most (con)temporary regions 'stretch' in space so that their social contents/relations are networked across borders. Such networking modifies and reconstitutes regions/borders, and gives rise to a complex, dynamic topology where distance and proximity fold in numerous ways (cf. Allen, 2016).

Some relational geographers go further and contend that to talk about bounded regions is a misconception of the networks and flows that actually exist and which are unduly 'reified' under the label of 'region'. Hence, talking about regions as bounded entities blinds one to this act of reification, since ' given actor–network is not confined to a finite, homogeneous territory demarcated by clear-cut boundaries; rather it carries the potential of infinite expansion due the unproblematic incorporation of all the kinds of actors, however different, the network may mobilize' (Pedersen, 2009, p. 140). However, many commentators have called for the need to move beyond the territorial/relational binary that has characterized such debates (Allen & Cochrane, 2007; Cochrane & Ward, 2012; Harrison, 2013; Varró & Lagendijk, 2013). Painter (2010), for example, suggests that 'territory' and 'network' are not incommensurable or rival principles of spatial organization.

For him, territory is primarily an effect – and such a 'territory effect' can best be understood as the result of networked socio-technical practices. Hence, the current resurgence of territory or region can be seen as itself a product of relational networks.

Of course the 'real-world' problem is – and this was sometimes perhaps under-estimated during the early period of relational thinking – that while in some cases boundaries are quite insignificant, in other cases they are more persistent and make a difference. A certain boundedness is often a 'fact of practice' since many regions are actually *territories* deployed within the processes of governance, and are made socially meaningful entities in processes characterized by multifaceted power relations. Recent research on the changing forms of regional governance has high-lighted the traversing and interrelated character of the 'territorial' and 'relational' rather than seeing them as separate or even opposite ontological realms (Cochrane & Ward, 2012; McCann & Ward, 2010). It is therefore crucial to scrutinize the territory/network constellation as embedded in social practice (planning, govern-ance, politics) rather than assuming an abstract ontological rupture between the territorial and relational. The functions of borders should be understood contextu-ally in relation to social practice in order to reveal their possible constitutive roles in the making, management and control of territorial spaces and social action (Paasi & Zimmerbauer, 2016). Respectively, regional planning, for example, operates more often with 'penumbral' rather than fixed borders: the former can be at the same time meaningful in some planning-related social practices and rather meaningless in some others. Thus, one has to ask how the region performed in relation to some entities and relations rather than other, at what time and place this occurs, and by whom such performativity is mobilized (Metzger, 2013). To learn from this, one needs to study how these relations play out in practice, where different conceptualizations of space in general, and regions in particular, have no problem of sitting beside one another and co-mingling, untroubled by academic tribulations and claims about their supposed mutual exclusivity (Metzger, 2013).

VARIETIES OF FETISHISM (AND THEIR CRITICS)

The conceptualization of the region is certainly not merely a 'what it is' problem in regional studies or even in social practice, but also pertains to the perhaps even more vexing question of 'what it does' (cf. Agnew, 1989). Is the region to be understood as a prime mover of action, i.e., does it have 'agentic capacities', or is it conceptualized as 'merely' mirroring other, supposedly more primary powers? This conundrum concerning 'what regions do' invites one to revisit debates about *spatial fetishism* that were opened up by critical geographers a long time ago, and then to look at some fresh alternatives.

The term 'fetishism' has, in a generic sense, been used in social science to denote some form of misattribution of agency, which in the broad Marxist tradi-tion of social science has also been associated with the notion of 'reification': an obfuscation of the relations that produce or sustain a specific entity or arrangement. In Marxist traditions of social science, this has primarily been discussed in terms of *commodity* fetishism, whereby the social relations that enable the production of a specific market goods become hidden from view when the product is inserted into market-based systems of exchange. This in turn generates relationship between goods that only become comprehendible in narrowly economic terms, i.e., as relative economic values, thus obscuring the social relations of production of the goods in question. *Spatial* fetishism, in turn, refers to an understanding in which the relations between social groups or economic classes are interpreted as relations between areas, as if one region (one section of 'space') would be, for example, exploiting another region or ultimately that a given social structure would be determined by spatial relations (Anderson, 1973; Urry, 1985). For Gregory (1978), the 'fetishism of area' refers to thinking of regions as entities that can interact with other regions, as if they constitute a world apart from society. Such fetishism also characterizes the discourse of competition between states, willingly used by politicians in their rhetoric.

Critiques of fetishism take various forms. For Marxists spatial fetishism reifies what in reality is the product of capital/class dynamics. For humanistic geographers it reifies what in reality are psychological–linguistic ideas that subjects employ to orientate themselves in the world. What unites these streams of critique is that they all disapprove of the direct or indirect attribution of agentic capacities to space or spatial entities such as regions in relation to the organization of social relations and meaning. They further point to how such fetishism often obscures the making, becoming and performativity of regions as results of societal power relations, struggles and ideologies. This complexity is an everlasting challenge for critical scholars and, as Soja (1989, p. 6) states:

> We must be insistently aware of how space can be made to hide consequences from us, how relations of power and discipline are inscribed into the apparently innocent spatiality of social life, how human geographies become filled with politics and ideology.

The key message of these commentators is that while regions seem to act and do things, in reality it is *other* forces, often among this group of authors assumed to be those of capital, that matter – and what are recognized as 'regions' are merely the material and/or ideological–fictitious reflections of such processes. Consequently, statements such as 'the region does this or that' or 'it is in the interest of the region' thus obfuscate the real interests and actors, e.g., of economic classes.

Fetishizing in regional practice and research

Who are, then, those criticized for generating spatial fetishism today? The recent resurgence of the region has led to a situation in which the region is increasingly taken for granted as a (bounded) setting or background for diverging social processes. It has been suggested above that this occurs not only in academic fields but also in regional media, education, planning and governance. To give some examples, in strategic regional planning it is characteristic to represent regions as actors that make decisions, struggle with each other or promote themselves (Bristow, 2010; Pike, 2011). In the media, regions, nations or cities are portrayed as partaking in a 'struggle' and 'beating each other' in economic issues and cultural achievements. Regional actors increasingly try to transform regions into products that are marketed as attracting packages to individuals, families or businesses that are seduced to regions in various roles: as tourists, workers, employees, etc. Marketing/ promotion everywhere uses such strategies in fetishizing the region/place.

Another form of fetishizing can be labelled as a 'pre-scientific' understanding of regions, wherein the region is taken for granted as a mere neutral background of social issues, discounting the political history and institutional biography of any region (Paasi, 2010). Such understandings are partly due to the position given to region in contexts such as governance, planning and regional development and is fed by different interpretations of the real-world needs for regionalization processes. The consolidating forms of governance in the European Union have markedly advanced such an understanding. One central medium was the creation of the European Union's NUTS (Nomenclature of Units for Territorial Statistics) region system, i.e., the authorization of spatial units that are used at various spatial scales as the basis for the creation and maintenance of statistical information on 'regions' and that standardizes a nested understanding of what are the European regions. The NUTS system was established by EUROSTAT in order to help governance, management and the 'harmonization' of the spatial practices in Europe. Formally, the 'Europe of regions' thus consists of given administrative regions represented in official statistics (Bristow, 2010; Paasi, 2010). The NUTS classification is powerful in 'objectifying' European regional spaces: it defines regional boundaries, and has been the base for the allocation of European Union structural aid.

In academic circles, the aforementioned forms of policy-related or 'lay' fetishisms to some degree constitute easy targets. However, things get more sensitive when the sharp edge of critique is instead turned towards one's own academic colleagues. Nonetheless, every new school of regional geography in one way or the other has criticized its predecessors of some form of essentialism or fetishism. In one of the most recent recurrences of such critiques, Suorsa's (2014) review of almost 100 articles on regional innovation systems research demonstrates that the conceptualization of region is typically marginalized in such studies; innovations systems are more often than not seen to be located in regional settings that are taken for granted. Christopherson and Clark (2007) have explicitly criticized the representation of regional units as 'actors in themselves' in economic geography, and Asheim (2009, p. 174), for his part, criticizes fetishizing the idea of 'learning region' and states that 'regions cannot learn, only firms and organizations can' (cf. Cumbers, Mackinnon, & McMaster, 2003; Hassink & Klaerding, 2012).

However, even though the critique of spatial fetishism is alive and well within regional studies – and further, one would argue, has functioned as a quilting point for many productive and important academic debates – critics of spatial fetishism are in turn criticized by social constructivists for essentializing and unduly privileging other drivers, such as capital dynamics, in their accounts. Complaints of essentialism are directed against the reduction of multifaceted, dynamic and complex realities to 'one or a few fundamental causes' (Graham, 1990, p. 54). Graham (1990) shows that generalizing accounts drawing on macro-level social or political economy explanations frequently comprise an essentialist element when directly or indirectly highlighting, e.g., capital accumulation, capitalist relations within production, the class struggle, production or profitability as *the* prime drivers of social and spatial change. The same broad critique of essentialization can of course be levelled against claims that firms and organizations, supposedly in contrast to regions, can 'learn' – given that many organizational scholars in turn would argue that they indeed cannot, and that only humans are capable of this. A conclusion which then again in itself would be questioned by social scientists influenced by post-humanist strands of philosophy, who would claim that such a statement would constitute a reification or essentialization of individual 'humans' as some form of autonomous units, which in turn would indicate a failure to recognize that any form of individual subjectivity in effect constitutes a relational arrangement of variegated sets of genetic material, social relations, cultural traditions, ideology, institutions, etc. Situating critiques against spatial fetishism within such a wider contextual frame sheds a light on how these arguments often have been underpinned by problematic un-interrogated assumption that humans (or capital, class, culture) are somehow integral and coherent actors, and in themselves not battlegrounds for various conflicting economic, political, cultural, ideological and biological drives, pushing their action in various directions. From such a vantage point, the positing of *anything* as an actor 'in itself' becomes problematic, and an example of what Haraway (1997) calls *corporeal* fetishism, which entails 'mistaking *heterogeneous* relationality for a fixed, seemingly objective thing', by way of which 'interactions among heterogeneous actors are mistaken for self-identical things to which actions might be applied' (Haraway, 1997, pp. 142–143, original emphasis).

Problematizing the notion of agency and the relational region

A stable and somehow fixed image of preceding traditions of regional geography seems to have become a caricature for the representatives of newer approaches. Thus, new approaches often accentuate the missing historical reflexivity in their earlier counterparts; complaining about their positing of the bounded character of regions and the fixity and inwards-looking orientation in the previous, supposedly more 'traditional' perspective. They in consecutive turns blame each other of a lack of scientific rigour or varieties fetishism. However, with some notable exceptions (e.g., Graham, 1990), what these critics often appear to be only dimly aware of is that they themselves generally all in turn implicitly lean against something supposedly firmer and 'more real', as a purportedly solid ontological ground that can be used as a leverage point to denounce the 'mere illusions' that are problematically reified by others. All could therefore in turn be criticized for propagating various forms of reductionism, and generating reifications of, if not regions in themselves, then classes in themselves, networks in themselves, capital in itself, etc. – enacting regions as mere reflections or symptoms of these supposedly more 'real' forces. Thus, it could be argued that critiques that only aim at debunking fetishisms do not really serve to foreground the region, but rather to background it; or more specifically, they foreground it momentarily, so that it can then be dismissed as a mere reflection of some supposedly more real, underlying force or agent such as 'globalization', 'capital', etc.

Could there be a way out of this vicious circle of critique, which to an external observer could sometimes appear as a dog chasing its own tail? A way out that does not rely on claiming some solid ontological ground as a basis for knocking the bottom out of others' conceptualizations? At least one attempt at providing such an 'irreductionist' approach is the version of actor–network theory (ANT) provided by Bruno Latour. In ANT, careful attention is paid so as not a priori to 'reify' or privilege any form of force or entity as more primary than another (Latour, 1988, 2005). Rather than taking terms such as 'actors' or 'networks' as given start- or endpoints of enquiry, ANT treat such concepts as practical handles on a world that is in itself always richer than our descriptions of it – but where the use of specific concepts make a difference by performatively bringing together and highlighting certain aspects and back grounding others (see also Latour, Jensen, Venturini, Grauwin, & Boullier, 2012; Mol, 2010; Paasi, 2008). It plays with the definition of, for example, 'networks' and 'actors', arguing that one often can learn new things about the world by approaching what one normally would call a 'network' as an 'actor', an entity that produces some form of agency; and then also turning this around to analyse an 'actor' instead as a 'network' made up of entangled, mutually affective heterogeneous components, stretching both within and outside of the boundaries of a recognized entity – and where agency is understood to be relationally produced in such networks (cf. Abrahamsson, Bertoni, Mol, & Martin, 2015; Johansson & Metzger, 2016; Latour, 2005).

From the vantage point of such an approach, 'reification' and 'fetishism', i.e., the 'picking out' and 'cutting loose' of singular objects from complex and entangled webs of constitutive relations, and then attributing some form of power of agency to them, become crucial human practices for navigating in a world marked by ubiquitous and wicked relational complexity. This is also the explicit argument made by Law (2015): in an in-itself messy and over-rich world of complexly overlapping similarities and differences, any conceptualization in academic or other context demands simplifications that foreground some sets of relations and attributes while backgrounding other. Humans simply must and do 'fetishize' all the time to get some manageable handles on a relationally complex world of open or semi-bounded systems.[4] Indeed, it becomes completely necessary to conduct such simplifications to ever be able to act in the world, or one would be constantly overcome by a sense of overwhelming complexity.

Following Law (2015), the question is how to conduct such conceptualizations, in the form of foregrounding and simplification, in a responsible way – by staying attentive to the effects of one's choices and making oneself conscious of what becomes made important and what is excluded from any particular way of conceptualizing some phenomenon. As a consequence, fetishization cannot be seen as an evil in itself.

However, what becomes tantamount is trying to make oneself aware of the practical consequences of any specific mode of fetishization or reification. The interesting question becomes how self-aware one is in doing so and also to stay attentive to the wider implications and consequences of just how one fetishizes or reifies.

What about regions in such a relational world? Social constructivist and poststructuralist approaches to regions have helped engender an understanding of these entities as composite actors, 'made to act by many others' (Latour, 2005, p. 46), where those 'others' lie topologically and topographically both 'inside' and 'outside' the everlastingly reconstructing, material and discursive socio-spatial process that becomes labelled as 'the region', and where variegated actors contribute to producing (often contested) accounts and narratives of such regions as to some degree constituting coherent and definable entities. Work of regionali-zation and 'region-building' is performed not only by economic, political and cultural/media elites in the production/reproduction of regions and identity narratives, but also in everyday practices and in the work of, for example, regional planners and developers, as well as through such mundane material structures such as transport infrastructures (Metzger, 2013; Paasi, 2013).

Regions are thus envisaged as complicated constellations of materiality, agency, social relations and power; as institutional structures and processes that are continuously 'becoming' instead of just 'being'. They are based on a complex interplay between non-discursive and discursive practices and patterns. Various time scales come together in such processes. Similarly, heterogeneous social insti-tutions such as culture, media and administration are crucial in these processes and in the production and reproduction of certain 'structures of expectations' for these units. Such structures are the basis for the narratives of identity, mobiliza-tion of collective memory, and they also constitute the visible and invisible social 'gel' based on values, norms and ideologies (Paasi, 1991).

So what is the point of the above, fairly extensive, digression into ANT-inspired conceptualizations of the region? Is it to argue that finally the 'right' and 'true' way to represent and conceptualize regions has now been found? Given the previously presented pragmatist sensibilities of this enquiry, any such idea would of course be completely off-hand. Rather, this approach has been recounted in some detail because it productively speaks to an identified weakness in previously dominant ways of conceptualizing regions. Specifically, in this case, it offers affordances for the researcher to extricate her analysis from the previously described fetishism–conundrum. Viewed from the vantage point of these previous debates, this way of rethinking the region may indeed appear to be sensible and pertinent, seeing that it offers a way around an identified problem that previous conceptualizations had trouble negotiating. However, this by no means implies that this way of conceptualizing regions somehow would be a complete, eternal or total solution. As long as the region remains an interesting category of social and scholarly practice, also this approach will with time most certainly be superseded as a consequence of increasingly obvious internal contradictions, and constantly growing lacunae with regards to its explanatory power vis-à-vis the continually evolving worldly processes it pertains to index and relate to.

Just to mention one such obvious and troubling weakness of an ANT-inspired way of conceptualizing the region, it can definitely be argued that in such a very broad and general definition of the nature of regions, what is gained in explanatory power is lost in specificity and context sensitivity. Hence, the question arises what the particular but common attributes (e.g., various institutions, practices, symbols) of the entities labelled as regions really are in contrast to any other type of spatial entity that arguably could be considered to be constituted and held together by similar attributes and mechanisms (cf. Paasi, 1991)? What is it that 'regions' have in common, which at the same time differentiates them from (or links them with), for example, 'nations', 'places' and 'localities'? For at the same time as the radical poststructuralist approaches suddenly enable analysts to label very many phenomena around the world as 'regions' of some kind and extent, the question nevertheless follows: what good does this do? That is, what difference does it make to conceptualize something as a 'region', 'carving it out' and labelling it as such, and not in a different way? This question can, of course, productively be posed in an analytical modality, turned towards, for instance, all the political and professional groups that throw this concept around in their everyday practice and discourse, asking what difference it appears to make in their practice to enact 'regions' in various ways; but the question also has a normative dimension that poses a challenge to regional studies as an academic pursuit.

CONCLUDING DISCUSSION

Academic debates about the development and refinement of various analytical spatial concepts do not only constitute esoteric wordplays. Rather, they are enmeshed in wider societal power dynamics in which the stakes often are high, even if not always directly visible. One such stake, which is fairly obvious, is certainly the fate and prospects of specific academic disciplines – which are dependent on prestige and apparent relevance, leading to funding and influence within and outside academia. Viewed from this angle, it could be argued that the subdisciplines of regional geography and regional studies, building upon the logic of the importance of 'foregrounding the region', in this regard are dependent upon a sustained interest in the concept of the 'region' and that which it purports to denote. This foundation has been put into doubt by claims set forth since the 19th century, suggesting that the region will fade away along with the consolidating modernity and related state-centric spatiality (Keating, 1998). It is obvious that such predictions have been if not completely erroneous then at least grossly premature (e.g., Addie & Keil, 2015; Parker & Harloe, 2015; Soja, 2015). Part of this perseverance is based on the intimate relation between the state and the region: the region, especially when conceptualized as a sub-state political territory, is a critical constituent of the territorial politics and governance of modern states and its rise into a privileged scale of activity is itself a result of politics, policies and power (Christopherson & Clark, 2007).

Thus, regions appear to have persistent relevance and allure, both for academics and policy practitioners alike. Then again, understandings of what a region is and does have shifted considerably in the course of decades. The region is today generally conceptualized as a flexible, malleable and mutable object of analysis. 'Unusual' regions (Deas & Lord, 2006) appear to pop up everywhere, if one just looks closely enough. This brings a new focus to the practical enactment of various ways of being/becoming a 'region' and, for lack of better terms, 'modes of regionality' or 'ways of becoming region'. If there is not anything that is basically 'regional', but nevertheless a whole lot of (contested) patterns out there in the world that seem meaningful to be labelled as 'regions' for some purposes, and that some groups of people also label as such, what is it that makes them hang together *as regions*? This certainly relates to some degree to the old question of 'regions in themselves' versus 'for themselves', but also demands the recognition of that there are then innumerable regions 'in themselves' out there all the time, criss-crossing in partial connections (Metzger, 2013). So the 'for themselves' becomes perhaps an even more pertinent question. This in turn brings back into focus the 'subject of regionality': who/what is ascribing regionality to an entity (or even de-/ascribing it as gifted with 'regional identity')? And what organizing work are actors performing to make the region become 'for itself' by holding steady, reworking or challenging aspects of their environment (in a very broad sense, including, for example, social and political environment)? This could be a group of practitioners, a group of residents, politicians, researchers, or any mix of these and others. The interesting thing is, of course, that they can all define this object in different ways, thus generating regions in the guise of often 'non-coherent' and 'fuzzy' 'multiple objects' that are 'more than one but less than many', and characterized by a curious 'fractional coherence' that is often fraught by frictions and contradictions (Law, 2004; Metzger, 2013).

Such an understanding further demands that academic analyses of regional issues do not only turn attention to when people 'out there' (e.g., activists or policy practitioners) are ascribing regionality, analysing why 'they' treat/define something as a region in practice, and looking at what difference does this make. It also highlights the need for the academic researcher to interrogate her own role in producing/reproducing ascriptions of regionality in her work, and to ask herself: what difference am I making – how am I intervening in worldly affairs – by doing this? If one recognizes that the world is much more complex than what can be grasped with the conceptual tools available at any given time (Paasi, 2008), and that there are always innumerable ways to analyse and correlate possible conceptual 'holds' on the world – what kind of scholarly practice would such an insight call for? To begin with, it would require of researchers in regional studies always to ask questions such as: What difference does it make if one conceptualizes some spatial entities as 'regions' or not? What difference does it make to package and enact a set of heterogeneous relations as a 'region'? What supplement does it add to see something, or rather – treat it – specifically as a 'region'?

Further, and perhaps somewhat more uncomfortably, it would perhaps also require turning the question 'what does it do?' not only towards *regions* and those who enact them within, for example, the spheres of politics and professional practice, but also towards the subdiscipline of *regional studies*. This certainly demands that the regional studies scholar interrogates, with critical (self)distance, her own research practices: in which concrete ways do specific approaches co-produce the objects of their interest? And further, how do they organize attention towards certain issues and away from others? What is being made absent/ present in various ways of analyzing regions, and to what consequences? More broadly: what are the explicit or implicit ontologies, epistemologies and normativities of a specific way of performing regional studies? And finally, as well as perhaps also most dauntingly: what are the situated but patterned ethico-political effects of performing the concept of 'region' specifically, and regional studies more generally, in this or that way?

ACKNOWLEDGEMENTS

The authors thank three anonymous reviewers for their comments.

DISCLOSURE STATEMENT

No potential conflict of interest was reported by the authors.

FUNDING

Anssi Paasi thanks the Academy of Finland for funding the RELATE Center of Excellence [project number 272168].

NOTES

1. This lack of concern with correspondence-based understandings of truth is one of the central components of pragmatist though, perhaps most succinctly expressed in William James's famous dictum that if 'no bell in us tolls to let us know for certain when truth is in our grasp, then it seems a piece of idle fantasticality to preach so solemnly our duty of waiting for the bell' (James, 1897, p. 30). That is, even if there were a 'right' or a 'wrong' way to grasp things, how would one ever know when one got it 'right' except by way of intersubjective agreement or pragmatic, experimental testing and application?
2. Our way of apprehending the term 'ontology' is influenced by the so-called 'ontological turn' within science and technology studies (e.g., Woolgar & Lezaun, 2013, 2015). Respectively, one does not approach the subject of ontology in a prescriptive–speculative sense by making claims about the supposed nature of reality, but rather one takes an interest in the study of 'ontology in practice' and its situated effects, that is, the ideas people hold about how the world works and the components that constitute it, and what difference such ideas make (cf. Johansson & Metzger, 2016; Joronen & Häkli, 2016).
3. It is characteristic for historians of geography to trace the differences between various national schools of thought and their views on what regions are and are regional geographers do. Such comparison is certainly fruitful (Agnew, 1989; Barnes, 2011). However, the focus of the following discussion is particularly upon contrasts and differences in key aspects of the conceptualization of regions. While one is well aware that the foregrounding of the region has occurred to some extent simultaneously on several interre-

lated, contested terrains, not neatly in the form of successive rounds of theorization, limitations of space here mean the process will be described in a manner that to some degree oversimplifies the national complexities of the historical unfolding of these developments.
4. Law (2015) does not explicitly use the term 'fetishize', but utilizes the terminology developed by Rittel and Webber (1973) to discuss the 'taming' of 'wicked problems'. However, see Latour (2010) on 'factishes'. Collinge (2005, p. 201) also makes what appears to be a related argument, based on Derrida's notion of the 'spectral logic of the fetish'.

REFERENCES

Abrahamsson, S., Bertoni, F., Mol, A., & Martin, R. I. (2015). Living with omega-3: New materialism and enduring concerns. *Environment and Planning D: Society and Space, 33*, 4–19. doi:10.1068/d14086p

Addie, J. P., & Keil, R. (2015). Real existing regionalism: The region between talk, territory and technology. International *Journal of Urban and Regional Research, 39*, 407–417. doi:10.1111/1468-2427.12179

Agnew, J. (1989). Sameness and difference: Hartshorne's the *Nature of geography* and geography as areal variation. In J. N. Entrikin & D. S. Brunn (Eds.), *Reflections on Richard Hartshorne's the Nature of geography* (pp. 121–139). Washington, DC: Association of American Geographers (AAG).

Allen, J. (2016). *Topologies of power*. London: Routledge.

Allen, J., & Cochrane, A. (2007). Beyond the territorial fix: Regional assemblages, politics and power. *Regional Studies, 41*, 1161–1175. doi:10.1080/00343400701543348

Allen, J., Cochrane, J., & Massey, D. (1998). *Rethinking the region*. London: Routledge.

Anderson, J. (1973). Ideology in geography: An introduction. *Antipode, 5*, 1–6. doi:10.1111/j.1467-8330.1985.tb00330.x

Asheim, B. (2009). Learning regions. In R. Kitchin & N. Thrift (Eds.), *International encyclopedia of human geography, Vol. 6* (pp. 172–178). London: Elsevier.

Barnes, T. J. (2008). American pragmatism: Towards a geographical introduction. *Geoforum, 39*, 1542–1554. doi.org/10.1016/j.geoforum.2007.02.013

Barnes, T. J. (2011). From region to space I. In J. Agnew & J. S. Duncan (Eds.), *A companion to human geography* (pp. 146–160). Oxford: Blackwell.

Blaut, J. (1962). Object and relationship. *Professional Geographer, 14*, 1–7. doi:10.1111/j.0033-0124.1962.146_1.x

Bristow, G. (2010). *Critical reflections on regional competitiveness*. London: Routledge.

Buttimer, A. (1979). Insiders, outsiders and the geography of regional life. In A. Kuklinski (Ed.), *Regional dynamics of socioeconomic change* (pp. 155–175). Tampere: Finnpublishers.

Christopherson, S., & Clark, J. (2007). *Remaking regional economies*. London: Routledge.

Cochrane, A., & Ward, K. (2012). Researching the geographies of policy mobility: Confronting the methodological challenges. *Environment and Planning A, 44*, 5–12. doi:10.1068/a44176

Collinge, C. (2005). The *différance* between society and space: Nested scales and the returns of spatial fetishism. *Environment and Planning D: Society and Space, 23*, 189–206. doi:10.1068/d360t

Crawshaw, R. (2013). Guest Editor. Introduction: Politics, economics and perception in regional construction. *Regional Studies, 47*, 1177–1180. doi:10.1080/00343404.2013.781427

Cumbers, A., Mackinnon, D., & McMaster, R. (2003). Institutions, power and space: Assessing the limits to institutionalism in economic geography. *European Urban and Regional Studies, 10*, 325– 342. doi:10.1177/09697764030104003

Deas, I., & Lord, A. (2006). From a new regionalism to an unusual regionalism? The emergence of non-standard regional spaces and lessons for the territorial reorganisation of the state. *Urban Studies, 43*, 1847–1877. doi:10.1080/00420980600838143

Deleuze, G., & Guattari, F. (1994). *What is philosophy?* London: Verso.

Entrikin, J. N. (Ed.). (2008). *Regions: Critical essays in human geography.* London: Ashgate.

Faludi, A. (2012). Multi-level (territorial) governance: Three criticisms. *Planning Theory and Practice, 13*, 197–211. doi:10.1080/14649357.2012.677578.

Fawn, R. (2009). 'Regions' and their study: Wherefrom, what for and whereto? *Review of International Studies, 35*(S1), 5–34. doi:10.1017/S0260210509008419

Graham, J. (1990). Theory and essentialism in Marxist geography. *Antipode, 22*, 53–66. doi:10.1111/j.1467-8330.1990.tb00197.x

Gregory, D. (1978). *Ideology, science and human geography.* New York: St. Martin's.

Hacking, I. (1999). *The social construction of what?* Cambridge, MA: Harvard University Press.

Haggett, P. (1965). *Locational analysis in geography.* London: Edward Arnold.

Haraway, D. J. (1997). *Modest_Witness@Second_Millennium. FemaleMan© _Meets_ OncoMouse™: Feminism and technoscience.* New York: Routledge.

Harrison, J. (2008). The region in political economy. *Geography Compass, 2*(3), 814–830. doi:10.1111/j.1749-8198.2008.00113.x

Harrison, J. (2013). Configuring the new 'regional world': On being caught between territory and networks. *Regional Studies, 47*, 55–74. doi:10.1080/00343404.2011.644239

Hassink, R., & Klaerding, C. (2012). The end of the learning region as we knew it; towards learning in space. *Regional Studies, 46*, 1055–1066. doi:10.1080/00343404.2012.705823

Haughton, G., & Allmendinger, P. (2015). Fluid spatial imaginaries: Evolving estuarial city–regional spaces. *International Journal of Urban and Regional Research, 39*, 857–873. doi:10.1111/1468-2427.12211

Hudson, R. (2002). *Producing places.* Oxford: Guilford.

Hudson, R. (2007). Regions and regional uneven development forever? Some reflective comments upon theory and practice. *Regional Studies, 41*, 1149–1160. doi:10.1080/00343400701291617

James, W. (1897) The will to believe. In *The will to believe and other essays in popular philosophy* (pp. 1–31). New York: Longmans, Green.

Jessop, B., Brenner, N., & Jones, M. (2008). Theorizing socio-spatial relations. *Environment and Planning D: Society and Space, 26*, 389–401. doi:10.1068/d9107

Johansson, N., & Metzger, J. (2016). Experimentalizing the organization of objects: Re-enacting mines and landfills. *Organization*, doi:1350508415624271.

Jonas, A. E. G. (2012). City-regionalism: Questions of distribution and politics. *Progress in Human Geography, 36*, 822–829. doi:10.1177/0309132511432062

Jones, M. (2009). Phase space: Geography, relational thinking, and beyond. *Progress in Human Geography, 33*, 487–506. doi:10. 1177/0309132508101599

Jones, M., & Paasi, A. (2013). Guest Editorial: Regional world(s): Advancing the geography of regions. *Regional Studies, 47*, 1–5. doi:10.1080/00343404.2013.746437

Joronen, M., & Häkli, J. (2016) Politicizing ontology. *Progress in Human Geography*. doi:0309132516652953.

Keating, M. (1998). *The new regionalism in Western Europe*. Cheltenham: Edward Elgar.

Keating M. (Ed.). (2004). *Regions and regionalism in Europe*. Cheltenham: Edward Elgar.

Kimble, G. H. T. (1951). The inadequacy of the regional concept. In L. D. Stamp & S. W. Woolridge (Eds.), *London: Essays in geography* (pp. 151–174). London: Longmans, Green.

Koselleck, R. (2002) *The practice of conceptual history: Timing history, spacing concepts*. Stanford: Stanford University Press.

Latour, B. (1988). *The pasteurization of France*. Cambridge, MA: Harvard University Press.

Latour, B. (2005). *Reassembling the social*. Oxford: Oxford University Press.

Latour, B. (2010). *On the modern cult of the factish gods*. Durham: Duke University Press.

Latour, B., Jensen, P., Venturini, T., Grauwin, S., & Boullier, D. (2012). 'The whole is always smaller than its parts' – a digital test of Gabriel Tardes' monads. British Journal of Sociology, 63, 590–615. doi:10.1111/j.1468-4446.2012.01428.x

Law, J. (2004). *After method: Mess in social science research*. London: Routledge.

Law, J. (2015). *Working well with wickedness* (CRESC Working Paper No. 135). Milton Keynes/Manchester: Centre for Research on Socio-Cultural Change (CRESC).

Massey, D. (1978). Regionalism: Some current issues. *Capital and Class, 2*, 106–125. doi:10.1177/030981687800600105

Massey, D. (1984). *Spatial divisions of labour*. Basingstoke: Macmillan.

Massey, D. (2005). *For space*. London: Sage.

McCann, E., & Ward, K. (2010). Relationality/territoriality: Toward a conceptualization of cities in the world. *Geoforum, 41*, 175–184. doi:10.1016/j.geoforum.2009.06.006

Metzger, J. (2013). Raising the regional leviathan: A relational–materialist conceptualization of regions-in-becoming as publics-instabilization. *International Journal of Urban and Regional Research, 37*, 1368–1395. doi:10.1111/1468-2427.12038

Metzger, J., & Schmitt, P. (2012). When soft spaces harden: The EU strategy for the Baltic Sea region. *Environment and Planning A, 44*, 263–280. doi:10.1068/a44188

Minshull, R. (1967). *Regional geography: Theory and practice*. Hutchinson: London.

Moisio, S., & Paasi, A. (2013). From geopolitical to geoeconomic? The changing political rationalities of state space. *Geopolitics, 18*, 267–283. doi:10.1080/14650045.2012.723287

Mol, A. (1999). Ontological politics: A word and some questions. In J. Law & J. Hassard (Eds.), *Actor–network theory: And after* (pp. 74–89). Oxford: Blackwell.

Mol, A. (2010). Actor–network theory: Sensitive terms and enduring tensions. *Kölner Zeitschrift für Soziologie und Sozialpsychologie, 50*, 253–269.

Murdoch, J. (2006). *Post-structuralist geography*. London: Sage.

Murphy, A. B. (2008). Rethinking multi-level governance in a changing European Union: Why metageography and territoriality matter. *GeoJournal, 72*, 7–18. doi:10.1007/s10708-008-9161-9

Paasi, A. (1986). The institutionalization of regions: A theoretical framework for understanding the emergence of regions and the constitution of regional identity. *Fennia – International Journal of Geography, 164*, 105–146. doi:10.11143/9052

Paasi, A. (1991).Deconstructing regions:Notes on the scales of spatial life. *Environment and Planning A, 23*, 239–256. doi:10.1068/a230239

Paasi, A. (2008). Is the world more complex than our theories of it? TPSN and the perpetual challenge of conceptualization. *Environment and Planning D: Society and Space, 26*, 405–410. doi:10.1068/d9107c

Paasi, A. (2010). Commentary: Regions are social constructs but who or what constructs them? Agency in question. *Environment and Planning A, 42*, 2296–2301. doi:10.1068/a42232

Paasi, A. (2011). From region to space II. In J. Agnew & J. S. Duncan (Eds.), *A companion to human geography* (pp. 161–175). Oxford: Blackwell.

Paasi, A. (2013). Regional planning and the mobilization of 'regional identity': From bounded spaces to relational complexity. *Regional Studies, 47,* 1206–1219. doi:10.1080/00343404.2012.661410

Paasi, A., & Zimmerbauer, K. (2016). Penumbral borders and planning paradoxes: Relational thinking and the question of borders in spatial planning. *Environment and Planning A, 48,* 75–93. doi:10.1177/0308518X15594805

Painter, J. (2010). Rethinking territory. *Antipode, 42,* 1090–1118. doi:10.1111/j.1467-8330.2010.00795.x

Parker, S., & Harloe, M. (2015). What place for the region? Reflections on the regional question. *International Journal of Urban and Regional Research, 39,* 361–371. doi:10.1111/1468-2427.12175

Pedersen, M. A. (2009). At home away from homes: Navigating the Taiga in Northern Mongolia. In P. W. Kirby (Ed.), *Boundless worlds* (pp. 135–152). Oxford: Berghahn.

Pike, A. (2007). Editorial: Whither regional studies? *Regional Studies, 41,* 1143–1148. doi:10.1080/00343400701675587

Pike, A. (Ed.). (2011) *Brands and branding geographies.* London: Edward Elgar.

Pred, A. (1984). Place as historically contingent process: Structuration and the time–geography of becoming places. *Annals of the Association of American Geographers, 74,* 279–297. doi:10.1111/j.1467-8306.1984.tb01453.x

Rittel, H.W., & Webber, M. M. (1973). Dilemmas in a general theory of planning. *Policy Sciences, 4,* 155–169. doi:10.1007/BF01405730

Sayer, A. (1989). The 'new' regional geography and problems of narrative. *Environment and Planning D: Society and Space, 7,* 253–276. doi:10.1068/d070253

Scott, A. J., & Storper, M. (2007). Regions, globalization, development. *Regional Studies, 41,* S191–S205. doi:10.1080/00343400032000108697

Soja, E. (1989). *Postmodern geographies.* London: Verso.

Soja, E. J. (2015). Accentuate the regional. *International Journal of Urban and Regional Research, 39,* 372–381. doi:10.1111/1468-2427.12176

Suorsa, K. (2014). The concept of 'region' in research on regional innovation systems. *Norsk Geografisk Tidsskrift – Norwegian Journal of Geography, 68,* 207–215. doi:10.1080/00291951.2014.924025

Taylor, P. J. (1988). World-systems analysis and regional geography. *Professional Geographer, 40,* 259–265. doi:10.1111/j.0033-0124.1988.00259.x

Thrift, N. (1983). On the determination of social action in space and time. *Environment and Planning D: Society and Space, 1,* 23–57. doi:10.1068/d010023

Urry, J. (1985). Social relations, space and time. In D. Gregory & J. Urry (Eds.), *Social relations and spatial structures* (pp. 20–48). London: Macmillan.

Varró, K., & Lagendijk, A. (2013). Conceptualizing the region – In what sense relational? *Regional Studies, 47,* 18–28. doi:10.1080/00343404.2011.602334

Williams, R. (1983). *Keywords.* London: Fontana.

Woolgar, S., & Lezaun, J. (2013). The wrong bin bag: A turn to ontology in science and technology studies? *Social Studies of Science, 43,* 321–340. doi:10.1177/0306312713488820

Woolgar, S., & Lezaun, J. (2015). Missing the (question) mark? What is a turn to ontology? *Social Studies of Science.* doi:0306312715584010.

Towards a theory of regional diversification: combining insights from Evolutionary Economic Geography and Transition Studies

Ron Boschma, Lars Coenen, Koen Frenken and Bernhard Truffer

ABSTRACT

Towards a theory of regional diversification: combining insights from Evolutionary Economic Geography and Transition Studies. *Regional Studies*. This paper develops a theoretical framework of regional diversification by combining insights from Evolutionary Economic Geography and Transition Studies. It argues that a theory of regional diversification should not only build on the current understanding of related diversification but also account for processes of unrelated diversification by looking at the role of agency in processes of institutional entrepreneurship, and at enabling and constraining factors at various spatial scales. This paper proposes a typology of four regional diversification trajectories by cross-tabulating related versus unrelated diversification with niche creation versus regime adoption, and it develops a number of propositions.

摘要

迈向区域多样化的理论：结合演化经济地理学与变迁研究的洞见。Regional Studies。本文透过结合演化经济地理学和变迁研究的洞见，建立一个区域多样化的理论架构。本文主张，区域多样化的理论，不应只是建立在当前对于相关多样化的理解之上，而应同时透过检视行动者在制度革新过程中的角色，以及在各种空间尺度上的协助与限制因素，考量非相关多样化的过程。本文透过将相关多样化相对于非相关多样化，以及利基创造相对于体制採纳进行交叉製表，提出四大区域多样化轨迹的类型学，并发展若干的主张。

RÉSUMÉ

Vers une théorie de la diversification régionale: combinant des aperçus provenant de la géographie économique évolutionniste et des études sur la transition. *Regional Studies*. Cet article développe un cadre théorique de la diversification régionale en combinant des aperçus provenant de la géographie économique évolutionniste et des études sur la transition. On affirme ici qu'une théorie de la diversification régionale devrait reposer non seulement sur la compréhension actuelle de la diversification associée mais devrait tenir compte aussi des processus de diversification sans rapport en examinant le rôle que joue la représentation dans les processus de l'esprit d'entreprise institutionnel, et les facteurs favorables et défavorables à diverses échelles spatiales. Cet article propose une typologie de quatre trajectoires de diversification régionale en effectuant une tabulation croisée de la diversification associée et la diversification sans rapport avec la création et l'adoption de créneaux, et on élabore un nombre de propositions.

ZUSAMMENFASSUNG

Auf dem Weg zu einer Theorie der regionalen Diversifizierung: Kombination von Erkenntnissen aus der evolutionären Wirtschaftsgeografie und von Übergangsstudien. *Regional Studies*. In diesem Beitrag entwickeln wir durch die Kombination von Erkenntnissen aus der evolutionären Wirtschaftsgeografie und von Übergangsstudien einen theoretischen Rahmen der regionalen Diversifizierung. Wir argumentieren, dass eine Theorie der regionalen Diversifizierung nicht nur auf dem derzeitigen Verständnis der verwandten Diversifizierung aufbauen, sondern auch Abläufe der unverwandten Diversifizierung berücksichtigen sollte, indem sie die Rolle der Wirkmächtigkeit in Abläufen des institutionellen Unternehmertums sowie ermächtigende bzw. einschränkende Faktoren auf verschiedenen räumlichen Ebenen untersucht. Vorgeschlagen wird eine Typologie von vier Abläufen der regionalen Diversifizierung durch Kreuztabellierung von verwandter im Vergleich zu unverwandter Diversifizierung mit Nischenbildung im Vergleich zu Regimeübernahme; ebenso wird eine Reihe von Vorschlägen entwickelt.

RESUMEN

Hacia una teoría de la diversificación regional: combinación de ideas de la geografía económica evolutiva y los estudios de transición. *Regional Studies*. En este artículo desarrollamos un marco teórico de la diversificación regional al combinar las ideas de la geografía económica evolutiva y los estudios de transición. Argumentamos que una teoría de diversificación regional no solo debe construirse sobre el actual concepto de diversificación relacionada sino también teniendo en cuenta los procesos de diversificación inconexa al considerar el papel de las actividades en los procesos de empresariado institucional, así como los factores permisivos y limitantes a diferentes escalas espaciales. Proponemos una tipología de cuatro trayectorias de diversificación regional mediante una tabulación cruzada de diversificación relacionada en comparación con diversificación inconexa y de una creación de nichos frente a la adopción del régimen, y presentamos una serie de propuestas.

INTRODUCTION

In recent times, scholars in economic geography have been preoccupied with the question how regions diversify into new industries (Neffke, Henning, & Boschma, 2011) and new technologies (Rigby, 2015), how regions develop new growth paths (Isaksen & Trippl, 2014; Martin, 2010), and why regions differ in their ability to do so (Boschma & Capone, 2015). Most empirical studies have focused on the process of related diversification and regional branching, and have shown that related diversification is the rule, while unrelated diversification is the exception (Boschma, 2016). Though regions display a clear tendency to diversity into related activities, some have argued that unrelated diversification is nevertheless important to secure long-term economic development, as the process of related diversification might eventually come to a halt due to a lock-in (Saviotti & Frenken, 2008). Hence, attention for related diversification should go hand in hand with attention for unrelated diversification.

Unrelated diversification is expected to stem from breakthroughs that emerge from recombining previously unconnected technologies into a new configuration (Castaldi, Frenken, & Los, 2015; Fleming, 2001). Such true Schumpeterian 'Neue Kombinationen', if successful, may provide a long-term source of competitiveness as other regions that do not share the same specialized capabilities being recombined will find it hard to copy such a success. Such a policy strategy can be combined with an explicit aim to address persistent societal challenges such as climate change, ageing, internet crime and youth unemployment (Coenen, Hansen, & Rekers, 2015). Hence, new solutions might be, to a considerable extent, unrelated to existing technologies as well as to institutions.

While some scholars have started working on the topic of unrelated diversification using both case studies (Binz, Truffer, & Coenen, 2016; Dawley, MacKinnon, Cumbers, & Pike, 2015) and statistical approaches (Boschma & Capone, 2015; Neffke, Hartog, Boschma, & Henning, 2014), insights from these studies have remained fragmented at best. The objective of this paper is to make a first step in filling this gap. In doing so, the role of agency in the current Evolutionary Economic Geography (EEG) framework on regional diversification will have to be better theorized (Neffke et al., 2014). Furthermore, as the prime focus has been on the enabling conditions embodied in related capabilities, too little emphasis has been on constraining factors embodied in vested interests. Such constraints stem from interests solidified into institutions at both the regional level (as embodied in policies, laws and regulations, but also cultures, policy styles and labour markets) and the global level (socio-technical regimes). A theory of regional diversification has therefore explicitly to address agency who purposefully strives to overcome constraints to diversification.

The transition literature provides inroads to address these issues (Bergek, Jacobsson, Carlsson, Lindmark, & Rickne, 2008; Geels, 2002; Rip & Kemp, 1998). Radical novelty is understood to depend on experimental alignment process of heterogeneous social and technical elements into new socio-technical configurations. In this perspective, actors are essentially forced to adopt a bricolage mode of innovation while having to cope with vested interests and technological and cognitive lock-ins within established socio-technical regimes. As a consequence, the focus is more on experimentation and how institutional entrepreneurship leads to institutional change (Coenen & Truffer, 2012). Whereas several economic geographers have criticized the limited attention in EEG to agency and institutions in processes of regional diversification (Boschma & Capone, 2015; Coe, 2011; Coenen, Asheim, Bugge, & Herstad, 2016; Hassink, Klaerding, & Marques, 2014; Kogler, 2015; MacKinnon, Cumbers, Pike, Birch, & McMaster, 2009; Neffke et al., 2014), few have made explicit theoretical suggestions how such limitations can be overcome. This motivated the authors to enrich EEG with insights from the transition literature, which shares evolutionary foundations with EEG, but rather focuses on the interplay between incremental versus disruptive processes of interrelated industrial, institutional and technological change. Hence, it offers a complementary perspective on regional diversification beyond aggregated firm-driven diversification, yet couched in evolutionary terminology (Truffer & Coenen, 2012).

This paper builds on both EEG and the transition literatures to develop a theoretical framework on regional diversification. Proposed is a theory of regional diversification that emphasizes agency in the processes of institutional entrepreneurship that underlie regional diversification, as well as the enabling and constraining factors at various spatial scales. From this, one can derive the buildings blocks of a theory of both related and unrelated diversification.

The paper is structured as follows. The second section discusses the EEG literature on regional diversification. Despite a few attempts, it is argued that a comprehensive theoretical framework on regional diversification in regions is still underdeveloped. The third section discusses elements from the transition literature that address a number of weaknesses in EEG in this respect. The fourth section presents the main features of the proposed theoretical framework on regional diversification. The fifth section concludes.

EVOLUTIONARY ECONOMIC GEOGRAPHY (EEG) AND REGIONAL DIVERSIFICATION

There is a rapidly growing interest in the question how regions develop new growth paths, and why regions differ in their ability to do so (Boschma & Frenken, 2006). The recent EEG literature on regional diversification looks at the presence of locally related activities as an enabling factor. Studies show that existing local capabilities condition which new activities are more likely to develop in regions (Berge & Weterings, 2014; Boschma, Balland, & Kogler, 2015; Boschma, Heimeriks, & Balland, 2014; Boschma, Minondo, & Navarro, 2013; Colombelli, Krafft, & Quatraro, 2014; Essleztbichler, 2015; Feldman, Kogler, & Rigby, 2015; Heimeriks & Balland, 2015; Kogler, Rigby, & Tucker, 2013; Neffke et al., 2011; Quatraro & Montresor, 2015; Rigby, 2015; Tanner, 2014, 2016) and countries (Bahar, Hausmann, & Hidalgo, 2014; Boschma & Capone, 2015; Hidalgo, Klinger, Barabasi, & Hausmann, 2007). These studies conclude that relatedness is an important driver of regional diversification, despite the fact that studies employ different dependent variables (like new products, industries, technologies), relatedness measures (e.g., product relatedness, technological relatedness, skill relatedness, input–output relatedness), spatial units of analysis (countries, regions, cities, labour market areas) and time periods (Boschma, 2016). So, related diversification is found to be a more common phenomenon in regions, but unrelated diversification also occurs, though more rarely.

From an evolutionary point of view, the finding that related diversification is much more common than unrelated diversification does not come as a surprise. Diversification in regions is a deeply uncertain process that can be reduced by relying on existing local capabilities when diversifying into new activities (Boschma & Frenken, 2011; Frenken, van Oort, & Verburg, 2007). For instance, it is less problematic for regions to move from motor cycles to trucks than from bananas to computers, as motor cycles and trucks require similar capabilities while bananas and computers require very different capabilities. Unrelated diversification occurs when a region develops a new activity that requires very different capabilities than existing local activities and, hence, tends to be driven by actors who built up their capabilities elsewhere (migrants, multinationals) and, in some cases, were supported by state policies (Dawley et al., 2015; Neffke et al., 2014). Alternatively, unrelated diversification may stem from within the region by recombining previously unconnected technologies leading to 'Neue Kombinationen' (Castaldi et al., 2015).

There is some research on enabling conditions for unrelated diversification. Xiao, Boschma, and Andersson (2016) showed that more knowledge-intensive regions in Europe are more likely to move in more unrelated activities, as compared with more knowledge-extensive regions in the European periphery. Other scholars are exploring the role of national institutions on related versus unrelated diversification. Boschma and Capone (2015) found that liberal market institutions (as compared with coordinated market institutions) favour more unrelated diversification at the country level. Cortinovis, Xiao, Boschma, and Van Oort (2016) did not find an effect of regional formal and informal institutions on the tendency of regions to diversify in related or unrelated activities. Scholars have also suggested that bridging networks and non-proximate links would favour unrelated diversification, but systematic evidence is still lacking (Crespo, Suire, & Vicente, 2014). In sum, this emerging literature on unrelated diversification is still fragmented and underdeveloped, often singling out one factor, and not providing a comprehensive theoretical framework.

A more fundamental limitation of the regional diversification literature has been its primary focus on the role of regional capabilities, without taking account of the role of agency at the micro-level (Boschma, 2016). In the late 1980s, the window of locational opportunity (WLO) approach made an early attempt to link human agency to new industry formation in place (Scott & Storper, 1987; Storper & Walker, 1989). This was regarded crucial when it is impossible for new industries to build on locally available capabilities. In that case, new industrial activities create their own economic and institutional conditions of support in place as to build regional capabilities, networks and regulations, or attract them from other places. In that sense, a favourable environment is more likely the result of, rather than a precondition for, such an emergent process. This does not imply that local capabilities do not play a role: some new industries rely more heavily on local generic resources than other industries (Boschma, 1997), but the emphasis in the WLO approach is clearly on the emergence process through which new industries create a conducive milieu, instead of the other way around. However, this WLO approach remained largely conceptual: it has not been subject to any systematic empirical research, nor did it specify in detail how and by whom institutional change comes about.

A key impulse to the development of a micro-perspective on regional diversification was given by Klepper in the 2000s. He considered the role of agency as crucial for the study of new industry formation by looking at the importance of individuals (spinoff entrepreneurs) and firms (diversifiers) that make regions diversify (Buenstorf & Klepper, 2009; Klepper, 2007). Klepper contributed to an agency-based explanation of regional diversification by focusing mainly on entrepreneurs spinning from and incumbents diversifying from related activities. His agency-based perspective was focused entirely on firms, not on other types of actors that affect the tendency of regions to diversify in new activities. Klepper's theory also paid little attention to the local environment as conditioning factor, and how actors actively shape their local environment.

In sum, what is still underdeveloped in EEG is a comprehensive theory on related and unrelated diversification in regions that (1) incorporates the role of human agency and their engagement with processes of institutional entrepreneurship in particular; (2) gives a full account of the role of constraining factors,[1] besides enabling factors, as the diversification process in regions is often contested by vested interests at various spatial levels; (3) moves beyond an exclusive focus on regional or national capabilities to account for influences from the outside; and (4) follows a co-evolutionary perspective in which regional diversification is conceptualized as a process based on the dynamic interplay between agency and its changing technological, institutional and spatial context.

TRANSITION THEORY: BRICOLAGE, SYSTEMIC ALIGNMENT AND NICHE SCALING

In this quest for a more comprehensive theory of regional diversification, it is argued that the transition literature provides useful and complementary concepts and insights. That literature has an explicit account of human agency that relies on concepts like bricolage and institutional entrepreneurship. Moreover, it proposes a meso-level account of diversification, as embodied in the creation of niches through systemic alignment that is attentive to both constraining and enabling factors internal and external to a region, and it addresses how niches for experimentation are mindfully created and scaled in the context of regimes through co-evolutionary processes of shielding, nurturing and empowerment. These topics are discussed below.

Bricolage as a core mechanism in unrelated diversification

In order to explain unrelated diversification, the analysis is broadened so one can ask how other resources, strategies and actors get mobilized to interrelate proximate and distant knowledge stocks in the generation of novelty. A well-known study on unrelated diversification 'avant la lettre' was presented by Garud and Karnøe (2003), contrasting the emergence of the wind turbine industry in Denmark and the United States. In EEG terms, they argued that the US pathway represented a typical knowledge intensive (high-tech) strategy trying to optimize for related variety (Frenken et al., 2007), and following a policy approach oriented at technological breakthrough narrowly defined. In Denmark, the wind industry developed through a process of trial and error, collaboration and mobilization of various resources (knowledge, financial and institutional) that involved a broad set of local actors. They consisted of firms, farmers, policy-makers, public research organizations and non-governmental organizations (NGOs), distributed across a wide spectrum of different (and, in terms of competences, unrelated) industries like mechanical equipment, electronics, farmers and energy utilities. Building on Lévi-Strauss' work on resource scarce innovation processes (Lévi-Strauss, 1967), Garud and Karnøe (2003) called this ideal type mode 'bricolage'. As they show, the Danish bricolage approach that begins with a low-tech design but ramps up progressively prevails over the US high-tech breakthrough approach.

The term 'bricolage' alludes to the consideration of a multiplicity of actors embedded in networks who collectively draw on a broad set of distributed resources such as money, material components, discourses, knowledge, legitimacy and skills, organizational arrangements and political regulation in order to create new industrial pathways through processes of mindful deviation (Baker & Nelson, 2005; Duymedjian & Rüling, 2010). The key ability of actors in bricolage is to enable the alignment of a heterogeneous set of actors, institutions and technologies in order to establish socio-technical 'configurations that work' (Callon, 1998; Rip & Kemp, 1998). Through bricolage, path creation is understood as an iterative construction process where networks of distributed actors jointly create new market segments and user profiles, adapt regulations, lobby for subsidies, or define new technical standards and thereby ultimately create the conducive environment that helps a new industry develop and prosper in a region (Garud & Karnøe, 2003; Garud, Kumaraswamy, & Karnøe, 2010). Thus, the notion of bricolage helps to specify further agency processes implicit in the aforementioned work in EEG on windows of locational opportunity (Storper & Walker, 1989) and firm-based perspectives on regional diversification (Klepper, 2007; Neffke et al., 2014). As a consequence, the generation of unrelated radical novelty is likely to be a messy, step-wise and experimental process. This requires entrepreneurship not only to be proficient in the relevant knowledge fields but also to be capable of embedding new ideas in a wider institutional environment. This is exactly what Hughes (1993) identified as 'system builders' being a crucial factor in the emergence of infrastructure sectors like electricity in the early 20th century.

The bricolage approach became very prominent in organization and management studies (Baker, Miner, Dale, & Eesley, 2003; Stinchfield, Nelson, & Wood,

2013). It has arguably been less developed for regional development and policy processes. Nonetheless, drawing on the work of Sabel (1996), previous research on EU regional innovation strategies has conceptualized these as 'regional experimentalism' in which:

> the state, firms and intermediaries work in small-scale repeated interactions in an attempt to (re)define regional development support services and priorities in a collective manner, establish specific targets and responsibilities and monitor outcomes in a way that facilitates learning on the part of those in a position to respond.
>
> (Henderson, 2000, p. 349; cf. Morgan & Henderson, 2002)

Similarly, albeit 15 years later, experimentalism and entrepreneurial discovery are emphasized in the policy framework of smart specialization (Foray, David, & Hall, 2009; Foray, David, & Hall, 2011). Here, the ability is crucial to combine and relate knowledge about science, technology and engineering with knowledge of market growth potential, potential competitors as well as the whole set of inputs and services required for launching a new activity.

What is highlighted in smart specialization, albeit somewhat implicitly, is that entrepreneurship is not just about 'taking a technology to the market' (Sotarauta & Pulkkinen, 2011). While traditionally entrepreneurship is considered key for experimentation in combinatorial knowledge dynamics for related diversification (Frenken & Boschma, 2007), what is equally emphasized through the notion of bricolage is the need for institutional entrepreneurship. Here, actors break with existing institutionalized rules and practices associated with the dominant institutional logics (see the concept of regime below) and institutionalize the alternative rules, practices or logics they are championing (Battilana, 2006; Garud, Hardy, & Maguire, 2007). Institutional entrepreneurs are typically heterogeneous actors including, but not limited to, firms or individual entrepreneurs who mobilize resources, competences and power to create new or transform existing institutions (Battilana, Leca, & Boxenbaum, 2009; Sotarauta & Pulkkinen, 2011).

In order to unpack how bricolage, experimentation and institutional entrepreneurship may give rise to new socio-technical pathways, the recent literature on socio-technical transitions proves to provide a number of relevant insights.

The initiation of new pathways through socio-technical alignment

Transition Studies represent a scholarly field that has emphasized the role of distributed agency in the development of new industries and the crucial role of socio-technical alignment. Its key focus concerns transformative shifts in systems of production and consumption that unfold as disruptive technological change co-evolves with changes in markets, user practices, policy, discourses and governing institutions (Geels, 2002; Kemp, Schot, & Hoogma, 1998; Markard, Raven, & Truffer, 2012; Rip & Kemp, 1998). Empirically, this literature has been primarily interested in understanding and explaining historical examples of long-term yet disruptive technological change such as the transition from sailing to steam ships (Geels, 2002). Furthermore, this literature is well known for its engagement in understanding and contributing to the more normative objective of radically improving societal systems of provision in order to comply with conditions of sustainability in, for example, energy, mobility, water, housing and food (Frantzeskaki, Castan-Broto, Coenen, & Loorbach, 2016; Fuenfschilling & Truffer, 2014; Geels, Kemp, Dudley, & Lyons, 2012; Grin, Rotmans, & Schot, 2011; Spaargaren, Oosterveer, & Loeber, 2012; Verbong & Geels, 2012).

Transition Studies emerged out of an evolutionary economics (Nelson & Winter, 1982) and a social–constructivist understanding of innovation processes (Rip & Kemp, 1998), emphasizing that successful socio-technical configurations have to be actively constructed and stabilized. Drawing furthermore on the Schumpeterian notion of creative destruction, research on socio-technical transitions is specifically concerned with the role of emergent technologies that challenge and struggle against incumbent actors who dominate a particular sector (Bergek et al., 2015; Markard et al., 2012). In analyzing this process, transitions research is heavily influenced by the concept of path dependency. Building on an earlier conceptualization of technological trajectories and regimes (Dosi, 1982; Nelson & Winter, 1977), as well as sociological insights on agency and structure (Giddens, 1984), the concept of the socio-technical regime accounts for the persistence and rigidity of structures within a system (Fuenfschilling & Truffer, 2014). It is defined as the 'coherent complex of scientific knowledge, engineering practices, production process technologies, product characteristics, skills and procedures, established user needs, regulatory requirements, institutions and infrastructures' (Rip & Kemp, 1998, p. 338). The 'structuration' of this complex, in terms of its internal alignment, is high, providing stable rules and coordinating effects on actors. As a consequence, sectors that have a strong regime are considered as hostile selection environments for disruptive innovations and radical (technological) change. Instead they are prone to lock-in and path dependency and largely geared to generate incremental innovations and gradual change.

Here, Transition Studies provides useful insights. Even though it emphasizes how (radical) novelty is constrained and contested by a regime, it specifies at the same time how such radical novelty emerges. This is mostly conceptualized through the notion of niches (Geels & Raven, 2006) or through work done in the field of technological innovation systems dealing with emergent (sustainable) technologies and industries (Bergek et al., 2008; Hekkert, Suurs, Negro, Kuhlmann, & Smits, 2007). Similar to previous work on bricolage and path creation (Garud et al., 2010; Karnøe & Garud, 2012; Sydow, Windeler, Müller-Seitz, & Lange, 2012), it subscribes to the notion that new paths do not emerge from external shocks but from the strategic agency in heterogeneous actor groups that jointly act upon locked-in structures and mobilize resources to create a new industry (Simmie, 2012).

Due to its strong focus on socio-technical alignment, Transition Studies have been, until recently, rather silent about the spatial structure and preconditions for these processes. Truffer and Coenen (2012) proposed three conceptual platforms where Transition Studies could address this shortcoming by engaging with the regional studies and economic geography literature: (1) emphasizing the local embedding of new industries and technologies by an integrated view on the joint alignment of socio-technical and socio-spatial structures; (2) the consideration of multi-scalar factors of transitions like trans-regional actors networks and institutions; and (3) an attentiveness to power relationships in these processes. Since these early proposals, a sizable number of studies have emerged which further elaborated the geography of transitions field (Hansen & Coenen, 2015; Murphy, 2015; Truffer, Murphy, & Raven, 2015). A recent review (Hansen & Coenen, 2015) has shown that the large majority of case studies dealing with the geography of transitions has zoomed in on the importance of place dependence for transition processes. This has helped to specify that niche formation in emergent clean technologies is contingent on place-specific factors such as local related variety, local natural resource endowments, local market formation, urban and regional visions and policies, and local informal institutions. While a higher level of sensitivity concerning the importance of place dependence is gained in these studies, it may have come with a bias towards emphasizing particularities found in single-case studies of distinct places. Another insight of this work holds that regimes, even though they can be considered as global structures, these may nevertheless exhibit a high degree of local variation (Späth & Rohracher, 2012). And niches, on the other hand, are not bound to the local scale, but often consist of globally interconnected sets of activities (Binz, Truffer, & Coenen, 2014; Quitzow, 2015; Sengers & Raven, 2015).

Proposing a more systematic framework regarding unrelated diversification, Binz, Harris-Lovett, Kiparsky, Sedlak, and Truffer (2016) suggested how the emergence of new industrial pathways in regions can be framed as a process of bricolage by mobilizing and aligning different resources, like knowledge, markets, investment and legitimacy. Rather than assuming that markets for new industrial pathways pre-exist, it treats (niche) markets as a resource for radically new technologies, products and services that have to be actively created through, for example, lobbying, regulation and standardization (Dewald & Truffer, 2012). Similarly, financial investment requires active mobilization through networking between entrepreneurs, investors and intermediary organization. Legitimacy, finally, is emphasized as a key resource for new industry formation as new products and processes are often not aligned with existing regulative, normative and cognitive institutions resulting in initial scepticism and lack of user acceptance (Aldrich & Fiol, 1994; Binz, Harris-Lovett, et al., 2016; Yeung & Coe, 2015). Therefore, actors promoting unrelated diversification have to engage in considerable institutional work either to adapt the industry to existing institutional structures or to adapt these structures to match the industry's needs better (Bergek et al., 2008; Fuenfschilling & Truffer, 2016). Drawing on a case study of industry formation for on-site water recycling in Beijing, Binz, Harris-Lovett, et al. (2016) found that such processes of resource mobilization and alignment are not confined to local interactions but depend on a complex interplay between local and global configurations.

Establishing pathways by scaling of niches

While the notion of bricolage, on the one hand, broadens the set of resources considered for new path creation, it also stresses the highly experimental nature of new path creation. Interestingly, experimentation is mentioned by Martin (2010) as a critical process for new path creation in regions, but this is not further elaborated. In contrast, research in Transition Studies has foregrounded the role of experimentation, particularly in connection to the concept of niches which are conceived as 'incubation spaces' for radically new technologies and/or practices characterized by high technological, institutional and market uncertainty. Such niches protect radical innovations against market selection and institutional pressures from a regime and allow actors to learn about these novelties and their uses through experimentation (Coenen, Raven, & Verbong, 2010; Geels, 2002). When niches gather sufficient momentum so that these relatively loose configurations become institutionalized they create capacity for emergent technologies and practices to challenge and substitute a regime and induce transitions.

In the transition literature, strategic niche management elaborates how heterogeneous experiments can be managed in order to support socio-technical alignment (Hoogma, Kemp, Schot, & Truffer, 2002; Schot & Geels, 2008). Three processes are distinguished for successful development of a niche: shielding, nurturing and empowerment (Smith & Raven, 2012). All three processes essentially enable different actors to try out new alignments between institutions, technologies and actors. Shielding refers to those activities that hold at bay selection pressures from a regime and that afford the protective space for path-breaking innovations to emerge. Nurturing refers to those activities that then support the development of path-breaking innovation (Schot & Geels, 2008) such as the processes of anchoring elaborated by Binz, Harris-Lovett, et al. (2016).

Experimental projects in real-life contexts are seen to be critical by bringing together actors from variation and selection environments in shared networking and learning activities. In these experiments, firms, research institutes, universities and governments search and explore the best possible combinations of innovations and their social and institutional embedding (Bulkeley & Castán Broto, 2013). A key challenge that these niche experiments are facing concerns how to upscale successful innovations and practices beyond their initial niche (Geels, Hekkert, & Jacobsson, 2008). Whereas initial attention has been paid primarily to the roles of 'shielding' and 'nurturing', Smith and Raven (2012, p. 1034) argue that more focus should be given to the 'empowering' role of niches, which 'involves processes that make niche innovations competitive within unchanged selection environments (fit and conform) or processes that change mainstream selection environments favourable to the path-breaking innovation (stretch and transform)'.

Summing up, it is suggested here that Transition Studies provide a suitable framework for analyzing processes of unrelated diversification in particular. In unrelated diversification, agency in the form of bricolage, institutional entrepreneurship or policy action comes more heavily to bear and successful attempts rely on experimental activities, strategies of resourceful actors, capabilities of 'system building' and partly also serendipity (Dawley, 2014; Dawley et al., 2015). Transition Studies have so far been less strong in formulating hypotheses about which individual actors, technologies, networks or institutions are more amenable to successful path creation. What the literature suggests, however, is to be attentive of which constellations of factors might be more or less amenable for conducting successful bricolage processes. Moreover, the transition literature has only started to look at the geography of niches and regimes, and what are the implications for (related and unrelated) diversification in regions. It is argued that regimes tend to be global as they depict a structural pattern of alignment between actors, institutions and technologies that has reached validity beyond specific territorial contexts and which is diffused through international networks (Fuenfschilling & Binz, 2016) though not equally present and institutionalized in all regions (Späth & Rohracher, 2012). A similar ambivalence may be found for the geography of niches which might emerge regionally, though often in parallel with global networks connecting them (Sengers & Raven, 2015).

TOWARDS A THEORY OF REGIONAL DIVERSIFICATION

In the foregoing, it has become clear that scholars in EEG and Transition Studies have a common interest to understand the nature, loci and radicalness of novelty. However, their perspectives, namely units of analysis, are different. In EEG, the notion of novelty is spatially defined and treated: looking from the perspective of a region, scholars distinguish between related and unrelated diversification. The more a new industry is unrelated to the capability base already built up in the *region*, the more a new industry marks a radical departure from a region's own past. The transition perspective, by contrast, looks at the construction of niches that challenge an existing socio-technical regime that is globally dominant in a particular *sector*. Here, the radicalness lies in the extent to which the niche differs from the globally institutionalized regime.

The notions of unrelated diversification and niche creation, thus, should not be confused. Unrelated diversification is defined with reference to a particular region with certain capabilities ('place'), while a new niche is defined with reference to a particular regime following a certain technological trajectory ('path'). Put differently, place and path dependence are two distinct dependencies in evolutionary processes (Heimeriks & Boschma, 2014; Martin & Sunley, 2006). *Place dependence* stems from the local reproduction of localized knowledge, territorial institutions and vested interests embedded in places, which tends to hamper processes of unrelated diversification of a regional economy. *Path dependence* stems from shared cognitive frames, standards and institutions embedded in global socio-technical regimes, which tends to hamper the development of new niches and their further development into alternative socio-technical regimes. So, place and path dependence relate to socio-spatial and socio-technical embedding respectively (Truffer & Coenen, 2012).

Though distinct, place and path dependence typically reinforce each other. A regime tends to be globally organized and hence present in many regions. In regions where a regime is both dominant and strongly aligned with localized knowledge, territorial institutions and vested interests, a change of regime will be very unlikely, as niche actors will have to deviate from their socio-spatial and socio-technical embedding. Having said this, regimes are neither monolithic nor fully globalized (Fuenfschilling & Binz, 2016; Späth & Rohracher, 2012). A regime may be strong in some regions and weaker in other. That is, regions differ in the extent to which a regime is adopted and the degree to which the regime is regionally institutionalized (Crouch & Voelzkow, 2009). Moreover, in some regions, a sector can be dominated by a single regime, while in other regions this sector may be characterized by co-existing regimes. Think, for example, of cities dominated by cars versus cities where cars, bikes and public transport co-exist and may be even made complementary. Hence, one can expect windows of opportunity to exist in regions where the regime is less dominant and only weakly institutionalized or hybridized.

The distinction between place and path dependence thus implies that the two processes of unrelated diversification at the regional level and niche creation at the sectoral level do not necessarily coincide. This is what is depicted in Table 1, where radicalness is distinguished along both the regional dimension (related versus unrelated) and the sectoral dimension (regime versus niche). Thus, in the case of regional diversification, a new industry is *new to the region*, while in the case of a niche creation it is *new to the world*. A region creating a new niche may do so via unrelated or related diversification. For example, Danish regions specialized in agriculture diversified into an unrelated niche of wind turbine production. An example of related diversification leading to a new niche would be Silicon Valley specialized in the information and communication technology industry currently creating a niche for self-driving cars. In both examples, a new-to-the-world niche was created through regional diversification.

The same possibilities of related and unrelated diversification hold when a region becomes active in an existing regime technology. That is, a region may diversify by entering a global regime through related or unrelated diversification. For example, it may diversify in a related manner from operating in the oil regime serving the transport sector into the (fossils-based) plastics regime serving the packaging industry. However, a region may also enter a regime that is unrelated to the capabilities already present in the region, like a desert region specialized in

Table 1 Typology of regional diversification.

		Region	
		Related	*Unrelated*
SECTOR	REGIME	Replication	Transplantation
	NICHE	Exaptation	Saltation

tourism that discovers oil and enters the oil regime. For each new industry created in a region, one can thus assess whether the industry is related or unrelated to the region's existing capability base and whether the industry is constituting a new niche in a particular sector, or whether it extends an already existing regime in a sector.

One can thus derive a typology of four different regional diversification processes. For each of the four diversification trajectories, the type and extent of institutional work involved, the expected driving actors and the spatial logics are further theorized below, as summarized in Table 2.

Replication stands for the most conservative diversification logic in which a region develops related industries by adopting a technology that is institutionalized in a global socio-technical regime. From the regime perspective, the process of replication entails the gradual process by which a regime diffuses at a global scale. Hence, the notion of replication follows from the theory of Winter and Szulanski (2001) about routine replication by organizations across regional contexts. In this diversification logic, a region replicates largely its existing capability base by branching out into related activities and at the same time largely replicates existing knowledge, institutions and interests embedded in an existing socio-technical regime. This strategy can be very successful since the region can become readily competitive in an existing global regime as it can leverage its experience in related industries (Boschma & Frenken, 2011).

Transplantation stands for a diversification trajectory in which a region develops an industry unrelated to its knowledge base and institutions, yet based on adopting a regime technology from the global system. The use here of the term 'transplantation' is in line with Martin and Sunley (2006), who mention transplantation as a primary mechanism of creating a 'new pathway of regional growth', while it also builds on the notion of institutional transplantation of policy institutions across countries (De Jong, Lalenis, & Mamadouh, 2002). This diversification logic is a more risky one as a region cannot build on its existing knowledge base and regional institutions while it has to compete with many other regions where the

Table 2 Characteristics of diversification trajectories.

Process	Relatedness	Level	Risk	Institutional work	Key actors	Spatial logic
Replication	Related	Regime	Low	Maintenance	Regional incumbents	Localized
Transplantation	Unrelated	Regime	Moderate	Creation (especially regionally)	Regime incumbents/ governments	Global to regional
Exaptation	Related	Niche	Moderate	Creation (especially globally)	New entrants	Regional to global
Saltation	Unrelated	Niche	High	Creation (all levels)	Broad range	Global to global

regime is already present. Hence, this strategy can only be successful if resources other than knowledge and institutions can be leveraged, such as location, connectivity, a critical natural resource or low labour costs. The latter two conditions are often present in developing countries, where regional and national governments follow a catch-up strategy through imitation of established technologies, that is, by diversifying into regimes that are unrelated to their pre-existing capability base.

Exaptation refers to a diversification logic where new applications are discovered for existing knowledge or technology (Dew, Sarasvathy, & Venkataraman, 2004). Innovation by exaptation has received considerable interest lately (Andriani & Cattani, 2016; Andriani & Cohen, 2013), and from various perspectives including psychology of perception (Felin, Kauffman, Mastrogiorgio, & Mastrogiorgio, 2016), niche construction theory (Dew & Sarasvathy, 2016) and a narrative approach (Garud, Gehman, & Giuliani, 2016). The canonical example of exaptation in biology is bird wings that initially evolved for insulation purposes but later developed into a means to fly. Similarly, many technologies find applications that were not foreseen when first developed. For example, technologies like the laser, the computer and plastics have continued to find new applications in very diverse sectors. Exaptation thus refers to a diversification logic where a region builds on an existing knowledge base and succeeds in entering many sectors by creating new niches. Silicon Valley and its ICT knowledge base is a perfect example, branching out in many sectors by developing new niche technologies with some of these successfully growing out into a new global regime (personal computers, online advertising, mobile telephony), while other (still) having a niche status (self-driving cars, home-sharing platforms, smart homes).

Finally, saltation (or leap) can lead to regional diversification. Saltation is a term used in biology to denote the process in which just a single mutation ('macromutation') can lead to speciation. In the context of our framework, the concept of saltation leading to a new niche would refer to an innovation that is not only new to the region but also new to the world. An example is the discovery of penicillin by Alexander Fleming in 1928 in London, which later became mass-produced in the United States to support Allied forces during the Second World War; another is Thomas Edison's light bulb and the subsequent rise of the New Jersey lamp industry (Smil, 2006). Even if the saltation idea in biology is contested and not widely accepted, the idea that a single innovation can sometimes lead to a whole new industry is widespread in innovation theory. In this context, scholars often speak of breakthrough innovations that differ in a fundamental sense from previous technologies and provide the basis for many incremental improvement later on (Ahuja & Lampert, 2001). In this context, some explicitly refer to the distinction between micro- and macro-mutations in biology, and speak analogously of micro- and macro-inventions in technological development (Mokyr, 1990). Related to the notion of saltation is the distinction between competence-enhancing and competence-destroying innovation (Anderson & Tushman, 1990), where the latter notion is in line with saltation as it highlights the radical departure from existing capabilities.

Going back to the agency perspective advocated by organization scholars and their theories of bricolage (Garud & Karnøe, 2003) and institutional entrepreneurship (Battilana et al., 2009), one can further specify the role of actors in the four diversification trajectories. Clearly, in the case of replication, actors operate in a context where they can build on (related) existing regional strengths and global regimes. The institutional work required, then, is one of maintaining existing institutions (Fuenfschilling & Truffer, 2014). These patterns are readily explained by the key notions of place and path dependence, respectively. In particular, one expects regional industry incumbents to be most active in this process, since related diversification into established regimes fits most firms' own strategy to grow and expand (Klepper, 2002; Neffke et al., 2014). Another reason why one expects large incumbent firms to be the typical actor in this process is that regime entry requires many resources and a long-term vision given the entry barriers in established regimes.

In the case of transplantation, institutional work has to be done at the regional level to adapt institutions such that globally accepted technologies, standards and regulations are accepted and implemented. One can expect that transplantation activities are guided regional and national government as an explicit development strategy, and to are carried out by actors who have both the capabilities and the interests to make the regime diffuse (i.e., regime incumbents), for example, global consultancies, multinational corporations and transnational government agencies. Given that vested interests in a region may well be threatened by the transplantation of regime technology by globally operating regime actors, conflicts may well arise. The introduction of a regime technology that is new to the region often leads to competition for scarce public and private resources. In this context, one can thus regard the regime incumbents as the institutional actor 'mindfully deviating' from regional institutions, and trying to mould them into global regime standards. Such changes will be more readily accepted if a sense of urgency to change exist (e.g., during a severe crisis) (De Jong et al., 2002), opening up windows for institutional entrepreneurship at the regional level (Battilana et al., 2009). Furthermore, one can expect transplantation to be more successful if the institutional distance between actors in the adopting region and in the global regime is small (De Jong et al., 2002; Gertler, 2004). In sum, transplantation is certainly actor led, and a key question holds in what contexts what actor(s) take up this role, how outcomes vary according to the actor(s) taking up this role, and what roles regional governments can play to resolve such conflicts.

Compared with transplantation, exaptation is much more a local process even if, as explained above, niche creation may well involve concurrent and networked processes across multiple regions. Here, the actors are expected to come from related industries in the region, as exaptation is a process of related diversification. Typically new entrants such as spinoffs, and to a lesser extent diversifying firms, are crucial to pioneer the formation of new industries that build on established ones (Klepper, 2007). The institutional work to be carried out is to get the new niche technology accepted through new regulations and social norms. Regime actors, either regional or global, tend to de-legitimize such efforts and to close windows for such institutional entrepreneurship. Hence, building on the theory of institutional entrepreneurship (Battilana et al., 2009), one expects that attempts to promote new niches by changing regime institutions to be most successful in regions where the regime is not well established or otherwise under pressure due to wider 'landscape pressures', as well as in regions where powerful regime actors are absent and powerful niche actors reside with global reach so as to get a niche globally aligned and legitimized. Regional governments can play this role as well by lobbying for the creation of supporting institutions at national and global levels.

Finally, a new niche created by saltation will be mostly driven by individual heterogeneous agents. Given that such leaps imply that the new path is both unrelated to a region's capabilities and challenging an existing global regime, agents have to deviate at two levels, from path dependence and place dependence. They not only break with established knowledge base and institutions and interests at the regional level, but also have to establish a niche in a global regime. While in transplantation and exaptation, either the regime or the region provide a supporting institutional structure, saltation requires a fundamental change of institutions in both dimensions, that is, both globally at the sectoral level and locally at the regional level. Here, one expects novelty to emerge in a distributed and rather unruly manner, with many heterogeneous agents involved and often located in different regions. As there are only few supporting structures at the regional or global level to build on, these actors have to engage in a collective alignment process emphasized by the notions of bricolage and collective institutional entrepreneurship, for example, as driven by a social movement (Sine & Lee, 2009).

CONCLUSIONS

This paper proposes a new typology of regional diversification that combines complementary logics from two different literatures that evolved in parallel, that is, the EEG literature on regional diversification and the transition literature on niche–regime interactions. In doing so, it has been able to tackle a number of weaknesses in both literatures as far as their view on diversification processes is concerned.

The EEG literature on regional diversification has revealed important insights into how regions diversify over time: its main research interest is to understand how regional capabilities enable diversification of regions. Its prime focus has been on related diversification in regions, and less so on unrelated diversification. However, the role of human agency (especially institutional entrepreneurs) has been poorly integrated in this EEG framework on regional diversification. The paper has also argued that EEG lacks a systematic focus on constraining factors (for an exception, see Hassink, 2005), neglects issues like power and conflicts stemming from contradictory interests among stakeholders (Boschma & Frenken, 2009; MacKinnon et al., 2009), and draws little attention to the process of institutional work by institutional entrepreneurs that is required to overcome such constraints (Battilana et al., 2009).

This paper has argued that the transition literature provides key insights on regional diversification. There is more focus on constraints and resistance from actors dominating established sectoral socio-technical regimes. There is also more focus on experimentation and the role of all sorts of actors including governments that enable, or not, niche formation and institutional change. In that sense, the transition literature provides complementary insights to EEG. However, Transition Studies have also been less keen on developing hypotheses about which actors and contexts are more conducive to regional diversification. There is also little systematic empirical evidence on the geographical configurations of niche formation and regimes so far, and its implications for processes of regional diversification.

A key result from this discussion holds that unrelated diversification and niche creation should be understood as distinct, as the units of analysis in EEG and Transition Studies are different. In EEG, the notion of novelty is spatially defined (new to the region). Here, the radicalness involves the extent to which a new activity in a region can or cannot build on existing related capabilities in the region. The transition perspective looks at the construction of niches that challenge an existing regime that is globally dominant in a particular sector. Here, the radicalness lies in the extent to which the niche differs from the globally institutionalized regime, or not. Based on these two dimensions, four types of regional diversification were derived. Related diversification in regions consist of two types: replication (within an existing socio-technical global regime) and exaptation (creating a niche that can grow out into a new global regime). This paper also distinguished between two types of unrelated diversification: transplantation involves a change in the regional capability base but within the boundaries of the existing socio-technical regime, while saltation stands for the most radical type of regional diversification, requiring not only a transformation of regional capabilities but also a complete regime change.

The authors believe this proposed framework opens up a lot of challenging avenues for future research. A first set of questions concerns the geography of diversification. A key question is how the geography of the four types of diversification trajectories would look like. Are there regions that would be good at in all diversification types? To what extent do regions specialize in one of the diversification trajectories, and why, and which regions fail to develop any type of diversification? This also confronts one with a methodological challenge if one would want to analyze diversification in a quantitative manner: how to operationalize the two dimensions (related/unrelated and niche/regime) in our proposed framework. For each new industry in a region, one needs to assess whether the new industry is related or unrelated to the region's capability base, and whether the new industry is constituting a new niche in a particular sector, or whether it extends an existing regime in a sector. Surely, the EEG literature on regional diversification has recently made progress in developing various relatedness measures, but it is still debating how to assess the degree of relatedness between new and existing local activities, and how to connect relatedness to specific capabilities (Boschma, 2016).

Another set of questions concerns the process of diversification and the role of various actors, such as firms, NGOs, citizen movements, trade associations and universities (Vallance, 2016). This paper has already theorized for all four types of diversification about the extent of agency required, and the likely agents to take up the role of institutional entrepreneurs. Further questions include what kind of strategies actors employ to carry out the institutional work required, at the regional, national and global levels, what types of conflicts can emerge, and how these may differ between the four types of regional diversification (replication, transplantation, exaptation and saltation)? Even in the extreme case of replication where new activities are related to capabilities and institutions at both regional and global levels, the process of diversification is unlikely to be a conflict-free process. In this particular case, it is highly probable that a new industry will take away resources from local related industries (including capital, skilled labour and public subsidies) because these are highly relevant (related) for the new industry. In the other diversification logics, however, actors will probably deal with other sorts of tensions, especially when the existing regime is seriously challenged. Hence, one expects the dynamics and mechanisms of each of the different diversification trajectories to be quite distinct.

A final set of questions addresses the regional contextual factors that condition the diversification trajectories in certain regions. Building on Battilana et al. (2009), this paper has already discussed the more specific institutional contexts that provide windows for institutional entrepreneurship. In general, regional contexts strongly support replication, and may well be hostile towards alternative, risky types of diversification trajectories. At the same time, in such processes of institutional change the institutional entrepreneurs still remain embedded in wider pre-existing institutions. Hence, one can further ask the question which more generic macro-institutional features favour experimentation and institutional entrepreneurship underlying transplantation, exaptation and saltation, respectively. Can one identify institutional conditions that enable such a culture of experimentation? How do different varieties of capitalism condition the different types of regional diversification processes (Boschma & Capone, 2015; Cortinovis et al., 2016)? Are certain regions better at running experiments, while others are better at scaling up? And how important are region–external linkages (Asheim & Isaksen, 2002; Neffke et al., 2014; Trippl, Grillitsch, & Isaksen, 2015)? And how can one relate strategies in global value chains with diversification strategies of countries and regions?

This brings the discussion to the specific role of public policy. The four different diversification logics will have implications for the design and implementation of public policy. So what could be the role of the state in all diversification types (Dawley et al., 2015; Mazzucato, 2013; Morgan, 2013)? How can one operationalize smart specialization policy in terms of these diversification strategies? And do countries/regions go through different types of diversification strategies, like developing countries may shift from a strategy based on catching-up in existing technological pathways (transplantation) to developing new pathways (like exaptation)? Do diversification strategies based on 'normal' innovations differ from those that are connected to 'grand challenges'? How can regions/countries moderate the strength of socio-technical regimes in order to enable niche experiments to emerge and to scale up? And what about the mix of niche promotion and regime weakening policies at regional, national and global levels? This wealth of questions – of theoretical, empirical and policy nature – suggests a fruitful future for research on regional diversification in the years to come.

DISCLOSURE STATEMENT

No potential conflict of interest was reported by the authors.

FUNDING

Ron Boschma and Lars Coenen gratefully acknowledge financial support from the Swedish Research Council [Linnaeus grant number 349200680] and Sweden's Innovation Agency Vinnova [grant agreement number 2010-07370].

NOTE

1. When paying attention to constraining factors, the EEG literature tends to refer almost exclusively to the specific case of old industrial regions in which different types of lock-in are perceived to prevent them shifting into new activities (Grabher, 1993; Hassink, 2005; Coenen, Moodysson, & Martin, 2015). An exception is a study on cities active in fashion design (Wenting & Frenken, 2011).

REFERENCES

Ahuja, G., & Lampert, C. M. (2001). Entrepreneurship in the large corporation: A longitudinal study of how established firms create breakthrough inventions. *Strategic Management Journal, 22*, 521–543. doi:10.1002/smj.176
Aldrich, H. E., & Fiol, C. M. (1994). Fools rush in? The institutional context of industry creation. *Academy of Management Review, 19*, 645–670.
Anderson, P., & Tushman, M. (1990). Technological discontinuities and dominant designs: A cyclical model of technological change. *Administrative Science Quarterly, 35*, 604–633.
Andriani, P., & Cattani, G. (2016). Exaptation as source of creativity, innovation, and diversity: Introduction to the special section. *Industrial and Corporate Change, 25*, 115–131. doi:10.1093/icc/dtv053
Andriani, P., & Cohen, J. (2013). From exaptation to radical niche construction in biological and technological complex systems. *Complexity, 18*, 7–14. doi:10.1002/cplx.21450
Asheim, B. T., & Isaksen, A. (2002). Regional innovation systems. The integration of local 'sticky' and global 'ubiquitous' knowledge. *Journal of Technology Transfer, 27*, 77–86.

Bahar, D., Hausmann, R., & Hidalgo, C. A. (2014). Neighbors and the evolution of the comparative advantage of nations: Evidence of international knowledge diffusion? *Journal of International Economics, 92*, 111–123.

Baker, T., Miner, A. S., Dale, B., & Eesley, T. (2003). Improvising firms: Bricolage, account giving and improvisational competencies in the founding process. *Research Policy, 32*, 255–276.

Baker, T., & Nelson, R. E. (2005). Creating something from nothing: Resource construction through entrepreneurial bricolage. *Administrative Science Quarterly, 50*, 329–366. doi:10.2189/asqu.2005.50.3.329

Battilana, J. (2006). Agency and institutions: The enabling role of individuals' social position. *Organization, 13*, 653–676. doi:10. 1177/1350508406067008

Battilana, J., Leca, B., & Boxenbaum, E. (2009). How actors change institutions: Towards a theory of institutional entrepreneurship. *Academy of Management Annals, 3*, 65–107.

Berge, M. van den, & Weterings, A. (2014). *Relatedness in eco-technological development in European regions*. The Hague: Planbureau voor Leefomgeving.

Bergek, A., Hekkert, M., Jacobsson, S., Markard, J., Sandén, B., & Truffer, B. (2015). Technological innovation systems in contexts: Conceptualizing contextual structures and interaction dynamics. *Environmental Innovation and Societal Transitions, 16*, 51–64. doi:10.1016/j.eist.2015.07.003

Bergek, A., Jacobsson, S., Carlsson, B., Lindmark, S., & Rickne, A. (2008). Analyzing the functional dynamics of technological innovation systems: A scheme of analysis. *Research Policy, 37*, 407–429. doi:10.1016/j.respol.2007.12.003

Binz, C., Harris-Lovett, S., Kiparsky, M., Sedlak, D. L., & Truffer, B. (2016). The thorny road to technology legitimation. Institutional work for potable water reuse in California. *Technological Forecasting and Social Change, 103*, 249–263. doi:10.1016/j.techfore.2015.10.005

Binz, C., Truffer, B., & Coenen, L. (2014). Why space matters in technological innovation systems – Mapping global knowledge dynamics of membrane bioreactor technology. *Research Policy, 43*, 138–155. doi:10.1016/j.respol.2013.07.002

Binz, C., Truffer, B., & Coenen, L. (2016). Path creation as a process of resource alignment and anchoring. Industry formation for on-site water recycling in Beijing. *Economic Geography, 92*, 172–200.

Boschma, R. (1997). New industries and windows of locational opportunity. A long-term analysis of Belgium. *Erdkunde, 51*, 12–22.

Boschma, R. (Forthcoming 2016). Relatedness as driver behind regional diversification: A research agenda. *Regional Studies*. http://dx.doi.org/10.1080/00343404.2016.1254767

Boschma, R., Balland, P.-A., & Kogler, D. F. (2015). Relatedness and technological change in cities: The rise and fall of technological knowledge in U.S. metropolitan areas from 1981 to 2010. *Industrial and Corporate Change, 24*, 223–250.

Boschma, R., & Capone, G. (2015). Institutions and diversification: Related versus unrelated diversification in a varieties of capitalism framework. *Research Policy, 44*, 1902–1914.

Boschma, R., & Frenken, K. (2006). Why is economic geography not an evolutionary science? Towards an Evolutionary Economic Geography. *Journal of Economic Geography, 6*, 273–302. doi:10. 1093/jeg/lbi022

Boschma, R., & Frenken, K. (2009). Some notes on institutions in Evolutionary Economic Geography. *Economic Geography, 85*, 151–158. doi:10.1111/j.1944-8287.2009.01018.x

Boschma, R., & Frenken, K. (2011). Technological relatedness and regional branching. In H. Bathelt, M. P. Feldman & D. F. Kogler (Eds.), *Beyond territory. Dynamic geographies of knowledge creation, diffusion and innovation* (pp. 64–81). London: Routledge.

Boschma, R., Heimeriks, G., & Balland, P.-A. (2014). Scientific knowledge dynamics and relatedness in biotech cities. *Research Policy, 43*, 107–114. doi:10.1016/j.respol.2013.07.009

Boschma, R., Minondo, A., & Navarro, M. (2013). The emergence of new industries at the regional level in Spain: A proximity approach based on product-relatedness. *Economic Geography, 89*, 29–51. doi:10.1111/j.1944-8287.2012.01170.x

Buenstorf, G., & Klepper, S. (2009). Heritage and agglomeration: The Akron tyre cluster revisited. *Economic Journal, 119*, 705–733. doi:10.1111/j.1468-0297.2009.02216.x

Bulkeley, H., & Castán Broto, V. (2013). Government by experiment? Global cities and the governing of climate change. *Transactions of the Institute of British Geographers, 38*, 361–375. doi:10.1111/j.1475-5661.2012.00535.x

Callon, M. (1998). An essay on framing and overflowing: Economic externalities revisited by sociology. In M. Callon (Ed.), *The laws of the markets* (pp. 244–269). Oxford: Blackwell.

Castaldi, C., Frenken, K., & Los, B. (2015). Related variety, unrelated variety and technological breakthroughs. An analysis of US state-level patenting. *Regional Studies, 49*, 767–781.

Coe, N. M. (2011). Geographies of production I: An evolutionary revolution? *Progress in Human Geography, 35*, 81–91. doi:10. 1177/0309132510364281

Coenen, L., Asheim, B. T., Bugge, M., & Herstad, S. J. (2016). Advancing regional innovation systems: What does Evolutionary Economic Geography bring to the policy table? *Environment and Planning. C, Government and Policy*. doi:10. 1177/0263774X16646583

Coenen, L., Hansen, T., & Rekers, J. V. (2015). Innovation policy for grand challenges. An economic geography perspective. *Geography Compass, 9*, 483–496. doi:10.1111/gec3.12231

Coenen, L., Moodysson, J., & Martin, H. (2015). Path renewal in old industrial regions: Possibilities and limitations for regional innovation policy. *Regional Studies, 49*, 850–865. doi:10.1080/00343404.2014.979321

Coenen, L., Raven, R., & Verbong, G. (2010). Local niche experimentation in energy transitions: A theoretical and empirical exploration of proximity advantages and disadvantages. *Technology in Society, 32*, 295–302. doi:10.1016/j.techsoc.2010. 10.006

Coenen, L., & Truffer, B. (2012). Places and spaces of sustainability transitions: Geographical contributions to an emerging research and policy field. *European Planning Studies, 20*, 367–374. doi:10.1080/09654313.2012.651802

Colombelli, A., Krafft, J., & Quatraro, F. (2014). The emergence of new technology-based sectors in European regions: A proximitybased analysis of nanotechnology. *Research Policy, 43*, 1681–1696. doi:10.1016/j.respol.2014.07.008

Cortinovis, N., Xiao, J., Boschma, R., & Van Oort, F. (2016). *Quality of government and social capital as drivers of regional diversification in Europe* (Papers in Evolutionary Economic Geography No. 16.10). Utrecht: Utrecht University.

Crespo, J., Suire R., & Vicente J. (2014). Lock-in or lock-out? How structural properties of knowledge networks affect regional resilience. *Journal of Economic Geography, 14*, 199–219. doi:10.1093/jeg/lbt006

Crouch, C., & Voelzkow, H. (2009). *Innovation in local economies: Germany in comparative context*. Oxford: Oxford University Press.

Dawley, S. (2014). Creating new paths? Offshore wind, policy activism, and peripheral region development. *Economic Geography, 90*, 91–112. doi:10.1111/ecge.12028

Dawley, S., MacKinnon, D., Cumbers, A., & Pike, A. (2015). Policy activism and regional path creation: The promotion of offshore wind in North East England and Scotland. *Cambridge Journal of Regions, Economy and Society, 8*, 257–272. doi:10.1093/cjres/rsu036

De Jong, M., Lalenis, K., & Mamadouh, V. D. (Eds.) (2002). *The theory and practice of institutional transplantation*. Dordrecht: Springer.

Dew, N., & Sarasvathy, S. D. (2016). Exaptation and niche construction: Behavioral insights for an evolutionary theory. *Industrial and Corporate Change*, *25*, 167–179. doi:10.1093/icc/dtv051

Dew, N., Sarasvathy, S. D., & Venkataraman, S. (2004). The economic implications of exaptation. *Journal of Evolutionary Economics*, *14*, 69–84.

Dewald, U., & Truffer, B. (2012). The local sources of market formation: Explaining regional growth differentials in German photovoltaic markets. *European Planning Studies*, *20*, 397–420. doi:10.1080/09654313.2012.651803

Dosi, G. (1982). Technological paradigms and technological trajectories. A suggested interpretation of the determinants and directions of technical change. *Research Policy*, *11*, 147–162.

Duymedjian, R., & Rüling, C.-C. (2010). Towards a foundation of bricolage in organization and management theory. *Organization Studies*, *31*, 133–151. doi:10.1177/0170840609347051

Essleztbichler, J. (2015). Relatedness, industrial branching and technological cohesion in US metropolitan areas. *Regional Studies*, *49*, 752–766. doi:10.1080/00343404.2013.806793

Feldman, M. P., Kogler, D. F., & Rigby, D. L. (2015). rKnowledge: The spatial diffusion and adoption of rDNA methods. *Regional Studies*, *49*, 798–817. doi:10.1080/00343404.2014.980799

Felin, T., Kauffman, S., Mastrogiorgio, A., & Mastrogiorgio, M. (2016). Factor markets, actors, and affordances. *Industrial and Corporate Change*, *25*, 133–147. doi:10.1093/icc/dtv049

Fleming, L. (2001). Recombinant uncertainty in technological space. *Management Science*, *47*, 117–132. doi:10.1287/mnsc.47.1.117. 10671

Foray, D., David, P. A., & Hall, B. (2009). *Smart specialisation – The concept* (Knowledge Economists Policy Brief No. 9). Brussels: European Commission.

Foray, D., David, P. A., & Hall, B. H. (2011). *Smart specialisation From academic idea to political instrument, the surprising career of a concept and the difficulties involved in its implementation* (MTEI-WORKING_PAPER-2011-001). Lausanne: Ecole Polytechnique Federale de Lausanne (EPFL).

Frantzeskaki, N., Castan-Broto, V., Coenen, L., & Loorbach, D. (Eds.) (2016). *Urban sustainability transitions*. London: Routledge.

Frenken K., & Boschma, R. A. (2007). A theoretical framework for economic geography: Industrial dynamics and urban growth as a branching process. *Journal of Economic Geography*, *7*, 635–649. doi:10.1093/jeg/lbm018

Frenken, K., van Oort, F. G., & Verburg, T. (2007). Related variety, unrelated variety and regional economic growth. *Regional Studies*, *41*, 685–697. doi:10.1080/00343400601120296

Fuenfschilling, L., & Binz, C. (2016). Global socio-technical regimes. Paper presented at the 50th SPRU Anniversary Conference, Brighton, UK, 7–9 September 2016.

Fuenfschilling, L., & Truffer, B. (2014). The structuration of sociotechnical regimes – Conceptual foundations from institutional theory. *Research Policy*, *43*, 772–791. doi:10.1016/j.respol.2013. 10.010

Fuenfschilling, L., & Truffer, B. (2016). The interplay of institutions, actors and technologies in socio-technical systems. An analysis of transformations in the Australian urban water sector. *Technological Forecasting and Social Change*, *103*, 298–312.

Garud, R., Gehman, J., & Giuliani, A. P. (2016). Technological exaptation: A narrative approach. *Industrial and Corporate Change*, *25*, 149–166. doi:10.1093/icc/dtv050

Garud, R., Hardy, C., & Maguire, S. (2007). Institutional entrepreneurship as embedded agency: An introduction to the special issue. *Organization Studies*, *28*, 957–969. doi:10.1177/0170840607078958

Garud, R., & Karnøe, P. (2003). Bricolage versus breakthrough: Distributed and embedded agency in technology entrepreneurship. *Research Policy, 32*, 277–300. doi:10.1016/S0048-7333 (02)00100-2

Garud, R., Kumaraswamy, A., & Karnøe, P. (2010). Path dependence or path creation. *Journal of Management Studies, 47*, 760–774. doi:10.1111/j.1467-6486.2009.00914.x

Geels, F. W. (2002). Technological transitions as evolutionary reconfiguration processes: A multi-level perspective and a case-study. *Research Policy, 31*, 1257–1274. doi:10.1016/S0048-7333 (02)00062-8

Geels, F. W., Hekkert, M. P., & Jacobsson, S. (2008). The dynamics of sustainable innovation journeys. *Technology Analysis and Strategic Management, 20*, 521–536. doi:10.1080/09537320802292982

Geels, F. W., Kemp, R., Dudley, G., & Lyons, G. (Eds.) (2012). *Automobility in transition? A socio-technical analysis of sustainable transport*. New York: Routledge.

Geels, F. W., & Raven, R. (2006). Non-linearity and expectations in niche-development trajectories: Ups and downs in Dutch biogas development (1973–2003). *Technology Analysis and Strategic Management, 18*, 375–392. doi:10.1080/09537320600777143

Gertler, M. S. (2004).*Manufacturing culture: The institutional geography of industrial practice*. Oxford: Oxford University Press.

Giddens, A. T. (1984). *The constitution of society. Outline of the theory of structuration*. Cambridge: Polity.

Grabher, G. (1993). The weakness of strong ties – The lock-in of regional development in the Ruhr area. In G. Grabher (Ed.), *The embedded firm.* (pp. 255–277). London: Routledge.

Grin, J., Rotmans J., & Schot, J. (2011). On patterns and agency in transition dynamics: Some key insights from the KSI programme. *Environmental Innovation and Societal Transitions, 1*, 76–81. doi:10.1016/j.eist.2011.04.008

Hansen, T., & Coenen, L. (2015). The geography of sustainability transitions: Review, synthesis and reflections on an emergent research field. *Environmental Innovation and Societal Transitions, 17*, 92–109. doi:10.1016/j.eist.2014.11.001

Hassink, R. (2005). How to unlock regional economies from path dependency? From learning region to learning cluster. *European Planning Studies, 13*, 521–535. doi:10.1080/09654310500107134

Hassink, R., Klaerding, C., & Marques, P. (2014). Advancing Evolutionary Economic Geography by engaged pluralism. *Regional Studies, 48*, 1295–1307. doi:10.1080/00343404.2014.889815

Heimeriks, G., & Balland, P.-A. (2015). How smart is specialisation? An analysis of specialisation patterns in knowledge production. *Science and Public Policy*. doi:10.1093/scipol/scv061

Heimeriks, G., & Boschma, R. (2014). The path- and place-dependent nature of scientific knowledge production in biotech 1986–2008. *Journal of Economic Geography, 14*, 339–364. doi:10.1093/jeg/lbs052

Hekkert, M. P., Suurs, R. A. A., Negro, S. O., Kuhlmann, S., & Smits, R. E. H. M. (2007). Functions of innovation systems: A new approach for analysing technological change. *Technological Forecasting and Social Change, 74*, 413–432. doi:10.1016/j.techfore.2006.03.002

Henderson, D. (2000). EU regional innovation strategies: regional experimentalism in practice?*European Urban and Regional Studies,7*,347–358.doi:10.1177/096977640000700404

Hidalgo, C. A., Klinger, B., Barabasi, A. L., & Hausmann, R. (2007). The product space and its consequences for economic growth. *Science, 317*, 482–487. doi:10.1126/science.1144581

Hoogma, R., Kemp, R., Schot, J., & Truffer, B. (2002). *Experimenting for sustainable transport. The approach of strategic niche management.* London: Spon.

Hughes, T. P. (1993). *Networks of power: Electrification in Western society, 1880–1930.* Baltimore: Johns Hopkins University Press.

Isaksen, A., & Trippl, M. (2014). *Regional industrial path development in different regional innovation systems: A conceptual analysis* (Papers in Innovation Studies No. 2014/17). Lund: Lund University, Centre for Innovation, Research and Competence in the Learning Economy (CIRCLE).

Karnøe, P., & Garud, R. (2012). Path creation: Co-creation of heterogeneous resources in the emergence of the Danish wind turbine cluster. *European Planning Studies, 20,* 733–752. doi:10. 1080/09654313.2012.667923

Kemp, R., Schot, J., & Hoogma, R. (1998). Regime shifts to sustainability through processes of niche formation: The approach of strategic niche management. *Technology Analysis and Strategic Management, 10,* 175–198. doi:10.1080/09537329808524310

Klepper, S. (2002). The capabilities of new firms and the evolution of the U.S. automobile industry. *Industrial and Corporate Change, 11,* 645–666.

Klepper, S. (2007). Disagreements, spinoffs, and the evolution of Detroit as the capital of the U.S. automobile industry. *Management Science, 53,* 616–631.

Kogler, D. F. (2015). Editorial: Evolutionary Economic Geography – Theoretical and empirical progress. *Regional Studies, 49,* 705–711.

Kogler, D. F., Rigby, D. L., & Tucker, I. (2013). Mapping knowledge space and technological relatedness in U.S. cities. *European Planning Studies, 21,* 1374–1391. doi:10.10 80/09654313.2012.755832

Lévi-Strauss, C. (1967). *The savage mind.* Chicago: University of Chicago Press.

MacKinnon, D., Cumbers, A., Pike, A., Birch, K., & McMaster, R. (2009). Evolution in economic geography: Institutions, political economy, and adaptation. *Economic Geography, 85,* 129–150. doi:10.1111/j.1944-8287.2009.01017.x

Markard, J., Raven, R., & Truffer, B. (2012). Sustainability transitions: An emerging field of research and its prospects. *Research Policy, 41,* 955–967. doi:10.1016/j. respol.2012.02.013

Martin, R. (2010). Roepke Lecture in Economic Geography – Rethinking regional path dependence: Beyond lock-in to evolution. *Economic Geography, 86,* 1–27. doi:10.1111/j.1944-8287. 2009.01056.x

Martin, R., & Sunley P. (2006). Path dependence and regional economic evolution. *Journal of Economic Geography, 6,* 395–437. doi:10.1093/jeg/lbl012

Mazzucato, M. (2013). *The entrepreneurial state. Debunking public vs. private sector myths.* London: Anthern.

Mokyr, J. (1990). *The lever of riches: Technological creativity and economic progress.* New York: Oxford University Press.

Morgan, K. (2013). Path dependence and the state: The politics of novelty in old industrial regions. In P. Cooke (Ed.), *Reframing regional development: Evolution, innovation, transition* (pp. 318–340). London: Routledge.

Morgan, K., & Henderson, D. (2002). Regions as laboratories: The rise of regional experimentalism in Europe. In M. Gertler & D. Wolfe (Eds.), *Innovation and social learning: Institutional adaptation in an era of technological change* (pp. 204–226). London: Palgrave Macmillan.

Murphy, J. T. (2015). Human geography and socio-technical Transition Studies: Promising intersections. *Environmental Innovation and Societal Transitions, 17,* 73–91. doi:10.1016/j. eist.2015.03.002

Neffke, F., Hartog, M., Boschma, R., & Henning, M. (2014). *Agents of structural change. The role of firms and entrepreneurs in regional diversification* (Papers in Evolutionary Economic Geography No. 14.10. Utrecht: Utrecht University.

Neffke F., Henning M., & Boschma, R. (2011). How do regions diversify over time? Industry relatedness and the development of new growth paths in regions. *Economic Geography*, *87*, 237–265. doi:10.1111/j.1944-8287.2011.01121.x

Nelson, R.R., & Winter, S. G. (1977). In search of useful theory of innovation. *Research Policy*, 6, 36–76. doi:10.1016/0048-7333 (77)90029-4

Nelson, R. R., & Winter S. G. (1982). *An evolutionary theory of economic change*. Cambridge, MA: Belknap.

Quatraro, F., & Montresor, S. (2015). Key enabling technologies and smart specialization strategies. Regional evidence from European patent data. Paper presented at the annual DRUID conference, Rome, Italy.

Quitzow, R. (2015). Dynamics of a policy-driven market: The coevolution of technological innovation systems for solar photovoltaics in China and Germany. *Environmental Innovation and Societal Transitions*, *17*, 126–148. doi:10.1016/j.eist.2014.12.002

Rigby, D. L. (2015). Technological relatedness and knowledge space. Entry and exit of US cities from patent classes. *Regional Studies*, *49*, 1922–1937.

Rip, A., & Kemp, R. (1998). Technological change. In S. Rayner & E. L. Malone (Eds.), *Human choice and climate change. Resources and technology* (pp. 327–399). Columbus: Battelle.

Sabel, C. F. (1996). A measure of federalism: Assessing manufacturing technology centers. *Research Policy*, *25*, 281–307. doi:10. 1016/0048-7333(95)00851-9

Saviotti, P. P., & Frenken, K. (2008). Export variety and the economic performance of countries. *Journal of Evolutionary Economics*, *18*, 201–218. doi:10.1007/s00191-007-0081-5

Schot, J., & Geels, F. W. (2008). Strategic niche management and sustainable innovation journeys: Theory, findings, research agenda, and policy. *Technology Analysis and Strategic Management*, *20*, 537–554. doi:10.1080/09537320802292651

Scott, A. J., & Storper, M. (1987). High technology industry and regional development. A theoretical critique and reconstruction. *International Social Science Journal*, *112*, 215–232.

Sengers, F., & Raven, R. (2015). Toward a spatial perspective on niche development: The case of bus rapid transit. *Environmental Innovation and Societal Transitions*, *17*, 166–182. doi:10.1016/j.eist.2014.12.003

Simmie, J. (2012). Path dependence and new path creation in renewable energy technologies. *European Planning Studies*, *20*, 729– 731. doi:10.1080/09654313.2012.667922

Sine, W. D., & Lee, B. H. (2009). Tilting at windmills? The environmental movement and the emergence of the US wind energy sector. *Administrative Science Quarterly*, *54*, 123–155. doi:10.2189/asqu.2009.54.1.123

Smil, V. (2006). *Transforming the twentieth century: Technical innovations and their consequences*. Oxford: Oxford University Press.

Smith, A., & Raven, R. (2012). What is protective space? Reconsidering niches in transitions to sustainability. *Research Policy*, *41*, 1025–1036. doi:10.1016/j.respol.2011.12.012

Sotarauta, M., & R. Pulkkinen (2011). Institutional entrepreneurship for knowledge regions: In search of a fresh set of questions for regional innovation studies. *Environment and Planning C*, *29*, 96–112. doi:10.1068/c1066r

Spaargaren, G., Oosterveer, P., & Loeber, A. (Eds.) (2012). *Food practices in transition: Changing food consumption, retail and production in the age of reflexive modernity*. New York: Routledge.

Späth, P., & Rohracher, H. (2012). Local demonstrations for global transitions. Dynamics across governance levels fostering sociotechnical regime change towards sustainability. *European Planning Studies, 20*, 461–479.

Stinchfield, B. T., Nelson, R. E., & Wood, M. S. (2013). Learning from Levi-Strauss' legacy: Art, craft, engineering, bricolage, and brokerage in entrepreneurship. *Entrepreneurship Theory and Practice, 37*, 889–921. doi:10.1111/j.1540-6520.2012.00523.x

Storper, M., & Walker, R. (1989). *The capitalist imperative: Territory, technology and industrial growth.* New York: Basil Blackwell.

Sydow, J., Windeler, A., Müller-Seitz, G., & Lange, K. (2012). Path constitution analysis: A methodology for understanding path dependence and path creation. *BuR – Business Research, German Academic Association for Business Research (VHB), 5*, 155–176.

Tanner, A. N. (2014). Regional branching reconsidered: Emergence of the fuel cell industry in European regions. *Economic Geography, 90*, 403–427. doi:10.1111/ecge.12055

Tanner, A. N. (2016). The emergence of new technology-based industries: The case of fuel cells and its technological relatedness to regional knowledge bases. *Journal of Economic Geography, 16*, 611–635. doi:10.1093/jeg/lbv011

Trippl, M., Grillitsch, M., & Isaksen, A. (2015). *External 'energy' for regional industrial change: Attraction and absorption of non-local knowledge for new path development* (Papers in Innovation Studies No. 2015/47). Lund: Lund University, Centre for Innovation, Research and Competence in the Learning Economy (CIRCLE).

Truffer, B., & Coenen, L. (2012). Environmental innovation and sustainability transitions in regional studies. *Regional Studies, 46*, 1–21. doi:10.1080/00343404.2012.646164

Truffer, B., Murphy, J. T., & Raven, R (2015). The geography of sustainability transitions: Contours of an emerging theme. *Environmental Innovation and Societal Transitions, 17*, 63–72. doi:10.1016/j.eist.2015.07.004

Vallance, P. (2016). Universities, public research, and Evolutionary Economic Geography. *Economic Geography, 92*, 355–377. doi:10.1080/00130095.2016.1146076

Verbong, G., & Geels, F. (2012). Future electricity systems: Visions, scenarios and transition pathways. In G. P. J. Verbong & D. Loorbach (Eds.), *Governing the energy transition: Reality, illusion or necessity?* (pp. 203–219). New York: Routledge.

Wenting, R., & Frenken, K. (2011). Firm entry and institutional lock-in: An organizational ecology analysis of the global fashion design industry. *Industrial and Corporate Change, 20*, 1031–1048. doi:10.1093/icc/dtr032

Winter, S. G., & Szulanski, G. (2001). Replication as strategy. *Organization Science, 12*(6), 730–743.

Xiao, J., Boschma, R., & Andersson, M. (2016). *Industrial diversification in Europe: The differentiated role of relatedness* (Papers in Evolutionary Economic Geography No. 16.27). Utrecht: Utrecht University.

Yeung, H. W., & Coe, N. M. (2015). Toward a dynamic theory of global production networks. *Economic Geography, 91*, 29–58. doi:10.1111/ecge.12063

Shifting horizons in local and regional development

Andy Pike, Andrés Rodríguez-Pose and John Tomaney

ABSTRACT

Shifting horizons in local and regional development. *Regional Studies*. This paper aims, first, to trace the evolution of thinking about local and regional development in order to situate current debates in their sometimes neglected historical context and, second, to outline the elements of a future research agenda suited to contemporary challenges informed by the fundamental question of what kind of regional development and for whom. It shows how local and regional development has become a global challenge, but also how the approaches to it reflect shifting theories and ideologies which are mediated through particular structures of government and governance that shape diverse types of policy intervention.

摘要

地方及区域发展改变中的地平线。区域研究。本文第一个目标在于追溯地方及区域发展的思考演变，以将目前的辩论置放于时而受到忽略的历史脉络中，第二个目标则是概要适合当前挑战的未来研究议程所包含的元素，而这些挑战则是由"什麼样的区域发展、为谁发展"此般根本的问题所告知。本文展现地方与区域发展如何成为全球的挑战，以及达到该目标的方法如何反映转变中的理论及意识形态，而这些理论及意识形态，则是透过形塑多样政策介入类型的政府与治理的特别结构所中介。

RÉSUMÉ

Les nouveaux horizons de l'aménagement du territoire. *Regional Studies*. Dans un premier temps, cet article cherche à dessiner l'évolution de la pensée à propos de l'aménagement du territoire pour situer les débats en cours dans un contexte historique, ce qui est souvent négligé, et dans un deuxième temps à esquisser les éléments d'un futur programme de recherche qui répond aux défis contemporains éclairés par la question primordiale, à savoir quel genre d'aménagement du territoire faut-il et pour qui? Il montre non seulement comment l'aménagement du territoire est devenu un défi mondial, mais aussi comment les façons de l'aborder reflètent des théories et des idéologies changeantes qui sont diffusées au moyen des structures de gouvernement et de gouvernance particulières qui déterminent divers moyens d'intervention politique.

ZUSAMMENFASSUNG
Veränderliche Horizonte in der Lokal- und Regionalentwicklung. *Regional Studies.* In diesem Beitrag versuchen wir erstens, die Evolution der Denkweise über Lokal- und Regionalentwicklung nachzuverfolgen, um die derzeitigen Debatten in ihren zuweilen vernachlässigten geschichtlichen Kontext zu stellen, und zweitens, die Elemente einer künftigen Forschungsagenda zu beschreiben, die auf die aktuellen Herausforderungen im Zusammenhang mit der grundlegenden Frage nach der Art und den Zielgruppen der Regionalentwicklung zugeschnitten ist. Wir zeigen auf, wie die Lokal- und Regionalentwicklung zu einer weltweiten Herausforderung geworden ist und wie zugleich die diesbezüglichen Ansätze das Spiegelbild von veränderlichen Theorien und Ideologien sind, die durch bestimmte Strukturen der Regierung und Governance vermittelt werden, welche unterschiedliche Arten politischer Maßnahmen prägen.

RESUMEN
Horizontes cambiantes en el desarrollo local y regional. *Regional Studies.* El objetivo de este artéculo es primero seguir la evolución del pensamiento sobre el desarrollo local y regional con el fin de situar los debates actuales en sus contextos históricos a veces ignorados y, segundo, destacar los elementos de una agenda futura de investigación que se ajuste al reto actual de abordar la cuestión fundamental de qué tipo de desarrollo y para quién. Demostramos el modo en que el desarrollo local y regional se ha convertido en un reto global, pero también cómo sus enfoques reflejan las teorías e ideologías cambiantes que están influenciadas por estructuras particulares de gobierno y gobernanza que dan forma a los diferentes tipos de intervención política.

INTRODUCTION

the play of forces in the market normally tends to increase, rather than to decrease, the inequalities between regions.

(Myrdal, 1957, p. 26)

Although the concern with the nature of 'development' and its geographies can be traced back to the earliest stages of industrialization and urbanization, it was in the second half of the 20th century that both the study of local and regional development and the range and scale of government interventions to support economic development expanded significantly. In the immediate post-war period policy-makers, in both the global North and South, placed great faith in the ability of the state to promote development and manage spatial inequalities. Only by the last quarter of the 20th century was a renewed emphasis placed on the role of market mechanisms in the allocation of resources across the economic landscape, although states continued to intervene to (re)shape economic geographies. This shift in policy approach coincided with the acceleration of globalization and trans-formations in the geopolitical order. Before the global financial crisis of 2008/09 free markets and globalization were associated with relatively high levels of economic growth and the expansion of a new middle class in emerging econo-mies, but also with a new, complex and uneven geography of inequality. In the aftermath of the Great Recession, a new normal of low global growth has created fresh challenges for thinking about uneven urban and regional development, including what is meant by 'development' itself and how its economic, social and environmental dimensions relate (Pike, Rodríguez-Pose, & Tomaney, 2016).

Shifting contexts, experiences and legacies have meant the focus of local and regional development studies has been constantly shifting. The key concepts that structure our understanding of what local and regional developments have been affected by the vagaries of academic fashion and examined through different scien-tific and ideological prisms reflecting dominant and insurgent knowledge claims and unequal power structures. Local and regional development has adopted a multi-plicity of forms in different historical and geographical contexts and this raises the question what new can be said about the factors that promote it. This paper aims, first, to trace the evolution of thinking about local and regional development in order to situate current debates in their sometimes neglected historical context and, second, to outline the elements of a future research agenda suited to contemporary challenges informed by the fundamental question of what kind of regional develop-ment and for whom (Pike, Rodríguez-Pose, & Tomaney, 2007; Pike et al., 2016). The paper organizes the discussion in relation to key themes in local and regional development: the global context; definitions of development and the values and principles that underpin them; frameworks of understanding; government and governance; policy and practice; and international experiences. This structure is intended to highlight how local and regional development has become a global chal-lenge, but how the approaches to it reflect shifting theories and ideologies which are mediated through particular structures of government and governance that shape diverse types of policy intervention by actors leading to variegated international practices and experiences of development locally and regionally.

LOCAL AND REGIONAL DEVELOPMENT IN
A GLOBAL CONTEXT

The growing integration of the global economy provides both the context within which local and regional development occurs and the ways in which it is understood analytically. As a broad multidisciplinary field, local and regional development studies typically have focused on localities and regions in the countries of the global North. Another multidisciplinary endeavour, development studies, has, by contrast, been concerned with less-developed and emerging economies in the global South. Such strands of work have tended to run in parallel with limited interaction and cross-fertilizations of theory, evidence and policy. The evolution of distinct disciplinary traditions, in part, reflects (and is reflected in) the categories through which the world has been classified for the purposes of analysis: 'First', 'Second' and 'Third World'; 'developed' and 'less developed countries'; 'high-', 'middle-' and 'low-income economies'; 'transition', 'emerging' and 'post-socialist' economies. But such fragmented conceptual, analytical and policy perspectives limit one's understanding of local and regional development in an increasingly globalized and interdependent world, constraining explanation, policy formulation and praxis (Pike, Rodríguez-Pose, & Tomaney, 2014). Scott and Storper (2003, p. 582) call for the development of a common theoretical language about local and regional development in all parts of the world in the context of globalization, while recognizing that 'territories are arrayed at different points along a vast spectrum of development characteristics'. For this reason, the present paper adopts a deliberately broad and international definition of what constitutes the literature on local and regional development, and what comprises its subjects and objects of enquiry.

Much analytical effort has been applied to understanding how accelerating global financial flows, direct investment in manufacturing, services and the built environment become 'embedded' in cities and regions and shape their development patterns. In one radical reading, mobile capital seeks a recurring 'spatial fix', reflecting capitalism's insatiable drive to overcome its inherent crises by geographical expansion and restructuring, implying (re)building spaces for accumulation that must be then be devalorized in order to make way for yet another 'spatial fix' (Harvey, 1985). Amin and Thrift attribute the embeddedness of economic activity to the presence of 'institutional thickness' – trust-based networks of interacting organizations that shape collective endeavour in cities and regions that 'hold down the global' (Amin & Thrift, 1994, p. 10). But a focus only on the endogenous characteristics of places as determinants of local growth draws attention away from other critically important and co-constitutive exogenous factors that shape local and regional development including the restructuring of international divisions of labour, national political economies and macro-economic shifts. Recent history provides ample evidence of the adverse impacts of globalization on local and regional development arising from a volatile financial system, uncertain trade and investment flows, resulting in ongoing embedding, disembedding and re-embedding of economic activity in global networks.

Scott and Storper (2003) stress the importance of global and historically persistent phenomena of such large-scale processes of urban agglomeration and regional economic specialization, which have accelerated with globalization, in understanding local and regional development processes, evolving configurations of economic concentration, and the uneven geography of inequality. For Glaeser (2012), globalization and technological changes underpinning urban agglomerations make cities more important because both increase productivity by accelerating returns to knowledge and innovation. Allowing economic activity to concentrate geographically – by limiting constraints to agglomeration – is interpreted as the key to economic growth. A corollary of the new scholarly and political focus on the productive potential of the largest cities is the need to accept that some cities and regions may face processes of economic decline, which public policy intervention will, and normatively should, do little to arrest. Glaeser, for instance, has argued in relation to Buffalo, New York:

> The truth is, the federal government has already spent vast sums of taxpayer money over the past half-century to revitalize Buffalo, only to watch the city continue to decay. Future federal spending that tries to revive the city will likely prove equally futile.
>
> (Glaeser, 2007, n.p.)[1]

Reflecting these ideas, the World Bank (2009) has emphasized the importance of 'economic concentration' (typically measured in terms of density) as a source and manifestation of productivity and growth. In the case of developing countries and perhaps echoing Hirschman's (1958) notion of 'unbalanced development', the World Bank advocates a policy of facilitating mass migration from lower income regions to large cities as the best means of accelerating growth, generating employment and maximizing overall welfare.

The view of the urban density and agglomeration as the drivers of local and regional development has come under scrutiny. Patterns of agglomeration vary widely depending on the mix of local circumstances and sectors, and the role of historical path dependencies in the evolution of regional economies. Hence, urban and regional systems contain a great variety of productivity enhancing conditions (Scott & Storper, 2003). Concepts such as globalization and agglomeration provide frameworks for analysing local and regional development rather than an iron cage which determines social and economic outcomes. The geographical sources of economic growth are varied, while the potential for development exists in a diversity of locations in places outside the economic cores (Organisation for Economic Co-operation and Development (OECD), 2012; Parkinson et al., 2012).

DEFINING THE PRINCIPLES AND VALUES OF LOCAL AND REGIONAL DEVELOPMENT

Referring to conceptions of 'development', Raymond Williams noted that 'very difficult and contentious political and economic issues have been widely obscured by the apparent simplicity of these terms' (Williams, 1983, p. 103). Definitions are a critically important and deceptively difficult starting point for understanding what is meant by local and regional development and are intertwined with conceptions of what development is for (Pike et al., 2007, 2016). Local and regional development has historically been dominated by economic concerns and, fundamentally, by growth. Since the early work of Kuznets – notwithstanding his own doubts about its value in this respect – national income growth has been the main measure of economic progress (Coyle, 2014). But, as Seers (1969, p. 1) observed 'development consists of much else besides economic growth' and should be measured along other axes such as poverty, unemployment, inequality, and the strength of education and rights of citizenship. He maintained that if these problems grew worse, 'it would be strange to call the result "development", even if per capita income doubled' (p. 3). Growth is not always the objective per se, but a means for achieving well-being, according to the social, economic, cultural and political conditions of particular populations in specific places. In this respect, definitions of local and regional economic development are inescapably context-dependent. The well-being target is unlikely to be the same for people living in New York or in Maputo; only the residents of New York or Maputo can define their objectives in the medium- and long-term (Canzanelli, 2001).

The limits of conventional measures of development have been amplified in recent debates focusing on the growth of wealth inequality. Stiglitz (2013) and especially Piketty (2014) have drawn attention to the increasing wealth gap between the top 1% and those at the bottom of the income pyramid. Rising inequality between and within regions also forms an important component of these broader inequalities (Ezcurra & Rodríguez-Pose, 2014), but, to date, has received comparatively little attention. For some, urban and regional inequality is an inevitable part – even a necessary motor – of urban dynamism (Glaeser, 2013). For others, by contrast, growing inequality, polarization and poverty, together with the emergence of a new 'precariat' (Savage, 2015), contribute to undermine the very foundations of urban development (Sassen, 2001, 2006). Rising inequality erodes any shared sense of citizenship, weakening social solidarity and entrenching the political power of elites (Crouch, 2013; Oxfam, 2014). Increasing inequalities also have wider economic impacts dragging upon further growth, limiting the expansion of demand and consumption by groups experiencing stagnating or declining relative incomes (Cingano, 2014; Morgan Stanley, 2014; Ostry, Berg, & Tsangarides, 2014; Standard & Poor, 2014). Moreover, inequality erodes trust, increases anxiety and illness, and even drives up crime and murder rates. In richer countries, a smaller gap between rich and poor means happier, healthier and more peaceful societies: people in more unequal states of the United States trust each other less, while homicide rates are higher in more unequal US states and Canadian provinces (Wilkinson & Pickett, 2010).

The sense of a loosening link between growth and development lies behind recent efforts to find new ways to define and measure development, notably the United Nations' Human Development Index (HDI),[2] Stiglitz, Sen and Fitoussi's Commission on the Measurement of Economic and Social Progress (2009), the European Commission's 'GDP and Beyond' project (European Commission, 2013), and the OECD's 'Global Project on Measuring the Progress of Societies', which led to the Better Life Index (OECD, 2013). These efforts have been mirrored at the local and regional scales in efforts to define development in terms of broader measures of well-being rather than economic output. Examples include the Genuine Progress Indicator in the states of Maryland[3] and Vermont[4] (Tomaney, 2015).

Perrons and Dunford (2013) and Morgan (2004) – following Sen (1999) – call for a distinction to be made between qualities that are 'instrumentally significant', such as jobs and income, and qualities and 'capabilities' that are 'intrinsically significant', such as health, education and civic participation. Such a distinction encourages a focus on matters of well-being and quality of life, the conditions of 'human flourishing', and whether and how growth can be rendered more equitable, inclusive and just (Benner & Pastor, 2012; Rodríguez-Pose & Wilkie, 2015).

In this vein, Perrons and Dunford (2013) highlight the growing gap since the mid-1990s between London (and the South East of England region) and other UK regions, as measured by gross value added (GVA) per head. Adapting the HDI, they propose a regional development index (RDI) for the UK, which includes measures of a healthy life, knowledge, economic standard of living and employment. Ranked in this way, London falls from first place (when measured by GVA per head) to seventh place in the new index. Developing the index further by adding a gender dimension, London falls to the bottom of the rankings, while the North East of England, which has a low rank in GVA per head, is placed highly in relation the gender-sensitive regional development index (GRDI). In considering the question 'what kind of regional development and for whom?', the definition of development can be further extended to the use of natural resources and environmental impacts of economic activity. Other considerations – what Sen (1999) terms aspects of 'human flourishing' – include the way that different forms of development impact on family life and children and contribute to active and committed forms of citizenship at the local and regional scales.

How one defines development determines one's perception of which territories can be ranked as 'developed'. The RDI and GRDI pose useful questions about how economic progress and the well-being of communities should be measured and assessed. For most people in the UK, it is counter-intuitive to place a region like the North East of England at the top of any development ranking because of its high unemployment, ill-health and problems of low productivity. UK regional policy has traditionally been based on a growth and innovation-oriented model of development, attempting to emulate aspects of London's almost uniquely configured experience and trajectory without a considered assessment of its real costs and benefits for different social groups and the very different contexts elsewhere in the UK.

FRAMEWORKS OF UNDERSTANDING: CONCEPTS AND THEORIES OF LOCAL AND REGIONAL DEVELOPMENT

Our understanding of the processes of local and regional development is constantly shifting and perennially contested. A range of theories variously employ hard, bounded and soft, unbounded conceptualization and theorization, inductive and/or deductive reasoning, narrow and closed as well as broader and more open assumptions about perfect or imperfect competition, macro- or microeconomic frameworks, varied geographies and conceptions of the 'local' and the 'regional', including macro- and cross-boundary regions, city-regions, cities, communities and neigh-bourhoods, quantitative and qualitative methods. They seek to explain trends in social and spatial disparities towards convergence or divergence or – in more recent language – towards a 'flat' or a 'spiky' world (McCann, 2008; Rodríguez-Pose & Crescenzi, 2008). Recurring issues concern: the extent to which local and regional growth has an endogenous and/or exogenous character; the quantitative extent and qualitative character of development; the role of constant, diminishing or increasing returns in the economic growth process; innovation and knowledge and technology diffusion, externalities, or spillovers; the impact of the economies and diseconomies of agglomeration; the relative roles of specialization and diversity in explaining local and regional economic performance; the nature of resilience, adaptation and adaptability in relation to disruptive change; and the balance between objectives of economic efficiency, social justice and environmental stewardship.

Academic concerns with theorizing the socially and geographically uneven forms of development generally emerge out of a dissatisfaction with neo-classical accounts founded upon assumptions of economic rationality, perfect mobility, information and competition, the role of diminishing returns, and that, all things being equal, the factors of production, responding to market signals, would be allocated efficiently between places ensuring a long-run equilibrium. Such ideas have had an enduring impact on public policy, despite the challenge of alternative theories that challenge assumptions of the rational choosing individual. In the 1980s, Margaret Thatcher's Conservative government in the UK, for example, argued that 'employment imbalances between areas should in principle be corrected by the natural adjustment of labour markets' (Department of Trade and Industry (DTI), 1983, pp. 3ff.) in order to justify reductions in regional policy expenditure.

Work in the 1950s and 1960s challenged the idea that the free play of market forces would lead to the long-run reduction of regional inequalities. Myrdal, Perroux and Hirschman all saw development as a socially and geographically uneven process. Myrdal (1957), drawing inspiration from Keynes' view that the economy has intrinsic disequilibrium tendencies, maintained that

> The system is by itself not moving towards any sort of balance between forces, but is constantly on the move away from such a situation. In the normal case a change does not call forth countervailing changes but, instead, supporting changes, which move the system in the same direction as the first change but much further. Because of such circular causation as a social process tends to become cumulative and often gather speed at an accelerating rate.
>
> (p. 13)

Much subsequent work can be seen as a series of extended elaborations of Myrdal's early observation, as researchers seek deeper explanations for these processes in order to understand their consequences better, and better inform policy-makers.

The 'New Economic Geography', for instance, emphasizes the role of increasing returns, agglomeration economies, multiplier effects and knowledge spillovers in shaping the distribution of economic activity (Krugman, 1998). It seeks to explain how places end up with geographically differentiated economic structures and income levels, and to ask whether spatial disparities are (in)efficient for overall national economic growth. In this perspective, economic activity tends to concentrate in a few dominant metropolitan areas, reflecting, in the first order, the presence of natural advantages such as physical resources, location and the concentration of talent. Concentration also reflects advantages derived from history and past policy interventions (e.g. the decision to create a capital city, to locate economic activities in certain areas of the country, responding to political and/or military needs, or the historical role of fiscal incentives). In the second order, the presence of agglomeration economies induces firms and labour to sort themselves over space and co-locate. Agglomeration economies arise, firstly, when co-location facilitates the sharing of local public goods that serve several individuals or firms, such as universities; and, secondly, when firms have demands for similar skills and seek to share risks or can draw upon the advantages of a thick labour market, allowing better matching of firms and workers. In addition, knowledge spillovers contribute to productivity improvements, through greater intensity of communication between local actors which can contribute to increased innovation and technological advances, and through enhanced learning among workers, particularly in agglomerations with dense geographical concentrations of skilled and specialized labour. Finally, external and agglomeration economies result from intra-industry specialization that allows finer inter-firm divisions of labour, multiplying the number of forward and backward industrial linkages locally and further afield.

Agglomeration economies provide an important explanation for patterns of local and regional development but do not deliver a complete account (Martin, 2015). Many intermediate and peripheral territories also display significant potential for growth and often make vital contributions to national growth – up to two-thirds in OECD countries in recent years. As defined by the OECD, predominantly rural regions, on average, enjoyed faster growth between 1995 and 2007 than much larger cities or even intermediate regions (OECD, 2012). Hence, while agglomeration matters, other factors, such as special endowments of human capital, institutional qualities, or the innovative capacity of firms and individuals may matter more for local and regional development in certain geographical settings and time periods.

A series of 'Schumpeterian' contributions emphasize the importance of innovation and the disruptive role of technological and organizational changes ('gales of creative destruction') in shaping patterns of local and regional development. Firms in some regions can take advantage of 'windows of locational opportunity' (Scott & Storper, 2003), exploiting first-mover advantages in new technologies. Successful regions contain firms that seize opportunities arising from technological transformations, often aided by farsighted public and private actors at the local and regional scale (Castells & Hall, 1994). Florida (2002) attributes regional growth to the rise of the 'creative class' – people who add economic value and generate novelty through their creativity and foster urban and regional growth through high levels of innovation and technology-based industries by congregating in 'tolerant places'. The role of innovation potential and performance as the key to understanding differential geographical patterns of local and regional development figured prominently in the 1980s and 1990s when attention was accorded to the 'resurgence of regional economies' (Storper, 1995) and attention was drawn to the performance of industrial districts (Piore & Sabel, 1984), local industrial systems (Saxenian, 1994), territorial innovation systems (Moulaert & Sekia, 2003) and learning regions (Cooke & Morgan, 1998), and how regional development was underpinned by the operation of 'untraded inter-dependencies' (Storper, 1995), 'social capital' (Coleman, 1988; Putnam, 1993; Trigilia, 2001), or reflected the extent to which the region acted as a 'nexus of learning' (Cooke & Morgan, 1998). A related body of research on existing industrial regions theorized economic decline in evolutionary terms and elaborated conceptions of economic, cognitive and institutional lock-ins which hindered development (Grabher, 1993).

Other contributions have been more sceptical of the extent to which the fate of localities and regions lies in their own hands, reflecting the enduring tension between exogenous and endogenous understandings of development. Massey's (1984) early intervention queried the extent to which geographical inequality should be defined as a 'regional problem', but rather as the outcome of capitalist processes of investment and divestment that produce 'spatial divisions of labour'. Similarly, Peck (2005, p. 764) chastises theories of the creative class as generators of economic development because they 'are peculiarly well suited to entrepreneurialized and neoliberalized urban landscapes', which both promote urban and regional inequality and commodified and hollowed-out forms of community life.

The global economic crisis of 2008 returned attention to the crisis-prone nature of capitalist development, its localized and systemic manifestations, and intensified patterns of inequality between and within cities and regions. The global financial crisis and the ensuing Great Recession posed new and profound challenges for concepts and theories in frameworks of understanding (e.g., Hadjimichalis & Hudson, 2014). Much contemporary theory was crafted in the 1990s, a period of relative stability, integration and growth that ended in economic crisis and was replaced by low growth, economic instability, new mass migrations and the rebuilding of borders around the world ('de-globalization'). Existing approaches are weak at explaining discontinuous change, suggesting the need to pay more attention to Minsky-style crisis theories to develop a better awareness of disruptive changes destabilizing existing models of local and regional development. This demands fresh thinking about viable, sustainable and scalable alternatives, and asks questions about adaptation, adaptability, and the adaptive capacity of actors and institutions in localities and regions to withstand, recover from or anticipate disruptive change (Pike, Dawley, & Tomaney, 2010). Together with the above discussion about inequality, the discussion here points to the need to pay greater attention to the relation and interaction of exogenous and endogenous causation, especially the macroeconomic and political factors that help to shape 'territorial competition', and their connections and interactions with local and regional development outcomes.

INSTITUTIONS: GOVERNMENT AND GOVERNANCE

The apparent global trend of decentralization and the empowerment of local, regional and city-regional institutions in pursuit of development has led to a broader consideration of their role. Amin and Thrift (1994) proposed the presence of 'institutional thickness' as an explanation of the superior performance of some regions. This claim gave birth to the 'new regionalism' that emphasized the capability of decentralized institutions to enable the apparent resurgence of regional economies. The new regionalism has been criticized for generalizing from the experience of a small number of economically successful regions (Lovering, 1999), overlooking questions of distribution, justice and ethics (Hadjimichalis, 2006), and neglecting how it is that the quality and performance of institutions rather than their number and density is what matters (Rodríguez-Pose, 2013; Tomaney, 2014). Very similar institutional settings work in different ways in different territories.

Concern with institutions has become a mode of investigation into the conditions that promote local and regional development reflecting a broader concern about how institutions shape economic development (Gertler, 2010). Analysis has involved the search for an elusive 'devolution dividend' (Pike, Rodriguez-Pose, Tomaney, Torrisi, & Tselios, 2012), while the role of institutions looms large in discussions of the 'learning region' (Morgan, 2004) or regional development agencies. Regional institutions have also been analysed in evolutionary approaches: often institutional 'lock-ins' account for the failure of territories to adapt to economic crises (Grabher, 1993). Moreover, under certain conditions, the trend to devolution has contributed to the growth of local and regional inequalities by empowering already strong regions (Rodríguez-Pose & Gill, 2004).

Institutions matter because they facilitate negotiation and dialogue, mobilize stakeholders and integrate them into the development processes, enhance policy continuity and strengthen territories' 'voice' (Pike et al., 2016). Differences in the performance of institutions play a central role in explaining patterns of local and regional growth (Storper, Kemeny, Makarem, & Osman, 2014). Development is hindered by 'institutional bottlenecks' such as poor mobilization of stakeholders, lack of continuity and coherence in the policy implementation, institutional instability, lack of a common and strategic vision, and capacity gaps in multilevel governance frameworks, which preclude a shift in the focus of policies away from subsidies towards policies aimed at mobilizing regions' own resources and assets (OECD, 2012). Institutions affect the resilience of territories and their adaptability in the face of economic change (Pike et al., 2010; North, 2005).

In policy terms, it is easy to draw misleading conclusions from the 'institutional turn' in local and regional development studies. Prescriptions such as the suggestion that strong mayors produce better urban social and economic outcomes (Barber, 2013) capture the attention of policy-makers but are poorly founded in evidence. The more important lessons lie in the recognition that markets are embedded in institutional and cultural frameworks at all spatial scales, and actors and institutions mediate how policies are formulated, developed and rendered mobile within geographically extensive and relational networks (Peck &

Theodore, 2015). Well-functioning institutions enable human flourishing in cities and regions, but they can also facilitate regressive and unproductive forms of development. Institutions are the arena for the production of social, economic, cultural and political values and are the subject of political contention as well as consensus. A key area for future research and action concerns the role of political institutions because of their fundamental and formative role in creating the frameworks and conditions for local and regional innovation and transformation.

LOCAL AND REGIONAL DEVELOPMENT POLICY AND PRACTICE

Government intervention to shape patterns of local and regional development expanded in different forms and guises in the global North and South, especially after the Second World War. In the global South, such interventions typically formed a part of post-colonial nation-building efforts. Myrdal, echoing the Polyanian sense of the 'double movement', argued that in the relatively prosperous democratic welfare states

> the stronger will be the urge and the capacity to counteract the blind market forces which tend to result in regional inequalities; and this, again, will spur economic development in the country, and so on and so on, in circular causation.
>
> (Myrdal, 1957, p. 41)

In the global North, the promotion of geographically balanced national development proceeded alongside the growth of the redistributive Keynesian welfare state. National governments sought to reallocate economic activity from faster growing regions with capacity constraints to slower growing regions with capacity surpluses ('Spatial Keynesianism') (Jessop, 2002; Brenner, 2004). Economic crisis, internationalized competition and the 'fiscal crisis of the state' (O'Connor, 1973) underpinned the erosion of the post-war settlement in many developed countries, contributing to a reduction in nationally directed regional policy and the concomitant rise in importance of local and regional institutions as modes of governance of local and regional development. For Harvey (1989), Spatial Keynesianism and urban 'managerialism' have been replaced by 'urban entrepreneurialism' which draws attention to the ways that nationally managed redistribution between cities and regions has been superseded by territorial competition for jobs and services. Such mechanisms of inter-territorial competition both shape local and regional development outcomes and generate macroeconomic consequences, reinforcing the notion that cities and regions are in competition with each other for investment, resources and people (Cheshire & Gordon, 1998; Brenner & Wachsmuth, 2013). The trope of 'regional competitiveness' is pervasive in the world of economic development policy, although this rests on a narrow conception territorial development and overemphasizes the importance of the firm to the region and the region to the firm, implying the existence of a collective territorial economic performance rather than developing a realistic understanding how particular economic activities take place in a given locality or region (Bristow, 2005).

National governments in the global North and South have developed an array of policies designed to stimulate local and regional development or deal with the consequences of geographically uneven economic decline and social stress. In the global South, the introduction of measures such as export processing zones, free-ports and, more recently, science and technology parks have been intended to kick-start the local and regional and, as a result, the national economy, but with uneven economic and social consequences (Rodríguez-Pose & Hardy, 2014). The geographical inequalities arising from such policies are the stimulus to a new engagement with regional policy in China (European Union/National Development and Reform Commission, 2011). In the global North, Spatial Keynesianism was manifested in the public support for urban and regional infrastructure and services, the provision of financial incentives to attract mobile investors to lagging regions, constraints on development in faster growing regions, efforts to build up the local export base, and the formation national spatial planning systems, while the welfare state redistributed resources through fiscal instruments that provided a set of 'automatic stabilizers' for regions (Kaldor, 1970).

Spatial Keynesianism generated improvements in output and employment and mitigated local and regional inequalities. But researchers highlighted the limits of these policy approaches, emphasizing how under certain conditions regional investment incentives were costly, had deadweight and displacement effects, and lacked additionality. Policies to attract mobile investments to lagging regions were heavily criticized because of their tendency to create 'branch plant economies' (Firn, 1975; Turok, 1993) that promoted development *in* the region but not *of* the region (Morgan & Sayer, 1985). Similarly, the heavy emphasis on 'hard' physical infrastructure investments (notably transport) as a stimulus to economic development has been criticized for ignoring the broader underlying human and 'softer' factors (such as skills, innovation and agglomeration) (Crescenzi & Rodríguez-Pose, 2012). Nevertheless, despite the ebbing of Spatial Keynesianism, physical infrastructure investments and incentives for mobile investments remain popular with policy-makers. They still remain central to the policy repertoire of local and regional development authorities across the world, making a reappearance after the global economic crisis and Great Recession in the late 2000s in the form of stimulus packages. In the face of austerity and tax payer resistance, the search for new forms of finance for regional development, including value-capture mechanisms, tax increment financing and other forms of 'financialization' are proliferating (O'Brien & Pike, 2015).

Partly reflecting the perceived weaknesses of 'top-down' and often externally oriented approaches and policies aimed at attracting mobile investors and building infrastructures, from the 1990s research refocused upon approaches aimed at promoting endogenous potential (Vázquez-Barquero, 2003) and 'development from below' (Stöhr, 1990). These ideas were typically translated into support for industrial clusters (Porter, 1998). Despite its enduring popularity with economic development practitioners, the cluster concept has been criticized for being too conceptually and geographically elastic and confused to be a useful guide to policy, and lacking in systematic and robust evidence of its effectiveness (Martin & Sunley, 2011). Recent attempts to overcome the bifurcations of policy approaches have focused on the attraction of exogenous resources, while at the same time promoting endogenous development in attempts to integrate better formerly separate 'top-down' and 'bottom-up' approaches (Crescenzi & Rodríguez-Pose, 2011). Researchers stress the importance of global production networks and value chains in shaping local and regional development outcomes and the potential of public policies to foster the 'strategic coupling' of (exogenous) global resources flows and (endogenous) local assets (Yeung & Coe, 2015). These debates find expression in the case for 'place-based' local and regional development policies that focus on the promotion of locally rooted human and knowledge-based assets through fine-gained locally conceived and executed development strategies that provide public goods aimed improving the local business environment: skills, technology and clusters (Barca, McCann, & Rodríguez-Pose, 2012; see also OECD, 2012).

While there are powerful voices stressing the limits of policy interventions at the local, regional and/or city-regional levels, the OECD (2012) has sought to draw together the elements of a 'new' paradigm that emphasizes a bottom-up initiative and responsibility, and the reconfiguration of centre and centre–regional/local relations toward self-sustaining/self-financing forms of development. Trends in this direction can be observed in many parts of the world. In some places, local and regional authorities have made virtue of the necessity of self-help with fewer resources available from central governments in wake of the global financial crisis and the Great Recession. But the new paradigm needs to be considered in relation to whether or not macro-economic and political contexts enable such approaches.

LOCAL AND REGIONAL DEVELOPMENT IN INTERNATIONAL CONTEXT

Local and regional development occurs amidst increasingly complex and interdependent global flows of resources, finance and people. Local and regional context continues to matter in shaping both patterns of development and variegated policy responses. Diversity and differentiation are ensured by, *inter alia*, legacies of inherited spatial divisions of labour, national and regional political economies and institutional capacities, and differing understandings of the values that should underpin policy. The growth of the 'Tiger' economies (Yeung, 2009), the rapid rise of China (European Union/National Development and Reform Commission, 2011), industrialization in Latin America (Guiliani et al., 2005), and the process of European integration (Dunford, 1993) demonstrate many different forms of local and regional development, patterns of inequality, and policy responses, as well as significant similarities.

The diversity of experience in the global North and South leads to the demand to 'provincialize' or 'dislocate' dominant theories of local and regional development.

In the aftermath of the Second World War – and still today – the promotion of economic development concepts, policy and practice continues to draw on experiences from the global North. Researchers contest the appropriateness of this one-way traffic (e.g. Connell, 2007; Roy, 2009). The rise of China as an economic power presents a political challenge to the tenets of what has been known as The Washington Consensus on development (Williamson, 1989; Stiglitz, 2002; Rodrik, 2007). Rather than any single and dominant origination of invention and wisdom, the future of local and regional development theory, policy and practice is more likely to take the form of diverse and myriad knowledge exchanges and dialogue and learning that interconnect and operate in multiple directions across the world in which learned societies can play a role. But in exploring the diversity of experience it is crucial to avoid an approach which lapses into 'irreducible complexity, limitless variety, grassroots creativity and effervescent potential' (Peck, 2015, p. 164). Local and regional development occurs within a system of institutionally 'variegated' capitalism (Peck & Theodore, 2007). Cities and regions make their own history, but not circumstances of their own choosing: they remain entangled in and constrained by global systems of political and economic power.

AGENDAS

An agenda for local and regional development studies calls for the recognition that the forces of globalization are pervasive but highly variegated in their unfolding, reach and impact. International flows of finance, investment, goods, services and people will continue to be mediated institutionally, politically and ideologically – perhaps more so in an age when borders are being rebuilt. Global trends in social and spatial inequality demand urgent responses, but the international debate about inequality has so far paid scarce attention to its geography, which tends to appear as backdrop rather than element. More investigation is required into the mutually constitutive role of macro-political and economic processes and patterns of local and regional development.

Rising inequality alongside economic turmoil raises the question of what is meant when one speaks of 'development'. Efforts to find new measures of local and regional development remain in their infancy, but there is enough work to suggest that rephrasing the question suggests new and/or reformed approaches that reconfigure the relationships between its economy, society and environment. Propositions such as the 'Foundational Economy', for instance, draw attention to the sheltered sectors that supply mundane but essential goods and services such as infrastructures, utilities, food processing, retailing and distribution; and health, education and welfare that are used by everyone regardless of income or social status (Bowman, Froud, Johal, Law, & Leaver, 2014). These sectors rarely figure in the theory and practice of local and regional development but can be reorganized in ways that generate welfare gains and diffuse prosperity amongst localities and regions with different and/or weaker sets of assets and resources.

Such approaches though require supportive political and economic frameworks, including multilevel systems of government and governance and fiscal redistribution. The 'institutional turn' in the study of local and regional development represents an important conceptual and theoretical advance. Institutions are critical to the embedding of development in places and ensuring the social and spatial distribution of its outcomes and impacts. But more work is needed, first, to understand the policy implications of the insights arising from this productive vein of research and, second, to develop suitable policy guidelines, especially for regions that have weak and/or dysfunctional institutional endowments.

In a period of political and economic turmoil, local and regional development is an urgent priority. But in many parts of the world, this debate takes place in contexts where citizens are increasingly distrustful of political leaders, public institutions and traditional modes of exercising power. The task of developing concepts, theory, policy, and practice in local and regional development remains both large and pressing but requires more extensive enrolment of actors in the global North and South and the building of mechanisms and networks to encourage, facilitate and promote dialogue, debate and deliberation about the common concerns and problems in the global North and South (Pike et al., 2014; Pike, Rodríguez-Pose, & Tomaney, 2015).

ACKNOWLEDGEMENTS

The authors would like to acknowledge the highly constructive comments made by two anonymous referees and the advice of the editors.

DISCLOSURE STATEMENT

No potential conflict of interest was reported by the authors.

NOTES

1. For a similar argument applied to Australia, see Daley (2012); and to northern English cities, see Leunig and Swaffield (2008).
2. See http://hdr.undp.org/en/content/human-development-index-hdi/.
3. See http://www.dnr.maryland.gov/mdgpi/.
4. See http://www.vtgpi.org/.

REFERENCES

Amin, A., & Thrift, N. (1994). Living in the global. In A. Amin, & N. Thrift (Eds.), *Globalization, institutions and regional development in Europe* (pp. 1–22). Oxford: Oxford University Press.
Barber, B. (2013). *If mayors ruled the world*. New Haven and London: Yale University Press.

Barca, F., McCann, P., & Rodríguez-Pose, A. (2012). The case for regional development intervention: Place-based versus place-neutral approaches. *Journal of Regional Science*, *52*, 134–152. doi:10.1111/j.1467-9787.2011.00756.x.

Barber, B. (2013). *If mayors ruled the world*. New Haven and London: Yale University Press.

Benner, C., & Pastor, M. (2012). *Just growth: Inclusion and prosperity in America's metropolitan regions*. London: Routledge.

Bowman, A., Froud, J., Johal, J., Law, J., & Leaver, A. (2014). *The end of the experiment? From competition to the foundational economy*. Manchester: Manchester University Press.

Brenner, N. (2004). Urban governance and the production of new state spaces in Western Europe, 1960–2000. *Review of International Political Economy*, *11*, 447–488. doi:10.10 80/0969229042000282864.

Brenner, N., & Wachsmuth, D. (2012). Territorial competitiveness: Lineages, practices, ideologies. In B. Sanyal, L. J. Vale, & C. D. Rosan (Eds.), *Planning ideas that matter* (pp. 179–206). Cambridge, MA: MIT Press.

Brenner, N., & Wachsmuth, D. (2013). Territorial competitiveness: Lineages, practices, ideologies. In B. Sanyal, L. Vale, & C. Rosan (Eds.), *Planning ideas that matter: Livability, territoriality, governance and reflective practice* (pp. 179–204). Cambridge, MA:MIT Press.

Bristow, G. (2005). Everyone's a 'winner': Problematising the discourse of regional competitiveness. *Journal of Economic Geography*, *5*, 285–304. doi:10.1093/jeg/lbh063.

Canzanelli, G. (2001). *Overview and learned lessons on local economic development, human development, and decent work*. ILO, Geneva, and Universitas Working Paper. Retrieved from http://www.ilo.org/public/english/universitas/publi.htm.

Castells, M., & Hall, P. (1994). *Technopoles of the world*. London: Routledge.

Cheshire, P., & Gordon, I. (1998). Territorial competition: Some lessons for policy. *Annals of Regional Science*, *32*, 321–346. doi:10.1007/s001680050077.

Cingano, F. (2014). *Trends in income inequality and its impact on economic growth*. Organisation for Economic Co-operation and Development (OECD) Social, Employment and Migration Working Papers No. 163. OECD Publ. Retrieved from http://dx.doi. org/10.1787/5jxrjncwxv6j-en.

Coleman, J. S. (1988). Social capital in the creation of human capital. *American Journal of Sociology*, *94*, S95–S120. doi:10.1086/228943.

Connell, R. (2007). *Southern theory: Social science and the global dynamics of Knowledge*. Cambridge: Polity.

Cooke, P., & Morgan, K. (1998). *The associational economy: Firms, regions, and innovation*. Oxford: Oxford University Press.

Coyle, D. (2014). *GDP: A brief but affectionate history*. London: Princeton University Press.

Crescenzi, R., & Rodríguez-Pose, A. (2011). Commentary. *Environment and Planning A*, *43*, 773–780. doi:10.1068/a43492.

Crescenzi, R., & Rodríguez-Pose, A. (2012). Infrastructure and regional growth in the European Union. *Papers in Regional Science*, *91*, 487–513. doi:10.1111/ j.1435-5957.2012.00439.x.

Crouch, C. (2013). From markets versus states to corporations versus civil society. In W. Streeck & A. Schafer (Eds.), *Politics in the age of austerity* (pp. 219–238). Cambridge: Polity.

Daley, J. (2012). *Critiquing government regional development policies*. Melbourne, VIC: Grattan Institute. Retrieved from http://grattan.edu.au/static/files/assets/f3f39109/142_ daley_oped_CEDA_regional_dev.pdf.

Department of Trade and Industry (DTI). (1983). *White Paper, Regional industrial policy (Cmnd 9111)*. London: HMSO.

Dunford, M. (1993). Regional disparities in the European community: Evidence from the REGIO databank. *Regional Studies, 27*, 727–743. doi:10.1080/003434093123313479 15.

European Commission. (2013). *Progress on 'GDP and beyond' actions*. Commission Staff Working Document, SWD(2013) 303 final. Brussels: European Commission. Retrieved from http://ec.europa.eu/environment/enveco/pdf/SWD_2013_303.pdf.

European Union/National Development and Reform Commission. (2011). *Regional policy in China and the EU. A comparative perspective*. Brussels: European Commission, Directorate-General for Regional Policy. Retrieved from http://ec.europa.eu/regional_policy/sources/cooperate/international/pdf/brochure_eu_china_v17_en.pdf.

Ezcurra, R., & Rodríguez-Pose, A. (2014). Trade openness and spatial inequality in emerging countries. *Spatial Economic Analysis, 9*, 162–182. doi:10.1080/17421772.201 4.891155.

Firn, J. (1975). External control and regional development: The case of Scotland. *Environment and Planning A, 7*, 393–414. doi:10.1068/a070393.

Florida, R. (2002). *The creative economy. The rise of the creative class: And how it is transforming work, leisure, community and everyday life*. New York: Basic Books.

Gertler, M. (2010). Rules of the game: The place of institutions in regional economic change. *Regional Studies, 44*, 1–15. doi:10.1080/00343400903389979.

Glaeser, E. (2007). Can Buffalo ever come back? *City Journal*. Retrieved from http://www.city-journal.org/html/17_4_buffalo_ny.html.

Glaeser, E. (2012). *Triumph of the city*. London: Pan Macmillan.

Glaeser, E. (2013, 13 October). A happy tale of two cities. *New York Daily News*.

Grabher, G. (1993). The weakness of strong ties: The lock-in of regional development in the Ruhr area. In G. Grabher (Ed.), *The embedded firm: On the socio-Economics of interfirm, relations* (pp. 255–277). London: Routledge.

Guiliani, E., Petrobelli, C., & Rabellotti, R. (2005). Upgrading in global value chains: Lessons from Latin American clusters. *World Development, 33*, 549–573. doi:10.1016/j.worlddev.2005.01.002.

Hadjimichalis, C. (2006). Non-economic factors in economic geography and in 'New Regionalism': A sympathetic critique. *International Journal of Urban and Regional Research, 30*, 690–704. doi:10.1111/j.1468-2427.2006.00683.x.

Hadjimichalis, C., & Hudson, R. (2014). Contemporary crisis across Europe and the crisis of regional development theories. *Regional Studies, 48*, 208–218. doi:10.1080/0034340 4.2013.834044.

Harvey, D. (1985). The geopolitics of capitalism. In D. Gregory & J. Urry (Eds.), *Social relations and Spatial structure* (pp. 128–163). London: Macmillan.

Harvey, D. (1989). From managerialism to entrepreneurialism: The transformation in urban governance in late capitalism. *Geografiska Annaler. Series B, Human Geography, 71*, 3–17. doi:10.2307/490503.

Hirschmann, A. (1958). *The strategy of economic development*. New Haven and London: Yale University Press.

Jessop, B. (2002). *The future of the capitalist state*. Cambridge: Polity.

Kaldor, N. (1970). The case for regional policies. *Scottish Journal of Political Economy, 17*, 337–348.

Krugman, P. (1998). What's new about New Economic Geography? *Oxford Review of Economic Policy, 14*, 7–17. doi:10.1093/oxrep/14.2.7

Leunig, T., & Swaffield, J. (2008). *Cities unlimited: Making urban regeneration work.* London: Policy Exchange.

Lovering, J. (1999). Theory led by policy: The inadequacies of the 'New Regionalism' (illustrated from the case of Wales). *International Journal of Urban and Regional Research, 23*, 379–395. doi:10.1111/1468-2427.00202.

Martin, R. (2015). Rebalancing the spatial economy: The challenge for regional theory. *Territory, Politics, Governance, 3*, 235–272. doi:10.1080/21622671.2015.1064825.

Martin, R., & Sunley, P. (2011). Conceptualizing cluster evolution: Beyond the life cycle model? *Regional Studies, 45*, 1299–1318. doi:10.1080/00343404.2011.622263

Massey, D. (1984). *Spatial division of labour.* London: Macmillan.

McCann, P. (2008). Globalization and economic geography: The world is curved, not flat. *Cambridge Journal of Regions, Economy and Society, 1*, 351–370. doi:10.1093/cjres/rsn002.

Morgan, K. (2004). Sustainable regions: Governance, innovation and scale. *European Planning Studies, 12*, 871–889. doi:10.1080/0965431042000251909.

Morgan, K., & Sayer, A. (1985). A 'modern' industry in a 'mature' region: The remaking of management-labour relations. *International Journal of Urban and Regional Research, 9*, 383–404. doi:10.1111/j.14682427.1985.tb00438.x.

Morgan Stanley. (2014). *US economics. Inequality and consumption* Retrieved from http://www.morganstanleyfa.com/public/projectfiles/02386f9f-409c-4cc9-bc6b-13574637ec1d.pdf.

Moulaert, F., & Sekia, F. (2003). Territorial innovation models: A critical survey. *Regional Studies, 37*, 289–302. doi:10.1080/0034340032000065442.

Myrdal, G. (1957). *Economic theory and under-developed regions.* London: Duckworth.

North, D. (2005). *Understanding the process of economic change.* Princeton: Princeton University Press.

O'Brien, P., & Pike, A. (2015). City deals, decentralisation and the governance of local infrastructure funding and financing in the UK. *National Institute Economic Review, 233*, R14–R26.doi:10.1177/002795011523300103.

O'Connor, J. (1973). *The fiscal crisis of the state.* New York: St. Martin's.

Organisation for Economic Co-operation and Development (OECD). (2012). *Promoting growth in all regions.* Paris: OECD.

Organisation for Economic Co-operation and Development (OECD). (2013). *How's life? Measuring well-being.* Paris:OECD.

Ostry, J. D., Berg, A., & Tsangarides, C. (2014). *Redistribution, inequality and growth.* IMF Staff Discussion Note No. SDN/14/02. Washington, DC: International Monetary Fund (IMF) Retrieved from https://www.imf.org/external/pubs/ft/sdn/2014/sdn1402.pdf.

Oxfam. (2014). *Working for the few: Political capture and economic inequality.* Oxfam Briefing Paper No. 178. Oxford: Oxfam.

Parkinson, M., Meegan, R., Karecha, J., Evans, R., Jones, G., Tosics, I., & Hall, P. (2012). *Second tier cities in Europe: In an age of austerity why invest beyond the capitals.* Liverpool: ESPON & Institute of Urban Affairs, Liverpool John Moores University.

Peck, J. (2005). Struggling with the creative class. *International Journal of Urban and Regional Research, 29*, 740–770. doi:10.1111/j.1468-2427.2005.00620.x.

Peck, J. (2015). Cities beyond compare? *Regional Studies, 49*, 160–182. doi:10.1080/00343404.2014.980801.

Peck, J., & Theodore, N. (2007). Variegated capitalism. *Progress in Human Geography, 31*, 731–772. doi:10.1177/0309132507083505.

Peck, J.. & Theodore, N. (2015). *Fast policy: Experimental statecraft at the thresholds of neoliberalism*. Minneapolis: University of Minnesota Press.

Perrons, D., & Dunford, R. (2013). Regional development, equality and gender: Moving towards more inclusive and socially sustainable measures. *Economic and Industrial Democracy, 34*, 483–499. doi:10.1177/0143831X13489044.

Pike, A., Dawley, S., & Tomaney, J. (2010). Resilience, adaptation and adaptability. *Cambridge Journal of Regions, Economy and Society, 3*, 59–70.

Pike, A., Rodríguez-Pose, A., & Tomaney, J. (2007). What kind of local and regional development and for whom? *Regional Studies, 41*, 1253–1269. doi:10.1080/00343400701543355

Pike, A., Rodríguez-Pose, A., & Tomaney, J. (2014). Local and regional development in the Global North and South. *Progress in Development Studies, 14*, 21–30. doi:10.1177/1464993413504346.

Pike, A., Rodríguez-Pose, A., & Tomaney J. (Eds.). (2015). *Major works in local and regional development*, 4 vols. London: Routledge.

Pike, A., Rodríguez-Pose, A., & Tomaney, J. (2016). *Local and regional development* (2nd ed.). London: Routledge.

Pike, A., Rodríguez-Pose, A., Tomaney, J., Torrisi, G., & Tselios, V. (2012). In search of the 'economic dividend' of devolution: Spatial disparities, spatial economic policy and decentralisation in the UK. *Environment and Planning C: Government and Policy, 30*, 10–28.

Piketty, T. (2014). *Capital in the twenty first century*. Cambridge, MA: Harvard University Press.

Piore, M., & Sabel, C. (1984). *The second industrial divide*. New York: Basic.

Porter, M. (1998). Clusters and the new economics of competition, *Harvard Business Review, November–December*, 77–90.

Putnam, R. (1993). *Making democracy work*. Princeton: Princeton University Press.

Rodríguez-Pose, A. (2013). Do institutions matter for regional development? *Regional Studies, 47*, 1034–1047. doi:10.1080/00343404.2012.748978.

Rodríguez-Pose, A., & Gill, N. (2004). Is there a global link between regional disparities and devolution? *Environment and Planning A, 36*, 2097–2117. doi:10.1068/a362

Rodríguez-Pose, A., & Crescenzi, R. (2008). Mountains in a flat world: why proximity still matters for the location of economic activity. *Cambridge Journal of Regions, Economy and Society, 1*, 371–388. doi:10.1093/cjres/rsn011.

Rodríguez-Pose, A., & Hardy, D. (2014) *Technology and industrial parks in emerging countries: Panacea or pipedream?* Heidelberg: Springer.

Rodríguez-Pose, A., & Wilkie, C. (2015). *Conceptualizing equitable economic growth in urban environments*. Cities Alliance Discussion Paper No. 2. Brussels.

Rodrik, D. (2006). Goodbye Washington consensus, hello Washington confusion? A review of the World Bank's economic growth in the 1990s: Learning from a decade of reform. *Journal of Economic Literature, 44*, 973–987. doi:10.1257/jel.44.4.973.

Rodrik, D. (2007). *One economics, many recipes: Globalization, institutions, and economic growth*. Princeton: Princeton University Press.

Roy, A. (2009). The 21st-century metropolis: New geographies of theory. *Regional Studies, 43*, 819–830. doi:10.1080/00343400701809665.

Sassen, S. (2001). *The global city: New York, London, Tokyo*. Princeton: Princeton University Press.

Sassen, S. (2006). *Cities in a World Economy*. London: Pine Forge.

Savage, M. (2015). *Social class in the 21st century*. London: Pelican.

Saxenian, A. (1994). *Local industrial systems regional advantage: Culture and competition in Silicon Valley and route 128*. Cambridge, MA: Harvard University Press.

Scott, A., and Storper, M. (2003). Regions. Globalization, development. *Regional Studies, 37*, 549–578. doi:10.1080/0034340032000108697a 579-593

Seers, D. (1967). The meaning of development. *IDS Communication, 44*, 1–26.

Seers, D. (1969). *The meaning of development*. IDS Communication No. 44. Brighton: Institute of Development Studies.

Sen, A. (1999). *Development as freedom*. Oxford: Oxford University Press.

Standard & Poor. (2014). *Economic research: How increasing income inequality is dampening U.S. economic growth, and possible ways to change the tide*. Retrieved from https://www.globalcreditportal.com/ratingsdirect/renderArticle.do?articleId=1351366&SctArtId=255732&from=CM&nsl_code=LIME&sourceObjectId=8741033&sourceRevId=1&fee_ind–&exp_date=20240804-19:41:13#ContactInfo.

Stiglitz, J. (2002). *Globalization and its discontents*. London: Penguin.

Stiglitz, J. (2013). *The price of inequality*. London: Penguin.

Stiglitz, J., Sen, A., & Fitoussi, J.-P. (2009). *Report by the Commission on the Measurement of Economic Performance and Social Progress*. Retrieved from http://www.insee.fr/fr/publications-et-services/dossiers_web/stiglitz/doc-commission/RAPPORT_anglais.pdf

Stöhr W. B. (Ed.). (1990). *Global challenge and local response. Initiatives for economic regeneration in contemporary Europe*. London: United Nations University/Mansell.

Storper, M. (1995). The resurgence of regional economies, ten years later: The region as a nexus of untraded interdependencies. *European Urban and Regional Studies, 2*, 191–221. doi:10.1177/096977649500200301.

Storper, M., Kemeny, T., Makarem, N., & Osman, T. (2014). *The rise and fall of urban economies lessons from San Francisco and Los Angeles*. Stanford: Stanford University Press.

Tomaney, J. (2014). Region and place I: Institutions. *Progress in Human Geography, 38*, 131–140. doi:10.1177/0309132513 493385.

Tomaney, J. (2015). Region and place III: Well-being, *Progress in Human Geography*. doi:10.1177/0309132515601775

Trigilia, C. (2001). Social capital and local development. *European Journal of Social Theory, 4*, 427–442. doi:10.1177/13684310122225244.

Turok, I. (1993). Inward investment and local linkages: How deeply embedded is 'Silicon Glen'? *Regional Studies, 27*, 401–417.doi:10.1080/00343409312331347655.

Vázquez-Barquero, A. (2003). *Endogenous development: Networking, innovation, institutions and cities*. London: Routledge.

Wilkinson, R., & Pickett, J. (2010). *The spirit level: Why equality is better for everyone*. London: Penguin.

Williams, R. (1983). *Keywords*. London: Pan.

Williamson, J. (1989). What Washington means by policy reform. In J. Williamson (Ed.), *Latin American readjustment: How much has happened?* Washington, DC: Institute for International Economics.

World Bank. (2009). *World development report 2009: Reshaping economic geography*. Washington, DC: World Bank.

Yeung, H. W. C. (2009). Regional development and the competitive dynamics of global production networks: an East Asian perspective. *Regional Studies, 43*, 325–351. doi:10.1080/00343400902777059.

Yeung, H. W. C., & Coe, N. M. (2015). Toward a dynamic theory of global production networks. *Economic Geography, 91*, 29–58.doi:10.1111/ecge.12063.

Transforming cities: does urbanization promote democratic change?

Edward L. Glaeser and Bryce Millett Steinberg

ABSTRACT

Transforming cities: does urbanization promote democratic change? *Regional Studies*. Could urbanization lead to more democracy and better government for the mega-cities of the developing world? This paper reviews three channels through which urbanization may generate political change. First, cities facilitate coordinated public action and enhance the effectiveness of uprisings. Second, cities may increase the demand for democracy relative to dictatorship. Third, cities may engender the development of 'civic capital' which enables citizens to improve their own institutions. History and empirics provide significant support for the first channel, but less evidence exists for the others. Urbanization may improve the quality of poor-world governments, but more research is needed to draw that conclusion.

摘要

转变中的城市：城市化会促进民主变革吗？ *Regional Studies*. 城市化能够为发展中世界的巨型城市带来更民主与更佳的治理吗？本文回顾城市化可能产生政治变革的三大管道。首先，城市促进协调的公共行动，并强化起义的效应。再者，城市可能增加相对于独裁的民主要求。第三，城市可能促成"公民资本" 的发展，该资本让公民得以改善其自身的制度。历史和经验主义为第一种管道提供显着的支持，但其他的管道则较少有支持的证据。城市化或能促进穷困世界的政府素质，但须有更多的研究才能获得该结论。

RÉSUMÉ

La transformation des grandes villes: est-ce que l'urbanisation promeut le changement démocratique? *Regional Studies*. L'urbanisation, pourrait-elle entraîner un brin de démocratie et une aubaine gouvernementale pour les méga-villes du monde en voie de développement? Cet article fait la critique de trois voies par lesquelles l'urbanisation pourrait engendrer le changement politique. Primo, les grandes villes permettent l'action publique coordonnée et améliorent l'efficacité des soulèvements. Secundo, il se peut que les grandes villes augmentent la demande de démocratie par rapport à la dictature. Tertio, les grandes villes pourraient engendrer le développement du 'capital civique', ce qui permet aux citoyens d'améliorer leurs propres institutions. L'histoire et les résultats empiriques apportent beaucoup de soutien en faveur de la première voie, mais plus rares sont les preuves en faveur des autres. L'urbanisation pourrait améliorer la compétence du gouvernement des pays pauvres, mais il faut davantage de recherches afin de tirer une telle conclusion.

ZUSAMMENFASSUNG

Wandel in den Städten: Fördert die Urbanisierung demokratische Veränderungen? *Regional Studies*. Könnte die Urbanisierung in den Megastädten der Entwicklungsländer zu mehr Demokratie und besseren Regierungen führen? In diesem Beitrag untersuchen wir drei Kanäle, über die Urbanisierung zu politischen Veränderungen führen kann. Erstens ermöglichen Städte koordinierte öffentliche Aktionen und verbessern die Wirksamkeit von Aufständen. Zweitens können Städte die Nachfrage nach Demokratie statt Diktatur erhöhen. Drittens können Städte zur Entwicklung von 'Bürgerkapital' führen, das Bürgern eine Verbesserung ihrer eigenen Institutionen ermöglicht. Die historischen und empirischen Daten sprechen in signifikantem Umfang für den ersten Kanal, während sich für die anderen Kanäle weniger Evidenz findet. Eine Urbanisierung kann die Qualität von Regierungen in armen Ländern verbessern, doch für diese Schlussfolgerung ist mehr Forschungsarbeit erforderlich.

RESUMEN

Transformar las ciudades: ¿fomenta la urbanización el cambio democrático? *Regional Studies*. ¿Podría la urbanización conducir a más democracia y una administración mejor en las mega-ciudades del mundo en desarrollo? En este artículo revisamos tres canales mediante los cuales la urbanización podría generar un cambio político. En primer lugar, las ciudades facilitan una acción pública coordinada y mejoran la eficacia de las revueltas. En segundo lugar, las ciudades podrían hacer aumentar la demanda de democracia en vez de dictadura. En tercer lugar, las ciudades podrían generar el desarrollo de la 'capital cívica' que permite a sus ciudadanos mejorar sus propias instituciones. Los datos históricos y empíricos proporcionan un apoyo significativo para el primer canal, pero existe menos evidencia para los otros. La urbanización podría mejorar la calidad de los Gobiernos del mundo pobre, pero es necesario llevar a cabo más estudios para llegar a esta conclusión.

INTRODUCTION

Massive urbanization of the poorer world inspires both awe and horror. China's spectacular post-1982 economic growth was accompanied, and perhaps made possible, by a 450 million-person increase in the number of Chinese urbanites. Yet the slums of Dhaka (Bangladesh), Kinshasa (D. R. of Congo) and

Port-au-Prince (Haiti) remain practically synonymous with disease, death and urban dysfunction. Will the growing cities of the developing world prove capable of promoting both future economic growth and positive political change?

This paper begins by reviewing the links between cities and economic development. Despite the growth of poor world urbanization, the cross-country link between urbanization and income is stronger than ever. Moreover, the urbanization level of poorer countries in 1960 is a potent predictor of economic growth since that time. The within-country literature on agglomeration economies typically finds that earnings increase by approximately 0.06 log points as density levels double, in both rich and poor countries alike (Chauvin, Glaeser, Ma, & Tobio, 2016).

While urban density is associated with higher incomes, contagious disease, crime, traffic congestion and high housing prices can also be features of urban life. The negative externalities that come with crowding typically require public management, but developing-world cities often have governments that are neither democratic nor competent. Poor-world cities will only become pleasant when their governments improve to the point where they can deliver clean water, public safety and reasonable commutes.

Will developing-world urbanization generate the political change that can help make developing-world cities more liveable? At a purely statistical level, countries that were more urbanized in 1960 experienced more democracy after that year, holding the initial level of democracy constant. This effect is particularly strong among countries that initially had low levels of democracy. The idea that cities promote democracy is termed the 'Boston Hypothesis', reflecting the seminal role that the city of Boston played in generating the American Revolution and the republic that followed.

Yet this correlation may be spurious or a side-effect of rising incomes in more urbanized places. To understand better whether urbanization will improve government or promote democracy, the channels through which urban density can promote regime change are analyzed.

The paper proceeds by discussing three ways in which urbanization relates to regime change and democracy. First, urbanization may enable uprisings and revolution by facilitating coordination and enhancing the power of organized action. A crowd in Cairo's Tahrir Square packs far more political punch than a group of farmers in a remote farming village. Wallace (2014) provides compelling empirical work showing that dictatorships face a far higher risk of regime change in urbanized societies.

Second, urbanization may increase the demand for democracy. To understand why populations may favour democracy or dictatorship, one can follow the framework of Djankov, Glaeser, La Porta, Lopez-de-Silanes, and Shleifer (2003) which emphasizes that different systems offer a trade-off between losses from overly strong governments, termed 'dictatorship', and losses from overly weak governments, termed 'disorder'. Cities enable trade and facilitate innovation, both of which can be stifled by dictatorial regimes. These upsides of urban existence should push residents to favour more democracy. Yet cities also facilitate negative social interactions, including crime and the spread of contagious disease. The need to reduce those threats should increase the demand for dictatorship.

Finally, this article discusses the possibility that urbanization may promote the social skills and connections that collectively compose 'civic capital': the ability of citizens to improve the quality of their government. Yet there is currently little empirical support for the view that civic capital is higher in cities.

Subsequently, the article reviews the history and empirics that are related to urbanization and democracy change. The hypothesis that cities abet revolutions against dictators seems relatively solid, supported by 26 centuries of urban revolts and Wallace's (2014) statistical work.

Empirical support for the idea that urbanization increases the demand for democracy relative to dictatorship is weaker. There are a number of important elections pitting democracy against dictatorship where urbanites voted for more democratic alternatives. Survey evidence from Latin America shows a weak correlation between urban residence and support for democracy.

The article concludes by emphasizing the need for more research on cities in the developing world, especially on the link between urbanization and governmental change.

THE ECONOMIC BENEFITS AND SOCIAL COSTS OF DENSITY

The developing world is urbanizing rapidly primarily because cities typically offer tangible economic benefits. This section first discusses those benefits and then turns to the costs of urbanization. It ends by emphasizing how the costs of density depend on the competence of the public sector.

Density and economic opportunity

Social scientists have been pondering the benefits of urbanization for centuries. When people and firms locate close to one another transportation costs fall (Krugman, 1991), which enhances productivity both directly and indirectly by increasing the diversity of input production (Ciccone & Hall, 1996). Adam Smith argued that urbanization enabled specialization, while in 'the highlands of Scotland, every farmer must be butcher, baker and brewer for his own family'. Johann Heinrich von Thünen emphasized the transportation cost savings in urban cores, which would then become the central agglomeration force in the New Economic Geography (Krugman, 1991). Alfred Marshall noted the free flow of knowledge within cities, and put forth the idea that workers can move from less to more productive firms in dense urban labour markets.

All these theories suggest that workers will be more productive in cities, and most of them also suggest that wages will also be higher.[1] The typical starting point for estimating agglomeration effects is an individual-level regression in which earnings are connected with metropolitan area size or density or both. From the worker's perspective, higher urban wages compensate for higher costs of living, but from the firm's perspective, higher wages must be offset by other urban advantages, typically called productivity. The marginal product of labour may be higher in cities either because workers produce more output in cities (which presumably must be true in export sectors), or because the price charged for that output is higher (which is more likely to be true for non-traded service industries).

A typical estimate from the United States is that the coefficient on agglomeration is about 0.06, meaning that earnings increase by 6% as metropolitan area size increases by 100% (Glaeser & Gottlieb, 2009). These effects are stronger for more initially skilled workers, suggesting that there is a complementarity between cities and skills (Glaeser & Resseger, 2010).

Yet these ordinary least squares (OLS) approaches to estimating agglomeration effects suffer from two well-known problems. First, more able workers and more productive firms may disproportionately sort in dense agglomerations. Second, some locations may be innately more productive than others and consequently attract more people. In both cases, estimated coefficients will be biased because the unobserved heterogeneity is correlated with agglomeration size and density.

Perhaps the simplest approach for improving estimation involves instrumenting for area size with past population or geography (Rosenthal & Strange, 2004, Combes et al., 2010). Another is to focus on land values, rather than earnings, because if firms are willing to pay more for land, then presumably that land brings the offsetting advantage of higher productivity (Dekle & Eaton, 1999). A third approach is to look at real wages, with or without individual fixed effects (Combes et al., 2008; Glaeser & Mare, 2001; Yankow, 2006). A final approach involves examining shocks to place, such as the opening of million-dollar plants in an area (Greenstone, Hornbeck, & Moretti, 2010). This better-identified literature typically confirms that agglomeration economies are important drivers of productivity.

While most of this literature uses data from the developed world, the correlation between urban density and earnings appears to be at least as strong in the developing world (Chauvin et al., 2016), which helps explain why urbanization is increasing so quickly in the world's poorer places.

Dynamics effects of density on income

Will urbanization bring dynamic benefits as well as static gains? Economics since Marshall have hypothesized that density can increase learning and the production of new ideas. Glaeser and Mare (2001) suggest that their wage evidence is compatible with the view that cities enable the formation of human capital that gradually leads to wage growth. De la Roca and Puga (2016) use administrative data from Spain to examine migrants and find quite substantial wage growth effects in cities.

But do cities generate wider economic growth? The correlation between income growth and initial metropolitan area–population size is quite dependent on the period studied. Over 1970–80, for example, the relationship is negative. Over 1980–2000, the relationship is positive. Figure 1 shows the correlation across metropolitan areas with a population in 1980 that is greater than 250,000. The coefficient depicted is 0.03, meaning that as population doubles, income grows by approximately 3% more between 1980 and 2000. City size may predict income growth over this period because economic changes during this era were kind to cities and increasingly restrictive housing supply regulations made it difficult to move into the more productive, larger metropolitan areas.

Urbanization is also correlated with income growth across countries. Table A1 in the supplemental data online shows the basic patterns using data from the World Bank. The first two regressions show the correlation between urbanization and the logarithm of per-capita gross domestic product (GDP).[2] The coefficient of 5.26 implies that a 20 percentage point increase in urbanization is associated with more than a doubling of income. In the second regression, which controls for total years of schooling and for continent, the coefficient drops to 3.5.

To examine growth effects, regression (3) relates per-capita growth between 1960 and 2010 with urbanization in 1960. The coefficient of 1.8 suggests that a 10 percentage point higher urbanization rate in 1960 is associated with about 20% greater income growth between 1960 and 2010. Regression (4) includes controls for initial income, initial schooling and continent dummies. The coefficient is essentially unchanged.

These growth regressions do not imply that urbanization always generates growth. Omitted area-level variables may well explain this correlation. Yet the

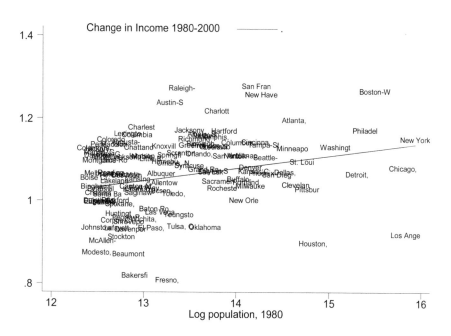

Figure 1 Metropolitan area size and income growth, 1980–2000.

Note: Based on US Census data on metropolitan-area incomes from 1980 to 2000 and metropolitan-area population in 1980. Metropolitan areas have been adjusted to have constant borders.

relationship is sufficiently strong that it is certainly plausible that urbanization might aid country-level growth. Cities might speed new idea formation and knowledge accumulation, especially by enabling the flow of technology across continents.[3] Urbanization may also promote growth by improving the quality of government.

The downsides of density: negative externalities in cities

Agglomeration economies are significant, but the downsides of density can also be large (Glaeser, 1998). When people crowd into a dense area, they transmit diseases more easily. Urban activity can pollute both the air and the water. Proximity also enables crime, and the abundance of potential perpetrators in cities makes solving crimes more difficult (Glaeser & Sacerdote, 1999). From medieval Paris to modern São Paulo, cities have sometimes become places of danger. Crowded streets make commutes longer. Building up is often more expensive than building out, which makes urban homes more expensive.

Most of these costs of density are negative externalities, which can be alleviated by effective government. Good policing can reduce crime. The public sector can provide infrastructure that moves waste from city streets and brings clean water into urban centres. A substantial literature now links investment in water and sewers with public health in the United States (Cutler & Miller, 2005; Alsan & Goldin, 2016). Street grids and good public transportation can make traffic congestion less painful. Expensive infrastructure projects require public competence, and in the hands of a bad government a road project becomes simply a source of corruption and patronage.

Addressing urban problems effectively often requires incentives as well as infrastructure. Singapore made its streets more valuable by using electronic road pricing to reduce congestion. The health benefits of water pipes and sewers fall if poorer people are not willing to pay to connect to the system. Effective government can also be necessary to nudge people to connect with the infrastructure using either fines or subsidies (Ashraf, Glaeser, & Ponzetto, 2016).

Consequently, the social costs of density depend on the quality of government. When the public sector is capable, as in Singapore or Sweden, infrastructure and incentives will make urban life less challenging. When the public sector is weak, urbanites will suffer more from the demons that come with density. The horrific quality of life in many developing world cities says as much about the failures of those cities' governments as it does about the intrinsic problems of city life.

If the downsides of density are costly enough, then restricting city growth can yield benefits that are large enough to offset the losses that come from smaller agglomeration economies and eliminating the option to migrate to the city. Yet there is a possible countervailing benefit of urbanization that will be explored next. Large cities may eventually lead to better governments that make cities more liveable. If urbanization yields a dividend of better government then the entire country may benefit from urbanization. The next sections discuss why urbanization might produce better government and democracy.

CITIES, DEMOCRATIZATION AND GOVERNMENT QUALITY

This section explores the Boston Hypothesis – the possible link between urbanization and democracy. It first notes the empirical link between urbanization in 1960 and increases in democracy after that point. It then turns to why urbanization may actually lead to democracy, by enabling regime change, increasing the demand for democracy and building civic capital.

Urbanization and the transition to democracy: cross-country evidence

Table A1, panel B, in the supplemental data online examines the link across countries between urbanization in 1960 and democracy between 1960 and 2000. Regressions (1) and (2) control only for democracy in 1960 and urbanization in 1960. Regressions (3) and (4) also control for 1960 per capita GDP, education and oil production. Regressions (1) and (3) show results for all countries; regressions (2) and (4) show results only for initially less democratic countries.

Countries that were more urbanized in 1960 have higher polity IV democracy scores between 1960 and 2000, conditional on democracy score in 1960. This relationship holds particularly strongly for countries with low levels of democracy in 1960 (democracy index <8). The results weaken when other characteristics are controlled for, but the coefficient on urbanization remains sizable and statistically significant at the 90% level. If income and education are partially the result of urbanization, then the results without controls may be more relevant than the results with the added controls.

While these results are hardly conclusive, they lend some credence to the idea that urbanization might be a contributing factor in any move towards democracy.

Will urbanization promote regime change?

Cities have often played a role in the toppling of dictatorial regimes. Urban proximity enables collaboration, and uprisings require people to act and plan together. As Blanksten (1960) writes, 'few interests arising in rural areas are capable of making themselves heard in politics', but in cities 'interest groups form more readily and give voice to the demands of urbanized sectors of the population'. A successful protest or revolution depends upon assembling enough participants, and cities make it easier to mass rebels.

Just as cities enable marriage markets (Costa & Kahn, 2000), cities enable revolutionary partnerships to emerge and grow. The partnership between John Hancock and Samuel Adams grew in pre-revolutionary Boston. Cities both lower travel costs and enable people with idiosyncratic preferences, such as the urge to topple the regime, to find each other.

In principle, urban concentration could also make it easier for dictators to monitor their own citizens. Yet while such effective surveillance may be possible in highly capable dictatorships, such as Nazi Germany or the Soviet Union at its height, such competence is beyond most modern developing world dictators. The typical despot, both today and in history, lacks the capacity to patrol effectively the hidden nooks and crannies that always exist in large cities.

Cities can also abet revolt by reducing the risks to protesters. The costs of protesting or revolting, like the costs of rioting, decline as the number of protesters increase because larger crowds make it harder for the police to target any individual protester (DiPasquale & Glaeser, 1998). Rural mobs are easy for the army to disperse or destroy. Urban mobs are harder to dislodge, partially because an abundance of urban structures make it harder for tanks and cavalry to manoeuvre.

Agrarian repression occurs far from the censoring attention of the world. Protests in large cities are particularly effective when cities are highly visible to the local and global press, and when the army actually cares about avoiding opprobrium, which appears to have been the case in Cairo in 2011. Urban proximity can also increase the efficacy of an uprising, if long-term urban contact between soldiers and citizenry has increased the army's sympathy for the protesters.[4]

Probably the most important impact of urban size on revolutionary success occurs in capital cities, where urban protesters are close to the seat of power. Consequently, protests have more ability to threaten or disrupt the existing government.[5] Even when revolution sparks in an outlying city, such as Sidi Bouzid in the Tunisian interior, governments rarely fall until the capital itself rises. President Zine El Abidine Ben Ali only left Tunisia after large protests and violence in Tunis itself.

These channels collectively make cities handmaidens to regime change, but even if a revolution starts with dreams of democracy, there are many cases, including the French and Russian revolutions, in which an initially more democratic regime yields to a more authoritarian counter-coup. A post-revolutionary shift to democracy may not occur because the ambitions of a few may trump the desires of the many, or because post-revolution, the population might decide that authoritarianism was better than its disorderly alternative. The next section turns to the question of whether a revolution leads to democracy, and it will take the optimistic view that a democratic outcome is somewhat more likely if the benefits of democracy are larger.

The demand for democracy

The paper analyzes the popular demand for democracy through the Djankov et al. (2003) framework that examines the trade-off between dictatorship and disorder. This framework helps one understand whether urbanization will promote the 'demand for democracy', which should increase the probability of revolt against a dictatorship and increase the probability that democracy emerges after regime. A democracy is more likely to survive after a revolution if there is widespread belief that popular sovereignty is worth a fight. Conversely, dictatorial counter-coups often need popular acceptance, which will be forthcoming when people believe that dictatorship is preferable to disorder. As Holland (1911, p. 167) writes about the Napoleon Bonaparte's coup, 'the 18th Brumaire was nevertheless condoned, nay applauded, by the French nation', who were 'weary of revolution' and 'sought no more than to be wisely and firmly governed'.

The paper now focuses on the social costs of disorder and dictatorship, which shape the demand for democracy. Djankov et al. (2003) argue that different regimes create different social losses relative to an imaginary first best of perfect governance. Highly autocratic regimes that tax, extort and spend on pet projects create losses through the public sector. Djankov et al. call these public sector related costs 'dictatorship'.

Yet without effective governance, ordinary thieves and armed brigands steal and destroy value. If polluters do not face regulation or Pigouvian taxes, the environment suffers. Djankov et al. collectively call the private sector costs created by weak government 'disorder'.

When nations choose their constitutions, they trade dictatorship against disorder. A more empowered executive may effectively stamp out petty crime, but will also create other abuses. A limited state may avoid corruption, but fail to protect property against theft. Djankov et al. argue that countries face an institutional possibilities frontier (IPF), illustrated in Figure 2, with a trade-off between democracy and dictatorship. That paper suggests that institutions such as common law, civil law, social democracy, and authoritarianism and totalitarianism represent points along that curve. Those five examples are placed moving along the curve from disorder to dictatorship.

Whenever new governments form after an uprising, countries must choose what type of government to have, which means choosing a point along that frontier. In Figure 2, the optimal choice of regime is illustrated by the tangency point between

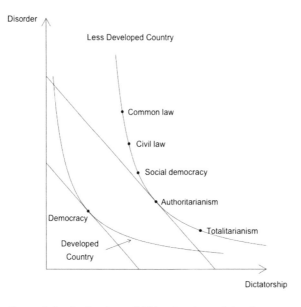

Figure 2 Institutional possibilities frontier and development.

the IPF and downward sloping 45° line, which minimizes the sum of total social losses from dictatorship and disorder. Countries might err and choose a point above the frontier, but by assumption they cannot choose a point within the frontier.

The form of the IPF depends on the level of economic conditions and the level of 'civic capital', which refers to the social conditions, which includes both education and culture that promote effective private and public solutions to problems. This section discusses whether urbanization increases the demand for dictatorship or disorder for a given level of civic capital. The following subsection discusses whether urbanization changes the level of civic capital.

Urbanization can lead to more democracy even if it does not directly increase the demand for democracy. If urbanization enables revolutions against dictators and if countries that have revolutions are likely to prefer something more democratic than the pre-revolutionary regime, then urbanization can promote democracy even if it does not make democracy more appealing. The existence of an uprising suggests that pre-revolutionary dictatorial institutions were seen as being problematic.[6] Consequently, if successful revolt topples a despot, then logically the public will typically want more, not less, democracy, and the optimal shift on the IPF is to the left.

Theory is ambiguous about cities and the demand for dictatorship. The positive interactions that can occur in cities are likely to suffer more from dictatorship, but negative urban interactions will also do more harm when governance is chaotic.

Figure 2 shows the positive case when urbanization increases the demand for democracy by increasing the scope for private sector activities. In a simple agricultural society, the losses created by an authoritarian government may be limited since choices are limited. When urbanization creates more upside potential from private interactions, including gains from trade and innovation, then the downsides of the abuse of government power increase.

Figure 2 captures this possibility by suggesting that urbanization has shifted the IPF downward and flattened the curve. With a flatter curve, reducing disorder requires large losses from dictatorship. The benefits of urbanization will be reduced by an authoritarian state that imposes widespread regulation and limits private activity.[7]

Yet cities also increase the scope for negative externalities. Urban density abets crime, contagious disease and traffic congestion. Limited, democratic government makes it harder to impose the restrictions that limit these negative externalities. The strong hand of Lee Kwan Yew allowed congestion pricing in Singapore long before more democratic places charged drivers for overusing city streets. In 2016, the Philippines elected Rodrigo Duterte, a tough-talking former mayor who has promised to use any means necessary to stamp out crime and drugs-related corruption.

If negative urban externalities increase the social costs of disorder, as shown in Figure 3, then urbanization will also increase the demand for dictatorship. The graph shows urbanization acting almost as a pure increase in the gains to dictatorship. That shift will make it less likely that uprisings end in democracy, and more likely that urbanites will support dictatorial coups that promise to rein in urban disorder.

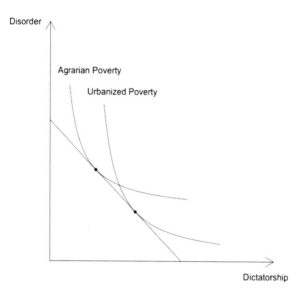

Figure 3 Institutional possibilities frontier and urban externalities.

Urbanization is more likely to increase the demand for democracy when the upsides from urban innovation are great and less likely when the costs of urban disamenities are more severe. The demand for democracy seems likely to be strong in commercial cities and weakest in industrial ones. Commercial cities, like the ports of America's Colonial Seaboard or the towns of medieval Flanders, exist primarily as places of trade and exchange. Restricting freedom reduces the merchant's ability to find profits in new forms of exchange, such as importing Dutch tea into 18th-century Boston. Industrial uprisings such as the Moscow uprising in the Revolution of 1905, are much more likely to focus on living conditions than freedom.

Conditions that magnify the downsides of density should decrease the demand for dictatorship. The chaotic conditions in some Middle Eastern cities, such as Cairo, may have increased the demand for strong leadership after the Arab Spring, such as the Muslim Brotherhood. Democracy may be less common in more ethnically fragmented societies (Alesina, Devleeschauwer, Easterly, Kurlat, & Wacziarg, 2003), because ethnically fragmented cities are typically more disorderly.[8] If tropical climates increase the risks of contagious disease in cities, then the demand for dictatorship would be higher in warmer parts of the globe.

As urbanization increases the scope for positive interactions, which may be squelched by a dictatorship, and the scope for negative interactions increases, which may be tamed by a dictator, urbanization may either increase or decrease the demand for democracy. However, even if urbanization does not make regime changes more likely to move towards democracy in the short run, it may still improve the quality of government by developing civic capital over time.

114

Urbanization and civic capital

Djankov et al. (2003) argue that countries can only shift the IPF downward if the level of 'civic capital' increases, where civic capital represents the capacity of the country to work collaboratively to produce effective government and to produce socially beneficial outcomes even in the absence of state action. Education is one part of civic capital. Years of schooling are reliably correlated with better functioning governments, both across countries (La Porta, Lopez-de-Silanes, Shleifer, & Vishny, 1999) and across US states (Glaeser & Saks, 2006). Education increases the capacity of individuals to understand their governments and to work together (Glaeser, Ponzetto, & Shleifer, 2007).

This subsection discusses the hypothesis that city living may also create civic capital. Interactions are the point of urban density. Cities enable and often require people to work together with others. By collaborating, people learn how to collaborate. For example, Fossett and Kiecolt (1989) show that support for racial integration is higher in larger cities and smaller among people with farm origins. Abrahamson and Carter (1986) document a broad correlation between tolerance and city size. As Wirth (1938) famously wrote:

> If the individual would participate at all in the social, political, and economic life of the city, he must subordinate some of his individuality to the demands of the larger community and in that measure immerse himself in mass movements.

Cities can enhance what Robert Putnam calls 'bridging social capital', the connectivity across different types of people, in at least two ways. First, there can just be learning by doing. By working with diverse people throughout a city, people may learn how to bridge social divides and create functional relationships despite differences in religion or ethnicity. Second, people can consciously invest in their ability to deal with different people in order to take advantage of the opportunities. They can learn different languages, or at least understand the idiosyncratic features of different ethnicities.

Naturally, this optimistic view of cities may not occur in reality. An urban slum can be as homogenous and isolated as a rural community. Urban political entrepreneurs can spread hatred towards an out-group in order to gain support among their own ethnicity. Still, the common Latin roots of civic, civilization and city are not accidental, for classical cities were seen as the civilizing influences that needed and produced good citizens.

SUGGESTIVE EVIDENCE ON URBANIZATION AND DEMOCRATIZATION

The previous section suggested that urbanization would be more likely to lead to democratization if (1) urbanization increased the probability that dictators would be toppled and dictators are typically replaced by something less dictatorial, or if (2) urbanization increased the demand for democracy. This section discusses whether history and statistics support either of these possibilities. It also discusses suggestive evidence on the link between urbanization and civic capital.

Does urbanization promote popular uprisings?

Cities have played a recurring role in revolutions throughout history, some of which were democratic. In 509 BCE, Lucius Junius Brutus gathered the people of Rome in the Forum and exhorted them to rise up against the last of the kings, Lucius Tarquinius Superbus. One year later, Cleisthenes led the people of Athens against the tyrant Hippias. These urban uprisings produced the Roman Republic and Athenian democracy, which provided the classical models of non-dictatorial governments in the west. The 17th-century Dutch Republic had its roots in urban anti-Catholic riots. Urban wealth then enabled the Dutch to pay for mercenaries.

Numerous historical works (Carp, 2007; Nash, 2009) have emphasized the outsized role that cities played in fomenting the American revolt. Parisian uprisings toppled kings in 1789, 1830 and 1848. Traugott (1995) describes how 'a popular insurrection in the capital was capable of bringing down the national government, virtually overnight and irrespective of popular sentiment in the provinces'. Dynasties were also ended by revolutions in Berlin, Lisbon and St Petersburg. Urban uprisings also helped end the remaining communist regimes in Czechoslovakia, Poland, East Germany, Bulgaria and Romania.

In the developing world, revolutions have also often had a distinctly urban component. Democratic movements in erstwhile African colonies like Zimbabwe often began in cities (Scarnecchia, 2008). French control over Algeria was shaken by urban guerrilla warfare carried on Algiers by the National Liberation Front. The People Power Revolution, largely in Manila, led to an end to the Marcos Regime. The occupation of prominent urban spaces like Tahrir Square ultimately led to the end of several authoritarian governments in the Arab Spring.

This anecdotal evidence is also supported by the empirical work of Wallace (2014), who looks at the link between urban size and the survival of non-democratic regimes. He finds that 'for the 235 regimes with urban concentration levels about the mean level in the data, the mean duration is 8.6 years and the annual regime death rate is 9.1 percent', but 'for the 198 regimes characterized by low levels of urban concentration, the incidence rate is only 5.7 percent and the mean duration is 12.2 years' (p. 194). The impact of urbanization on regime survival is large and statistically significant, and remains effectively unchanged when he controls for a bevy of other variations. The impact of very large cities is particularly striking.

There is an older literature on revolutions and coups that finds significantly more mixed results on the link between urbanization and uprisings. Wallace's finding that 'large cities are dangerous for non-democratic regimes' is at odds with studies that found that urbanization was either irrelevant or actually promoted executive stability (Auvinen, 1997). That previous work typically focused on revolutions everywhere, not just in non-democratic regimes. Since urbanites can effect political change at the ballot box in a democracy, there is far less reason for them to revolt. Consequently, one should expect big cities to lead to revolt primarily in non-democratic polities, which is exactly what Wallace finds. Our reading of this evidence is that the theoretical arguments that urbanization desta-bilizes autocracies, discussed above, have reasonable support in history and more modern statistical work.

Does urbanization increase the demand for democracy?

Urban revolts may produce democracies accidentally, because anything that comes after a dictatorship is likely to be more democratic, but it is possible that urbanization actually increases the demand for democracy. Wantchekon and Garcia-Ponce (2016) show that African countries that experienced urban insur-gency movements at the time of colonial independence are more likely to have democratic regimes today than those that experienced rural insurgencies. They argue that urban movements tended to involve peaceful protests, while rural movements were often based around armed conflict.

This pattern may reflect the higher costs of organizing in rural areas. Since peaceful protesters can easily be dispersed in rural areas, regime opponents need to be armed. Since the costs of armed revolt are high, revolutionaries need to be promised large tangible rewards, which can more easily be delivered by a subse-quent dictatorship.

Voigtländer and Voth (2012) show that support for the National Socialist German Workers' ('Nazi') Party in Germany was lower in large cities after 1928, suggesting that the demand for dictatorship was somewhat lower in urban areas. In Mexico's 2000 election that ended 71 years of one-party rule, the opposition candidate, Vincente Fox, did far better in and around Mexico City than he did in the country as a whole. In Zimbabwe, the Movement for Democratic Change almost swept the capital city of Harare in its 2008 attempt to defeat Robert Mugabe's strongman regime, while failing to secure a national majority.[9]

Additional evidence on urbanization and the demand for democracy is provided by Latinobarometro, a survey of beliefs and attitudes about democracy from several countries across Latin America. Panel A of Table A2 in the supplemental data online shows the relationship between support for democracy and urban residence. In the first regression, the dependent variable equals 1 if respondents answered that 'democracy is always the best type of government', and 0 otherwise. In the next regression, the dependent variable equals 1 if respondents answered that 'some-times authoritarian governments are necessary', and 0 otherwise. These outcomes both come from the same question and consequently the categories are mutually exclusive. (The omitted category was 'the type of government doesn't matter'.)

The key independent variable is an indicator variable that takes on a value of 1 if the respondent inhabits a city of more than 100,000 people or in the capital. The regressions control for years of education and country-fixed effects. Together, the regressions show a modest but statistically significant link with support for democracy and a negative relationship with support for autocracy. These results modestly support the hypothesis that, at least in Latin America today, urbaniza-tion is positively associated with the demand for democracy.

Some additional support for the hypothesis that urbanization increases the demand for democracy is found in the urban crowds that occasionally emerge to demand democracy and to protect democracy from dictatorial subversion. In Moscow urban crowds stopped a military coup d'état in 1991. Berliners fought against the Kapp Putsch in 1920. King Gyanendra's attempt to replace constitutional monarchy in Nepal with direct royal rule was thwarted by waves of protests and strikes in Kathmandu.

Hong Kong's 2014 Umbrella Revolution was an urban movement protesting the Chinese Communist Party's perceived interference in Hong Kong elections. The Ukrainian Orange Revolution of 2004, centred largely in Kiev, effectively reversed the rigging of a national election. The 2013 Gezi Park protests in Istanbul objected to the concentration of power by President Recep Tayyip Erdoğan.

Urbanization and civic capital

Does urbanization actually create more civic capital? There are certainly examples of urbanites coming together to discipline rather than overthrow governments. In 1871, New Yorkers assembled in Cooper Union to organize against the rampant theft of the Tweed Ring. Twenty years later, the Progressive Era would begin as municipal reformers throughout the United States organized to improve the quality of city government. Nineteenth-century Paris was the hub of the global public health movement that advocated for sewers, clean water and improvements in housing quality. The Generation of 1837 was a cluster of talent in Buenos Aires that organized to promote democracy and better government in Argentina. Guatemala's anti-corruption movement engineered a protest of over 100,000 people in Guatemala City and eventually forced the resignation of President Otto Pérez Molina.

Yet there is little evidence that urbanization is positively linked with political engagement. Oliver (2000) finds that political engagement, including both voting and attending meetings, actually declines with city size within the United States. This finding supports the view that smaller jurisdictions are more accessible to citizens, but since American suburbanites are not dispersed agrarians, it does not exactly disprove the view that urbanization will promote civic capital in the developing world.

Latinobarometro data, shown in panel B of Table A2 in the supplemental data online allows one to examine these relationships in a less developed context. A set of indicators of political engagement is regressed on a dummy for whether the respondent lives in an urban area (as described above). As in panel A, the regressions control for education and country-fixed effects and here show only the coefficient on living in the capital city with more than 100,000 inhabitants. Urban residents are less likely to vote or work for a party or candidate, but more likely to be interested in politics or talk about politics and more likely to have participated in a protest. One interpretation of these results is that urbanites in the developing world are more likely to work for regime change but less likely to work within the system.

These existing results do not support a strong connection between urbanization and political investments at the individual level. Thomas Jefferson put more hope in the voting habits of yeomen farmers than urbanites, and perhaps he was right. Yet the existing research in this area is so limited that this article must leave the final word to future researchers.

CONCLUSIONS: MAPPING A RESEARCH AGENDA

The bulk of urban research has focused on the wealthy world, yet the biggest urban problems occur in the developing world. In almost every area, there is a need for significant regional research in the developing world. The most important questions continue to be the need to understand the nature of agglomeration economies and how those economies are being shaped by new technologies.

One also needs to understand better the downsides of density in the developing world. What interventions can improve housing quality cheaply in the slums of poor world mega-cities? What public health interventions can effectively improve longevity? What transportation innovations are effective at reducing hellish commutes?

This paper emphasized the role that cities can play in fomenting political change, but acknowledged that this is a hypothesis, not a fact. It highlighted three primary channels through which urbanization might promote democracy and good government. All three merit further investigation. Despite Wallace (2014), there is little consensus that urbanization promotes regime change among dictatorships.

The question of whether urbanization increases the demand for democracy is also unresolved. This paper presented some suggestive evidence, but since cities can also require firm management there are surely cases where urbanization increases the demand for dictatorship. In this case, it is important to map out when urbanization has made democracy more appealing and when city size has strengthened the hands of despots.

Finally, the speculative question was raised about whether urban life increases civic capital, defined as the capacity and taste for organized political action. The modest amount of existing evidence does not support this claim, yet it still seems possible that cities are more likely than subsistence farms to produce effective political actors. The world is rapidly urbanizing and it is necessary to understand better the widespread effects of that change.

ACKNOWLEDGEMENTS

Edward Glaeser thanks the Taubman Center for State and Local Government. Three referees and an associate editor provided excellent comments.

DISCLOSURE STATEMENT

No potential conflict of interest was reported by the authors.

SUPPLEMENTAL DATA

Supplemental data for this article can be accessed at http://dx.doi.org/10.1080/00343404.2016.1262020

NOTES

1. One prominent exception is the Krugman (1991) model where workers are paid less because they receive the benefit of being able to buy goods cheaply.
2. Results are shown using current exchange rates. Results adjusting for purchasing power parity are quite similar.
3. Jaffe, Trajtenberg, and Henderson (1993) document more patenting activity per capita in large cities and that patents are more likely to cite other patents that are geographically close. Audretsch and Feldman (1996) show that new product innovations are more common in large cities.
4. Urban interactions between Louis XVI's 'French Guard' and civilians apparently increased their sympathy for protesters, which reduced the royal ability to rout the revolutionaries with force. Prussian kings, keenly aware of such risks, housed their army away from civilians.
5. This proximity effect may explain why dictatorships have disproportionately large capital cities, because dictators may transfer extra resources to the residents of their capitals to keep them happy, which in turn attracts more people to the capital and creates more instability for the dictator (Ades & Glaeser, 1995).
6. Moreover, if the popular sentiment was that the pre-revolutionary regime needed to be more dictatorial, then many, if not most, leaders would be happy to oblige.
7. Some of the most successful modern Asian dictatorships have allowed significant economic freedom, which should reduce the demand for democracy.
8. While there are many cases in which different ethnicities peaceably co-exist in cities, ethno-linguistic fractionalization is positively correlated with murder rates (Hansmann & Quigley, 1982) and riots (DiPasquale & Glaeser, 1998).
9. The Movement for Democratic Change's success in Harare is all the more remarkable considering the widespread allegations of electoral abuse.

REFERENCES

Abrahamson, M., & Carter, V. J. (1986). Tolerance, urbanism and region. *American Sociological Review, 51*(2), 287–294. doi:10. 2307/2095522

Ades, A. F., & Glaeser, E. L. (1995). Trade and circuses: Explaining urban giants. *Quarterly Journal of Economics, 110*(1), 195–227. doi:10.2307/2118515

Alesina, A., Devleeschauwer, A., Easterly, W., Kurlat, S., & Wacziarg, R. (2003). Fractionalization.*Journal of Economic Growth,8*(2),155–194.doi:10.1023/A:1024471506938

Alsan, M., & Goldin, C. (2016). *Watersheds in infant mortality: The role of effective water and sewerage infrastructure, 1880 to 1915* (NBER Working Paper No. 21263, June 2015). Cambridge, MA: National Bureau of Economic Research (NBER). doi:10. 3386/w21263.

Ashraf, N., Glaeser, E. L., & Ponzetto, G. A. (2016). Infrastructure, incentives, and institutions. *American Economic Review, 106*(5), 77–82. doi:10.1257/aer.p20161095

Audretsch, D., & Feldman, M. (1996). R&D spillovers and the geography of innovation and production. *American Economic Review*, *86*(3), 630–640.

Auvinen, J. (1997). Political conflict in less developed countries 1981–89. *Journal of Peace Research*, *34*(2), 177–195. doi:10.1177/0022343397034002005

Blanksten, G. I. (1960). The politics of Latin America. In G. A. Almond and J. S. Coleman (Eds.), *The politics of the developing areas* (pp. 455–531). Princeton: Princeton University Press.

Carp, B. L. (2007). *Rebels rising: Cities and the American Rolution*. Oxford: Oxford University Press.

Chauvin, J. P., Glaeser, E., Ma, Y., & Tobio, K. (2016). What is different about urbanization in rich and poor countries? Cities in Brazil, China, India and the United States. *Journal of Urban Economics*. doi:10.1016/j.jue.2016.05.003

Ciccone, A., & Hall, R. E. (1996). Productivity and the density of economic activity. *American Economic Review*, *86*(1), 54–70.

Combes, P.-P., Duranton, G., & Gobillon, L. (2008). Spatial wage disparities: Sorting matters! *Journal of Urban Economics*, *63*(2), 723–742. doi:10.1016/j.jue.2007.04.004

Combes, P.-P., Duranton, G., Gobillon, L., & Roux, S. (2010). Estimating agglomeration economies with history, geology, and worker effects. In E. L. Glaeser (Ed.), *Agglomeration economics* (pp. 15–66). Chicago: University of Chicago Press.

Costa, D. L., & Kahn, M. E. (2000). Power couples: Changes in the locational choice of the college educated. *Quarterly Journal of Economics*, *115*(4), 1287–1315. doi:10.1162/003355300555079

Cutler, D. M., & Miller, G. (2005). The role of public health improvements in health advances: The twentieth-century United States. *Demography*, *42*(1), 1–22. doi:10.1353/dem.2005.0002

De la Roca, J., & Puga, D. (Forthcoming 2016). Learning by working in big cities. *Review of Economic Studies*.

Dekle, R., & Eaton, J. (1999). Agglomeration and land rents: Evidence from the prefectures. *Journal of Urban Economics*, *46*(2), 200–214. doi:10.1006/juec.1998.2118

DiPasquale, D., & Glaeser, E. L. (1998). The Los Angeles riot and the economics of urban unrest. *Journal of Urban Economics*, *43*(1), 52–78. doi:10.1006/juec.1996.2035

Djankov, S.,Glaeser, E., La Porta, R., Lopez-de-Silanes, F., & Shleifer, A. (2003). The new comparative economics. *Journal of Comparative Economics*, *31*(4), 595–619. doi:10.1016/j.jce.2003.08.005

Fossett, M. A., & Kiecolt, K. J. (1989). The relative size of minority populations and white racial attitudes. *Social Science Quarterly*, *70* (4), 820–835.

Glaeser, E. L. (1998). Are cities dying? *Journal of Economic Perspectives*, *12*(2), 138–160. doi:10.1257/jep.12.2.139

Glaeser, E. L., & Gottlieb, J. D. (2009). The wealth of cities: Agglomeration economies and spatial equilibrium in the United States. *Journal of Economic Literature*, *47*(4), 983–1028. doi:10. 1257/jel.47.4.983

Glaeser, E. L., & Mare, D. C. (2001). *Cities and skills. Journal of Labor Economics*, *19*(2), 316–342. doi:10.1086/319563

Glaeser, E. L., Ponzetto, G. A., & Shleifer, A. (2007). Why does democracy need education? *Journal of Economic Growth*, *12*, 77–99. doi:10.1007/s10887-007-9015-1

Glaeser, E. L., & Resseger, M. G. (2010). The complementarity between cities and skills. *Journal of Regional Science*, *50*(1), 221–244. doi:10.1111/j.1467-9787.2009.00635.x

Glaeser, E. L., & Sacerdote, B. (1999). Why is there more crime in cities? *Journal of Political Economy*, *107*(S6), S225–S258. doi:10. 1086/250109

Glaeser, E. L., & Saks, R. E. (2006). Corruption in America. *Journal of public Economics*, *90*(6), 1053–1072. doi:10.1016/j.jpubeco. 2005.08.007

Greenstone, M., Hornbeck, R., & Moretti, E. (2010). Identifying agglomeration spillovers: Evidence from winners and losers of large plant openings. *Journal of Political Economy*, *18*(3), 409–432.

Hansmann, H. B.,& Quigley, J. M. (1982). Population heterogeneity and the sociogenesis of homicide. *Social Forces*, *61*(1), 206–224. doi:10.1093/sf/61.1.206

Holland, A. W. (1911). French Revolution. In H. Chisholm (Ed.), *Encyclopædia Britannica* (11th ed.). Cambridge: Cambridge University Press. Retrieved from https://en.wikisource.org/wiki/1911_Encyclop%C3%A6dia_Britannica/French_Revolution,_The#Coup_d.27.C3.A9tat_of_the_18th_Brumaire/.

Jaffe, A. B., Trajtenberg, M., & Henderson, R. (1993). Geographic localization of knowledge spillovers as evidenced by patent citations. *Quarterly Journal of Economics*, *108*(3), 577–598. doi:10. 2307/2118401

Krugman, P. (1991). Increasing returns and economic geography. *Journal of Political Economy*, *99*(3), 460–482.

La Porta, R., Lopez-de-Silanes, F., Shleifer, A., & Vishny, R. (1999). The quality of government. *Journal of Law, Economics, and Organization*, *15*(1), 222–279. doi:10.1093/jleo/15.1.222

Nash, G. B. (2009). *The urban crucible: The northern seaports and the origins of the American Revolution* (abridged ed.). Cambridge, MA: Harvard University Press.

Oliver, J. E. (2000). City size and civic involvement in metropolitan America. *American Political Science Review*, *94*(2), 361–373. doi:10.2307/2586017

Rosenthal, S. S., & Strange, W. C. (2004). Evidence on the nature and sources of agglomeration economies. *Handbook of Regional and Urban Economics*, *4*, 2119–2171. doi:10.1016/S1574-0080 (04)80006-3

Scarnecchia, T. (2008). *The urban roots of democracy and political violence in Zimbabwe: Harare and Highfield, 1940–1964* (Vol. 35). Rochester: University of Rochester Press.

Traugott, M. (1995). Capital cities and revolution. *Social Science History*, *19*(1), 147–168. doi:10.1017/S0145553200017259

Voigtländer, N., & Voth, H.-J. (2012). Persecution perpetuated: The medieval origins of anti-Semitic violence in Nazi Germany. *Quarterly Journal of Economics*, *127*(3), 1339–1392. doi:10. 1093/qje/qjs019

Wallace, J. (2014). *Cities and stability: Urbanization, redistribution, and regime survival in China*. Oxford: Oxford University Press.

Wantchekon, L., & Garcia-Ponce, O. (2016). *Critical junctures: Independence movements and democracy in Africa* (Mimeo). Retrieved from http://wrap.warwick.ac.uk/id/eprint/59346

Wirth, L. (1938). Urbanism as a way of life. *American Journal of Sociology*, *44*(1), 1–24. doi:10.1086/217913

Yankow, J. J. (2006). Why do cities pay more? An empirical examination of some competing theories of the urban wage premium. *Journal of Urban Economics*, *60*(2), 139–161. doi:10.1016/j.jue. 2006.03.004

Uneven and combined development

Michael Dunford and Weidong Liu

ABSTRACT

Uneven and combined development. *Regional Studies.* The concept of uneven and combined development (U&CD) interprets dynamic historical change and comparative geographical differentiation in terms of the co-existence of tendencies towards differentiation and equalization of the conditions of production, consumption, distribution and exchange, deriving from capital accumulation and political multiplicity. U&CD entails a conception of the global system as a constellation of interdependent, national institutional configurations and interests that shape international/national/regional trends. To explain geographies of industrialization and urbanization and current trends towards a pluri-centric world, U&CD requires, however, a specification of the underlying causal mechanisms, examined in economic geography, international relations and developmental state theories.

摘要

不均与联合发展。 *Regional Studies.* 不均与联合发展(U&CD)的概念，从资本积累和政治多元化中衍生出的迈向生产、消费、分配和交换条件的差异化和均值化的共存趋势，诠释历史变迁动态和相对地理差异。U&CD导致了全球系统作为形塑国际／国家／区域趋势的相互依赖之国家制度配置与利益之汇聚的概念。但为了解释工业化与城市化，以及当前迈向多核心世界的地理，U&CD需要以经济地理学、国际关系和发展型国家理论进行检视的基础因果机制之明确说明。

RÉSUMÉ

Le développement déséquilibré et combiné. *Regional Studies.* La notion de développement déséquilibré et combiné (uneven and combined development; U&CD) cherche à interpréter l'évolution historico-dynamique et la différenciation comparative géographique en termes de la co-existence des tendances à la différenciation et à l'égalisation des conditions de production, de consommation, de distribution et d'échange, ce qui provient de l'accumulation du capital et de la multiplicité politique. L'U&CD suppose une notion du système mondial comme une myriade de configurations institutionnelles, nationales, interdépendantes qui façonnent les tendances régionales/nationales/internationales. Afin d'expliquer les géographies de l'industrialisation et de l'urbanisation et les tendances actuelles à un monde pluricentrique, l'U&CD nécessite toutefois une spécification des mécanismes sous-jacents en jeu, examinés dans le cadre de la géographie économique, des relations internationales et des théories du développement des états.

ZUSAMMENFASSUNG

Ungleichmäßige und kombinierte Entwicklung. *Regional Studies*. Bei dem Konzept der ungleichmäßigen und kombinierten Entwicklung werden der dynamische historische Wandel und eine vergleichende geografische Differenzierung hinsichtlich der Koexistenz von Tendenzen zur Differenzierung und Ausgleichung der durch Kapitalansammlung und politische Multiplizität entstehenden Bedingungen für Produktion, Verbrauch, Verteilung und Austausch interpretiert. Die ungleichmäßige und kombinierte Entwicklung beinhaltet eine Konzeption des globalen Systems als Konstellation ineinandergreifender nationaler institutioneller Konfigurationen und Interessen, die die internationalen, nationalen und regionalen Trends prägen. Zur Erklärung der Geografien der Industrialisierung und Urbanisierung sowie der aktuellen Trends hin zu einer plurizentrischen Welt benötigt das Konzept der ungleichmäßigen und kombinierten Entwicklung jedoch eine Spezifizierung der zugrundeliegenden kausalen Mechanismen, die in den Theorien der Wirtschaftsgeografie, der internationalen Beziehungen und des entwicklungsfördernden Staates untersucht werden.

RESUMEN

Desarrollo combinado y desequilibrado. *Regional Studies*. El concepto del desarrollo combinado y desequilibrado interpreta el cambio histórico dinámico y la diferenciación geográfica comparativa en cuanto a la coexistencia de tendencias hacia la diferenciación y ecualización de las condiciones de producción, consumo, distribución e intercambio, que se derivan de la acumulación de capital y la multiplicidad política. El desarrollo combinado y desequilibrado implica una concepción del sistema global como una constelación de configuraciones institucionales y nacionales interdependientes e intereses que determinan las tendencias internacionales, nacionales y regionales. Para explicar las geografías de la industrialización y la urbanización así como las tendencias actuales hacia un mundo pluricéntrico, el desarrollo combinado y desequilibrado requiere no obstante una especificación de los mecanismos causales subyacentes, que se analizan en las teorías de la geografía económica, las relaciones internacionales y el Estado desarrollista.

INTRODUCTION

The crisis of neo-liberal globalization, the progressive slowdown of the economies of the North and of Japan that led global economic growth up to the 1970s, the end of the third wave of multiparty representative democracy, the rise of new powers with distinctive social models and the erosion of a unipolar world and Western global leadership are a set of interconnected trends. These trends are fundamentally changing the macro-geographies (Dunford et al., 2016; Peck, 2016) of the world and require a rethinking of the ideas that are used to understand international, national, regional and urban development.

A central argument of this article is that these macro-geographies are consequences of uneven and combined development (U&CD), making U&CD an important overarching concept. U&CD derives from geographically and historically differentiated processes of industrialization and urbanization and the underlying mechanisms through which infrastructures, jobs, people, income and wealth are concentrated in hierarchical systems of interconnected city-regions. These underlying mechanisms have been examined in numerous studies of modernization, dependency, modes of production, world systems, developmental states and economic/urban and regional geography (for recent accounts, see Haggard, 2015; Makki, 2015; Sheppard, 2016).

Analysis of these processes, it will be argued, should draw on a twofold conception of the evolving global system as (1) a set of processes of capital accumulation, unfolding at a variety of scales; and (2) an assemblage/constellation of interacting and asymmetrically integrated/interconnected national institutional configurations and interests that shape economic trends and can result in 'tectonic spatial shifts' (see also Aoyama, 2016) These economic, political and cultural drivers are associated with specific mechanisms of differentiation and equalization of the conditions of production, distribution, consumption and exchange (see also Smith, 1984), whose relative weight and character shape comparative development. In capitalist societies enterprises/institutions/countries that are less developed are pressured and able to appropriate technical and social gains from the more advanced. These gains are combined with existing conditions, jumping over intermediate steps, yet generating new contradictions. Outcomes depend on institutional/governance capacities and the degree of support from/ability to resist more advanced rivals. Outcomes involve an unfolding combination/articulation of different stages of development/modes of production and differentiated historical pathways to modernization (geographical variety).

To develop this argument, the next section will outline Leon Trotsky's original concept of U&CD and its recent impact on international relations. The third and fourth sections will present a set of stylized macroeconomic geographies, identifying the current map of U&CD and recent and long-term trends/modernization paths. To explain these geographies of global divergence and convergence, the remaining sections will examine mechanisms driving the reproduction of inequality (uneven development) and contender catch-up (combined development). The fifth and sixth sections draws on economic geography and economic history to examine the roles of capital accumulation, savings and investment. The seventh section draws on recent research especially in international relations to consider the role of political multiplicity and governance capacity as drivers of differentiation, equalization and comparative development. The final section concludes.

UNEVEN AND COMBINED DEVELOPMENT (U&CD)

Recently there has been a renewal of interest in several fields of research in U&CD. The concept/law was introduced by Leon Trotsky (Trotsky, 1928) who used it to explain the 'peculiarities' of the economic, political and cultural development of Russia before the 1917 Bolshevik Revolution (Trotsky, 1930). More specifically, it served, first, to criticize stages views of historical development. Stage theories claimed that less developed countries should undergo a 'democratic' revolution and then, only after a phase of capitalist development, a socialist revolution, and that less developed countries will repeat completely the processes of industrialization and modernization of advanced countries. Second, it helped explain Tsarist Russia's peculiar combination of state-promoted modern industry, a small industrial working class and a vast rural peasantry.

For Trotsky, Russian backwardness was an expression of the law of unevenness, which he later argued governed the whole history of mankind, explaining 'the extreme diversity in the levels attained, and the extraordinary unevenness in the rate of development of the different sections of mankind during the various epochs' (Trotsky, 1928, pt 1(4)).

Trotsky argued, however, that there is a related law of combined development.

> Capitalism finds various sections of mankind at different stages of development, each with its profound internal contradictions. . . . In contrast to the economic systems which preceded it, capitalism inherently and constantly aims at economic expansion . . . and equalizes the economic and cultural levels of the most progressive and the most backward countries.

Backward countries were compelled to follow after advanced countries ('the whip of external necessity'), but do not 'take things in the same order. The privilege of historic backwardness . . . compels the adoption of whatever is ready in advance of any specified date, skipping a whole series of intermediate stages'. The outcome of this dialectic of compulsion and privilege was 'the drawing together of different stages of the journey, a combination of the separate steps, an amalgam of archaic with contemporary forms' (Trotsky, 1928, pt 1(4)).

The most striking recent recovery of the concept of U&CD has occurred in the field of international relations where it serves as a foundation stone of geopolitical economy, non-realist accounts of the existence of a multiplicity of states and socially grounded interpretations of state systems, contemporary imperialism, and geopolitical and geo-economic conflict/cooperation (Allinson & Anievas, 2009;

Callinicos, 2009; Cooper, 2013; Desai, 2015; Harvey, 2003; Kiely, 2012; Rosenberg, 2010).

This research is important in that it draws attention to the causal role of state actions and inter-state relations and counters the exaggerations of 1990s' theories of globalization which suggested that increasing interconnectedness was leading to the replacement of the sovereign state system by a multilayered, multilateral system of 'global governance'.

More fundamentally, the concept of development as uneven/differentiated and intrinsically interactive grounds world history, world geography and international relations in multiple social structures and agency, and grounds the development of individual societies not in their internal structures and agents alone but also in their interconnectedness with other societies. U&CD accordingly undermines traditional social theories and Euro-centric concepts of development and modernity, as it recognizes the role of external and non-Western sources of internal change (Anievas & Matin, 2016). In the words of J. Rosenberg: 'all societies coexist with and interact with others, and . . . this [interaction] super-adds a lateral field of causality over and above the "domestic" determinations arising from each and every one of the participant societies' (Callinicos & Rosenberg, 2008, p. 88).

Rosenberg has argued that U&CD is an abstract universal category relating to the differentiated peopling of the earth and exploitation of first and second nature, the interaction of different communities and political multiplicity. Critics argue that conceptualizations of U&CD should be more sensitive to the specific mechanisms associated with different types of social order (Davidson, 2009; Kiely, 2012), or that the distinct causal repercussions of inter-societal competition are only fully activated under capitalism (Allinson & Anievas, 2009).

In urban and regional research uneven development received sustained attention in the late 1970s and 1980s (Dunford, 1979; Dunford & Perrons, 1983; Harvey, 1982; Lipietz, 1977; Massey, 1984; Smith, 1984). Recently, the concept of 'combined and uneven development' (*sic*) has re-emerged (Hadjimichalis & Hudson, 2014; Hudson, 2016; Peck, 2017; Rowthorn, 2010). The early analyses of the uneven production of nature and industrial and urban space have, however, much to learn from subsequent urban and regional research and especially from the international relations tradition: although spatial interdependence was highlighted, development was seen as combined and uneven rather than vice versa, and these studies failed to appreciate the significance of political multiplicity.

For Trotsky, combined 'grows out of the first [uneven development] and completes it' (cited in Davidson, 2012, p. 295). As Anievas and Nisancioglu (2015, p. 45) argue, 'combination . . . refers to the ways in which the internal relations of any given society are determined by their interactive relations with other developmentally differentiated societies'. In polities that are less developed, these interactions are sources of constraint and innovation/creativity. Material and non-material aspects of more advanced societies are grafted on and combined, in the absence of the social relations from which they emerged, with internal social relations to produce and reproduce in ever-changing forms 'amalgamated socio-political institutions, socio-economic systems, ideologies and material practices' (Anievas &

Matin, 2016, p. 45), which in turn react upon more developed societies (Matin, 2013). These differing combinations of 'native' and 'foreign', 'advanced' and 'backward', 'new' and 'old', 'modern' and 'traditional' relate to economics, politics and culture, and make development interactively multi-linear and geographically differentiated. Methodologically, therefore, U&CD theorizes not just general mechanisms governing social life (necessity) but also the necessity of multiple outcomes (contingency) and the openness of processes of development (Cooper, 2013).

In international relations these ideas are employed mainly to examine state formation and geopolitical rivalries and conflicts. What this research lacks, however, is a developed theorization and detailed empirical analysis of differential industrialization, urbanization and connectivity and of the role of capital accumulation: of, in other words, the objects of urban and regional research which can themselves be examined in the light of U&CD. For these reasons there are important potential synergies between these two fields of study, to which this article seeks to make a small contribution by examining geographies of *longue durée* industrialization and urbanization and contender catch-up in the light of U&CD (Rolf, 2015).

U&CD: SOME OUTLINE MACROECONOMIC GEOGRAPHIES

At present wide geographical disparities in labour productivity and output per head prevail, while growth involves phases of relatively sustained growth punctuated by phases of instability and crisis.

In 2014, measured in per capita gross domestic product (GDP) in 1990 purchasing power parity (PPP) US$ (Figure 1), there were wide differences between the Western offshoots of North America, Australia and New Zealand (US$31,599), the Asian Tiger economies (US$26,406), Japan (US$22,700), and Western Europe (US$20,964) and the rest of the world (ROW). The Gulf oil states averaged US$9233. In sub-Saharan Africa other than South Africa (US$5678) and Nigeria (US$2119), per capita GDP stood at just US$1205. China (US$9966) and India (US$3975) had moderate to relatively low levels of income per head. With 1.26 billion inhabitants, however, China was the largest economy in the world, with a GDP of US$13.590 trillion, compared with US$10.424 trillion for the United States and US$8.772 trillion for Western Europe.

This geography is a result of long-term processes. Considering the years since 1950 (Figure 2), growth rates were generally fastest in the 1950–73 Golden Age. After the Second World War, Western and Southern Europe grew rapidly. In each subsequent economic cycle Western European growth rates were less than half of Golden Age rates and close to zero in 2008–14. GDP growth of the Western offshoots also slowed down. Communist Eastern Europe grew rapidly in 1960–73. A rapid transition to capitalism in 1989–97 saw output decline on average at 5.1% per year. In 1997 and 2014 output stood at just 66.2% and 132% of its 1989 level. China's growth averaged 8.9% per year from 1979 to 2010 and is one of the reasons for the growth of Asia at 5.4%, 6.1% and 6.1% per year in the last three cycles from 1989 until 2014. In those years, the growth first of Japan and then of the Tiger economies slowed markedly. In Latin America, sub-Saharan Africa and the Middle East and North Africa (MENA), relatively high growth rates in 1950–73 gave way to much slower growth in 1973–97. In Latin America, sub-Saharan Africa and formerly Communist Eastern Europe, slowdown/decline reflected the implementation of Washington Consensus measures. Many of these countries progressively lost competitiveness in world markets, and some came to depend on natural resource/food exports. In growing rapidly Japan, the Four Tigers, China, India and Vietnam violated virtually all the rules of neoliberalism.

The roots of these disparities lie further in the past in the Great and Little Divergence. The Great Divergence in GDP per capita dates from the start of the Industrial Revolution and the subsequent wave of colonial and imperial expansion. International inequality increased very strongly from 1820 until 1950, when the share of world GDP of Western Europe and Western offshoots peaked (Figure 3). From 1950 until 1990 between-country inequality grew more slowly from a Theil coefficient of 0.51 to 0.54, after which it declined rapidly to 0.26 in 2014 (albeit with a brief increase after the 1997–98 Asian financial crisis) due to relatively rapid emerging economy growth (van Zanden, Baten, Foldvari, & van Leeuwen, 2014).[1]

These trends in global inequality reflect the evolving geography of industrialization and urbanization. Before the Industrial Revolution, Western Europe dominated a set of commercial empires around the Atlantic, Indian and Asian oceans, while Asia was the centre of world manufacturing (Figure 4). With the onset of the Industrial Revolution, a number of regions in Western Europe emerged as centres of modern manufacturing, from which economic development diffused to the rest of Europe and white-settler countries. Of them the United States pioneered

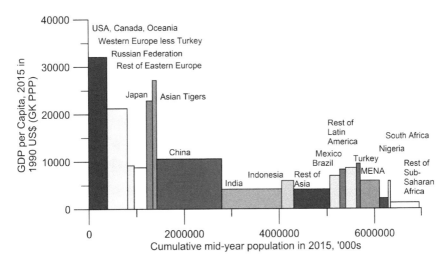

Figure 1 Gross domestic product (GDP), GDP per head and population in 2015 by major world regions and countries.

Source: Elaborated from The Conference Board (2016).

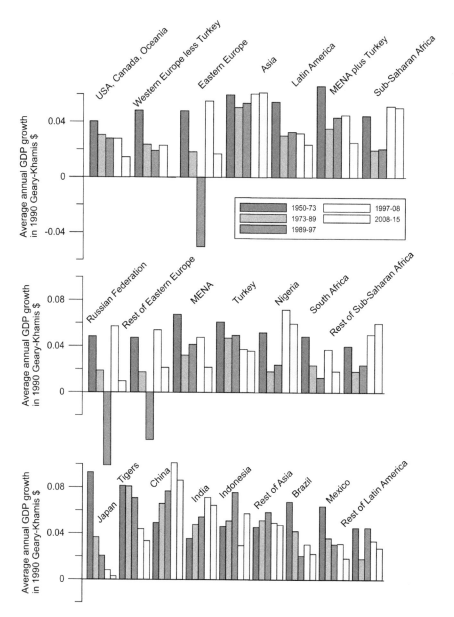

Figure 2 Average annual rates of growth, 1950–2015.
Source: Elaborated from The Conference Board (2016).

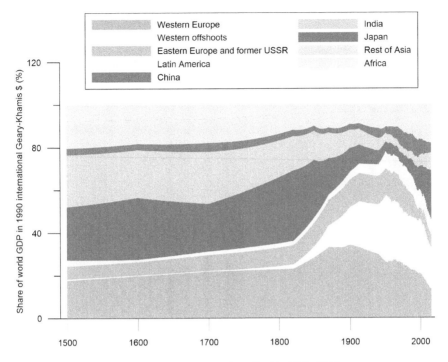

Figure 3 World shares of gross domestic product (GDP), 1500–2015.
Sources: Elaborated from Maddison (2003) and The Conference Board (2016).

mass production, and replaced Great Britain as the hegemonic global power. This polarization of the geography of industry started to change with the rise of Japan and the Asian Tigers, and the Fordist crisis of the 1970s which opened the way for financialization and the hollowing out of advanced capitalist country manufacturing (Dunford, 2005, pp. 156–157), a global shift/offshoring of manufacturing to emerging economies (Dicken, 2010) and eventually debt-financed trade imbalances in Western countries. Although industrial movement at first involved unskilled manufacturing rather than product design and marketing, export-oriented Asian economies progressively moved up the value chain.

In the last 250 years what distinguishes economically advanced economies from the ROW is sustained growth. In Great Britain the growth of a number of industrial regions and the country's commercial, financial, political and cultural capital made it the first modern industrial nation (Figure 5). Modern economic growth started some 200–230 years ago. Growth spread to other regions in Europe and white-settler territories. After the Meiji Restoration Japan embarked on modern industrial growth. Japanese growth accelerated after defeat in the Second World War, enabling it to join the group of advanced capitalist economies in the 1980s. The Soviet Union grew rapidly from the 1920s, and after massive Second

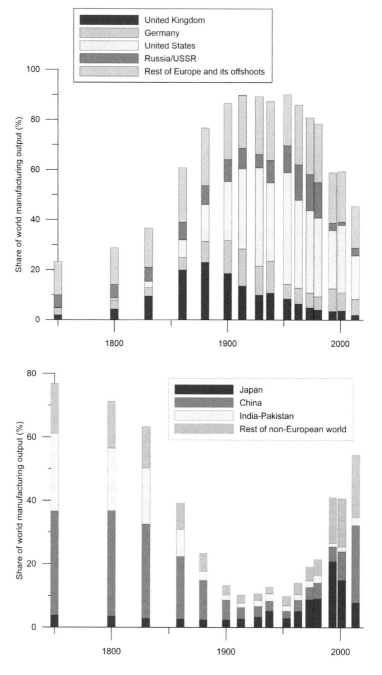

Figure 4 First and second industrial divides.

Sources: Elaborated from data from (Bairoch, 1997) and United Nations Industrial Development Organization (UNIDO) (2016).

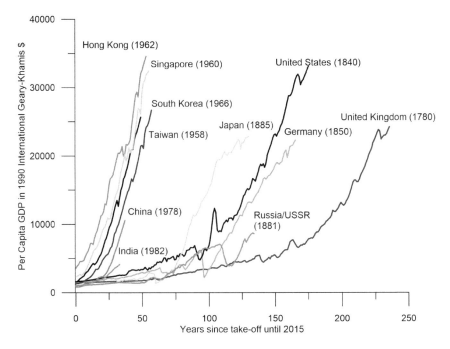

Figure 5 Take-off and relatively sustained growth up to 2015.
Source: Elaborated from data from Maddison (2003) and The Conference Board (2016).

World War destruction and population loss. Growth, however, petered out in the 1970s due to the ageing of the fixed capital stock and the inability of the centrally planned economy to replace retiring equipment and infrastructure (Popov, 2014). In the 1960s growth spread from Japan to four small Asian Tiger economies. Until the 1960s, the economies that acquired, adopted and developed advanced technologies and achieved relatively high levels of affluence were few in number and small in size. Although growth spurts occurred, and islands/enclaves of modernization emerged, most economies could not sustain high growth rates and remained relatively backward until the rise of China and India.

In each case growth involved the transformation of predominantly agrarian and rural into industrial and urban societies. These transformations generate profound dislocation and conflict as rural populations are uprooted, agricultural productivity increases, cities grow and new technologies and ways of life are generalized (combined development). As Figure 5 shows, the speed of these changes has accelerated. Achieving a five-fold increase in initial real GDP per capita took Great Britain more than 160 years, Germany more than 108, the United States more than 100 and Japan more than 75. Similar increases took just over 22 years in South Korea, 28 in Hong Kong, 24 in Taiwan and 26 in Singapore. Mainland China has so far taken just over 25 years, transforming the lives of some one-fifth of the world's population, compressing what had taken centuries into a few decades, and carrying it out on an unprecedented scale.

The gap that opened up with the Great Divergence was itself, however, laid upon an earlier gap, that had opened up in the early modern period, with the Little Divergence between the most advanced parts of Europe – Flanders, Holland and England – and the ROW. The ROW included not just China and other parts of Asia where the real wages of labourers were close to subsistence levels (Allen, 2009) but also Eastern and Southern Europe where Spanish and Italian GDP per head had gone into long-term decline from 1500.

THE REGIONAL FOUNDATIONS OF NATIONAL DEVELOPMENT

An examination of these changes in the map of economic development plays a significant role in regional and urban research, as these national differences are results of underling regional/urban differences, interregional and international relationships (commerce, investment, migration), and national institutional configurations. The Little Divergence between the North Sea area and the rest of Europe was regional/urban in character:

> In the 14th–15th centuries Flanders formed the urban core of this economic system – and England its 'periphery'. In the 16th century Brabant (and in particular Antwerp) took over the role of being the core. After 1585 the urban centre moved to Holland, a switch that resulted in the Dutch 'Golden Age' of the 17th century. After about 1650 London gradually replaced Amsterdam as the central hub in the commercial network of North-Western Europe, and the urban core switched to England.
>
> (de Pleijt & van Zanden, 2013, p. 2)

This divergence was driven in part by external factors. In 1620 Francis Bacon stated that the modern world was marked off from the past by the impact of three innovations (gunpowder, the printing press and the magnetic compass) which did more than any empire or religion to lift Europe out of the Dark Ages (Rosenberg, 2016). All three were transferred to Europe from China. Other external drivers also played a part (Anievas & Nisancioglu, 2015).

The subsequent Industrial Revolution occurred in a number of regional economies. In Great Britain in 1760–1800, the most important innovative changes occurred in about 10 small islands of industrialization near localized resource deposits or in areas of traditional industry: Cornwall, Shropshire, North Wales, upland Derbyshire, Tyneside, the Clyde Valley, South Staffordshire, the West Riding of Yorkshire and South Lancashire. Strong national performance was a result of the growth of a number of strong regional economies, although their growth ruined traditional industrial areas (such as Irish linen in the 1820s contributing to male migration to Britain and the United States and depopulation).

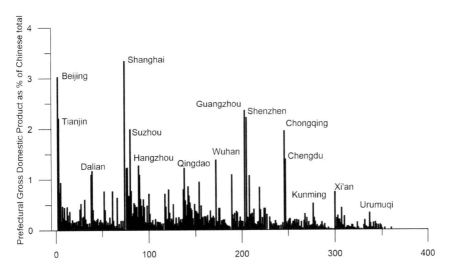

Figure 6 Prefecture-level gross domestic product (GDP) in China, 2013.
Source: Elaborated from data from the National Bureau of Statistics (NBS), various years.

National structures and trends are underpinned therefore by development within countries that is also uneven and combined.

Figure 6 plots the GDP in 2013 of four municipalities and 337 prefecture-level entities (essentially city-regions containing smaller county-level cities, townships and villages) in China. In 2013 five cities in Eastern China (Shanghai, Beijing, Guangzhou, Shenzhen and Tianjin) out of 341 accounted for 10.9% of GDP. The top 20, which included two cities in Western China (Chongqing and Chengdu) and three in Central China (Wuhan, Changsha and Zhengzhou), accounted for 32.2%, while 48 accounted for 50.4%. As throughout the world, wealth creation is strongly concentrated spatially in a relatively small number of city-regions.

Variations in GDP and GDP per capita differ enormously (and are subject to constant change). In 2013, in the case of these Chinese city-regions, GDP varied by 1173:1 whereas GDP per capita varied by 5.6:1, simply because the population was also concentrated in cities/mega-cities. These differences in labour productivity and per-capita income and in the underlying geography of economic activities and population are also results of development that is uneven and combined.

CAPITAL ACCUMULATION AND THE DIFFERENTIATION AND EQUALIZATION OF THE CONDITIONS OF PRODUCTION, DISTRIBUTION, CONSUMPTION AND EXCHANGE

The evidence presented in the last two sections points to the constancy of differences in development in the double sense of the unequal development of different parts of the surface of the earth (synchronic, geographical differences in labour productivity and income per head) and of change at varying speeds of relative positions (diachronic historical differences). In this sense there is a law of uneven development. Such a law is, however, essentially an empirical generalization as it does not fully specify causal mechanisms. Adding the idea that development is combined draws attention to the ways dynamic interdependence/connectedness near-compels enterprises/areas that are less developed to emulate more advanced rivals and reduce differences, articulating the old and the new. Again, however, the underlying causal mechanisms require specification.

As Lewis (1954, p. 54) indicated,

> the central problem in the theory of economic development is to understand the process by which a community which was previously saving and investing 4 or 5% of its national income or less, converts itself into the economy where voluntary saving is running at about 12 to 15% of national income or more … [showing that] the central fact of economic development is capital accumulation.

And as (Feinstein, 1981) noted,

> without an ability both to organize the process of production so as to incorporate the new techniques in appropriate assets, and to save a sufficient sum to provide the finance for those acquiring capital goods . . . [a society would not be able] to benefit from technical progress however readily the knowledge might be available. In this sense at least the process of capital accumulation must still occupy a central role in any explanation of the growth of output and productivity.

Capital assets includes tangible productive capital, intangible human capital and natural capital (reminding one of the importance of the metabolism of humanity with nature). In capitalist modes of production, natural and productive assets assume the form of private property. Capital itself is value in motion: money capital is advanced to purchase means of production and labour power, which transforms purchased inputs into products that are subsequently offered for sale (Harvey, 2016). The surpluses realized if products are sold for more than the sum advanced are in part reinvested, generating an outward spiral in which rapid increases in the production of goods and services create a need for increasing consumption (which itself depends on the way income is distributed) to recover costs and value added (see also Cox, 2008).

Growth and development themselves involve two interrelated longer-term processes of structural change (Kuznets, 1955): the transformation of societies that are predominantly agricultural and rural into societies in which (1) industry and services are the main sources of output and employment, and (2) the population is predominantly urban. Throughout most of human history these processes unfolded slowly, with many reverses.

These historically and geographically differentiated processes of industrialization and urbanization are a result of drivers of U&CD and in particular of differentiated investments in the conversion of land from rural to urban use and from one urban use to another, in urban and rural infrastructure, in agricultural restructuring to increase productivity and commercialized food production, in export-oriented 'basic' industries and 'non-basic services for the residential population and visitors, and their impacts on rural–urban migration and population change (Figure 7). The specific ways in which these drivers operate and evolve depend on their geographical and economic, political/institutional and cultural settings (e.g., Campolina Diniz & Vieira, 2016; Liu, Dunford, Song, & Chen, 2016; Turok, 2016). In capitalist societies most involve the investment of financial resources with a view to creating income streams permitting cost recovery, the repayment of credits and the realization of profits.

In urban and regional research these processes are examined in a wide range of theories. All, however, presuppose the existence of savings and investment. In capitalist societies the main starting point is the (agricultural, industrial, commercial, property (real estate) and financial) enterprise, its profit, growth and upgrading strategies (an M-C-Má circuit) and its changing relationships with its evolving external environment. These strategies give rise to social, technical and spatial

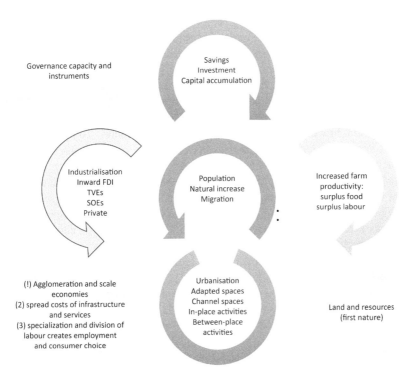

Figure 7 Drivers of urbanization and economic development.

divisions of labour (STSDL) (Massey, 1984) that increase productivity and differentiate and equalize the conditions of production, distribution, consumption and exchange.

Differentiation itself derives from growth and accumulation (and requires new modes of integration/coordination). Growth is a strategic objective not simply as a result of choice but due to the existence of competitors and the need ('the whip of external necessity') to grow/adjust to survive. Achieving this objective may involve introducing a new good or a new quality of a known good, a new method of production or mode of management or a new source of labour, opening up of a new market, conquering a new source of raw materials or semi-finished goods and/or establishing new organizational models. All are examples of innovation, deriving from dedicated research and development or from spillovers of knowledge and capabilities.

Outcomes include investment in new plant and equipment, increases in the scale of production (that spread fixed costs over a large volume of output), a more detailed division of labour (that increases productivity as it permits the introduction and use of machines, generating increasing returns) and an increased variety of intermediate and final goods. Geographically, scale/scope, agglomeration and urbanization economies result in the concentration of investments in places that are accessible and have large and extensive markets. In phases of growth, this increased differentiation of industrial activities leads to cumulative and rapid increases in productivity and strengthens the competitiveness of certain firms/regions (especially if reinforced by differences in the elasticity of demand for their products). These enterprises/areas grow rapidly and, aided by revolutions in transport, communications and connectivity, press for greater interregional and international integration to secure raw materials, cheaper inputs including labour and access to new or expanded markets, exposing other enterprises and parts of the world to greater competition.

Competition, however, gives rise to equalization tendencies. To remain profitable and survive, enterprises/areas that are left behind must adjust/copy/adapt, introducing new products and/or technologies, securing cheaper inputs or entering new markets so as to match/surpass their competitors, rivals and adversaries. Failure implies relative decline/bankruptcy and is reflected in company/industry life cycles. Success enables survival, and can involve catch-up or even overtaking, perhaps as a result of latecomer advantage and major shifts in technology and industrial structure. Geographically, moreover, there are limits to concentration with dispersal and equalization arising from higher living, wage and land costs in developed areas (Myrdal, 1957).

Trends in industrial development (and in urbanization) depend on the relative strength of these two sets of forces. Generally speaking, capital accumulation gives rise to greater socio-economic inequality reflected in the concentration and centralization of capital and increased income inequality. Geographically, divergence (uneven development) often prevailed for two reasons. First, companies in some areas introduced more complex divisions of labour and new technologies sooner and more extensively than those in others. Second, structural and geographical asymmetries emerged: different areas specialized in sectors (agriculture, industry or finance) with different returns to scale and demand elasticities or different functional roles (research, design, management, manufacture or marketing) that generated differences in per capita value added. Many less developed areas found themselves dependent, for example, on primary goods which do not yield dynamic increases in productivity in the way that manufacturing does, increasing disparities.

The completion of these circular movements of capital (M-C-Má) often encounters limits. These movements can spiral out of control giving rise to crises of different durations, reflecting underlying contradictions/disequilibria and changing secular trends. These chronological trends are also instances of U&CD. In economically developed parts of the world, for example, secular stagnation set in from the 1970s (Figure 2) due to a decline in the expected profitability of further investment after a long period of capital accumulation. To offset this downturn, a number of measures were adopted (an attack on wages and trade unions, the integration of political and economic power, the privatization of public assets, the accumulation of public and private debt, asset inflation and financialization). The interplay of these crisis tendencies and counter-tendencies generated several waves of expansion followed by severe contractions, at first in some peripheral parts of the world, in Japan, in Southeast Asia and finally in the core of the world economy (Streeck, 2016).

INEQUALITY, CAPITAL ACCUMULATION AND U&CD

In the last section ideas from economic geography are brought together to identify mechanisms through which capital accumulation causes a constant differentiation and equalization of socio-economic development. An analysis of the varying weight of these forces helps explain the trends in global development outlined above.

Capital investment depends, however, upon the availability of savings. Throughout most of human history savings were insufficient. Some 250 years ago, in the North Sea area this restriction was lifted in a sustained manner. The ways in which it was subsequently lifted in other parts of the world varied, contributing to different pathways to development.

In pre-industrial societies average income was close to subsistence levels, and traditional institutions and social relations (Asian values) restricted inequality. Significant inequality (beyond a small ruling elite) was incompatible with the survival of the population. As a result, there was little scope to raise savings rates. North Sea economies overcame this constraint by destroying traditional institutions and establishing social relations of capitalist production (private property, a wage-earning class separated from the means of production, capitalist agriculture and merchant capitalist structures) and international divisions of labour. As a result income inequality increased, allowing for the redistribution of income in favour of savings and investment (Popov, 2014).

In 1500–1800 throughout Europe there was a secular decline in real wages. In the North Sea area, however, there was a secular increase in GDP (Figure 8

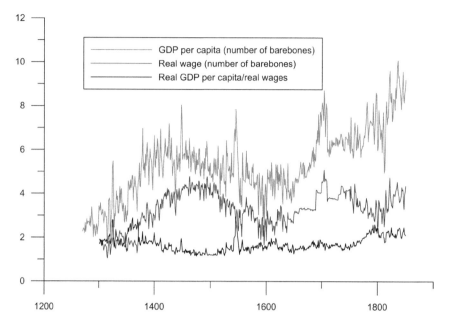

Figure 8 Real gross domestic product (GDP) and wages in England, 1270–1850.

Sources: Data are from www.iisg.nl/hpw and https://www.nuffield.ox.ac.uk/People/sites/Allen/SitePages/Biography.aspx/.

shows the English case). As GDP increased, middle- and upper-class incomes increased (Saito, 2015), at the expense of greater inequality and depression of the real living standards of wage earners, but without driving wage earners beneath the subsistence minimum or overturning the system Increased upper- and middle-class incomes enabled savings and investment to increase (Figure 9).

Capitalism is founded on inequality. In the Netherlands and England the fact that wages were several multiples of subsistence permitted a compression of real living standards. As Figure 10 shows, real wages in London and Amsterdam fell from the early stages of industrialization until 1812 and 1863 respectively, but were considerably higher than in Milan and Beijing, enabling these areas to pull cumulatively away from the ROW.

In Japan the first phase of industrialization occurred in the era of late 19th-century globalization after the Meiji Restoration of imperial rule. At that time Japan was a relatively egalitarian society. Growth, however, was accompanied by a strong rise in inequality, as is expected as rural societies are initially transformed into urban/industrial societies (Kuznets, 1955). In Japan, however, development combined modern industry with a traditional, non-proletarianized agriculture (combining/articulating several modes of production). Although powerful

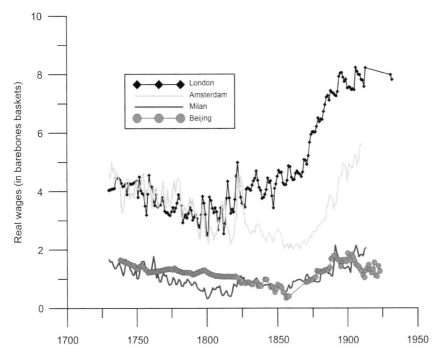

Figure 9 Real wages in Amsterdam, Beijing, London and Milan, 1730–1910.

Sources: Data are from www.iisg.nl/hpw; and https://www.nuffield.ox.ac.uk/People/sites/Allen/
    SitePages/Biography.aspx/.

landlords emerged, rural society predominantly comprised small rural cultivating landlords and tenant cultivators supplementing labour and land-intensive farm-work with proto-industrial and off-farm occupations (Saito, 2015).

Countries that industrialized later pursued different paths (Gerschenkron, 1962), and these paths involved different institutional and real wage evolutions. Centrally planned economies in Eastern Europe and China mobilized domestic savings for investment without high inequalities and started to catch up. After the Second World War, a slow increase in income and considerable US support enabled Japan and the Asian Tigers to increase savings rates and investment and achieve sustained economic growth, with degrees of inequality that were signifi-cantly smaller than in Europe and Latin America, and without a reduction in real living standards. China more recently embarked on a transformation which saw inequality increase but the real incomes and consumption of almost all sections of the population rise and millions lifted out of poverty, contrasting sharply with the experience of the first countries to industrialize. As in other Asian countries, however, the speed and sustained character of growth derive from exceptionally high rates of saving, investment and capital accumulation (Figure 10).

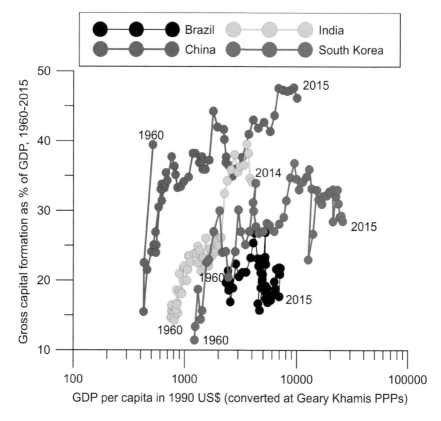

Figure 10 Gross capital formation as a share of gross domestic product (GDP).
Sources: Elaborated from World Bank (2016) and The Conference Board (2016).

POLITICAL MULTIPLICITY, GOVERNANCE CAPACITY, AND EQUALIZATION AND DIFFERENTIATION OF THE CONDITIONS OF PRODUCTION, CONSUMPTION, DISTRIBUTION AND EXCHANGE

These contrasting ways in which income distribution, savings and investment influenced growth are just one aspect of the institutional/political mediation of capital accumulation. The world is divided into a multiplicity of states with different institutional/civilizational/social configurations. These configurations evolve in the light of national reforms/revolutions and the internalization of inter-national influences. These states themselves adopt development strategies that serve to increase and reduce disparities. At each point in time these states also function as differentially endowed centres of development. Japan, for example, has acted as an important driver of combined development in Asia. China is emerging as a driver of combined development in Eurasia, and, through development cooperation and investment, in Africa.

In a world of multiple polities developed states competitively/collaboratively and individually/collectively assert their dominance over other countries. Countries that are less developed are enmeshed in asymmetrical webs of economic, political and military dependence that can impede/enhance their growth and development. A century of humiliation from the first Opium War to 1949 saw China, for example, go backwards economically to become the poorest country in the world. After the Second World War the United States supported the development of its allies in East Asia and Western Europe.

Contender countries sought to close development gaps. Commercial and military rivalries played a part in the 19th- and early 20th-century growth of European economies and the initial rise of Japan. In the second-half of the 20th century East Asian contender countries aided by the United States caught up quickly. To counter relative under-development, contender countries usually start with import substitution policies that see newly created industries crowd out foreign goods from the domestic market. At an appropriate point, emerging countries must switch to export orientation. Countries/regions that have established some domestic nodes of industrialization positioned in the early stages of development nonetheless find the challenge to grow from their initial positions extremely difficult. Industrial investment often depends on incoming transnational corporations that are very resistant to domestic content and technology transfer requirements and use their influence with international organizations and their domestic governments to unravel policy restrictions.

State-directed development of the productive forces is a driver of combined development, designed to jump steps and move progressively in the direction of a relationship of *similarity* with more developed economies by grafting on aspects of modernity. The aim is not to accept an about-to-be-established relationship of *complementarity*, involving sustained occupation of a subordinate position in an international capitalist division of labour that reproduces unevenness (Desai, 2015; Rolf, 2015).

An ability to overcome the aforementioned constraints and move in the direction of similarity depends in part on the strength of national identify, state domestic and international governance capacity, underlying social relationships/capability (Abramovitz, 1986) and the international context including relations among states. Of these determinations, state capacity depends on state strength and scope. State strength denotes the capacity of a government to enforce laws cleanly and transparently, implement effective policies and ensure compliance with the state's monopoly of violence and economic regulation. State scope denotes the range of functions that a government can effectively accomplish (Popov, 2014).

Great Britain's rise involved the use of protectionism and free-trade policies along with the resources and markets of its empire to promote industrialization. The development of contender countries such as the United States, Germany and Japan all involved state-supported capitalist industrialization and catch-up: the United States used tariffs, import controls, subsidies, tax exemptions and state investment in infrastructure. The initial development of the Soviet Union and China involved state-planned socialist models. The catch-up of Western and Southern Europe was shaped by varied systems of governance that often involved significant state investment/intervention. East Asian catch-up was shaped by a variety of developmental states that mobilized domestic and international financial resources and supported strategic industries. In none of these cases did development occur in the context of a minimalist multi-party representative state.

These cases are studied in terms of the rise and decline of nations/regions or the rise and decline of institutions: in Trotsky's theory of U&CD these questions are combined (van der Linden, 2007). An implication is that, alongside economic mechanisms, national institutions and the strength and capacity of states play an important role in driving catch-up industrialization/combined development. Popov (2014) has argued that state capacity depends on historical evolutions and in particular on the impact of colonization (combination) on traditional community structures. State capacity was/is strong where traditional institutions were completely destroyed and replaced by Western institutions in white-settler countries (except South Africa), weak where they were destroyed but only partially replaced in Latin America, sub-Saharan Africa and, to a lesser extent, South Asia, and strong where they (Asian values) survived as in parts of East Asia. Consequent differences in institutional conditions and economic inequality played a central role in explaining catch-up industrialization.

As Trotsky argued, economic and cultural capacities of adaptation and assimilation have performed an important role in determining the extent to which latecomers take advantage of the privilege of backwardness to appropriate what is relatively advanced (through investment, learning and acquisition), avoid steps on the path (through stage skipping investment), create combinations with a higher preponderance of modern elements and generate these effects quickly and strongly (Figure 5). The mirror image of the privilege of backwardness is the handicap of a head start. If a head start results in rigidities that impede progress as, for example, by restricting the scrapping of old and investment in new assets that are possibly interdependent and under the (uncoordinated) control of different owners, a relative latecomer leap forward is more likely (van der Linden, 2007).

Cases of latecomer advantage in contemporary China reflect both a privilege of backwardness for China and a handicap of a head start for more developed areas. China's rail system was largely developed after the Second World War. Its rolling stock was predominantly steam-driven until the 1980s. In the new millennium, however, China acquired all the patents worldwide for trains capable of exceeding 250 14;km/h, and in 2003–15 constructed a 20,000 14;km high-speed rail system. China had great difficulty in establishing a wired telephone network, yet was able to jump into the era of wireless and digital communication. Although Western countries and South Korea were at the forefront of third-generation cellphone technologies, China was an early player in fourth- and fifth-generation technologies. Chinese financial institutions still use large amounts of paper, yet internet banking has developed at an extraordinary speed. In the absence of a high-quality incumbent legacy retail system at all levels of the urban system, online shopping has taken off explosively and is highly innovative.

Catch-up and overtaking depend, however, on governance and economic and cultural capacities of adaptation and assimilation, making the attention paid in regional and urban development studies to institutional variety and performance increasingly vital. Attention has been paid to varieties of capitalism, variegated governance (Peck & Theodore, 2007) and varieties of 'plan rational' developmental states (Haggard, 2015).

Although identification of these types contributes to causal accounts of comparative development and critiques of more generalized models, these categories do not capture the diversity, multiplicity and particularity of social configurations and development pathways. In an unevenly developed world, the diffusion of ideas, knowledge and values and the imperatives of geopolitical and geo-economic competition result in interaction and in reproduction in each and every territory/polity of a unique variety of social structures.[2] In these interacting multi-scalar contexts, joint transformations of social structures and institutions are designed to move forward while dealing with contradictions, generating as many development paths as there are places.

CONCLUSIONS

The theory of U&CD emphasizes the ways in which the evolution of a world made up of differentiated societies/polities depends not just on their internal structures and agents but also mechanisms deriving from their interconnectedness/ combination. In a world of societies in which the capitalist mode of production predominates, mechanisms that constantly create new forms of unevenness coexist with mechanisms that equalize development. These mechanisms are economic and political. Economic mechanisms derive from competition, the accumulation of capital, the expansion of demand and institutional adaptation. Political mechanisms derive from political multiplicity and depend on whether relationships are competitive or collaborative and on governance capacity. Acting at multiple geographical scales and changing over the course of time, the relative weight of mechanisms of differentiation and equalization drive comparative development, while the combination of inherited conditions with whatever is in advance at any point in time gives rise to complex articulations of modern and non-modern modes of production and ways of life and multi-linear development.

In this article this concept of U&CD was elaborated to provide an interpretation of the Little and Great Divergences and of macro-geographies of catch-up industrial and urban development. Considerable attention was paid to (1) differential capital accumulation; (2) the impact of income distribution on the availability of savings to finance infrastructure, acquire capital goods and develop/acquire and exploit human knowledge and capabilities; and (3) the political capacity to implement catch-up development.

Uneven development is a central concept in urban and regional research. A weakness of this concept compared with U&CD is that it pays insufficient attention to interactivity/connectivity and political multiplicity. U&CD combines the analysis of dynamic change over historical time and comparative differences across geographical space (Rosenberg, 2006). U&CD embraces the analysis of multi-scalar and historical processes of capital accumulation and the associated movements of money, people, goods, income and wealth that serve to widen/ reduce disparities of all kinds. U&CD involves a conception of the global system as a constellation of interacting, national institutional configurations and interests that shape economic trends in part through state development strategies. The asymmetric integration and interaction of national models of development and the way they interact with global processes modifies their internal dynamics and generates international/sub-national disequilibria.

These ideas have much to contribute to urban and regional research and its relationships with cognate disciplines. More specifically, U&CD provides a powerful overarching framework for the analysis of urban and regional dynamics: the specific socially mediated processes of catching up, falling behind, overtaking and surging ahead that generate geographical variety and comparative regional/urban evolutions. This framework requires, however, further specification of the underlying causal drivers and repercussions of the concentration of infrastructures, jobs, people, income and wealth in hierarchical systems of interconnected city-regions. The extant literature already contains numerous insights as does research in cognate disciplines, although analysis must deal not with generic (indeterminate) categories/mechanisms but with the forms they assume in different institutional and social contexts.

ACKNOWLEDGEMENTS

The authors thank the referees for their detailed and extremely valuable comments made on an earlier version of this paper; and the editors for their guidance.

DISCLOSURE STATEMENT

No potential conflict of interest was reported by the authors.

FUNDING

The authors acknowledge the support of the National Natural Science Foundation of China [NSFC grant number 41530751] and The Leverhulme Trust Emeritus Fellowship.

NOTES

1. In 1910–50 and especially in 1950–80, intra-country social inequality declined due to an egalitarian revolution associated with the rise of Communism and the Golden Age

decline in income inequality in Europe and the United States. After 1980, within-country social inequality increased strongly.

2. China, for example, has combined inherited and imported elements in new ways to mix state-owned enterprises, solely owned direct foreign investment, joint ventures, township and village enterprises, private enterprises, a rural household responsibility system, state/collective ownership of land, massive public assets, a unified state with strong political decentralization and fierce inter-jurisdictional competition, elite consultative democracy, a cadre responsibility system, a combination of Confucian, socialist and consumerist values, and a distinctive model of international relations, amongst others.

REFERENCES

Abramovitz, M. (1986). Catching up, forging ahead, and falling behind. *Journal of Economic History*, *46*(2), 385–406. doi:10.1017/S0022050700046209

Allen, R. C. (2009). Agricultural productivity and rural incomes in England and the Yangtze Delta, *c.*1620–*c.*1820 (1). *Economic History Review*, *62*(3), 525–550. doi:10.1111/j.1468-0289.2008.00443.x

Allinson, J. C., & Anievas, A. (2009). The uses and misuses of uneven and combined development: An anatomy of a concept. *Cambridge Review of International Affairs*, *22*(1), 47–67. doi:10.1080/09557570802680132

Anievas, A., & Matin, K. (Eds.). (2016). *Historical sociology and world history. Uneven and combined development over the Longue Durée*. London: Rowman & Littlefield International.

Anievas, A., & Nisancioglu, K. (2015). *How the West came to rule: The geopolitical origins of capitalism*. London: Pluto.

Aoyama, Y. (2016). Reorienting the drivers of development: Alternative paradigms. *Area Development and Policy*, *1*(3), 295–304. doi:10.1080/23792949.2016.1239507

Bairoch, P. (1997). *Victoires et Déboires. Histoire économique et sociale du monde du XVIème siècle à nos jours*. Paris: Gallimard.

Callinicos, A. (2009). How to solve the many-state problem: A reply to the debate. *Cambridge Review of International Affairs*, *22*(1), 89–105. doi:10.1080/09557570802682518

Callinicos, A., & Rosenberg, J. (2008). Uneven and combined development: The social–relational substratum of 'the international'? An exchange of letters. *Cambridge Review of International Affairs*, *21* (1), 77–112. doi:10.1080/0955757 0701828600

Campolina Diniz, C., & Vieira, D. J. (2016). Brazil: Accelerated metropolization and urban crisis. *Area Development and Policy*, *1*(2), 155–177. doi:10.1080/23792949.2016.1202085

The Conference Board. (2016). *The Conference Board total economy database™*. Retrieved June 2016 from http://www.conferenceboard.org/data/economydatabase/

Cooper, L. (2013). Can contingency be 'internalized' into the bounds of theory? Critical realism, the philosophy of internal relations and the solution of 'uneven and combined development'. *Cambridge Review of International Affairs*, *26*(3), 573–597. doi:10.1080/09557571.2013.814045

Cox, K. R. (2008). Globalization, uneven development and capital: Reflections on reading Thomas Friedman's the world is flat. *Cambridge Journal of Regions, Economy and Society*, *1*(3), 389–410. doi:10.1093/cjres/rsn017

Davidson, N. (2009). Putting the nation back into 'the international'. *Cambridge Review of International Affairs*, *22*(1), 9–28. doi:10.1080/09557570802683920

Davidson, N. (2012). *How revolutionary were the bourgeois revolutions?* Chicago: Haymarket.

De Pleijt, A. M., & van Zanden, J. L. (2013). *The story of two transitions: Unified growth theory and the European growth experience, 1300–1870.* Paper presented at the Long-Run Growth: Unified Growth Theory and Economic History, University of Warwick, Coventry, 2013. Retrieved from http://www2.warwick.ac.uk/fac/soc/economics/research/centres/cage/events/conferences/longrungrowth/vanzanden.pdf

Desai, R. (2015). *Introduction: From the neoclassical diversion to geopolitical economy* (Vol. 30A. Research in Political Economy) (pp. 1–44). Bingley: Emerald Group. doi:10.1108/S0161-72302015000030A009

Dicken, P. (2010). *Global shift* (6th Ed.). New York: Guilford.

Dunford, M. (1979). Capital accumulation and regional development in France. *Geoforum, 10*(1), 81–108. doi:10.1016/0016-7185(79)90015-0

Dunford, M. (2005). Old Europe, new Europe and the USA: Comparative economic performance, inequality and market-led models of development. *European Urban and Regional Studies, 12*(2), 149–176. doi:10.1177/0969776405053742

Dunford, M., Aoyama, Y., Campolina Diniz, C., Kundu, A., Limonov, L., Lin, G., . . . Turok, I. (2016). Area development and policy: An agenda for the 21st century. *Area Development and Policy, 1*(1), 1–14. doi:10.1080/23792949.2016.1158621

Dunford, M. F., & Perrons, D. C. (1983). *The arena of capital.* London: Macmillan.

Feinstein, G. H. (1981). Capital accumulation and the Industrial Revolution. In R. A. M. D. N. Floud (Ed.), *The economic history of Britain since 1700* (Vol. 1, pp. 128–142). Cambridge: Cambridge University Press.

Gerschenkron, A. (1962). *Economic backwardness in historical perspective.* Cambridge, MA: Harvard University Press.

Hadjimichalis, C., & Hudson, R. (2014). Contemporary crisis across Europe and the crisis of regional development theories. *Regional Studies, 48*(1), 208–218. doi:10.1080/00343404.2013.834044

Haggard, S. (2015). The developmental state is dead: Long live the developmental state! In J. A. T. Mahoney & A. Kathleen (Eds.), *Comparative historical analysis in contemporary political science* (pp. 39–66). Cambridge: Cambridge University Press.

Harvey, D. (1982). *The limits to capital.* Oxford: Basil Blackwell.

Harvey, D. (2003). *The new imperialism.* Oxford: Oxford University Press.

Harvey, D. (2016). *Space and time of capital.* Beijing: Beijing Capital Normal University.

Hudson, R. (2016). Rising powers and the drivers of uneven global development. *Area Development and Policy, 1*(3), 279–294. doi:10.1080/23792949.2016.1227271

Kiely, R. (2012). Spatial hierarchy and/or contemporary geopolitics: What can and can't uneven and combined development explain? *Cambridge Review of International Affairs, 25*(2), 231–248. doi:10.1080/09557571.2012.678299

Kuznets, S. (1955). Economic growth and income inequality. *American Economic Review, 45*, 1–28.

Lewis, W. A. (1954). Economic development with unlimited supplies of labour. *Manchester School, 22*, 139–191. doi:10.1111/j.1467-9957.1954.tb00021.x

Lipietz, A. (1977). *Le capital et son espace (Capital and space).* Paris: François Maspero.

Liu, W., Dunford, M., Song, Z., & Chen, M. (2016). Urban–rural integration drives regional economic growth in Chongqing, Western China. *Area Development and Policy, 1*(1), 132–154. doi:10.1080/23792949.2016.1151758

Maddison, A. (2003). *The world economy: Historical statistics.* Paris: Organisation for Economic Co-operation and Development (OECD).

Makki, F. (2015). Reframing development theory: The significance of the idea of uneven and combined development. *Theory and Society, 44*(5), 471–497. doi:10.1007/s11186-015-9252-9

Massey, D. (1984). *Spatial divisions of labour.* London: Macmillan.

Matin, K. (2013). International relations in the making of political Islam: Interrogating Khomeini's 'Islamic government'. *Journal of International Relations and Development, 16*(4), 455–482. doi:10.1057/jird.2012.15

Myrdal, G. (1957). *Economic theory and underdeveloped regions.* London: Gerald Duckworth.

Peck, J. (2016). Macroeconomic geographies. *Area Development and Policy, 1*(3), 305–322. doi:10.1080/23792949.2016.1237263

Peck, J. (2017). Uneven regional development. In D. Richardson, N. Castree, M. F. Goodchild, A. Kobayashi, A. W. Liu, & R. A. Marston (Eds.), *The Wiley-AAG international encyclopedia of geography.* Oxford: Wiley-Blackwell.

Peck, J., & Theodore, N. (2007). Variegated capitalism. *Progress in Human Geography, 31*(6), 731–772. doi:10.1177/0309132507083505

Popov, V. (2014). *Mixed fortunes. An economic history of China, Russia and the West.* Oxford: Oxford University Press.

Rolf, S. (2015). *Locating the state: Uneven and combined development, the states system and the political* (Vol. 30A. Research in Political Economy) (pp. 113–153). Bingley: Emerald Group. doi:10.1108/S0161-72302015000030A009

Rosenberg, J. (2006). Why is there no international historical sociology? *European Journal of International Relations, 12*(3), 307–340. doi:10.1177/1354066106067345

Rosenberg, J. (2010). Basic problems in the theory of uneven and combined development. Part II: Unevenness and political multiplicity. *Cambridge Review of International Affairs, 23*(1), 165–189. doi:10.1080/09557570903524270

Rosenberg, J. (2016). Uneven and combined development: 'The international' in theory and history. In A. Anievas & K. Matin (Eds.), *Historical sociology and world history. Uneven and combined development over the Longue Durée* (pp. 17–30). London: Rowman & Littlefield International.

Rowthorn, R. (2010). Combined and uneven development: Reflections on the North–South divide. *Spatial Economic Analysis, 5*(4), 363–388. doi:10.1080/17421772.2010.516445

Saito, O. (2015). Growth and inequality in the great and little divergence debate: A Japanese perspective. *Economic History Review, 68*(2), 399–419. doi:10.1111/ehr.12071

Sheppard, E. (2016). *Limits to globalization: The disruptive geographies of capitalist development.* Oxford: Oxford University Press.

Smith, N. (1984). *Uneven development: Nature, capital and the production of space.* Oxford: Basil Blackwell.

Streeck, W. (2016). Does capitalism have a future? On the dismal future of capitalism. The future of capitalism. Unfettered capitalism eats itself. The next industrial revolution calls for a different economic system. *Socio-Economic Review, 14*(1), 163–183. doi:10.1093/ser/mwv037

Trotsky, L. (1928). *The Third International after Lenin.* Retrieved from https://www.marxists.org/archive/trotsky/1928/3rd/index.htm

Trotsky, L. (1930). *The history of the Russian Revolution.* Retrieved from https://www.marxists.org/archive/trotsky/1930/hrr/

Turok, I. (2016). Getting urbanization to work in Africa: The role of the urban land–infrastructure–finance nexus. *Area Development and Policy, 1*(1), 30–47. doi:10.1080/23792949.2016.1166444

United Nations Industrial Development Organization (UNIDO). (2016). *MVA 2016.* Vienna: UNIDO. Retrieved from http://stat.unido.org/

Van der Linden, M. (2007). The 'law' of uneven and combined development: Some underdeveloped thoughts. *Historical Materialism–Research in Critical Marxist Theory, 15*(1), 145–165. doi:10.1163/156920607X171627

Van Zanden, J. L., Baten, J., Foldvari, P., & van Leeuwen, B. (2014). The changing shape of global inequality 1820–2000; exploring a new dataset. *Review of Income and Wealth, 60*(2), 279–297. doi:10.1111/roiw.12014

The city as innovation machine

Richard Florida, Patrick Adler and Charlotta Mellander

ABSTRACT

The city as innovation machine. *Regional Studies*. This paper puts cities and urban regions at the very centre of the processes of innovation and entrepreneurship. It combines the insights of Jane Jacobs and recent urban research on the role of the city with the literature on innovation and entrepreneurship going back to Joseph Schumpeter. Innovation and entrepreneurship and their geography privileges the firm, industry clusters and/or the individual and poses the city as a container for them. By marrying Jacobs' insights on cities to those of Schumpeter on innovation, it is argued that innovation and entrepreneurship do not simply take in place in cities but in fact require them.

摘要

城市作为创新机器。*Regional Studies*。本文将城市与城市区域置放在创新与创业过程的核心。本文结合了简．雅各布斯与晚近对于城市角色的城市研究之洞见，以及可追溯至乔瑟夫．熊彼得的创新及创业精神之文献。创新和创精神及其地理，偏好企业、产业集群和／或个人，并将城市作为其容器。本文透过结合雅各布斯对城市的洞见和熊彼得对创新的洞见，主张创新和创业精神并不仅是在城市发生，而是无法脱离城市产生。

RÉSUMÉ

La ville en tant que moteur de l'innovation. *Regional Studies*. Cet article met les grandes villes et les régions urbaines au coeur des processus de l'innovation et de l'esprit d'entreprise. On associe les aperçus de Jane Jacobs et les recherches urbaines récentes sur le rôle de la ville à la documentation sur l'innovation et l'esprit d'entreprise remontant jusqu'à Joseph Schumpeter. L'innovation et l'esprit d'entreprise et leur géographie favorisent l'entreprise, les clusters d'industries et/ou l'individu et présentent la ville comme leur foyer. En associant les aperçus de Jacobs à propos des villes à ceux de Schumpeter au sujet de l'innovation, on affirme que

151

l'innovation et l'esprit d'entreprise ne se produisent pas tout simplement dans les villes mais en ont besoin en effet.

ZUSAMMENFASSUNG

Die Stadt als Innovationsmaschine. *Regional Studies*. In diesem Beitrag stellen wir Städte und Stadtregionen in den Mittelpunkt der Prozesse der Innovation und des Unternehmertums. Hierfür kombinieren wir die Erkenntnisse von Jane Jacobs und die aktuelle urbane Forschung über die Rolle der Stadt mit der Literatur über Innovation und Unternehmertum bis zurück zu Joseph Schumpeter. Innovation und Unternehmertum sowie ihre Geografie privilegieren die Firma, Branchencluster und/oder den Einzelnen und verwandeln die Stadt in einen Behälter dafür. Wir verbinden die Erkenntnisse von Jacobs über Städte mit denen von Schumpeter über Innovation und argumentieren, dass Innovation und Unternehmertum nicht einfach nur in Städten stattfinden, sondern diese vielmehr benötigen.

RESUMEN

La ciudad como máquina de innovación. *Regional Studies*. En este artículo se considera que las ciudades y las regiones urbanas son parte vital de los procesos de innovación y la iniciativa empresarial. Aquí combinamos las ideas de Jane Jacobs y los recientes estudios urbanos sobre el papel de la ciudad con la bibliografía sobre innovación e iniciativa empresarial desde Joseph Schumpeter. La innovación y la iniciativa empresarial, así como su geografía, conceden preferencias a la empresa, las aglomeraciones industriales y/o el individuo y convierten a la ciudad en su contenedor. Combinamos las ideas de Jacobs sobre las ciudades con las de Schumpeter sobre la innovación, y argumentamos que la innovación y la iniciativa empresarial no solo tienen lugar en las ciudades sino que las necesitan.

INTRODUCTION

Any way you slice it, innovation and entrepreneurship power economic growth. But most theories of economic growth and development dating back to the classical economists, Karl Marx and Joseph Schumpeter, and forward to modern growth theory associated with Robert Solow, Paul Romer and others, pose them as processes that operate at the firm or individual level. Entrepreneurship, after all, is typically viewed as the product of visionary business leaders from Thomas Edison and Henry Ford to Steven Jobs, Bill Gates, Larry Page and Sergey Brin, and Mark Zuckerberg. Innovation is seen as the product of forward-looking and resource-rich firms from DuPont and IBM to Apple, Microsoft and Google or great universities with their substantial research and development (R&D) efforts. Similarly, the human creativity that lies behind both innovation, a form of techno-logical creativity, and entrepreneurship, the application of human creativity for

more instrumental economic ends, is typically posed as the product of great creative individuals like the above or their artistic counterparts from Beethoven and
Mozart, Da Vinci and Michelangelo to Picasso and Warhol, Stravinsky, Armstrong
and Coltrane, McCartney and Lennon, and Hendrix. But recent research finds that
all three – innovation, entrepreneurship and creativity – are social processes that
involve groups of people and build off one another historically.

This paper extends a simple but provocative argument. It posits that the innovative
activities are the products of cities or regions (the terms 'city', 'region' and 'urban
region' are used throughout to refer to urban agglomerations or metropolitan areas).

The key processes that motivate technical advance, economic growth and
human progress writ large are the product not just of forward-looking individuals
and leading-edge firms, but of cities and urban regions. Cities and urban regions
are not just mere containers for innovative activities – but actively involved in the
generation of new ideas, new organizational forms and new enterprise.

In advancing this argument, one seeks to integrate the contributions of Schumpeter on innovation (Schumpeter, 1934a, 1934b) with those of Jane Jacobs on
cities (Jacobs, 1969), and also draw off the sizeable and growing literatures on the
geography of innovation, entrepreneurship and creativity. It is argued that under
knowledge-based capitalism the city and the region have emerged as the key
organizing unit for innovative activities, bringing together the firms, talent and
other regional institutions necessary for them.

Jacobs famously theorized that prevailing theories of innovation and economic
development going back to Smith (1776/1937) emphasize efficiency and the division of labour, but fail to account for the key inputs that drive innovation. Those,
she argued, were less a product of firms and more a product of cities and urban
regions which bring together the diversity of economic assets and actors required
for innovative and entrepreneurial activity. This paper brings together these
insights on the central role of cities and urban regions in the processes of innovation, creativity and entrepreneurship with the broader research literatures on their
industrial and geographical dynamics, essentially combining the insights of
Jacobs on cities with Schumpeter on the central role of innovation and entrepreneurship in economic growth and development.

The paper is organized as follows. It begins with a reprisal of Schumpeter's
theories of innovation and entrepreneurship, then turns to geography, with sections
on the more recent literature on the geography of innovation and the geography of
entrepreneurship. By innovation, this paper refers to technological progress that
expands to create new inventions, new products, new businesses and industries in
the form of new ideas, new inventions or new business practices and models.

By entrepreneurship this paper refers to the creation of new firms or start-up businesses that scale rapidly and have disruptive effects on their industries and/or the
economy broadly. It is less concerned with more routine process innovations or
small business start-ups that are created by necessity by entrepreneurs or take the
form of proverbial 'mom and pop' businesses. The paper then makes the broader
case that it is the city or region itself that lies at the very heart of the processes of
innovation and entrepreneurship. Here the fundamental insights of Jacobs on the

role of the city as the very source of innovation and growth are married with Schumpeter and his disciples' research on innovation, entrepreneurship and growth. The contention is that the city and region are the key social and economic organizing units for these processes, bringing together the diverse array of firms, talent, regional knowledge institutions, infrastructure and other inputs required for them to occur. In essence, innovation, entrepreneurship and creativity are less individual or firm-level processes and more quintessentially urban and regional ones.

SCHUMPETER'S INFLUENCE ON THEORIES OF INNOVATION AND ENTREPRENEURSHIP

The theory of innovation with its connection to economic growth dates back to Marx (1867/2012) and Schumpeter (1934a, 1934b, 1954). Marx argued that the rise of capitalism made technology an ongoing and disruptive force for economic growth. In his view the progress of capitalism was limited by the fundamental contradiction between growth and the flourishing of the forces of production and the constraints of the relations of production. Schumpeter updated Marx to take into account the processes of innovation and entrepreneurship. Instead of stalling out, falling into crisis and breaking out into class struggle, for Schumpeter innovation and entrepreneurship gave capitalism the possibility to reinvent itself continuously. Like Marx, he saw innovation and economic change as a disruptive, evolutionary process that occurs in bursts and cycles (Rosenberg, 2011).

Schumpeter saw innovation and entrepreneurship as the key factors in resetting the economy for new, long cycles of waves of economic growth. The uneven trajectory of economic change is propelled by processes within the 'development' sector of the economy – an area to be distinguished from equilibrium-governed 'circular flow' sector. At the centre of development are the visionary innovators or entrepreneurs who are motivated by more than just profit, but a desire for independence, distinction and accomplishment. The entrepreneur does not take technology as given, but instead seeks to shape its trajectory. Innovation is the dynamic in capitalism that allows it to transform itself in bursts of change.

In *The Theory of Economic Development*, Schumpeter (1934b) emphasized the role of smaller new firms, founded by entrepreneurs, in generating innovations. Small firms were said to better embody innovations which would replace older technologies and firms. His view changed in his later *Capitalism, Socialism, and Democracy* (Schumpeter, 1934a), a product of the rise of the rise of the large, vertically integrated enterprise, to focus on the central role of such large firms with their internal large R&D laboratories in the innovation process, something that he worried might dampen the innovation impetus over time.

In his work on *Business Cycles*, Schumpeter (1939) further argued that economic growth is highly cyclical and that innovation occurs in clusters or swarms of activity. Powered by innovation, economic growth and development is a discontinuous process that occurs in fits and starts and takes the form of a transition between disequilibrium states. As he put it later, 'the problem that is usually visualized is how capitalism administers existing structures, whereas the relevant problem is how it creates and destroys them' (Schumpeter, 1954, pp. 1734–1735). His felicitous phrase for this process was 'creative destruction'.

Schumpeter's theories of innovation, entrepreneurship and economic growth have been widely influential in economics, economic geography and regional studies. His treatment of innovation as endogenous to the economic system was early theoretical inspiration for more empirical work by Griliches (1957) and Schmookler (1966) as well as the broader theory of economic growth (Aghion & Howitt, 1992; Grossman & Helpman, 1993). Schumpeter's insights also lie at the heart of evolutionary economics à la Nelson and Winter (1982), and helped to shape the theory of industry life cycles (Klein, 1977; Klepper, 1996; Utterback & Abernathy, 1975; Vernon, 1966), some of which have been directly applied to regional development (Audretsch & Feldman, 1996). The basic insight here is that that industries and innovations each have more or less set lifetimes. The intensity of an industry's innovativeness is frontloaded in time toward the early part of its life. Eventually dominant organizational forms and product designs are established, products become standardized and both innovation and economic growth ebbs.

THE GEOGRAPHY OF INNOVATION

Geographers and regional scientists have brought a missing spatial dimension to the study of innovation and entrepreneurship. Research on the geography of innovation and entrepreneurship seeks to understand the geographical distribution of innovation, the spatial correlates of innovative regions, and the local processes that shape these geographical patterns. Innovation has numerous trace elements including codifiable knowledge (patents, copyrights), product improvements and venture capital. Across each of them, geographers and regional scientists have found innovation be highly concentrated across and within cities and metro areas.

Jaffe, Trajtenberg, and Henderson (1993) find that innovation (measured by patents and patent citations) are heavily concentrated in a relatively small number of university regions and corporate R&D centres. Innovation is also highly localized, finding that local patents were more likely to be cited by an inventor than similar patents from beyond a labour market (see also Acs, Audretsch, & Feldman, 1992; Anselin, Varga, & Acs, 1997; Jaffe, 1989; Jaffe et al., 1993; Thompson, 2006; Trajtenberg, 1990).

Innovation is considerably more geographically concentrated than traditional production or manufacturing activities (Feldman & Kogler, 2010). Across the world, innovative activity, whether measured through patents or scientific publication, is far more clustered and concentrated than population and/or production activity (Florida, 2002, 2005). Early-stage economic activities, which are tied to innovation, are more likely to require clustering and agglomeration. Research, design, testing and even the manufacture of new products and technologies arise in clustered environments where industrial actors congregate together. As these products become mature and more standardized, however, the benefits of co-location and agglomeration ebb, and production activities can be spread out across space (Ellison & Glaeser, 1999).

But patents are but one measure of innovation. Acs and Audretsch (1988, 1990) developed an alternative approach to measuring commercial innovation based on product innovation. Their research found commercial product innovations to be more concentrated in space than patents. Feldman and Florida (1994) used the same data and approach to examine the geography of innovation. Innovation varies greatly over space, they found, and is connected to a region's underlying 'technological infrastructure', which they defined as the level of local R&D activity, as well as its support services and localization of related research and commercialization activity.

Venture capital investment is another way of measuring commercially relevant innovation. Regional scientists have examined the geographical variation in flows of venture capital investment (Martin, Sunley, & Turner, 2002; Saxenian & Sabel, 2008). Venture capital is a crucial link in the division of labour that attends radical innovation. Venture and angel investment firms play the part of Schumpeterian financiers, connecting new process innovations with investment capital in the hope of realizing super profits. Florida and Kenney (1988, 2000) show that venture capital investment is spatially concentrated, with Silicon Valley winning the highest absolute and relative concentrations, and a handful of other regions rounding out the absolute rankings. Venture capital is found to flow between a discrete set of regions, for instance from finance-intensive New York, to technology-based Silicon Valley. These connections tend to be more network based than in other parts of the economy. Lead investors for local investment syndicates will closely monitor new opportunities. Regions with high levels of venture capital, then, tend to contain these networks, which themselves are structured to support the localization of venture capital (Powell, Koput, Bowie, & Smith-Doerr, 2002).

Theorizing on the clustering and localization of innovative economy activity dates back to Alfred Marshall (Marshall, 1890). He identified three mechanisms for why agglomeration in industrial districts would increase productivity: access to a thicker and more specialized labour market, access to more specialized services, and access to non-excludable knowledge. As he famously put it, 'The mysteries of the trade become no mystery: but are as it were, in the air.'

The Marshallian model has been influential on students of the geography of innovation. The non-excludable properties of knowledge allow them to spill more freely within the local region than within the national or international innovation system. There is extensive literature devoted to the Marshallian industrial district (Becattini, 1990; Cooke, Uranga, & Etxebarria, 1997; Saxenian, 1990, 1996; Storper & Walker, 1989). An industrial district can be distinguished as a fertile area for innovation due to its sharing of intermediate goods and financing, and its strong actor/networks which both match firms and labour and that help to efficiently transmit codified knowledge.

From the perspective of urban economics, there is Marshall–Arrow–Romer (MAR) theory that agglomerations of firms benefit primarily from knowledge spillovers between proximate firms in the same industry. This work recognizes not just the contributions of Marshall but also Arrow (1962) and Romer (1990) who created formal models that explained growth through the non-rivalrous, non-excludable nature of knowledge.

Another explanation for the clustering of innovation comes from the so-called New Economic Geography (NEG) (Fujita & Thisse, 1996; Krugman, 1990, 1991, 1998; Venables, Fujita, & Krugman, 1999). Its core–periphery model considers how price effects inside the firm can act to promote agglomeration. Firms huddle together near the most customers in order to minimize the final costs of their products. Hysteresis is a key feature of NEG models. When trade costs are intermediate there can be one of two equilibrium outcomes, either agglomeration or dispersion, depending on the existing level of agglomeration.

Still another approach comes from evolutionary economics and its applications to geography. New industries owe their spatial pattern to specific firms' behaviours, which have considerable spatial inertia (Dosi, 1997; Essletzbichler & Rigby, 2007; Frenken, Van Oort, & Verburg, 2007; Hodgson & Knudsen, 2004). The creation of new technologies and products is path dependent and tends to occur in places which already have considerable technological capacity. The firm itself is a collection of routines that repeat themselves over time. Location is one such behaviour. But radical new innovations emerge in new locations, where the lock-in effects of old technology can be avoided. Storper and Walker (1989) note that radical technologies open 'new windows of locational opportunity' and lead to more dramatic changes in the urban hierarchy. The window of location opportunity closes as firm routines are replicated in space.

Jacobs (1969) provides yet another view, arguing that economic diversity stimulates innovation and urban growth. Here meaningful innovation is seen as the recombination of disparate inputs, the most meaningful knowledge spillovers cross industry boundaries. There is strong empirical support for the Jacobs' theory. Glaeser, Kallal, Scheinkman, and Shleifer (1991) find variety, not specialization, is related to urban growth. Carlino, Chatterjee, and Hunt (2007) find that employment density predicts patents per capita. Bettencourt, Lobo, Helbing, Kühnert, and West (2007) show that patenting scales super-linearly with city size. Strumsky, Lobo, and Fleming (2005) find that the influence of local co-patenting networks on agglomeration of innovation is dwarfed by the influence of urbanization. Research on related variety (Boschma & Iammarino, 2009; Frenken et al., 2007) shows the influence of activities in distinct but related industries.

Duranton and Puga's (2001) 'nursery city' model makes the important point that cities act as incubators of innovation. Their framework marries the industry life cycle to theories of MAR and Jacobs, identifying two kinds of places: specialized places where all final and intermediate producers belong in the same industry, and diverse places where there is an equal share of agents from all sectors.

THE GEOGRAPHY OF ENTREPRENEURSHIP

Geographers and regional scientists have also brought a key spatial dimension to understanding entrepreneurship. Entrepreneurship is measured in various ways by looking at rates of firm formation, small business formation, technology-intensive business formation and clustering, high-tech start-ups and venture capital investment, and other measures. As noted above, the focus here is mainly on disruptive entrepreneurship of the Schumpetarian variety.

Like innovation, entrepreneurial activity is found to be heavily clustered in space (Armington & Acs, 2002; Sternberg, 2009). Entrepreneurial success itself is found to be clustered around existing agglomerations. New ventures within established clusters have higher employment growth and revenue across a range of industry contexts (Canina, Enz, & Harrison, 2005; Gilbert, McDougall, & Audretsch, 2006; Porter, 1998). Entrepreneurial failure seems to be similarly clustered (Folta, Cooper, & Baik, 2006; Shaver & Flyer, 2000).

The idea that some places are more attractive to entrepreneurship has been around for a while. Baumol (1968) was among the first to focus on the supply of entrepreneurs, and factors that affect entrepreneurial incentives. Baumol, Litan, and Schramm (2007) condense the recipe for entrepreneurial success to four factors: high returns, low start-up costs, disincentives for rent-seeking and competitive pressures on winning entrepreneurs.

Chinitz (1961) originally identified significant geographical variation in entrepreneurial activity. He compared New York and Pittsburgh and found their different growth trajectories to turn on differences in the diversity of their industries, the former being oriented toward greater diversity and more smaller, entrepreneurial firms, the latter being dominated by large, vertically integrated companies in a single industry. Glaeser, Kerr, and Ponzetto (2010) found substantial evidence for Chinitz theory: the economies with diverse clusters of small and medium-sized firms outperform those dominated by large firms.

The composition of the regional talent base or labour force has been found to influence the regional distribution of entrepreneurial activities. Human capital has been found to be closely associated with entrepreneurship at an individual level in studies from North America (Evans & Leighton, 1989; Roberts, 1991) and Europe (Bosma & Sternberg, 2014; Fritsch, Brixy, & Falck, 2006; Hundt & Sternberg, 2016; Wyrwich, Stuetzer, & Sternberg, 2016). Glaeser (2007) finds that roughly half the geographical variation in entrepreneurship can be explained by human capital along with industry structure compared with just 7% of entrepreneurship at the individual level.

Differences in regional labour supply or talent also affect the supply of entrepreneurs. Immigration (Froschauer, 2001; Kloosterman & Rath, 2001; Saxenian, 1999) can help improve entrepreneurial success by establishing essential network connections between the entrepreneur and foreign expertise/markets. Lee, Florida, and Acs (2004) find that firm formation across US metros is related to creativity as well as an index of diversity, which measures the openness of an area to outsiders.

A separate research stream differentiates between so-called 'opportunity-oriented' and 'necessity-oriented' entrepreneurship (Bosma & Sternberg, 2014; Short, Ketchen, Shook, & Ireland, 2009; Stam, 2007, 2015). In a European Study, Bosma and Sternberg (2014) found that entrepreneurship which is pulled by the promise of profit tends to be more clustered in cities than that which is compelled by a lack of options. Regional entrepreneurial opportunity has been found to be related to several elements of regional structure including R&D availability (Feldman, 2001; Fritsch & Wyrwich, 2014) and industrial structure (Glaeser, 2007).

In addition to theories and studies that explain geographical differences in entrepreneurship through the supply of human capital, there are others that examine regional treatment effects. The formation of new firms has been described as a 'regional event' (Feldman, 2001), which is launched from conditions that operate across and around firms. The region itself thus acts as a spur to entrepreneurial activity.

PUTTING THE CITY AND THE REGION AT THE CENTRE OF THE PROCESS OF INNOVATION

The paper now turns to the centrepiece of its argument. Advances in geographical and regional theory have helped one better understand the quintessential spatial dynamics of both innovation and entrepreneurship. Both activities are seen as concentrated in space and taking shape through geographically clustered processes. The argument builds from these advances to put the city and region at the centre of innovative and entrepreneurial activity. The city and region thus provide the basic platform for organizing the firms, individuals, talent, and other institutions and services that drive these critical processes. Essentially, innovation and entrepreneurship are more quintessentially spatial processes as opposed to firm- or individual-level ones. Indeed, it is contended that *place* has replaced the industrial corporation as the key economic and social organizing unit in the modern-day knowledge economy.

There is a longstanding literature that places cities at the centre of the creative process. New innovations, routines and industries tend to start in the urban 'nursery' (Duranton & Puga, 2001). Cities are simultaneously a place where skilled workers assemble and interact, and an organizational technology for that interaction. Regional theorists are accustomed, in their day-to-day lives, to describing cities as the catchment areas for a common set of rules and other institutions. In the authors' view, the city is the ultimate enabler of innovation, entrepreneurship and growth.

Jacobs (1969) stands out as the theorist who has come closest to expressing how cities and regions actively spur innovation and entrepreneurship. Whereas mainstream economics sets developments stories at the scale of the firm, the entrepreneur and the national economy, Jacobs put cities at the centre of the processes of innovation, entrepreneurship and economic growth. This rescaling involves a move away from specialization and cost reduction as mechanisms for development. The urban economy is not governed by a single production function, nor can it optimize within that. If firms have an intensive margin for growth, cities have an extensive margin. Scope and diversity trump scale and specialization. The city collects skills, firms and physical capital and provides a physical platform for them to be recombined into new and productive forms. Together, all these insights set up a distinctly urban model of growth. In fact, Jacobs summarized her own central contribution as follows (Stiegerwald, 2001):

> If I were to be remembered as a really important thinker of the century, the most important thing I've contributed is, 'What makes economic expansion happen?' This is something that has puzzled people always. I think I've figured out what it is, and expansion and development are two different things. Development is differentiation – new differentiation of what already existed. Practically every new thing that happens is a differentiation of a previous thing. Just about everything – from a new shoe sole to changes in legal codes – all of those things are differentiations. Expansion is an actual growth in size or volume of activity. That is a different thing.
>
> (Jacobs, 2001)

Specialization is the second-nature advantage that predicts continued growth. Since Adam Smith's classic *The Wealth of Nations* (1776), growth has been assumed to follow from a more intensive division of labour. Ricardo's slightly later vision of comparative advantage rooted national growth in the ability of countries to specialize and trade (Ricardo, 1817/1965). An emphasis on specialization and trade has resurfaced in the disciplines of regional science and regional economic geography, which each tend to prize the ability of regions to develop specialized economic bases.

Specialization involves lowering unit costs through an expansion of scale. A region would support this process by providing lower transaction costs to its firms. Lower taxes, subsidized infrastructure and business services are all attempts to stimulate the development process by reducing the cost of doing business. A place-centred theory of innovation, entrepreneurship and economic growth stands in opposition to views that emphasize efficiency and specialization, and can more comfortably account for the way these processes actually occur.

Here, the parallels between Jacobs and Schumpeter are striking. Expansion is the humdrum growth dimension that Schumpeter would have called 'circular flow'. Growth is achieved through an expansion of output, and bigger and smaller places are distinguished by mere quantitative differences in their output levels. Jacobs and Schumpeter each prized a second, radical type of growth that was propelled by innovation, not specialization. Novelty was seen as the mechanism for growth, not specialization; the production of new things was seen as crucial when compared with the production of more things at lower cost. Diversity in inputs is seen as crucial. The big city, in addition to having more costs and people, has a more complex set of functions that become self-organized. Urban growth is an emergent process that unfolds endogenously according to the related parameters of size and diversity.

In his Nobel Prize-winning work on growth, Lucas (1998, p. 7) placed Jacobs' work on the city at the very the centre of the process of economic growth itself:

I will be following very closely the lead of Jane Jacobs, whose remarkable book, *The Economy of Cities*, seems to me mainly and convincingly concerned (although she does not use this terminology) with the external effects of human capital.

Lucas's focus on these 'Jane Jacobs externalities' led him to an endogenous theory of growth that privileged interactions between people that occur in cities. Cumulative and everyday knowledge spillovers between agents led to dynamic growth. As Lucas framed it, the city – as it attracts and pushes together talented and creative people – is itself the central factor and unit of analysis in innovation, entrepreneurship and economic growth:

> If we postulate only the usual list of economic forces, cities should fly apart. The theory of production contains nothing to hold a city together. A city is simply a collection of factors of production – capital, people and land – and land is always far cheaper outside cities than inside. . . . It seems to me that the 'force' we need to postulate to account for the central role of cities in economic life is of exactly the same character as the 'external human capital.' . . . What can people be paying Manhattan or downtown Chicago rents for, if not for being near other people?
>
> (p. 39)

The factors of production: labour, capital and technical expertise were important in the way that are the ingredients of a recipe. However, the recipe itself – the way in which these interact – is determinative of growth. For Jacobs, Lucas and the authors, cities are a more conducive environment for this, the place the recipe gets made.

There are clear indications that innovative and entrepreneurial activities, which have long been understood to be spatially clustered and concentrated, are now becoming more quintessentially urban and place based.

First, innovation (measured by patents) has become increasingly concentrated in one place: the San Francisco Bay Area. Forman, Goldfarb, and Greenstein (2016) show that the Bay Area has accounted for virtually all the increase in patenting in the United States since the mid-1970s, while patenting in all other large metros either stagnated or declined.

Second, entrepreneurship measured as start-up activity has become even more concentrated than innovation. The Bay Area's share of venture capital-backed start-ups increased from roughly 22% in 1995 to more than 45% by 2015. The only other US metro to see its share of start-ups increase over this period was New York (Florida & Mellander, 2014).

Third, the past couple of decades have seen a massive shift in entrepreneurial start-up activity of the high-tech Schumpetarian variety away from traditional suburban locations to urban centres. Early research on high-tech industry and venture capital finance start-ups noted their concentration in suburban areas, or 'nerdistans' like Silicon Valley, the Route 128 suburbs outside Boston, or the suburbs of Austin and Seattle. Across the United States, more than half of all start-up neighbourhoods are urban, with 57% of start-up companies and 54% of venture capital investments located in urban zip codes. In effect, start-up activity has shifted back to dense cities and urban areas, which have the talent and diversity to generate them. It is likely that the previous suburban orientation of high-tech and start-ups was an aberration caused by the large corporate structures of the industrial age. Now innovation and start-up activity is, in effect, shifting back to denser urban areas which are more predisposed to it and serve as the key organizing unit for it (Florida & Mellander, 2014).

Fourth, high-tech start-up activity is not only concentrated at the metro level but also massively concentrated in neighbourhood-level micro-clusters. Just the top 20 zip codes across the United States account for more than US$10 billion in venture capital investment – roughly one-third of the national total. Furthermore, less than 1% (0.2%) of all zip codes, or 83 neighbourhoods, attract more than US$100 million in venture capital investment, representing over 60% of all venture capital investment nationwide. There are two small neighbourhoods in downtown San Francisco that attract more than US$1 billion in venture capital each, more than any other nation in the world outside the United States. This research indicates that these micro-clusters have formed in older, underutilized and, in many cases, formerly derelict urban neighbourhoods where no existing firm clusters were located. In other words, these micro-clusters emerged in relative isolation from existing firm- or individual-level capabilities. They are self-generating from the place itself (Florida & Mellander, 2014).

This is even more the case for high-quality entrepreneurial firms. Guzman and Stern (2015) chart the geographical distribution and distribution of high-quality entrepreneurial activity in the regions of Boston, San Francisco and Miami, showing that the centre of gravity for entrepreneurship has shifted from the exurban Route 128 area to downtown Boston and dense transit-served areas of Cambridge around MIT and Harvard, and Silicon Valley to the downtown and adjacent areas of San Francisco. While these regions had high levels of both overall entrepreneurship and geographical change, Miami, a city with high levels of self-employment, did not. They attribute these changes to entrepreneurial quality, concluding that low-quality entrepreneurial ecosystems will not *become* urbanized over time, while high-quality ecosystems become more highly urbanized.

The weight of this evidence thus supports the central contention that the city and the region lie at the very centre of the processes of innovation and entrepreneurship and form the basic spatial platform for these processes. It is the city itself that brings together the firms, individuals, talent, and other institutions and services that drive these critical processes. Essentially, innovation and entrepreneurship are more quintessentially urban or regional processes than firm- or individual-level ones.

Indeed, in the authors' view, place has come to replace the industrial corporation as the key economic and social organizing unit of our time. Cities have always been important engines of economic growth, but they are assuming an even greater importance in today's knowledge-driven innovation economy, where place-based ecosystems are critical to economic growth. But brainpower alone only tells part of the story. Even more key is the aptitude for marshalling and focusing all that raw intelligence that is on tap. Cities are not just containers for smart people: they are the enabling infrastructure where connections take place, networks are built and innovative combinations are consummated.

The relationship dates back through history, with the exception of the aberration of the industrial age. Over the course of history, certain cities have been fonts of innovative, creative and entrepreneurial activity. The Swedish regional scientist Åke E. Andersson frames it thus: 'Creative people need creative cities' (Andersson, 2011, p. 39). He focuses on how fifth-century BCE Athens, Renaissance Florence, Enlightenment London and fin-de-siècle Vienna became platforms for disruptive creative output:

> In the course of the past 2,500 years, a small number of relatively large cities have functioned as hotbeds of revolutionary creativity. These cities attracted a disproportionate share of migrants with creative inclinations, and they also facilitated the growth of creativity among those already present. Such cities were both used as arenas for presenting findings from elsewhere and as fertile locations for developing new ideas in collaboration with other creative people.

But, even this might understate the relationship between agglomeration and human ingenuity. Archaeological research finds that some of humankind's earliest technological and cultural early advances occurred in parts of the Middle East and Africa which had the highest population densities at that point in development (Shennan, 2002; Shennan et al., 2013). Other research finds a close link between early advances in primitive tool-making and the density of human settlement. In both cases, additive changes in the density of the local population can be said to create qualitative changes in technological and economic development. It is worth remembering that these breakthroughs happened in an environment with lower-than-modern levels of trade and specialization (Boyd & Richerson, 1988).

The city can be seen as a meso-level *treatment* for their residents, an active influence on how the mind of a creative worker forms. They do this in two ways. As Simonton (2011) notes, they assemble personal role models, who can influence the development of the young, more plastic mind. They also provide the diverse ideational milieu that will allow the creative mind to better overcome blocks in the creative process. It is common for the creative mind to return to ordinary life in the moments when it cannot solve an important problem. In the urban environment, there are many more diverse, but related, influences that might trigger a solution via what is commonly understood as a eureka moment. These insights challenge the idea that creation is a solitary pursuit and an outgrowth of some preformed genius.

Modern society instead *enables* creative output by organizing actors in conducive arrangements. The research laboratory, so prominent in late Schumpeter, is actually only a more artificial and limited example of such an arrangement. The city with its greater levels of density and diversity is the more eternally conducive environment for generating the human creativity that underpins innovation, entrepreneurship and economic growth.

This paper has contrasted literature on the geography of creativity with that of innovation and entrepreneurship. It has argued that radical innovation, in the Schumpeterian sense, is more a function of scope economies and diversity than scale economies and specialization and, in this sense, that innovation and entrepreneurship do not simply take in place in but *require* cities.

The authors would like to encourage future research on the geography of creativity, innovation and entrepreneurship across several dimensions. For one, it is useful to consider innovation more broadly than technological innovation per se to include innovations in businesses processes, service industries, and occupations as well as industries. Such a broader view of innovation opens up new sources of data and expands the focus to other sectors of the economy and society where much is to be learned about the clustering and geography of creativity and innovation. Much of the literature has focused on innovative industries. But there is much to be learned from the geographical concentration of innovative occupations. In is important to know not just where high-tech industries are clustered but where the talent that underpins them is concentrated: do they co-locate or are there different locational centres? Do some places specialize in certain dimensions of the spatial division of innovative talent? Furthermore, research on the spatial distribution of creative industries like music and the arts and creative occupations like musicians and artists can help one better understand how and why creativity and innovation cluster in environments which have virtually no physical constraints of the sort that shape the geography of traditional or even high-tech industries, such as access to raw materials, or location near ports and harbours, or access to universities per se. The music industry illustrates the central role of the city in organizing the creative process. Musicians today need little more than a laptop and an internet connection to record and distribute music. There is, moreover, a local music market in every large village or city that provides musical instruments, lessons and performances. One might expect this industry to 'fly apart' in Lucas's terms, yet exactly the opposite is observed. Music is among the most highly concentrated of all activities (Adler, 2014; Agrawal, Catalini, & Goldfarb, 2011; Currid, 2007; Florida & Jackson, 2010; Florida, Mellander, & Stolarick, 2010, 2012; Markusen & Schrock, 2006; Storper & Christopherson, 1987). Understanding why will better inform our theories of the geography of creativity and innovation.

The authors further encourage research to focus on the competition for space that stems from the concentration of innovation, entrepreneurship and creativity in a relatively small number of superstar cities and knowledge hubs. Alonso (1964) long ago outlined a general model of the competition for space. For much of history, firms and corporations competed for land at the centre of the city with households located further afield. The modern city is now the subject of an attenuated competition for space which Scott dubs the 'urban land nexus' (Scott, 1980). A key question then becomes: to what degree, then, might this heightened competition for space eventually displace creativity and innovation from established cities (Florida, 2017)? As Jacobs once said, 'when a place gets boring even the rich people leave'. An improved model of urban innovation and entrepreneurship with place at its centre would better identify how the cyclicality of the urban land market can enable and disable creative activity, explaining in part the tendency of innovations to swarm and the broader rise and decline of specific places as centres for innovation, entrepreneurship and economic growth.

This paper has argued that the firm has been too much the centre of the literature on the geography of innovation and entrepreneurship and that it is time to put the city at the very centre. As shown in this paper, the city, the region and the place are not just the containers where innovation and entrepreneurship happen, they are the key mechanisms which enable them.

DISCLOSURE STATEMENT

No potential conflict of interest was reported by the authors.

REFERENCES

Acs, Z. J., & Audretsch, D. B. (1988). Innovation in large and small firms: An empirical analysis. *American Economic Review, 78*(4), 678–690.

Acs, Z. J., & Audretsch, D. B. (1990). *Innovation and small firms*. Cambridge, MA: MIT Press.

Acs, Z. J., Audretsch, D. B., & Feldman, M. P. (1992). Real effects of academic research: comment. *American Economic Review, 82*(1), 363–367.

Adler, P. (2014). From capitol to Coachella: Exploring the role of Coachella in LA's music cluster. *California Policy Options, 19*, 165–191.

Aghion, P., & Howitt, P. (1992). *A model of growth through creative destruction* (NBER Working Paper No. 3223). Cambridge, MA: National Bureau of Economic Research (NBER). Retrieved from http://www.nber.org/papers/w3223

Agrawal, A. K., Catalini, C., & Goldfarb, A. (2011). *The geography of crowdfunding* (NBER Working Paper No. 16820). Cambridge, MA: National Bureau of Economic Research (NBER). Retrieved from http://www.nber.org/papers/w16820

Alonso, W. (1964). *Location and land use. Toward a general theory of land rent.* Cambridge, MA: Harvard University Press.

Andersson, Å. E. (2011). Creative people need creative cities. In D. Andersson, Å. E. Andersson, & C. Mellander (Eds.), *Handbook of creative cities* (pp. 14–55). Cheltenham: Edward Elgar.

Anselin, L., Varga, A., & Acs, Z. (1997). Local geographic spillovers between university research and high technology innovations. *Journal of Urban Economics, 42*(3), 422–448. doi:10.1006/juec. 1997.2032

Armington, C., & Acs, Z. J. (2002). The determinants of regional variation in new firm formation. *Regional Studies, 36*(1), 33–45. doi:10.1080/00343400120099843

Arrow, K. J. (1962). The economic implications of learning by doing. *Review of Economic Studies, 29*, 155–173. doi:10.2307/2295952

Audretsch, D. B., & Feldman, M. P. (1996). R&D spillovers and the geography of innovation and production. *American Economic Review*, *86*(3), 630–640.

Baumol, W. J. (1968). Entrepreneurship in economic theory. *American Economic Review*, *58*(2), 64–71.

Baumol, W. J., Litan, R. E., & Schramm, C. J. (2007). Sustaining entrepreneurial capitalism. *Capitalism and Society*, *2*(2), 1–36. doi:10.2202/1932-0213.1026

Becattini, G. (1990). The Marshallian industrial as a socio-economic notion. In F. Pyke (Ed.), *Industrial districts and inter-firm co-operation in Italy* (pp. 37–52). Geneva: International Institute of Labour Studies.

Bettencourt, L. M., Lobo, J., Helbing, D., Kühnert, C., & West, G. B. (2007). *Growth, innovation, scaling, and the pace of life in cities. Proceedings of the National Academy of Sciences*, *104*(17), 7301–7306. doi:10.1073/pnas.0610172104

Boschma, R., & Iammarino, S. (2009). Related variety, trade linkages, and regional growth in Italy. *Economic Geography*, *85*(3), 289–311. doi:10.1111/j.1944-8287.2009.01034.x

Bosma, N., & Sternberg, R. (2014). Entrepreneurship as an urban event? Empirical evidence from European cities. *Regional Studies*, *48*(6), 1016–1033. doi:10.1080/00343 404.2014.904041

Boyd, R., & Richerson, P. J. (1988). *Culture and the evolutionary process*. Chicago: University of Chicago Press.

Canina, L., Enz, C. A., & Harrison, J. S. (2005). Agglomeration effects and strategic orientations: Evidence from the US lodging industry. *Academy of Management Journal*, *48*(4), 565–581. doi:10.5465/AMJ.2005.17843938

Carlino, G. A., Chatterjee, S., & Hunt, R. M. (2007). Urban density and the rate of invention. *Journal of Urban Economics*, *61*(3), 389–419. doi:10.1016/j.jue.2006.08.003

Chinitz, B. (1961). Contrasts in agglomeration: New York and Pittsburgh. *American Economic Review*, *51*(2), 279–289.

Cooke, P., Uranga, M. G., & Etxebarria, G. (1997). Regional innovation systems: institutional and organisational dimensions. *Research Policy*, *26*(4), 475–491. doi:10.1016/ S0048-7333 (97)00025-5

Currid, E. (2007). *The Warhol economy: How fashion, art, and music drive New York City*. Princeton: Princeton University Press.

Dosi, G. (1997). Opportunities, incentives and the collective patterns of technological change. *Economic Journal*, *107*(444), 1530–1547. doi:10.1111/j.1468-0297.1997. tb00064.x

Duranton, G., & Puga, D. (2001). Nursery cities: Urban diversity, process innovation, and the life cycle of products. *American Economic Review*, *91*(5), 1454–1477. doi:10.1257/ aer.91.5.1454

Ellison, G., & Glaeser, E. L. (1999). The geographic concentration of industry: Does natural advantage explain agglomeration? *American Economic Review*, *89*(2), 311–316. doi:10.1257/aer. 89.2.311

Essletzbichler, J., & Rigby, D. L. (2007). Exploring evolutionary economic geographies. *Journal of Economic Geography*, *7*, 549–571. doi:10.1093/jeg/lbm022

Evans, D. S., & Leighton, L. S. (1989). Some empirical aspects of entrepreneurship. *American Economic Review*, *79*(3), 519–535.

Feldman, M. P. (2001). The entrepreneurial event revisited: firm formation in a regional context. *Industrial and Corporate Change*, *10*(4), 861–891. doi:10.1093/ icc/10.4.861

Feldman, M. P., & Florida, R. (1994). The geographic sources of innovation: Technological infrastructure and product innovation in the United States. *Annals of the*

Association of American Geographers, *84*(2), 210–229. doi:10.1111/j.1467-8306.1994.tb01735.x

Feldman, M. P., & Kogler, D. F. (2010). Stylized facts in the geography of innovation. *Handbook of the Economics of Innovation*, *1*, 381–410. doi:10.1016/S0169-7218(10)01008-7

Florida, R. (2002). *The rise of the creative class*. New York: Basic Books.

Florida, R. (2005). The world is spiky. *Atlantic Monthly, October*, 48–51.

Florida, R. (2017). *The new urban crisis*. New York: Basic Books.

Florida, R., & Jackson, S. (2010). Sonic city: The evolving economic geography of the music industry. *Journal of Planning Education and Research*, *29*(3), 310–321. doi:10.1177/0739456X09354453

Florida, R., & Mellander, C. (2014). *Rise of the startup city: The changing geography of the venture capital financed innovation* (Working Paper). CESIS, Royal Institute of Technology. Retrieved from https://static.sys.kth.se/itm/wp/cesis/cesiswp377.pdf/.

Florida, R., Mellander, C., & Stolarick, K. (2010). Music scenes to music clusters: The economic geography of music in the US, 1970–2000. *Environment and Planning A*, *42*(4), 785–804. doi:10.1068/a4253

Florida, R., Mellander, C., & Stolarick, K. (2012). Geographies of scope: An empirical analysis of entertainment, 1970–2000. *Journal of Economic Geography*, *12*(1), 183–204. doi:10.1093/jeg/lbq056

Florida, R. L., & Kenney, M. (1988). Venture capital-financed innovation and technological change in the USA. *Research Policy*, *17*(3), 119–137. doi:10.1016/0048-7333(88)90038-8

Florida, R., & Kenney, M. (2000). Transfer and replication of organizational capabilities: Japanese transplant organizations in the United States. In G. Dosi, R. Nelson, & S. Winter (Eds.), *The nature and dynamics of organizational capabilities*. Oxford: Oxford University Press.

Folta, T. B., Cooper, A. C., & Baik, Y. (2006). Geographic cluster size and firm performance. *Journal of Business Venturing*, *21*(2), 217–242. doi:10.1016/j.jbusvent.2005.04.005

Forman, C., Goldfarb, A., & Greenstein, S. (2016). Agglomeration of invention in the Bay area: Not just ICT. *American Economic Review*, *106*(5), 146–151. doi:10.1257/aer.p20161018

Frenken, K., Van Oort, F., & Verburg, T. (2007). Related variety, unrelated variety and regional economic growth. *Regional Studies*, *41*(5), 685–697. doi:10.1080/00343400601120296

Fritsch, M., Brixy, U., & Falck, O. (2006). The effect of industry, region, and time on new business survival: A multi-dimensional analysis. *Review of Industrial Organization*, *28*(3), 285–306. doi:10.1007/s11151-006-0018-4

Fritsch, M., & Wyrwich, M. (2014). The long persistence of regional levels of entrepreneurship: Germany 1925–2005. *Regional Studies*, *48*(6), 955–973. doi:10.1080/00343404.2013.816414

Froschauer, K. (2001). East Asian and European entrepreneur immigrants in British Columbia, Canada: Post-migration conduct and pre-migration context. *Journal of Ethnic and Migration Studies*, *27*(2), 225–240. doi:10.1080/13691830020041589

Fujita, M., & Thisse, J.-F. (1996). Economics of agglomeration. *Journal of the Japanese and International Economies*, *10*(4), 339– 378. doi:10.1006/jjie.1996.0021

Gilbert, B. A., McDougall, P. P., & Audretsch, D. B. (2006). New venture growth: A review and extension. *Journal of Management*, *32*(6), 926–950. doi:10.1177/0149206306293860

Glaeser, E. L. (2007). *Entrepreneurship and the city* (No. w13551). Cambridge, MA: National Bureau of Economic Research (NBER).

Glaeser, E. L., Kallal, H. D., Scheinkman, J. A., & Shleifer, A. (1991). *Growth in cities* (NBER Working Paper No. 3787). Cambridge, MA: National Bureau of Economic Research (NBER). Retrieved from http://www.nber.org/papers/w3787

Glaeser, E. L., Kerr, W. R., & Ponzetto, G. A. (2010). Clusters of entrepreneurship. *Journal of Urban Economics, 67*(1), 150–168. doi:10.1016/j.jue.2009.09.008

Griliches, Z. (1957). Hybrid corn: An exploration in the economics of technological change. *Econometrica, 25*(4), 501–522. doi:10. 2307/1905380

Grossman, G. M., & Helpman, E. (1993). *Innovation and growth in the global economy.* Cambridge, MA: MIT Press.

Guzman, J., & Stern, S. (2015). *Nowcasting and placecasting: Entrepreneurial quality and performance* (NBER Working Paper No. 13493). Cambridge, MA: National Bureau of Economic Research (NBER). Retrieved from http://www.nber.org/chapters/c13493.pdf

Hodgson, G. M., & Knudsen, T. (2004). The firm as an interactor: firms as vehicles for habits and routines. *Journal of Evolutionary Economics, 14*(3), 281–307. doi:10.1007/s00191-004-0192-1

Hundt, C., & Sternberg, R. (2016). Explaining new firm creation in Europe from a spatial and time perspective: A multilevel analysis based upon data of individuals, regions and countries. *Papers in Regional Science, 95*(2), 223–257. doi:10.1111/pirs.12133

Jacobs, J. (1969). *The economy of cities.* New York: Vintage.

Jacobs, J. (2001). [Interview with Bill Steigerwald]. *City Views, June.* Retrieved from http://reason.com/archives/2001/06/01/cityviews/.

Jaffe, A. B. (1989). Real effects of academic research. *American Economic Review, 79*(5), 957–970.

Jaffe, A. B., Trajtenberg, M., & Henderson, R. (1993). Geographic localization of knowledge spillovers as evidenced by patent citations. *Quarterly Journal of Economics, 108*(3), 577–598. doi:10. 2307/2118401

Klein, B. H. (1977). *Dynamic economics.* Cambridge, MA: Harvard University Press.

Klepper, S. (1996). Entry, exit, growth, and innovation over the product life cycle. *American Economic Review, 86*(3), 562–583.

Kloosterman, R., & Rath, J. (2001). Immigrant entrepreneurs in advanced economies: Mixed embeddedness further explored. *Journal of Ethnic and Migration Studies, 27*(2), 189–201. doi:10. 1080/13691830020041561

Krugman, P. (1990). *Increasing returns and economic geography* (NBER Working Paper No. 3275). Cambridge, MA: National Bureau of Economic Research (NBER). Retrieved from http://www.nber.org/papers/w3275

Krugman, P. (1991). History and industry location: The case of the manufacturing belt. *American Economic Review, 81*(2), 80–83.

Krugman, P. (1998). What's new about the New Economic Geography? *Oxford Review of Economic Policy, 14*(2), 7–17. doi:10.1093/oxrep/14.2.7

Lee, S. Y., Florida, R., & Acs, Z. (2004). Creativity and entrepreneurship: A regional analysis of new firm formation. *Regional Studies, 38*(8), 879–891. doi:10.1080/0034340042000280910

Lucas, R. E. (1998). On the mechanics of economic development. *Journal of Monetary Economics,* 38–39.

Markusen, A., & Schrock, G. (2006). The artistic dividend: Urban artistic specialisation and economic development implications. *Urban Studies, 43*(10), 1661–1686. doi:10.1080/00420980600888478

Marshall, A. (1890). *Principles of economics* (8th Ed.). London: Macmillan.

Martin, R., Sunley, P., & Turner, D. (2002). Taking risks in regions: The geographical anatomy of Europe's emerging venture capital market. *Journal of Economic Geography*, *2*(2), 121–150. doi:10.1093/jeg/2.2.121

Marx, K. (1867/2012). *Das Kapital: A critique of political economy*. New York: Regnery.

Nelson, R. R., & Winter, S. G. (1982). *An evolutionary theory of economic change*. Boston: Belknap/Harvard University Press.

Porter, M. E. (1998). Cluster and the new economics of competition. *Harvard Business Review, December*, 77–90.

Powell, W. W., Koput, K. W., Bowie, J. I., & Smith-Doerr, L. (2002). The spatial clustering of science and capital: Accounting for biotech firm–venture capital relationships. *Regional Studies*, *36*(3), 291–305. doi:10.1080/00343400220122089

Ricardo, D. (1965). *The principles of political economy and taxation* [1817] (London: J. M. Dent & Son).

Roberts, E. B. (1991). *Entrepreneurs in high technology: Lessons from MIT and beyond*. Oxford: Oxford University Press.

Romer, P. M. (1990). Human capital and growth: Theory and evidence. *Carnegie-Rochester Conference Series on Public Policy*, *32*, 251–286. doi:10.1016/0167-2231(90)90028-J

Rosenberg, N. (2011). Was Schumpeter a Marxist? *Industrial and Corporate Change*, *20*(4), 1215–1222. doi:10.1093/icc/dtr037

Saxenian, A. (1990). Regional networks and the resurgence of Silicon Valley. *California Management Review*, *33* (1), 89–112. doi:10.2307/41166640

Saxenian, A. (1996). *Regional advantage*. Cambridge, MA: Harvard University Press.

Saxenian, A. (1999). *Silicon Valley's new immigrant entrepreneurs*.

San Francisco: Public Policy Institute of California. Retrieved from http://wee.ppic.org/content/pubs/report/R_699ASR.pdf

Saxenian, A., & Sabel, C. (2008). Roepke Lecture in Economic Geography: Venture capital in the 'periphery=': The new Argonauts, global search, and local institution building. *Economic Geography*, *84*(4), 379–394. doi:10.1111/j.1944-8287.2008.00001.x

Schmookler, J. (1966). *Invention and economic growth*. Cambridge, MA: Harvard University Press.

Schumpeter, J. A. (1934a). *Capitalism, socialism, and democracy*. London: Allen & Unwin.

Schumpeter, J. A. (1934b). *The theory of economic development: An inquiry into profits, capital, credit, interest, and the business cycle*. Cambridge, MA: Harvard University Press.

Schumpeter, J. A. (1939). *Business cycles: A theoretical, historical, and statistical analysis of the capitalist process*. New York: McGraw-Hill.

Schumpeter, J. A. (1954). *History of economic analysis*. London: Allen & Urwin.

Scott, A. (1980). *The urban land nexus and the state*. London: Pion.

Shaver, J. M., & Flyer, F. (2000). Agglomeration economies, firm heterogeneity, and foreign direct investment in the United States. *Strategic Management Journal*, *21*(12), 1175–1193. doi:10.1002/1097-0266(200012)21:12<1175::AID-SMJ139>3.0.CO;2-Q

Shennan, S. (2002). *Genes, memes, and human history: Darwinian archaeology and cultural evolution*. Cambridge: Cambridge University Press.

Shennan, S., Downey, S. S., Timpson, A., Edinborough, K., Colledge, S., Kerig, T., . . .Thomas, M. G. (2013). Regional population collapse followed initial agriculture booms in Mid-Holocene Europe. *Nature Communications*, *4*, 1–8. doi:10.1038/ncomms3486

Short, J. C., Ketchen, D. J., Shook, C. L., & Ireland, R. D. (2009). The concept of 'opportunity=' in entrepreneurship research: Past accomplishments and future challenges. *Journal of Management, 34*, 1053–1079. doi:10.1177/0149206308324324

Simonton, D. K. (2011). Big-C creativity in the big city. In D. Andersson, Å. E. Andersson, & C. Mellander (Eds.), *Handbook of creative cities* (pp. 72–84). Cheltenham: Edward Elgar.

Smith, A. (1776/1937). *The wealth of nations*, ed. E. Cannan. New York: Modern Library.

Stam, E. (2007). Why butterflies don't leave: Locational behavior of entrepreneurial firms. *Economic Geography, 83*(1), 27–50. doi:10.1111/j.1944-8287.2007.tb00332.x

Stam, E. (2015). Entrepreneurial ecosystems and regional policy: A sympathetic critique. *European Planning Studies, 23*(9), 1759–1769. doi:10.1080/09654313.2015.1061484

Sternberg, R. (2009). Regional dimensions of entrepreneurship. *Foundations and Trends in Entrepreneurship, 5*(4), 211–340. doi:10.1561/0300000024

Stiegerwald, B. (2001). City views: Urban studies legend Jane Jacobs on gentrification, the new urbanism, and her legacy. *Reason, June*.

Storper, M., & Christopherson, S. (1987). Flexible specialization and regional industrial agglomerations: The case of the U.S. motion picture industry. *Annals of the Association of American Geographers, 77*(1), 104–117. doi:10.1111/j.1467-8306.1987. tb00148.x

Storper, M., & Walker, R. (1989). *The capitalist imperative: Territory, technology, and industrial growth*. Oxford: Blackwell.

Strumsky, D., Lobo, J., & Fleming, L. (2005). *Metropolitan patenting, inventor agglomeration and social networks: A tale of two effects* (Technical Report No. LAUR-04-8798). Los Alamos: Los Alamos National Laboratory

Thompson, P. (2006). Patent citations and the geography of knowledge spillovers: Evidence from inventor- and examiner-added citations. *Review of Economics and Statistics, 88*(2), 383–388.doi:10.1162/rest.88.2.383

Trajtenberg, M. (1990). A penny for your quotes: Patent citations and the value of innovations. *Rand Journal of Economics, 21*(1), 172–187. doi:10.2307/2555502

Utterback, J. M., & Abernathy, W. J. (1975). A dynamic model of process and product innovation. *Omega, 3*(6), 639–656. doi:10.1016/0305-0483(75)90068-7

Venables, A. J., Fujita, M., & Krugman, P. R. (1999). *The spatial economy: Cities, regions, and international trade*. Cambridge, MA: MIT Press.

Vernon, R. (1966). International investment and international trade in the product cycle. *Quarterly Journal of Economics, 80*(2), 190–207. doi:10.2307/1880689

Wyrwich, M., Stuetzer, M., & Sternberg, R. (2016). Entrepreneurial role models, fear of failure, and institutional approval of entrepreneurship: A tale of two regions. *Small Business Economics, 46*(3), 467–492. doi:10.1007/s11187-015-9695-4

Global investments and regional development trajectories: the missing links

Riccardo Crescenzi and Simona Iammarino

ABSTRACT

Global investments and regional development trajectories: the missing links. *Regional Studies*. Regional economic development has been long conceptualized as a non-linear, interactive and socially embedded process: these features were traditionally regarded as spatially mediated and highly localized. However, unprecedentedly fast technological change coupled with the intensification of global economic integration has spurred the need to place regional development in a truly open and interdependent framework. Despite substantial progress in the academic literature, rethinking regional development in this perspective still presents a number of challenges in terms of concepts, empirical evidence and policy approaches. Following an interdisciplinary assessment of how openness and connectivity – proxied by one of the many cross-border flows, i.e., global investments – interact with regional economic development trajectories, this paper presents a picture of the geography of foreign investments from and to the European regions and its change after the financial and economic crisis in 2008. This simple exercise sheds some initial light on how the operationalization of regional connectivity can improve one's empirical understanding of the evolution of regional economies and the policy approach needed to support their reaction to change.

摘要

全球投资与区域发展轨迹：遗失的连结。*Regional Studies*。 区域经济发展长期以来被概念化为非线性、互动且镶嵌于社会的过程；这些特徵传统上被认为受到空间中介且高度在地化。但前所未有的快速科技变迁，伴随着全球经济整合的加剧，刺激了将区域发展置放于真正开放且相互?依赖的架构之需求。尽管学术文献已有了实质的进展，但透过上述观点再思考区域发展，仍然在概念、经验证据与政策方法上呈现诸多挑战。本文追随开放性与连结性——由诸多全球投资的跨界流动之一进行代理 ——如何与区域经济发展轨迹互

171

动的跨领域评估，呈现一个来自欧洲区域与进入欧洲区域的外国投资地理图像，及其在2008年金融与经济危机之?后的改变。此一简易的操作，对区域连结的操作化如何能够促进我们对区域经济的演化之经验性理解，以及支持其回应变迁所需的政策方法，提供若干的初步说明。

RÉSUMÉ

Les investissements mondiaux et les trajectoires de l'aménagement du territoire: les chaînons manquants. *Regional Studies*. Depuis longtemps le développement économique régional a été conceptualisé comme un processus interactif non-linéaire qui est bien intégré sur le plan social: par le passé ces caractéristiques-là étaient considérées très influencées par l'espace et par la localisation. Cependant, l'évolution technologique à un rythme sans précédent conjointement avec l'intensification de l'intégration économique mondiale a stimulé la nécessité de mettre l'aménagement du territoire au sein d'un cadre vraiment ouvert et interdépendant. En dépit du progrès significatif évident dans la litérature spécialisée, repenser l'aménagement du territoire de ce point de vue pose un nombre de défis en termes des notions, des preuves empiriques, et des approches politiques. Suite à une évaluation interdisciplinaire de comment l'ouverture et la connexité -représentées par l'un des nombreux flux transfrontaliers – interagissent avec les trajectoires du développement économique régional, cet article présente une image de la géographie des investissements étrangers en provenance et à destination des régions européennes, et de son évolution depuis la crise financière et économique de 2008. Cette simple analyse éclaircit dans un premier temps comment l'opérationalisation de la connectivité régionale permet de mieux comprendre empiriquement le développement des économies régionales et de l'approche politique qu'il faut pour soutenir leur réaction au changement.

ZUSAMMENFASSUNG

Abläufe von globalen Investitionen und regionaler Entwicklung: die fehlenden Verbindungsglieder. *Regional Studies*. Die regionale Wirtschaftsentwicklung wurde lange als nichtlinearer, interaktiver und gesellschaftlich eingebetteter Prozess aufgefasst: diese Merkmale galten traditionell als räumlich vermittelt und hochgradig lokalisiert. Aufgrund des sich schneller denn je vollziehenden technischen Wandels – gekoppelt mit der Intensivierung der weltweiten wirtschaftlichen Integrationsprozesse – ist es jedoch notwendig geworden, die Regionalentwicklung in einen wirklich offenen Rahmen von Wechselbeziehungen zu stellen. Trotz erheblicher Fortschritte in der akademischen Literatur ist eine Neuorientierung der Regionalentwicklung an dieser Perspektive nach wie vor mit einer Reihe von Herausforderungen verbunden, was Konzepte, empirische Belege und politische Ansätze anbelangt. Im Anschluss an eine interdisziplinäre Bewertung der Frage, wie Offenheit und Verbundenheit – vertreten durch einen von zahlreichen grenzüberschreitenden Strömen, nämlich weltweiten Investitionen – mit den Abläufen der regionalen Wirtschaftsentwicklung zusammenwirken, wird in diesem Beitrag ein Abbild der Geografie ausländischer Investitionen von und in europäische Regionen sowie ihrer Veränderungen nach der Finanz- und Wirtschaftskrise von 2008 vorgestellt. Diese einfache Aufgabe ermöglicht eine erste Klärung der Frage, wie die Operationalisierung der regionalen Verknüpfungen das empirische Verständnis der Evolution regionaler Ökonomien und des erforderlichen politischen Ansatzes zur Unterstützung ihrer Reaktionen auf Veränderungen verbessern kann.

RESUMEN

Trayectorias de inversiones globales y desarrollo regional: los eslabones perdidos. *Regional Studies*. El desarrollo económico regional suele ser conceptualizado como un proceso no lineal, interactivo y socialmente integrado: estas características se solían considerar como espacialmente mediadas y altamente localizadas. Sin embargo, debido al rápido cambio técnico sin precedentes junto con la intensificación de la integración económica global, ha surgido la necesidad de colocar el desarrollo regional en un marco realmente abierto e interdependiente. Aunque en la bibliografía académica se han realizado grandes avances, el replanteamiento del desarrollo regional a este respecto todavía presenta una serie de retos en términos de conceptos, evidencia empírica y enfoques políticos. Tras una valoración interdisciplinaria sobre cómo la transparencia y la conectividad -representadas por uno de los muchos flujos transfronterizos, es decir, las inversiones globales – interactúan con las trayectorias regionales de desarrollo económico, en este artículo presentamos una imagen de la geografía de las inversiones extranjeras desde y hacia las regiones europeas, así como de los cambios después de la crisis financiera y económica en 2008.Este simple ejercicio nos permite una primera aclaración de la cuestión de cómo la operacionalización de la conectividad regional puede mejorar el entendimiento empírico de la evolución de las economías regionales y el enfoque político necesario para apoyar su reacción al cambio.

INTRODUCTION

The recent literature on regional economic development has reached a consensus on the idea that spatial proximity, density and localized processes should be placed in the wider context of economic globalization by accounting for other forms of proximity between local and non-local agents (e.g., Crescenzi, Nathan, & Rodríguez-Pose, 2016b; Huber, 2012; Uyarra, 2011). Regional economic and innovation trajectories do not depend exclusively on localized productive and knowledge assets, but need to combine 'local buzz' (Storper & Venables, 2004) and 'global pipelines' (Bathelt, Malmberg, & Maskell, 2004). The latter are non-spatially bounded linkages and networks that channel and diffuse new and valuable knowledge across space. For the development of these links geographical proximity constitutes 'neither a necessary nor a sufficient condition' (Boschma,

2005, p. 62), while other non-spatial relations – i.e., cognitive, organizational, social and institutional – play a crucial role as complements and/or substitutes of physical closeness (e.g., Crescenzi et al., 2016b; D'Este, Guy, & Iammarino, 2013).

A significant role in the establishment and governance of such pipelines is attributed to multinational enterprises (MNEs) as major 'flagships', or connectors, in global production networks (GPNs) (e.g., Coe, Hess, Yeung, Dicken, & Henderson, 2004, 2008; Dicken, 1994, 2003, 2007; Dicken & Henderson, 2003; Ernst & Kim, 2002; Henderson, Dicken, Hess, Coe, & Yeung, 2002; Hess & Yeung, 2006; Hobday, Davies, & Prencipe, 2005; Wrigley, Coe, & Currah, 2005; Yeung, 2009). The GPN approach combines the insights of various similar perspectives that capture the spread of value-added creation and distribution across firm boundaries and geographical borders, such as those of global commodity chains (GCCs) and global value chains (GVCs) (e.g., Gereffi, 2005; Gereffi & Kaplinsky, 2001; Gereffi & Korzeniewicz, 1994; Gereffi, Humphrey, & Sturgeon, 2005).[1]

Despite considerable academic advances in reconciling firms' cross-borders organizational networks with space-specific assets and institutional structures – i.e., the 'strategic coupling' process that ultimately drives contemporary regional economic development (e.g., Coe et al., 2004, 2008; Yeung, 2009, 2016) – still substantial gaps are left in the literature, particularly when looking for global–local frameworks for the 'diagnosis' of local economic conditions and the design of public policies. This paper contributes to filling this gap by conceptually and critically discussing the heterogeneity of regional openness and connectivity – here intended in terms of global investment flows – through the lenses of an 'integrated framework' for the analysis of local economic development (Crescenzi & Rodríguez-Pose, 2011) that systematically links localized regional assets and socio-institutional features with global connectivity. As an empirical example of how global investment flows are connected to regional trajectories and their change, the paper describes the relative position of the sub-national regions of the European Union (EU) in the inflows and outflows of greenfield foreign direct investment (FDI) to and from the area. By using information from the fDi Markets-*Financial Times* database for 2003–14, the paper follows up on previous work and classifies regions in a dynamic perspective, looking in particular at different stages of the value chain, or functions (e.g., Crescenzi, Pietrobelli, & Rabellotti, 2014; Sturgeon, 2008), before and after the 2008 financial crisis. The heterogeneity of (short-term) regional development trajectories and global connectivity patterns can offer some initial insights towards a more critical and nuanced interpretation of how regions react to shocks, and sheds some initial light on the importance of a more careful coordination of bottom-up and top-down place-based development policies.

The paper is organized as follows. The following section provides a snapshot of the academic debate on the interdependence of corporate and geographical connections and linkages, and highlights similarities in governance issues that both firms and regions are confronting. It focuses on three dimensions of connectivity – spatial extent, nature and directionality – and relates the concept with regional economic development. The third section presents some descriptive evidence of the geography of foreign investment flows in and from the EU over 2003–14, attempts a dynamic classification of EU regions in terms of connectivity measured by these flows before and after the recent financial and economic crisis, and tentatively links these regional typologies to regional development trajectories. The fourth section concludes, highlighting some possible implications for public policies and the challenges ahead in the analysis of global–local interdependence.

GLOBAL FIRMS' NETWORKS AND REGIONAL CONNECTIVITY

Connectivity and global investment flows: spatial extent, nature and directionality

Three key features of the current phase of economic globalization have direct geographical implications (Iammarino & McCann, 2013). First, the share of developing and emerging economies on global FDI flows has grown steadily and, for the first time in history, accounted for more than half the world's total inflows in 2012 (55% in 2014), and more than one-third of total outflows in 2014, confirming a massive transformation in the geography of foreign investment worldwide (United Nations Conference on Trade and Development (UNCTAD), 2015), and in European regions in particular (Crescenzi, Pietrobelli, & Rabellotti, 2016c). Second, the majority of these cross-border flows span neighbouring economies, rather than being genuinely global transactions. This global regionalism is also characterized by the slicing up and recombination of GVCs in which establishments and groups of activities are 'unbundled' (Baldwin, 2011) primarily across groups of neighbouring economic systems (e.g., Guy, 2009, 2015; Rugman, 2005). Third, around two-thirds of global FDI stocks are now in service industries (63% in 2012), with the remaining one-third involving manufacturing. Services liberalization, their increasing tradability due to information and communication technology (ICT) technologies, and the steady rise of GPNs/GVCs spurring the internationalization of services related to manufacturing, have all implied a substantial redistribution of comparative advantages across countries and regions, mirroring that of global gross domestic product (GDP) (UNCTAD, 2015).

Vertical disintegration, international outsourcing and offshoring have emerged as predominant modes of control and coordination of MNE activities, giving rise to what has been labelled the 'concentrated dispersion' of geographical production and knowledge networks (Ernst, 1997, 1998; Ernst & Kim, 2002; Ernst, Guerrieri, Iammarino, & Pietrobelli, 2001). GPNs integrate the dispersed supply and customer bases of MNEs, that is their subsidiaries, affiliates and joint ventures, suppliers and subcontractors, distribution channels and value-added resellers, as well as their research and development (R&D) collaborations and different kinds of cooperative agreements. MNEs break down the value chain into a variety of discrete functions, operations and transactions, and locate them where they can be carried out most effectively, improving firms' access to new intangible assets, and facilitating entry into new markets. The main purpose is to tap into location-specific resources and capabilities that are complementary to the firm's own, at the same time broadening its capacity of knowledge transfer to individual nodes of the GPN (Coe et al., 2004; Ernst et al., 2001; Ernst & Kim, 2002). Such linkages open up new development and upgrading opportunities for the regions and firms involved. Indeed, GPNs in particular industries – such as electronics – have actually shifted to global innovation networks (GINs), with the integration of functions such as engineering, product development, design and research within inter-firm networks situated for the most part in emerging locations in newcomer economies (Ernst, 2010).

Corporate networks have dramatically altered regional connectivity and inter-dependence around the world. MNE networks have spurred spikier geographies and uneven regional development, depending on the variation across urban and regional innovative and institutional capabilities to cash in on the presence of global 'gatekeepers' to build new absolute and comparative advantages. When competitive advantages are seen through the lenses of a fine-grained economic geography and perceived as simultaneously firm- and place-specific (Iammarino & McCann, 2017; Ietto-Gillies, 2012; Young, Hood, & Peters, 1994), the balance between endogenous and exogenous (to the region) knowledge sources and the overall degree of *connectivity* become far more relevant issues. It is not the simple regional *connectedness* – i.e., the architecture of transport and communication infrastructure – but rather the broader connectivity that matters: the capability of individuals, firms, organizations and institutions to interact and engage across geographical space and within networks (Iammarino & McCann, 2017). Regional connectivity is the degree of two-way (inward and outward) openness that shapes the regional churn of skills, talent, competences and business functions/value chain stages (Crescenzi et al., 2014). Even when inflows and outflows are balanced, suggesting that an 'equilibrium' has been reached by the regional economy, the dynamic recombination of key cognitive and productive local assets leads to the enduring capability of cities and regions to adapt, react and develop in an ever-changing global environment.

The literature on the impacts of foreign investment flows – just one, albeit very important, of the many cross-border flows associated with the new international division of labour – has emphasized the importance of the spillovers from global firms to their host locations (e.g., Blomström & Kokko, 1998; Blomström & Persson, 1983; Javorcik, 2004; Javorcik & Spatareanu, 2008; Kokko, 1996). Conversely, the influence of region-specific advantages on the growth and evolution of the 'hosted' MNEs as well as of the 'sending' regions has remained underexplored. An emerging body of literature indicates that while domestic outsourcing of value-added services such as R&D and design is relatively less diffused than that of production, the externalization of such innovation-intensive functions is more likely to span internationally, suggesting that firms' concerns about local competition are compensated by new streams of knowledge sourced in more distant regional systems (e.g., Cusmano, Morrison, & Rabellotti, 2010; Malecki, 2010). The impressive surge of both inward and outward FDI to and from developing and emerging locations – until recently characterized by very low or even null connectivity (UNCTAD, 2015) – supports the idea that economic development requires increasing and simultaneous two-way connectivity.

Following this line of argument, regional economic development is shaped by the co-existence and co-evolution – in the same functionally integrated spatial unit – of flows diversified in terms of their *spatial extent, nature* and *directionality*. First, not only do spatially bounded (intra- and inter-firm) regional flows matter to regional development trajectories: alternative non-spatial proximities make the geographical extent of these flows extra-local, international and global (*spatial extent*). Second, the *nature* of the flows is highly diverse: capital, skills and knowledge are bundled in the intra- and inter-firm connections that form GPNs/GVCs. The actual combination of their constituent elements and their sophistication/complexity depend on the function (or value chain stage) pursued by the agents 'connected' by each flow (e.g., the networks generated in order to pursue R&D activities in different locations might be more intensive in skills and knowledge than those driven by capital-intensive production activities). Third, local economies can be simultaneously origin and/or destination of the flows of investment by MNEs. If openness has been extensively associated to economic development and growth (e.g., Baldwin, 2006; Fagerberg & Srholec, 2008), it is the simultaneous exposure to inflows and outflows (bi-*directionality*) in places – like most of the EU – where the concepts of 'host' and 'home' overlap and blur that identifies the capability of cities and regions constantly to renew their competitive advantage and to react to shocks, shaping their long-term socio-economic performance, welfare and resilience.

Connectivity and regional economic development

Following the above line of argument, regional economic development trajectories can be reconceptualized and analysed in terms of the degree of local connectivity through global investment flows (among a variety of other channels) of varying spatial extent, nature and directionality. Connectivity does not operate (and is not formed) in a territorial vacuum; it is part of a set of geographical, economic and socio-institutional features that interactively shape both innovation and regional development. Networks (and the corresponding flows) based on alternative, non-spatial proximities interact with four other 'keystones' of regional development in an integrated framework (Crescenzi & Rodríguez-Pose, 2011, 2012): (1) the link between local innovative efforts and knowledge generation; (2) the geographical diffusion of knowledge spillovers and the region's industrial specialization; (3) the genesis and structure of local and regional policies; and (4) the existence and efficiency of regional innovation systems and supportive socio-institutional environments. The interaction of these five pillars determines the evolutionary trajectories of countries and regions by: (1) shaping the capability of local actors to establish relations based on both spatial and non-spatial forms of proximity and defining the connectivity of each region and its position in global networks; and (2) influencing how global knowledge and resources made available by regional connectivity are decoded and put into productive use in the regional economy, as well as how local resources and the results of local innovative efforts are 'channelled' into global markets (Crescenzi, 2014).

How does connectivity – here intended as linkages provided by global investment flows – change consolidated views of local economic development? The existing literature has mainly compared MNE subsidiaries with domestic firms in order to identify the potential advantages of the former: MNEs tend to be more productive, invest more in R&D and generate more knowledge than other firms (e.g., Castellani & Zanfei, 2007; Criscuolo, Haskel, & Slaughter, 2010; Dicken, 2007). On the other hand, the attention has been focused on the identification of the channels of spillovers from MNEs to domestic firms with a net separation between inter- and intra-industry effects. Intra-industry channels include demonstration, competition and labour market effects. Demonstration effects rely on the benefits coming from the exposure to the superior technology of MNEs subsidiaries (e.g., Girma, Greenaway, & Wakelin, 2001); competition effects build on the idea that the competitive pressure caused by the entry of foreign firms may act as an incentive for domestic firms to use available resources and existing technology more efficiently (e.g., Blomström & Lipsey, 1989); finally, labour market effects are mainly mediated by labour mobility (e.g., Driffield & Taylor, 2000). Inter-industry knowledge diffusion is based on backward and forward linkages and/or technological complementarity: firms operating in different industrial segments that are vertically connected and/or share technological bases with each other are in fact more likely to benefit from positive externalities (Boschma, 2005; Ernst & Kim, 2002; Javorcik, 2004).

The analysis of these mechanisms has not led to a consensus in the literature on the overall balance between these forces. Various studies have highlighted significant barriers to the absorption of new technologies by domestic firm (e.g., Castellani & Zanfei, 2002), 'market stealing effects' at the expenses of domestic firms (e.g., Aitken & Harrison, 1999), and limited labour mobility due to higher wages paid by foreign enterprises. As also highlighted by Coe et al. (2004, p. 481) 'the developmental impact of the coupling process is highly variable and contingent, and by no means automatically beneficial for the region'.[2]

On the other hand, outward investment may have both direct and indirect effects on domestic firms and the home economy (for a review, see Barba Navaretti & Venables, 2006). The direct benefits of firms' engagement in production activities abroad are those intrinsic in multinationality, i.e., higher efficiency, productivity and innovativeness of domestic MNEs. Similarly, indirect effects are related to both forward/backward linkages and knowledge spillovers of domestic MNEs on the rest of the home economy. However, the overall impact on the home country (region) remains ambiguous: it depends on the net balance between delocalized activities and reconfiguration of home production (Castellani & Zanfei,

2007; Castellani & Pieri, 2016). The theoretical literature has emphasized the crucial relevance of the *nature* of FDI: domestic firms may gain from the relocation of production towards relatively less advanced economies by triggering specialization by function within each industry, rather than by sector (Baldwin & Robert-Nicoud, 2007; Robert-Nicoud, 2008). Consistently, existing evidence shows that more intense outward FDI are associated, at least in the short run, with lower productivity and employment destruction – especially unskilled – at home. However, compensation effects of higher value-added productions and job creation in the home economy are also likely to emerge, particularly in the case of FDI towards regions and countries with a relatively lower level of development (e.g., Barba Navaretti, Castellani, & Disdier, 2010; Castellani & Pieri, 2016; Driffield, Love, & Taylor, 2009; Gagliardi, Iammarino, & Rodriguez-Pose, 2015; Grossman & Rossi-Hansberg, 2006). Positive effects may be strengthened over time thanks to efficiency gains linked to the geographical rationalization of production along the value chain, and to the dynamic benefits stemming from tapping into new sources of innovation and technical knowledge elsewhere (Cantwell & Iammarino, 2003; Castellani & Pieri, 2013; Crescenzi, Gagliardi, & Iammarino, 2015).

However, as pointed out by Castellani and Pieri (2016), the impact on the home economy of internationalization through investment abroad by domestic firms has until recently been rarely considered as a factor affecting regional development and growth, due to the lack of both strong conceptual frameworks and accurate information on the *spatial scale and extent* of outward FDI (see also Mudambi, 2007). Adjustment costs associated with the transition towards models of internationalization based on bi-*directional* global investment flows may be particularly relevant for less resilient peripheral regions, raising important questions about the spatial distribution of the benefits from the globalization of production in advanced economies (e.g., Elia, Mariotti, & Piscitello, 2009; Kemeny & Rigby, 2012).

The bulk of innovation studies posits that corporate dynamic capabilities, and therefore firm growth, are associated with both the openness of firms to their external knowledge environments, and with their internal knowledge-generating capacity (e.g., Fontana, Geuna, & Matt, 2006). The increasing empirical evidence on firm heterogeneity has also been acknowledged by the New Economic Geography (Ottaviano, 2011), casting doubt on the overarching power of the 'comparative advantage' concept, strictly reliant on a broad and static sectoral view of gains and losses in the competitive contest (Bailey & Driffield, 2007; Camagni, 2002; Kitson, Martin, & Tyler, 2004). Firm heterogeneous performance, even in the same industry and national economy, shows that advantages can be absolute, i.e., based on innovation and social capabilities, institutional capacity, and rooted in open and well-connected locations.

Thus, an interesting parallel can be drawn between the micro-level of the firm and the meso-level of the region with respect to dynamic capabilities. The main advantage of today's MNEs is to master system integration – i.e., complex coordination of activities combining different products, services, technologies and knowledge across spatial and functional boundaries (Malecki, 2010). Similarly, 'systemic integration' at the regional level involves coordinating and balancing a diverse structure of 'value networks' – which refers to trade flows, human capital and skills mobility, innovation linkages, foreign and domestic multinational presence, etc. – some of which rely on geographical proximity, whilst others are based on other forms of vicinity.

Openness and interrelatedness, as manifested in the global corporate organization network, have been largely considered at the national system level, often proxied by involvement in international trade, but still fail to be recognized as an essential engine of development in the case of regions (Gambardella, Mariani, & Torrisi, 2009). Complementarity and relatedness between old and new knowledge, and between local and extra-local capabilities and networks, are all necessary conditions for ensuring 'diversity for growth' (Jacobs, 1961, p. 194) in economic systems at different levels of geography (e.g., Boschma & Iammarino, 2009; Fagerberg & Srholec, 2008). The local institutional capacity to blend internal and external sources of knowledge and assets – thus, to master 'systemic integration', building absolute advantages and resilience – underlie interregional inequality and the formation of new spatial hierarchies, particularly visible in a context such as that of the EU, leading to 'more similar but less equal' (Paci, 1997) patterns of regional development.

The relative importance of the embeddedness of foreign firms into the local fabric (e.g., Turok, 1999) – traditionally seen as crucial for their positive impact on the regional economy – becomes a second-order concern relative to the effective coordination of different 'value networks' by local firms, organizations and institutions. In fact, vertical disintegration through outsourcing and offshoring may indeed threaten the thickness of localized networks and relational density, strengthening the asymmetric effects of openness across space (e.g., Cusmano et al., 2010).

A more complete, critical and nuanced consideration of global connectivity would enhance one's understanding of local economic development trajectories, including the response of regions to shocks, which has prompted lively debates in scholarly and policy circles in the aftermath of the financial and economic crisis of the end of the 2000s. Evolutionary economic geography has interpreted resilience in terms of the historical capacity of regions to reconfigure their socio-economic and institutional structures, enabling new development paths (for all, see Boschma, 2015; Martin & Sunley, 2014). Although a few attempts have been made in order to incorporate the role of knowledge (Boschma, 2005) and trade networks into the concept (Thissen, van Oort, Diodato, & Ruijs, 2013), there is currently neither conceptual integration nor systematic evidence on the link between regional connectivity via global investment flows and regional resilience. The assessment of the balance between inward and outward flows, in terms of creation/destruction of economic activities, sectors and functions, employment, skills and innovation, is all the more urgent to advance one's understanding of regional development trajectories and resilience and the ways to enhance them.

REGIONS *ON THE MOVE*: A BROAD-BRUSH PICTURE OF REGIONAL CONNECTIVITY THROUGH GLOBAL INVESTMENT FLOWS IN EUROPE

Direction and change of FDI in and from the European regions

Regional connectivity is key to local and regional economic trajectories. As argued above, the *spatial extent*, *nature* and *directionality* of the flows connecting each region to the rest of the global economy are fundamental, although often overlooked, diagnostic tools for local economic development analysis. In order to provide an initial and evocative hint on this dimension, this section looks into FDI in and from the European regions. As already mentioned, FDI by no means can capture the complexity of flows and exchanges that form the multiscalar web of global interregional connectivity neither can it fully proxy the complexity of GPNs/GVCs. However, MNEs do play a leading role in the development and control of GPNs/GVCs, with FDI being a significant (and in some sectors predominant) mode of governance of such organizational and governance structures. And – even more relevant for practical purposes – FDI leaves 'paper trails' that can be more easily followed and analysed across large samples of cities and regions than other components of GPNs/GVCs. Detailed and comparable data on other (more flexible) forms of networking between firms (e.g., subcontracting, outsourcing, joint ventures, trade, knowledge and skills exchange) would be ideal for present purposes but, unfortunately, they are not available at the sub-national level for multiple countries.

Therefore, in order to grasp at least prima facie the connectivity of European regions, this paper relies on fDi Markets-*Financial Times* data, comprising records of individual greenfield foreign investment 'projects' in all European regions across all sectors and classified by main business function. The dataset includes city-level information on the origin of the investment (or 'sending city/region') and its destination (or 'receiving city/region'). The analysis covers the period between 2003 (the starting year of data collection) and 2014 (the most recent post-crisis year with complete data), and includes all cross-border green- and brownfield investment[3] inward and outward between Europe and the rest of the world (including intra-Europe flows). In what follows 'Europe' is defined as: EU-28,[4] European Free Trade Association (EFTA) countries,[5] and candidate countries (CCs).[6]

The figures that follow offer a broad-brush picture of the connectivity of the European regions through global investment flows, its directionality and evolution over time.

Figures 1 and 2 map the spatial distribution of inward (Figure 1) and outward (Figure 2) FDI cumulative capital expenditure (CapEx)[7] in the EU regions (at territorial level (TL) 2 of the Organisation for Economic Co-operation and Development (OECD) regional classification[8]) over 2003–14. The spatial distribution of the non-normalized value of FDI inflows (Figure 1) highlights a consolidated geography of foreign presence in Europe. The well-established core–periphery patterns in the distribution of overall economic activity overlap only in part with

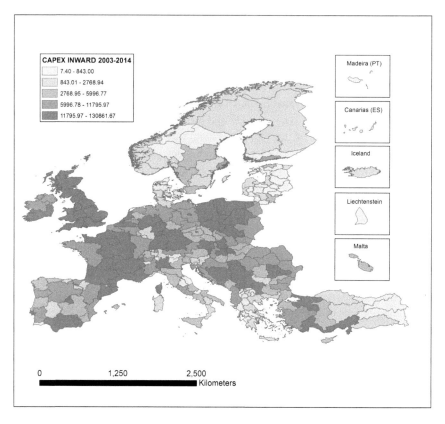

Figure 1 Foreign direct investment towards the regions of Europe (cumulative inward capital expenditure, 2003–14, US$ millions).

Source: Authors' elaboration of fDi Markets data.

the location of inward of FDI. 'Core' EU-15 regions are large recipients of FDI together with the most developed regions in Central and Eastern European members. However, a number of more peripheral regions in Poland, Romania, Bulgaria and the CCs are also relevant hotspots for the attraction of FDI. The geography of regional outward FDI (Figure 2) is concentrated in the 'Blue Banana' of Europe and in capital cities, confirming the spatial selectivity of active internationalization processes. A simple descriptive analysis of the change in the spatial extent, nature and directionality of these flows offers relevant insights on these multilayered geographies and links with regional trajectories.

In order to capture the (short-term) evolution of the connectivity of the EU regions – as a preliminary indication of their capacity to reconfigure their position in global investment flows in response to shocks – Figures 3 and 4 look respectively at the relative variation of FDI cumulative capital expenditure inflows and outflows between the pre-crisis (2003–08) and the post-crisis (2009–14) periods.

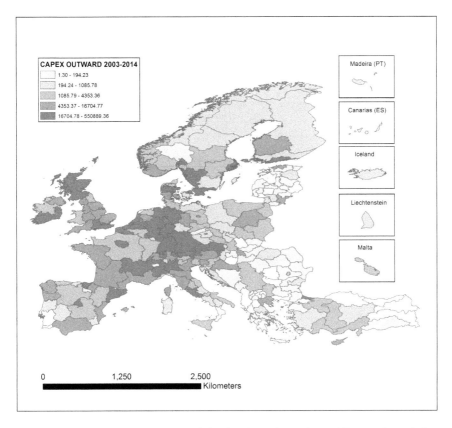

Figure 2 Foreign direct investment originating from the regions of Europe (cumulative outward capital expenditure, 2003–14, US$ millions).

Source: Authors' elaboration of fDi Markets data.

Different colours mark different positions of the regions in the distribution of the possible reactions to the 2008 crisis in terms of inward and outward FDI flows. The classification is based on the distribution of the normalized change in the capital invested between the two periods: each colour-coded category identifies a quintile of the distribution.[9] A sixth category – the green colour with orange dots – is included in the maps to identify outliers. The latter are regions characterized by a relative variation of FDI in the post-crisis period larger than 300%: this is mostly associated with regions with pre-crisis investment values close to zero that inflate the percentage change even with modest increases in the following period. Whilst focusing on the individual maps can shed a light on the evolution of investment flows over time (changes in connectivity across space), a comparison of the two maps offers a first description of the directionality of the flows and their relative balance.

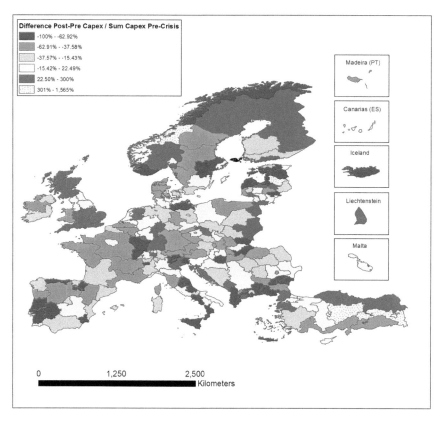

Figure 3 Changes in foreign direct investment towards the regions of Europe after the crisis (differences in capital expenditure between 2003–08 and 2009–14).

Source: Authors' elaboration of fDi Markets data.

Both maps mark in yellow the regions that can be classified as *stayers*, i.e., those that maintained a similar magnitude of FDI inflows and/or outflows before and after the crisis (percentage change close to zero). Figure 3 shows that, in terms of inflows, the *stayers* are localized: (1) around the central axis of Europe from the North (Yorkshire and the Humber, North East, and North West England), to the Centre (the regions of Île-de-France, Southern and Western Netherlands, those in north-west Germany, and Lombardia, Liguria and Emilia-Romagna in Northern Italy), and the South (Apulia and Basilicata in the Italian Mezzogiorno); and (2) in Eastern Europe, with regions in Hungary (Central and Western Transdanubia, Northern Hungary), Lithuania (Kaunas, Ŝiauliai and Vilnius counties), Romania (Sud-Muntenia and Sud-Est) and in the CCs of the Balkans (Albania and Kosovo) and Turkey (East Marmara, Istanbul, West Anatolia). Turning to FDI outflows in Figure 4, the *stayers* are concentrated in the north (Scotland, Northern Ireland, North West England) and south (South East and East of England) of the UK; north

184

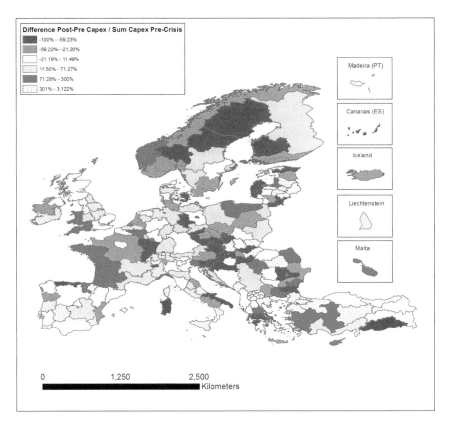

Figure 4 Changes in foreign direct investment originating from the regions of Europe after the crisis (differences in capital expenditure between 2003–08 and 2009–14).

Source: Authors' elaboration of fDi Markets data.

of Italy (Lombardy, Veneto, Trentino-Alto Adige); and a large part of Spain (e.g., Galicia, Madrid, Castile and León, Aragon, Catalonia, Andalusia). The regions of Paris (Île-de-France), Milan (Lombardy) and those in north-west Germany are the most noticeable *stayers* in terms of both inflows and outflows, suggesting a fundamental resistance to external shocks in terms of inward attractiveness and outward reach. Different is the pattern of regions such as Scotland, South East and East England, Northern Netherlands, or Friuli-Venezia Giulia in Italy: they retain their position in terms of outflows but improve their capacity to attract foreign investments. Other regions, such as Północno-Zachodni in north-west Poland, Castilla-La Mancha in Spain, Lazio, Emilia-Romagna and Liguria in Italy, Yorkshire and the Humber and North East England in the UK, and Central Greece, manifest the opposite pattern, i.e., being *stayer* in attractiveness toward foreign capital but experiencing increases in outflows.

While in fact some regions are *stayers* in terms of their FDI connectivity, others are *climbers*, improving their position in terms of inflows and/or outflows after the crisis. *Climbers* are marked in different shades of blue in the two figures depending on their position in the distribution of the relative change of their in/out flows before and after the crisis. If one focuses on the dark blue areas, one can identify those regions that gained the most after the 2008 shock. Figure 3 presents a rather disappointing picture: very few EU regions have been able to exceed their pre-crisis performance and – considering the fast growth of developing and emerging economies in the same period – it is clear that the shock has so far taken a conspicuous toll in terms of attractiveness of foreign capital. *Climbers* are some of the historically most attractive regions of Europe – South East and South West England, Scotland, Baden-Wurttemberg and the south of Norway – but also 'new entries' in the East of Europe that started from very low levels before the crisis, e.g., the eastern regions of Poland, some regions in Romania and Bulgaria, in the Baltic States, and in part of Turkey. Figure 4 shows instead a very different picture: many more regions have increased their outward investment projects after the crisis, possibly due to concurrent technological and organizational forces spurring the rationalization of MNE operations and boosting the offshoring of an increasing number of functions. Indeed, in almost all EU 'old' member state regions are investing more abroad than they did before the crisis: South West and Wales in the UK, West and South West in France, some Italian regions in the north and the centre of the peninsula. However, outward *climbers* are to be found also in Eastern Europe, e.g., the northern regions in Poland, and in CCs such as Serbia and Turkey.

Climbers with respect to both outward and inward flows are harder to find, with a few notable exceptions such as Baden-Wurttemberg and Hessen in Germany, the South of England and the Midlands in the UK, traditionally regarded as European regional *winners*; emerging *winners* may be found in Adriatic Croatia and in the region Wschodni in Poland. In line with the conceptual discussion developed above, the *winners* show a remarkable increase in the magnitude of their flows that is coupled with bi-directionality, providing local actors with unparalleled connectivity and, as a result, with growing opportunities for the renewal of local and regional industrial structures.

The regions that experienced a contraction in their connectivity after the crisis – here labelled *slippers* – are depicted in shades of red in both figures. Figure 3 confirms that large part of the European regions have still not recovered from the crisis: *slippers* are located in the entire periphery of Europe – Portugal, Spain, Southern Italy and Greece[10] – although with different intensities, but also in France (East France), Sweden (East Middle Sweden) and Central (Mecklenburg-Western Pomerania in Germany) and Eastern EU members (especially in some regions of Bulgaria, Estonia, Hungary, Latvia, Lithuania and Slovakia). Figure 4 indicates that the reduction in outward investment has remained confined to the eastern part of France (East France), Southern Italy (Apulia, Molise and Sardinia), Sweden (Middle and Upper Norrland), Easter Austria, and many of the eastern EU members.

Overall, the combined picture provided by both maps for *slippers* indicates that many peripheral European regions can be classified as *losers*, having lost their overall connectivity (inward and outward) through MNE investment flows.

Spatial extent and nature of FDI flows in and from the European regions

A balanced connectivity – albeit only partially captured with FDI data – may be considered a first indicator of the relative trajectory of the regional economies and their long-term resilience. However, *magnitude* and *directionality* of FDI flows need to be assessed jointly with their *spatial extent* and *nature* in order to develop a full diagnosis of local economic development trajectories and potential. Table 1 provides some relevant insights on the *spatial extent* of the FDI connectivity of the EU regions by showing the share of investment targeting and originating from three different categories of regions: the economic 'core', the 'periphery' of Europe[11] and the rest of the world.

Table 1 shows that the spatial extent of intra-EU FDI flows has remained largely unchanged after the crisis and that significant new emerging trends concern, instead, the position of EU regions with reference to extra-EU flows. An increasing share of investment from the core of Europe – that was previously targeting the periphery – has been diverted towards locations outside the EU boundaries. The periphery is not only losing ground in terms of intra-EU (and even intra-periphery) flows, but also investment from outside Europe is more concentrated in the core regions after the financial crisis. When looking at changes in the total magnitude of flows to and from these groups of regions, it becomes apparent that the 'core' of Europe is able to gain in relative terms from the increase of the spatial extent of its connectivity, which has evolved targeting locations in the rest of the world in order to compensate for the relative economic decline experienced by the European periphery during and after the crisis (Crescenzi, Luca, & Milio, 2016a).

The nature – in terms of business activities – of these FDI flows for *stayers*, *climbers* and *slippers* is captured by Tables 2 (pre-crisis) and 3 (post-crisis) for inward FDI, and Tables 4 (pre-crisis) and 5 (post-crisis) for outward FDI. The tables show the business function composition of investment into/from regions in different positions with respect to the distribution of the post-crisis change in FDI (where class 1 is the bottom quintile of the distribution and class 5 is the top quintile: these classes correspond to the colour-coding in Figures 3 and 4). For investments targeting the regions of Europe the comparison of Tables 2 and 3 shows that regions in the *slippers* category (classes 1–3 in the tables) are those experiencing the most significant change in the nature of their incoming FDI, with a marked reduction in 'production' activities in favour of 'services, sales and logistics' and 'headquarters': Brandeburg, Bratislavský kraj and Południowo-Zachodni are some examples of such trends.[12] In a context of shrinking connectivity these regions remain relevant targets for market-seeking investment and managerial functions. Conversely, the *climbers* (class 5 in Tables 2 and 3) lose in 'services' but gain in 'production' FDI, unveiling some capacity to attract production investment projects notwithstanding their relative cost disadvantage. The asset-seeking nature of these investment projects is more likely to produce development-enhancing effects in the local economy reinforcing the intrinsic advantages of an improved overall connectivity. Northern Holland, Eastern Holland and East England are all *climbers* that record a substantial increase in 'production' FDI with a corresponding decrease in 'services, sales and logistics'.

Similar changes in the functional composition of FDI can be observed for outward FDI in Tables 4 and 5. The *slippers* (in these tables corresponding to classes 1 and 2) tend to delocalize abroad relatively more of their 'headquarters' and 'services, sales and logistic' and less of their 'production', suggesting that the latter tends to become progressively more local/less connected for these regions. Examples here include the North West in the UK, Bassin Parisien in France, Asturias and Comunidad Valenciana in Spain, Attica in Greece, and Sardinia in Italy. The opposite trend is instead in place for the top *climbers* (class 5) in outward FDI: the composition of FDI flows from these regions is becoming more oriented towards 'production' activities. This trend – visible in regions such as Bratislavský kraj in Slovakia, Castilla-La Mancha and Extremadura in Spain, West and South West of France, and Friuli-Venezia Giulia in Italy – might correspond to very diverse underlying economic forces. On the one hand, it may be linked to the offshoring of existing local production with potentially negative effects on local employment and economic activity. On the other, this may be an indicator of a stronger internationalization capacity of local firms that, by expanding abroad, might be able to gain in terms of productivity and upgrading along the value chain. The actual combination of these opposite outcomes depends on how outflows are matched by inflows as well as on other local competitiveness factors that would need to be assessed jointly with connectivity in an integrated diagnostic framework.

Table 1 Spatial extent of foreign direct investment (FDI) in the regions of the European Union (EU) (changes in FDI to/from different groups of regions)

	Capital expenditure (CapEx) (core–periphery–extra Europe) shares								
	From the core			From the periphery			From extra-EU		
	Pre-crisis	Post-crisis	Growth rate	Pre-crisis	Post-crisis	Growth rate	Pre-crisis	Post-crisis	Growth rate
To the core	20%	18%	−16%	19%	13%	−32%	72%	79%	1%
To the periphery	12%	9%	−31%	28%	16%	−43%	28%	21%	−34%
To extra-EU	68%	74%	2%	53%	71%	34%			

Source: Authors' elaboration of fDi Markets data.

Table 2 Nature of foreign direct investment (FDI) inflows in the regions of Europe before the crisis (shares of business activities by class of change in capital expenditure (CapEx))

Europe destination – business activities only pre-crisis (2003–08) – shares

Quintile of change in CapEx	Headquarters	Innovative activities	Production	Services, sales and logistics
1	2%	2%	78%	18%
2	4%	4%	74%	18%
3	8%	4%	64%	24%
4	11%	2%	60%	27%
5	14%	4%	58%	24%

Source: Authors' elaboration of fDi Markets data.

Table 3 Nature of foreign direct investment (FDI) inflows in the regions of Europe after the crisis (shares of business activities by class of change in capital expenditure (CapEx))

Europe destination – business activities only post crisis (2009–14) – shares

Quintile of change in CapEx	Headquarters	Innovative activities	Production	Services, sales and logistics
1	6%	3%	65%	26%
2	7%	4%	61%	28%
3	12%	5%	55%	28%
4	12%	3%	56%	29%
5	14%	3%	64%	20%

Source: Authors' elaboration of fDi Markets data.

Table 4 Nature of outward foreign direct investment (FDI) originating from the regions of Europe before the crisis (shares of business activities by class of change in capital expenditure (CapEx)).

Europe source – business activities only pre crisis (2003–08) – shares

Quintile of change in CapEx	Headquarters	Innovative activities	Production	Services, sales and logistics
1	6%	0%	76%	17%
2	5%	2%	74%	19%
3	7%	3%	71%	19%
4	6%	2%	76%	16%
5	8%	2%	64%	26%

Source: Authors' elaboration of fDi Markets data.

Table 5 Nature of outward foreign direct investment (FDI) originating from the regions of Europe after the crisis (shares of business activities by class of change in capital expenditure (CapEx))

Europe source – business activities only post-crisis (2009–14) – shares				
Quintile of change in CapEx	Headquarters	Innovative activities	Production	Services, sales and logistics
1	11%	1%	63%	25%
2	9%	3%	62%	26%
3	9%	3%	62%	25%
4	8%	3%	68%	21%
5	8%	1%	73%	18%

Source: Authors' elaboration of fDi Markets data.

Connectivity and regional development trajectories: some initial insights

An in-depth analysis of the association between the spatial extent, nature and directionality of FDI flows and regional development trajectories would require the availability of regional indicators on a variety of social and economic dimensions, as well as the use of advanced statistical methods. While this approach is beyond the scope of this paper (and of the special issue in which it is hosted) some initial descriptive statistics offer preliminary insights on the link between connectivity and regional economic trajectories. Tables 6 and 7 show the levels and changes of regional GDP per capita (purchasing power standards – PPS) and unemployment rates – crude proxies for regional development – for *slipper* and *climber* regions identified in the third section, focusing on the first and fifth quintiles in the distribution of the changes in inward/outward flows before and after the crisis. Table 6 (looking at inward FDI) suggests that *climbers* have generally higher levels of GDP per capita; interestingly, both *climbers* and *slippers* in the attraction of FDI show similar reactions to the crisis with comparable positive changes in GDP following the shock. The key difference between the two groups of regions is in their highly differentiated capacity to reabsorb unemployed workers: after the crisis, unemployment increased substantially more in the *slippers* than in the *climbers*. Whilst in the former group unemployment increased by 3.94 percentage points, against an average increase in the EU-28 regions by 1.49 percentage points over the same period, the climber group experienced a rise in unemployment by 1.1 percentage points, outperforming the EU-28 average. When regions are categorized looking at changes in their FDI outflows (Table 7), *climbers* show slightly higher levels of GDP per capita but also more favourable GDP adjustment patterns (6.65%) when compared with *slippers* (4.84%) and to the EU-28 average (4.71% over the same period). Conversely, changes in unemployment rates are more homogenous between the two groups (and in line with the EU-28 average), confirming the potentially ambiguous link between active internationalization and domestic employment.

Table 6 Changes in inward foreign direct investment (FDI) flows and short-term regional economic trajectories

Quintile of change in CapEx	Number of regions	Category	Europe destination						
			GDP pc PPS, 2005–08	GDP pc PPS, 2009–14	Δ GDP PPS pc	Unemployment rate, 1999–2008	Unemployment rate, 2009–15	Δ Unemployment rate
			Average GDP pc, €, PPS	Average GDP pc, €, PPS	Rate of growth, 1999–2008 versus 2009–15, %	Unemployment rate, 15 years or over, %	Unemployment rate, 15 years or over, %	Difference 1999–2008 versus 2009–15, %
(1)	24	Slippers	24,158.33	24,327.08	0.70	8.48	12.42	3.94
(5)	16	Climbers	27,975.00	28,153.13	0.64	6.36	7.47	1.11

Notes: The number of regions in each class is lower than in previous tables due to the exclusion of outliers and missing data for gross domestic product (GDP) and/or unemployment. The Slippers category only includes the regions in the bottom quintile of the change in capital expenditure (CapEx) distribution as discussed in the text. PPS, purchasing power standards; pc, per capita.

Source: Authors' elaboration of EUROSTAT data.

Table 7 Changes in outward foreign direct investment (FDI) flows and short-term regional economic trajectories

			Europe source							
Quintile of change in CapEx	Number of regions	Categories	GDP pc 2005–08 Average GDP pc, €, PPS	GDP pc 2009–14 Average GDP pc, €, PPS	Δ GDP pc Rate of growth, 1999–2008 versus 2009–15, %	Unemployment rate, 1999–2008 Unemployment rate, 15 years or over, %	Unemployment rate, 2009–15 Unemployment rate, 15 years or over, %	Δ Unemployment rate Difference 1999–2008 versus 2009–15, %
(1)	25	Slippers	19,516.00	20,460.00	4.84	9.20	11.08	1.89
(5)	28	Climbers	21,189.29	22,597.62	6.65	8.77	10.51	1.74

Notes: The number of regions in each class is lower than in previous tables due to the exclusion of outliers and missing data for gross domestic product (GDP) and/or unemployment. The Slippers category only includes the regions in the first quintile of the change in capital expenditure (CapEx) distribution, while the Climbers category only includes the regions in the fifth quintile of the change CapEx distribution as discussed in the text.

PPS, purchasing power standards; pc, per capita.

Source: Authors' elaboration of EUROSTAT data.

Finally, Table **8** explores the bi-directionality of FDI flows by looking at GDP and unemployment for *winners* and *losers* (i.e., climbers/slippers simultaneously for both inward and outward FDI). The key difference between *winners* and *losers* is not in GDP per capita levels (both groups are in line with the EU-28 average), confirming that the suggested classification does not reflect 'simple' disparities in income levels. Conversely, notwithstanding the similarity in initial conditions, *winners* benefit from more favourable post-crisis trajectories (at least in the short-run) both in terms of GDP and unemployment. Favourable changes in two-way connectivity are generally associated with higher positive changes in GDP per capita and – in particular – to very modest increases in unemployment rates. The *winners* suffered an increase in their unemployment rate by 0.41 percentage points against an average increase by 1.79 percentage points in the *losers* and 1.49 in the EU-28. This provides tentative support to the initial intuition that two-way connectivity and its nature are fundamental elements for the understanding of regional trajectories, and should be carefully assessed in their interactions with other 'keystones' of regional development in an integrated (analytical and policy) framework.

GLOBAL AND REGIONAL INTERDEPENDENCY: RETHINKING POLICY TARGETS AND STRATEGIES

Connectivity is an essential dimension of regional economic development and is key to the diagnosis of development bottlenecks and untapped potential. In order to capture the way in which each region balances the costs of and benefits from connectivity, one needs to consider not only its intensity/magnitude but also its spatial extent, directionality and nature in terms of business functions.

The consequences of global connectivity crucially depend on the capacity of the regions to actually implement and govern systemic integration, involving the coordination of a diverse structure of 'value networks', both localized and non-spatial: this in turn requires capacity to manage institutional change (Rodríguez-Pose, 2013; Rodríguez-Pose & Di Cataldo, 2015). A more accurate understanding of the consequences of regional attractiveness towards inward flows – and the long-term processes of specialization and diversification able to reconfigure local economic and institutional advantages – must be coupled with the study of regional outward reaching, from both domestic MNEs and small and medium-sized enterprises (SMEs), which can provide new knowledge links and a reorientation of the local industry structure and economic functionality. Indeed, European regional *winners* seem to benefit from their balanced connectivity in terms of inward and outward FDI flows – possibly managing in a more effective way systemic integration between intra- and extra-region networks – and show more favourable post-shock adjustment trajectories both in terms of GDP and unemployment.

The empirical evidence based on the growing availability (though still inade-quate in terms of range and comparability of indicators to capture openness) of

Table 8 'Winners' and 'losers' in bi-directional connectivity and short-term changes in regional economic trajectories

Number of regions	Category	Europe source and destination							
		GDP pc, 2005–08	Average GDP pc, €, PPS	GDP pc, 2009–14	Average GDP pc, €, PPS	Δ GDP pc Rate of growth 1999–2008 versus 2009–15, %	Unemployment rate, 2000–08 Unemployment rate, 15 years or over, %	Unemployment rate, 2009–15 Unemployment rate, 15 years or over, %	Δ Unemployment rate Difference 2000–08 versus 2009–15, %
10	Winners Average	23,785		24,451.67		2.80	7.35	7.76	0.41
35	Losers Average	22,515		22,797.86		1.26	9.15	10.88	1.73

Note: PPS, purchasing power standards; pc, per capita. Source: Authors' elaboration of EUROSTAT data.

micro- and territorial statistical data shows a wide heterogeneity of firm and place trajectories. At the same time, the complexity of global flows and their dynamics highlights polarization processes at both individual and spatial level: while the channels for knowledge diffusion are more than ever diversified and tend to produce convergence effects, the creation of new knowledge and technology is highly concentrated, spurring divergence. The cross-border network-based organization of economic activities leads to connectivity as well as isolation, strengthening or disrupting the path dependency of regional development trajectories with ambivalent winner–loser impacts for spatial (and individual) equity (e.g., Mudambi & Santangelo, 2015).

Heterogeneity and complexity require composite, diversified and tailored development policies, based on modular combinations of public and private actions, from both local and global sources. The modularity concept has been recently proposed as a base for 'regional integrated policy platforms' (Cooke, 2007, 2013). The Schumpeterian 'recombinative' innovation process needs to focus not only on 'old' and 'new' knowledge, but also on 'local' and 'global'. In the same way as for individual firms, what is new to one region might not be to others: new (re)combinations (and their cognitive building blocks) can be attracted or tapped into by ensuring connectivity at the micro and meso levels. Modularity implies integrated intervention, i.e., micro-level support to individuals and firms – as, for example, in skills provision, training, innovativeness and openness encouragement – designed in conjunction with place-sensitive policies through the assessment of meso-level characteristics of industries/functions within regions, looking at economic, technological, social and institutional structures. Conversely, the national and international macro-levels should provide the broad framework conditions for the regulation of global flows – with respect, for example, to sustainability, social responsibility, tax regimes and human rights, and the integration with other forms of public intervention, e.g., social policy.

As highlighted in recent contributions (e.g., Bannò, Piscitello, & Varum, 2015), there is still scant appreciation of both region-specific factors and policy measures that influence local firms' and other agents' propensity to internationalize, offshore and outsource, or to overcome the 'liability of foreignness' (Zaheer, 1995; see also Massini & Miozzo, 2012). As noted above, for example, on the side of outward flows most attention has been devoted to trade, manufacturing and the building of territorial comparative advantages, with limited consideration of how to promote general openness, stimulating individual and organizational risk propensity for 'going global', and spurring regional connectivity as a whole. Financial incentives and access to capital are necessary but not anymore sufficient to support connectivity: institutional capacity-building, technical, legal, fiscal and administrative assistance, targeted and timely information, provision of specialized skills, all support individuals' and firms' decisions to invest abroad, helping regions creating absolute advantages – or 'knowledge monopolies' (Malecki, 2010) – and offsetting growing territorial inequality (Bannò et al., 2015).

The acknowledgement and evaluation of openness and heterogeneity across geographical space (Gambardella et al., 2009), especially in the case of European regions, is likely to improve the rather modest achievements of traditional economic development policies still firmly grounded on the maximization of 'inward FDI no matter what'. New actions aimed at making a region less 'provincial' (Gambardella et al., 2009) – therefore increasing its overall international integration – have become pressing. More generally, any 'new' industrial or regional strategy in Europe should be framed as both vertically and horizontally integrated platforms of place-sensitive development policies to aim simultaneously at different targets, including individual and social isolation across geographical space, following 'a coherent industrial strategy at various levels of governance, whether regional and/ or national' (Bailey & Driffield, 2007, p. 189). Interdependence and connectivity make public policy particularly important (see also Neilson, 2014; Phelps, 2008) both by 'looking up' – i.e., lobbying to address global negative externalities that need be corrected through international regulation – and by 'looking down' – i.e., supporting regional systemic integration and institutional capacity building for development and equity. In this context, successful interventions are premised on the availability of meso-level integrated frameworks and diagnostic tools that fully account for the relevance of connectivity and its multifaceted nature, transmission mechanisms and (asymmetrical) impacts.

ACKNOWLEDGMENTS

The authors thank Sebastiano Comotti for his excellent research assistance with foreign direct investment data. They are also grateful to Vassilis Monastiriotis for his comments made to earlier drafts of this paper. The authors remain solely responsible for any errors contained in the article.

DISCLOSURE STATEMENT

No potential conflict of interest was reported by the authors.

FUNDING

The research leading to these results received funding from the Economic and Social Research Council/Joint Programming Initiative Urban Europe [grant agreement number ES/M008436/1], and from the European Research Council under the European Union's Horizon 2020 Programme [grant agreement number 639633-MASSIVE-ERC-2014-STG].

NOTES

1. Although there is substantial similarity among the concepts (GPNs, GVCs, GCCs), there are also important differences. The distinction is, however, not bounding for

present purposes, as the argument does not relate to any particular structures and governance of such networks; for an insightful discussion, see Coe, Dicken, and Hess (2008).

2. See also Narula and Dunning (2010, p. 283): 'Quite apart from the dangers of crowding-out and the problems of stage-inappropriate MNE activities, it is not clear that increased MNE activity in terms of stock or flows necessarily implies a proportional increase in spillovers and linkages.'

3. In the database, joint ventures are tracked only when they lead to new operations, whereas mergers and acquisitions as well as other equity investment are not included. Foreign firms' operations are identified by *Financial Times* analysts through a wide variety of sources, including nearly 9000 media sources, project data from over 1000 industry organizations and investment agencies, and data purchased from market research and publication companies. Furthermore, each project is cross-referenced across multiple sources and more than 90% of investment projects are validated with company sources. In addition, Crescenzi et al. (2014) and Ascani, Crescenzi, and Iammarino (2016) show that investment projects recorded in fDi Markets are highly correlated with other macro-level data on FDI from UNCTAD, the International Monetary Fund (IMF) and the World Bank.

4. The EU-28 includes Austria, Belgium, Bulgaria, Croatia, Cyprus, the Czech Republic, Denmark, Estonia, Finland, France, Germany, Greece, Hungary, Ireland, Italy, Latvia, Lithuania, Luxembourg, Malta, the Netherlands, Poland, Portugal, Romania, Slovakia, Slovenia, Spain, Sweden and the UK. Andorra, Greenland, Monaco and San Marino are also included.

5. EFTA includes Iceland, Liechtenstein, Norway and Switzerland.

6. Candidate countries include Albania, Bosnia-Herzegovina, Kosovo, Macedonia, Montenegro, Serbia and Turkey.

7. The relative variation of FDI cumulative inflows and outflows between the pre- and post-crisis periods could also be expressed in terms of the number of projects and/or employment. However, capital expenditure (i.e., the capital invested) offers a more accurate picture of the evolution of FDI flows. On the one hand, the distribution of the number of projects is strongly skewed (for Europe both as a source and as a destination). On the other hand, the relative variation of estimated employment generated by the new FDI projects could be misleading. For many investment projects, particularly in outflows from Europe, the number of jobs created is an estimate of the 'expected' number of employees who will be hired in the new subsidiary: as a result, this information is often missing in the database.

8. This classification has a direct correspondence to the EUROSTAT Regional Classification based on the Nomenclature des Unités Territoriales Statistiques (NUTS) regions, but has the advantage of better capturing regional units with institutional and functional coherence. OECD TL2 regions correspond to EUROSTAT NUTS-1 regions in the following countries: Austria, Belgium, Cyprus, France, Germany, Luxembourg, Malta, the Netherlands, Poland, Turkey and the UK. Conversely, TL2 regions correspond to NUTS-2 regions in Bulgaria, Croatia, the Czech Republic, Denmark, Finland, Greece, Hungary, Ireland, Italy, Norway, Portugal, Romania, Slovakia, Slovenia, Spain, Sweden and Switzerland. NUTS-3 regions are instead the relevant units in Estonia, Iceland, Latvia, Lithuania and Macedonia. No relevant sub-national classification is defined in Albania, Andorra, Bosnia-Herzegovina, Greenland, Kosovo, Liechtenstein, Monaco, Montenegro, San Marino and Serbia. For those countries with no sub-national classification provided by the EUROSTAT 2013 NUTS shapefile (e.g., Albania), the data have been allocated at the national level (the shapefile can be downloaded from: http://www.baruch.cuny.edu/geoportal/data/esri/esri_intl.htm).

9. The distributions for inward and outward FDI are skewed in different directions and the classification of the regions across quintiles reflects these differences, resulting in a different colour coding in the two maps catered around zero. Moreover, when a region did not receive/made any investment in 2003–14 it is white coloured.

10. Most regions in Greece seem not to be hit by the crisis as they are not coloured in shades of red. However, this is the outcome of the limited number of investment targeting these regions already before 2008. Looking only at regions with at least 10 FDI projects before the crisis, it can be seen that both of them – Attica and Central Macedonia – experienced a strong decrease in the amount of FDI received.
11. The core–periphery distinction is based on the Structural Funds – European Regional Development Fund (ERDF) and European Social Fund (ESF) – eligibility 2014–2020 adopted by the European Commission. Regions classified as less developed (GDP/head <75% of the EU-27 average) are labelled as peripheral areas, while regions above that threshold are instead defined as core areas. For regions in countries excluded from the Structural Funds classification the following applied: Core: Andorra, Greenland, Iceland, Liechtenstein, Monaco, Norway, San Marino and Switzerland; and Periphery: Albania, Bosnia-Herzegovina, Kosovo, Macedonia, Montenegro, Serbia and Turkey.
12. There are also several other regions following similar patterns, but to a lesser extent, especially in Spain (País Vasco, Galicia, Andalusia, Isles Baleares, Castilla y León and La Rioja), Italy (Abruzzo and Toscana), Portugal (Centro and Lisbon), Germany and some regions in the Eastern Countries.

REFERENCES

Aitken, B. J., & Harrison, A. E. (1999). Do domestic firms benefit from direct foreign investment? Evidence from Venezuela. *American Economic Review, 89*(3), 605–618. doi:10.1257/aer.89.3.605

Ascani, A., Crescenzi, R., & Iammarino, S. (2016). What drives European multinationals to the European Union neighbouring countries? A mixed-methods analysis of Italian investment strategies. *Environment and Planning C: Government and Policy, 34*, 656–675. doi:10.1177/0263774X16628180

Bailey, D., & Driffield, N. (2007). Industrial policy, FDI and employment: Still 'missing a strategy'. *Journal of Industry, Competition and Trade, 7*(3–4), 189–211. doi:10.1007/s10842-006-7185-8

Baldwin, R. E. (2006). Multilateralising regionalism: Spaghetti bowls as building blocs on the path to global free trade. *World Economy, 29*(11), 1451–1518. doi:10.1111/j.1467-9701.2006.00852.x

Baldwin, R. E. (2011). *Trade and industrialisation after globalisation's 2nd unbundling: How building and joining a supply chain are different and why it matters* (Working Paper No. w17716). Cambridge, MA: National Bureau of Economic Research (NBER).

Baldwin, R., & Robert-Nicoud, F. (2007). *Offshoring: General equilibrium effects on wages, production and trade* (No. w12991). Cambridge, MA: National Bureau of Economic Research (NBER).

Bannò, M., Piscitello, L., & Varum, C. (2015). Determinants of the internationalization of regions: The role and effectiveness of public policy measures. *Regional Studies, 49*(7), 1208–1222. doi:10.1080/00343404.2013.821570

Barba Navaretti, G., Castellani, D., & Disdier, A. C. (2010). How does investing in cheap labour countries affect performance at home? Firm-level evidence from France and Italy. *Oxford Economic Papers, 62*(2), 234–260.

Barba Navaretti, G., & Venables, A. (2006). *Multinational firms in the world economy.* Princeton: Princeton University Press.

Bathelt, H., Malmberg, A., & Maskell, P. (2004). Clusters and knowledge: Local buzz, global pipelines and the process of knowledge creation. *Progress in Human Geography, 28*(1), 31–56. doi:10.1191/0309132504ph469oa

Blomström, M., & Kokko, A. (1998). Multinational corporations and spillovers. *Journal of Economic Surveys*, *12*(3), 247–277. doi:10.1111/1467-6419.00056

Blomström, M., & Lipsey, R. E. (1989). The export performance of US and Swedish multinationals. *Review of Income and Wealth*, *35*(3), 245–264. doi:10.1111/j.1475-4991.1989.tb00592.x

Blomström, M., & Persson, H. (1983). Foreign investment and spillover efficiency in an underdeveloped economy: Evidence from the Mexican manufacturing industry. *World Development*, *11*(6), 493–501. doi:10.1016/0305-750X(83)90016-5

Boschma, R. (2005). Proximity and innovation: A critical assessment. *Regional Studies*, *39*(1), 61–74. doi:10.1080/0034340052000320887

Boschma, R. (2015). Towards an evolutionary perspective on regional resilience. *Regional Studies*, *49*(5), 733–751. doi:10.1080/00343404.2014.959481

Boschma, R., & Iammarino, S. (2009). Related variety, trade linkages, and regional growth in Italy. *Economic Geography*, *85*(3), 289–311. doi:10.1111/j.1944-8287.2009.01034.x

Camagni, R. (2002). On the concept of territorial competitiveness: Sound or misleading? *Urban studies*, *39*(13), 2395–2411. doi:10.1080/0042098022000027022

Cantwell, J. A., & Iammarino, S. (2003). *Multinational corporations and European regional systems of innovation*. London: Routledge.

Castellani, D., & Pieri, F. (2013). R&D offshoring and the productivity growth of European regions. *Research Policy*, *42*(9), 1581–1594. doi:10.1016/j.respol.2013.05.009

Castellani, D., & Pieri, F. (2016). Outward investments and productivity: Evidence from European regions. *Regional Studies*, *50*(12), 1945–1964. doi:10.1080/00343404.2014.981149

Castellani, D., & Zanfei, A. (2002). Multinational experience and the creation of linkages with local firms: Evidence from the electronics industry. *Cambridge Journal of Economics*, *26*(1), 1–25. doi:10.1093/cje/26.1.1

Castellani, D., & Zanfei, A. (2007). Internationalisation innovation and productivity: How do firms differ in Italy? *World Economy*, *30*(1), 156–176. doi:10.1111/j.1467-9701.2007.00875.x

Coe, N. M., Dicken, P., & Hess, M. (2008). Global production networks: Realizing the potential. *Journal of Economic Geography*, *8*(3), 271–295. doi:10.1093/jeg/lbn002

Coe, N. M., Hess, M., Yeung, H. W. C., Dicken, P., & Henderson, J. (2004). 'Globalizing' regional development: A global production networks perspective. *Transactions of the Institute of British geographers*, *29*(4), 468–484. doi:10.1111/j.0020-2754.2004.00142.x

Cooke, P. (2007). To construct regional advantage from innovation systems first build policy platforms. *European Planning Studies*, *15*(2), 179–194. doi:10.1080/09654310601078671

Cooke, P. (2013). *Complex adaptive innovation systems: Relatedness and transversality in the evolving region* (Vol. 55). Abingdon: Routledge.

Crescenzi, R. (2014). Changes in economic geography theory and the dynamics of technological change. In M. M. Fisher, & P. Nijkamp (Eds.), *Handbook of regional science* (pp. 649–666). Berlin: Springer. doi:10.1007/978-3-642-23430-9_35

Crescenzi, R., Gagliardi, L., & Iammarino, S. (2015). Foreign multinationals and domestic innovation: Intra-industry effects and firm heterogeneity. *Research Policy*, *44*(3), 596–609. doi:10.1016/j.respol.2014.12.009

Crescenzi, R., Luca, D., & Milio, S. (2016a). The geography of the economic crisis in Europe: National macroeconomic conditions, regional structural factors and short-term economic performance. *Cambridge Journal of Regions, Economy and Society*, *9*, 13–32. doi:10.1093/cjres/rsv031

Crescenzi, R., Nathan, M., & Rodríguez-Pose, A. (2016b). Do inventors talk to strangers? On proximity and collaborative knowledge creation. *Research Policy*, *45*(1), 177–194. doi:10.1016/j.respol.2015.07.003

Crescenzi, R., Pietrobelli, C., & Rabellotti, R. (2014). Innovation drivers, value chains and the geography of multinational corporations in Europe. *Journal of Economic Geography*, *14*(6), 1053–1086. doi:10.1093/jeg/lbt018

Crescenzi, R., Pietrobelli, P., Rabellotti, R. (2016c). Regional strategic assets and the location strategies of emerging countries' multinationals in Europe. *European Planning Studies*, *24*(4), 645–667. doi:10.1080/09654313.2015.1129395

Crescenzi, R., & Rodríguez-Pose, A. (2011). *Innovation and regional growth in the European Union*. Berlin: Springer Science & Business Media.

Crescenzi, R., & Rodríguez-Pose, A. (2012). An 'integrated' framework for the comparative analysis of the territorial innovation dynamics of developed and emerging countries. *Journal of Economic Surveys*, *26*(3), 517–533.

Criscuolo, C., Haskel, J. E., & Slaughter, M. J. (2010). Global engagement and the innovation activities of firms. *International Journal of Industrial Organization*, *28*(2), 191–202. doi:10.1016/j.ijindorg.2009.07.012

Cusmano, L., Morrison, A., & Rabellotti, R. (2010). Catching up trajectories in the wine sector: A comparative study of Chile, Italy, and South Africa. *World Development*, *38*(11), 1588–1602. doi:10.1016/j.worlddev.2010.05.002

D'Este, P., Guy, F., & Iammarino, S. (2013). Shaping the formation of university–industry research collaborations: What type of proximity does really matter? *Journal of Economic Geography*, *13*(4), 537–558. doi:10.1093/jeg/lbs010

Dicken, P. (1994). Roepke Lecture in Economic Geography: Global–local tensions: Firms and states in the global space-economy. *Economic Geography*, *70*, 101–128. doi:10.2307/143650

Dicken, P. (2003). *Global shift: Reshaping the global economic map in the 21st century*. London: SAGE.

Dicken, P. (2007). *Global shift: Mapping the changing contours of the world economy*. London: SAGE.

Dicken, P., & Henderson, J. (2003). *Making the connections: Global production networks in Britain, East Asia and Eastern Europe* (Final Report on ESRC Research Project R000238535).

Driffield, N. L., Love, J. H., & Taylor, K. (2009). Productivity and labour demand effects of inward and outward foreign direct investment on UK industry. *Manchester School*, *77*(2), 171–203. doi:10.1111/j.1467-9957.2008.02093.x

Driffield, N., & Taylor, K. (2000). FDI and the labour market: A review of the evidence and policy implications. *Oxford Review of Economic Policy*, *16*(3), 90–103. doi:10.1093/oxrep/16.3.90

Elia, S., Mariotti, I., & Piscitello, L. (2009). The impact of outward FDI on the home country's labour demand and skill composition. *International Business Review*, *18*, 357–372. doi:10.1016/j.ibusrev.2009.04.001

Ernst, D. (1997). *From partial to systemic globalization: International production networks in the electronics industry* (Working Paper No. 98). Berkeley Roundtable on the International Economy.

Ernst, D. (1998). High-tech competition puzzles – How globalization affects firm behavior and market structure in the electronics industry. *Revue d'Économie Industrielle*, *85*(1), 9–30. doi:10.3406/rei.1998.1722

Ernst, D. (2010). Upgrading through innovation in a small network economy: Insights from Taiwan's IT industry. *Economics of Innovation and New Technology*, *19*(4), 295–324. doi:10.1080/10438590802469560

Ernst, D., Guerrieri, P., Iammarino, S., & Pietrobelli, C. (2001). New challenges for industrial clusters and districts: Global production networks and knowledge diffusion. In

P. Guerrieri, S. Iammarino, & C. Pietrobelli (Eds.), *The global challenge to industrial districts* (pp. 131–144). Cheltenham: Edward Elgar.

Ernst, D., & Kim, L. (2002). Global production networks, knowledge diffusion, and local capability formation. *Research Policy, 31*(8), 1417–1429. doi:10.1016/S0048-7333(02)00072-0

Fagerberg, J., & Srholec, M. (2008). National innovation systems, capabilities and economic development. *Research Policy, 37*(9), 1417–1435. doi:10.1016/j.respol.2008.06.003

Fontana, R., Geuna, A., & Matt, M. (2006). Factors affecting university–industry R&D projects: The importance of searching, screening and signalling. *Research Policy, 35*(2), 309–323. doi:10.1016/j.respol.2005.12.001

Gagliardi, L., Iammarino, S., & Rodriguez-Pose, A. (2015). *Outward FDI and the geography of jobs: Evidence from the UK* (CEPR Discussion Paper No. 10855, September). London: Centre for Economic Policy Research (CEPR).

Gambardella, A., Mariani, M., & Torrisi, S. (2009). How 'provincial' is your region? Openness and regional performance in Europe. *Regional Studies, 43*(7), 935–947. doi:10.1080/00343400801932268

Gereffi, G. (2005). The global economy: Organization, governance, and development. *Handbook of Economic Sociology, 2,* 160–182.

Gereffi, G., Humphrey, J., & Sturgeon, T. (2005). The governance of global value chains. *Review of International Political Economy, 12*(1), 78–104. doi:10.1080/09692290500049805

Gereffi, G., & Kaplinsky, R. eds. (2001). *The value of value chains: Spreading the gains from globalisation* (Vol. 32). Brighton: Institute of Development Studies (IDS), University of Sussex.

Gereffi, G., & Korzeniewicz, M. (Eds.). (1994). *Commodity chains and global capitalism.* London: Praeger.

Girma, S., Greenaway, D., & Wakelin, K. (2001). Who benefits from foreign direct investment in the UK? *Scottish Journal of Political Economy, 48*(2), 119–133. doi:10.1111/1467-9485.00189

Grossman, G. M., & Rossi-Hansberg, E. (2006). *Trading tasks: A simple theory of offshoring* (Working Paper Number No. w12721). Cambridge, MA: National Bureau of Economic Research (NBER).

Guy, F. (2009). *The global environment of business.* Oxford: Oxford University Press.

Guy, F. (2015). Globalisation, regionalization and technological change. In D. Archibugi & A. Filippetti (Eds.), *The handbook of global science, technology and innovation* (pp. 575–596). Oxford: Wiley-Blackwell.

Henderson, J., Dicken, P., Hess, M., Coe, N. M., & Yeung, H. W. C. (2002). Global production networks and the analysis of economic development. *Review of International Political Economy, 9,* 436–464. doi:10.1080/09692290210150842

Hess, M., & Yeung, H. W. C. (2006). Whither global production networks in economic geography? Past, present and future. *Environment and Planning A, 38*(6), 1193–1204.

Hobday, M., Davies, A., & Prencipe, A. (2005). Systems integration: A core capability of the modern corporation. *Industrial and Corporate Change, 14*(6), 1109–1143. doi:10.1093/icc/dth080

Huber, F. (2012). On the role and interrelationship of spatial, social and cognitive proximity: Personal knowledge relationships of R&D workers in the Cambridge information technology cluster. *Regional Studies, 46*(9), 1169–1182. doi:10.1080/00343404.2011.569539

Iammarino, S., & McCann, P. (2013). *Multinationals and economic geography: Location, technology and innovation.* Cheltenham: Edward Elgar.

Iammarino, S., & McCann, P. (Forthcoming 2017). Network geographies and geographical networks. Co-dependence and co-evolution of multinational enterprises and space. In G. L. Clark, M. P. Feldman, M. S. Gertler, & D. Wójcik (Eds.), *The New Oxford handbook of economic geography*. Oxford: Oxford University Press.

Ietto-Gillies, G. (2012). *Transnational corporations and international production: Concepts, theories and effects*. Cheltenham: Edward Elgar.

Jacobs, J. (1961). *Death and life of great American cities*. New York: Random House.

Javorcik, B. S. (2004). Does foreign direct investment increase the productivity of domestic firms? In search of spillovers through backward linkages. *American Economic Review, 94*(3), 605–627. doi:10.1257/0002828041464605

Javorcik, B. S., & Spatareanu, M. (2008). To share or not to share: Does local participation matter for spillovers from foreign direct investment? *Journal of Development Economics, 85*(1), 194–217. doi:10.1016/j.jdeveco.2006.08.005

Kemeny, T., & Rigby, D. (2012). Trading away what kind of jobs? Globalization, trade and tasks in the US economy. *Review of World Economics, 148*, 1–16. doi:10.1007/s10290-011-0099-5

Kitson, M., Martin, R., & Tyler, P. (2004). Regional competitiveness: An elusive yet key concept? *Regional Studies, 38*(9), 991–999. doi:10.1080/0034340042000320816

Kokko, A. (1996). Productivity spillovers from competition between local firms and foreign affiliates. *Journal of International Development, 8*(4), 517–530. doi:10.1002/(SICI)1099-1328(199607)8:4<517::AID-JID298>3.0.CO;2-P

Malecki, E. J. (2010). Global knowledge and creativity: New challenges for firms and regions. *Regional Studies, 44*(8), 1033–1052. doi:10.1080/00343400903108676

Martin, R., & Sunley, P. (2014). On the notion of regional economic resilience: Conceptualization and explanation. *Journal of Economic Geography*. doi:10.1093/jeg/lbu015

Massini, S., & Miozzo, M. (2012). Outsourcing and offshoring of business services: Challenges to theory, management and geography of innovation. *Regional Studies,, 46*(9), 1219–1242. doi:10.1080/00343404.2010.509128

Mudambi, R. (2007). Offshoring: Economic geography and the multinational firm. *Journal of International Business Studies, 38*(1), 206–210.

Mudambi, R., & Santangelo, G. D. (2015). From shallow resource pools to emerging clusters: The role of multinational enterprise subsidiaries in peripheral areas. *Regional Studies, 50*(12), 1965–1979. doi:10.1080/00343404.2014.985199

Narula, R., & Dunning, J. H. (2010). Multinational enterprises, development and globalization: Some clarifications and a research agenda. *Oxford Development Studies, 38*(3), 263–287. doi:10.1080/13600818.2010.505684

Neilson, J. (2014). Value chains, neoliberalism and development practice: The Indonesian experience. *Review of International Political Economy, 21*(1), 38–69. doi:10.1080/0969 2290.2013.809782

Ottaviano, G. I. (2011). 'New' New Economic Geography: Firm heterogeneity and agglomeration economies. *Journal of Economic Geography, 11*(2), 231–240. doi:10.1093/jeg/lbq041

Paci, R. (1997). More similar and less equal: Economic growth in the European regions. *Review of World Economics, 133*(4), 609–634. doi:10.1007/BF02707405

Phelps, N. A. (2008). Cluster or capture? Manufacturing foreign direct investment, external economies and agglomeration. *Regional Studies, 42*(4), 457–473. doi:10.1080/00343400701543256

Robert-Nicoud, F. (2008). Offshoring of routine tasks and (de)industrialisation: Threat or opportunity – And for whom? *Journal of Urban Economics, 63*(2), 517–535.

Rodríguez-Pose, A. (2013). Do institutions matter for regional development? *Regional Studies*, *47*(7), 1034–1047. doi:10.1080/00343404.2012.748978

Rodríguez-Pose, A., & Di Cataldo, M. (2015). Quality of government and innovative performance in the regions of Europe. *Journal of Economic Geography*, *15*(4), 673–706. doi:10.1093/jeg/lbu023

Rugman, A. M. (2005). *The regional multinationals*. Cambridge: Cambridge University Press.

Storper, M., & Venables, A. J. (2004). Buzz: Face-to-face contact and the urban economy. *Journal of Economic Geography*, *4*(4), 351–370. doi:10.1093/jnlecg/lbh027

Sturgeon, T. J. (2008). Mapping integrative trade: Conceptualising and measuring global value chains. *International Journal of Technological Learning, Innovation and Development*, *1*(3), 237–257. doi:10.1504/IJTLID.2008.019973

Thissen, M., van Oort, F., Diodato, D., & Ruijs, A. (2013). *Regional competitiveness and smart specialization in Europe: Place-based development in international economic networks*. Cheltenham: Edward Elgar.

Turok, I. (1999). Localisation or mainstream bending in urban regeneration? European experience. *Local Economy*, *14*(1), 72–86. doi:10.1080/02690949908726476

United Nations Conference on Trade and Development (UNCTAD). (2015). *Trade and development report*. New York: United Nations.

Uyarra, E. (2011). Regional innovation systems revisited: Networks, institutions, policy and complexity. In T. Herrschel, & P. Tallberg (Eds.), *The role of the regions, networks, scale, territory* (pp. 169–194). Gothenburg: Region Skane.

Wrigley, N., Coe, N. M., & Currah, A. (2005). Globalizing retail: Conceptualizing the distribution-based transnational corporation (TNC). *Progress in Human Geography*, *29*(4), 437–457. doi:10.1191/0309132505ph559oa

Yeung, H. W. C. (2009). Regional development and the competitive dynamics of global production networks: An East Asian perspective. *Regional Studies*, *43*(3), 325–351. doi:10.1080/00343400902777059

Yeung, H. W. C. (2016). *Strategic coupling: East Asian industrial transformation in the new global economy*. Ithaca: Cornell University Press.

Young, S., Hood, N., & Peters, E. (1994). Multinational enterprises and regional economic development. *Regional Studies*, *28*(7), 657–677. doi:10.1080/00343409412331348566

Zaheer, S. (1995). Overcoming the liability of foreignness. *Academy of Journal*, *38*(2), 341–363. doi:10.2307/256683

Geographical linkages in the financial services industry: a dialogue with organizational studies

Eric Knight and Dariusz Wójcik

ABSTRACT

Geographical linkages in the financial services industry: a dialogue with organizational studies. *Regional Studies*. This article proposes a conceptualization of the geographical linkages in the financial services sector based on boundary-spanning activities. In doing so, it seeks to open a dialogue between organizational sociology and regional development that goes beyond an analysis of financial transactions and asset prices to the informational content shared between organizations within a city, country or region. This conceptual approach offers new insights into why and how geographical linkages emerge within and between financial services organizations. This article foreshadows the utility of this approach by way of an illustrative case of HSBC, the 'world's local bank'.

摘要

金融服务业中的地理连结：与组织研究对话。*Regional Studies*。本文根据跨越边界之活动，概念化金融服务部门中的地理连结。本文旨在藉此开启组织社会学与区域发展的对话，该对话超越对金融交易和资产价格的分析，并进一步分析一个城市、国家或区域的组织之间共享的信息内容。本概念方法对于地理连结为何以及如何在金融服务组织之中与之间浮现，提出崭新的洞见。本文透过"世界的在地银行"HSBC这个具说明性的案例研究，预示此一方法的效用。

RÉSUMÉ

Les liens géographiques au sein du secteur des services financiers: engager un dialogue avec les études organisationnelles. *Regional Studies*. Cet article propose une conceptualisation des liens géographiques au sein du secteur des services financiers fondée sur des activités d'expansion (à savoir boundary-spanning activities). Ce faisant, on cherche à engager un dialogue ouvert entre la sociologie organisationnelle et l'aménagement du territoire qui va au-delà d'une analyse des opérations financières et le prix des actifs jusqu'au contenu instructif partagé entre des organisations au sein d'une ville, d'un pays ou d'une région. Cette approche conceptuelle permet de mieux comprendre l'apparition des liens géographiques entre et en-dedans des organisations du secteur des services financiers. Cet article présage l'utilité de cette approche au moyen d'une étude de cas, à savoir HSBC, qui se positionne comme la 'banque locale du monde'.

ZUSAMMENFASSUNG

Geografische Verknüpfungen im Finanzdienstleistungssektor: ein Dialog mit den Organisationsstudien. *Regional Studies*. In diesem Beitrag wird eine Konzeptualisierung der geografischen Verknüpfungen im Finanzdienstleistungssektor auf der Grundlage von grenzüberschreitenden Aktivitäten vorgeschlagen. Hierdurch soll ein Dialog zwischen der Organisationssoziologie und der Regionalentwicklung angeregt werden, der über die Analyse von Finanztransaktionen und Vermögenspreisen hinausgeht und auch die informationellen Inhalte erfasst, die zwischen Organisationen innerhalb einer Stadt, eines Landes oder einer Region ausgetauscht werden. Dieser konzeptuelle Ansatz bietet neue Einblicke in die Frage, warum und wie geografische Verknüpfungen innerhalb und zwischen Organisationen des Finanzsektors entstehen. Der Nutzen dieses Ansatzes wird anhand des Fallbeispiels von HSBC, der 'lokalen Bank der Welt', illustriert.

RESUMEN

Vínculos geográficos en el sector de los servicios financieros: un diálogo con los estudios organizativos. *Regional Studies*. En este artículo proponemos una conceptualización de los vínculos geográficos en el sector de los servicios financieros basándonos en las actividades transfronterizas. De este modo, se pretende estimular un diálogo entre la sociología organizativa y el desarrollo regional que vaya más allá de un análisis de las transacciones financieras y los precios de bienes para incorporar el contenido informativo compartido entre las organizaciones de cada ciudad, país o región. Este enfoque conceptual brinda una nueva perspectiva sobre porqué y cómo surgen los vínculos geográficos dentro y entre las organizaciones de los servicios financieros. En este artículo presagiamos la utilidad de este enfoque mediante un caso ilustrativo del HSBC, el 'banco local del mundo'.

INTRODUCTION

In June 2016 following Britain's decision to leave the European Union, Douglas Flint, Chairman of HSBC, one of the world's largest commercial banks, confirmed that senior management would not reconsider its decision to retain London as its global headquarters. After 10 months of internal deliberations, the bank had announced in February 2016 that it would end discussions about relocating to Hong Kong, despite Asia representing a large and rapidly growing share of the company's profits and revenue. That same week, the company also announced that it planned to relocate 1000 mid-office jobs from London to Paris as a result of the 'Brexit' decision. Thus, a mixed message emerged about how changes in the environmental context shaped the geographical footprint of the bank, both showing how radical shifts in the macro-policy setting impacted some service functions (e.g., mid-office staff) but not others (e.g., headquarters' location).

What drives the strategic location decisions of financial services organizations? Or, more specifically, what is the right unit of analysis for mapping the services performed with, and within, transnational commercial banks? Mainstream economics and finance has tended to view the economic activity of commercial banks predominantly through the lens of financial *transactions*, treating banks as vehicles for the efficient and effective flow of capital across boundaries (Knight & Sharma, 2016; Wilhelm & Downing, 2001). However, economic geographers and institutional scholars have increasingly sought to reframe the economic signifi-cance of financial services organizations through a multi-scalar approach, pointing to the role that transnational communities (Beaverstock, 2004), cities (Cassis, 2006; Jones, 2002), and even the internal routines within banks (as organizations) themselves (Faulconbridge, 2008) can play in shaping the flow and concentration financial services activity across the global economy.

Whilst each of these spatial scales enriches one's overall understanding of how transnational commercial banks, and organizations more broadly, become embedded within regions, less is known about why organizations *move between* regions once they have become embedded. This is important, since there is growing recognition that regions do not represent static entities with inherent traits or characteristics, but are rather living socio-technical constructions or 'networks of learning' in which the relational dynamics between an organization and its regional context are constantly shifting and being negotiated (Boschma, 2004). This is no more prescient than in the case of Brexit in which the relational dynamics regarding Britain's place within the European Union arguably changed overnight. Given these contingencies, this article argues that what is needed is a richer appreciation of the mechanisms by which organizations not only cluster in particular regions but also shift the types and concentration of services within and between regions in response to environmental cues.

This article explores this issue in the specific case of transnational commercial banking. Transnational commercial banks (hereafter 'transnational banks') play a vital role in the economy by intermediating the relationship between retail and corporate borrowers and savers, and diversifying risk globally. Since these organ-izations already have a presence across multiple cities, countries and regions, the strategic decision to shift resource allocation between offices and service providers offers an interesting opportunity to conceptualize why organizations shift their regional focus over time in response to particular types of environmental cues. Here, regions are understood in a socially constructed sense in terms of how organizational actors frame geographical boundaries in terms of time zones. These enable actors to delineate each others' activities in terms of how they frame management reporting and trading activities internally, as well as how they configure their financial reporting to external audiences.

By bringing together organizational sociology and regional development in the context of transnational banks, this article limits its contribution to three areas. First, it shows why different activities are performed at the corporate centre versus the periphery, based on their informational content. Second, by illustrating how this informational content changes over time, it accounts for why organizations *change* their regional presence based on the functions they perform in different regions. Finally, it proposes a methodological contribution to geography scholars beyond an analysis of financial transactions by examining the information sharing processes of organizational actors.

TRUSTWORTHINESS AND EFFICIENCY SHAPING THE LOCATION DECISIONS OF TRANSNATIONAL BANKS

There is now widespread recognition amongst scholars of regional development and strategic management that geographical context shapes the location decisions of organizations. In order to compete, firms do not merely draw on the cognitive and experiential knowledge resources of employees, but also rely on how this knowledge is embedded within a macro-level cultural and institutional context (Gertler, 2003; Lawson & Lorenz, 1999).

A classic reference point for linking geographical context to strategic decision-making within organizations is Sassen's (2001) theory of global city-regions, which focuses on the agglomeration activities of advanced producer services organizations. This is closely related to Castells' theory of an information society, which recognizes the role of the 'metropolitan region' (Castells, 2010; Sassen, 2001). Sassen's and Castells' work both theorize the role of cities in building 'trusted settings' which facilitate and harmonize inter-organizational relations. This is supported, for example, through face-to-face interactions, co-location and co-presence, which increase the opportunity for accidental meetings amongst a vetted, credible set of partners (Bathelt, Malmberg, & Maskell, 2004). Advanced producer service organizations, such as commercial banks, therefore co-locate in particular cities because of the ability to discern more quickly the legitimacy of strategic interactions at the very top of organizations (Sassen, 2001). Broadly, then, this approach argues that location decisions are based on the richness of relational context in which proximity enhances the trust between actors.

Other studies, such as on transnational corporations and tacit knowledge, have extended this work by focusing on the 'likeness' of shared activities and processes between organizations within a particular geographical context. Building on the organizational routines literature, these studies argue that territorial clustering arises from certain 'norms of reciprocity' in which inter-firm collaboration is aided by shared approaches, common language and mutually agreed 'rules of the game' that enable firms within a particular region to work closely together (Faulconbridge, 2006; Lawson & Lorenz, 1999). These studies have described these mechanisms at multiple scales, including learning regions (Maskell & Malmberg, 1999), shared 'communities of practice' (Beaverstock, 2004), 'global cluster regions' (Bathelt & Li, 2013), as well as amongst certain types of individuals (Gertler, 2003). In each case, the focus is on the replicability of systems and processes between organizations in a shared, relational context. This approach has been expanded through concepts such as global production networks, which articulates the role of particular types of organizations (e.g., 'lead firms') in orchestrating the coordination of 'like' or 'related' actors (Coe, Dicken, & Hess, 2008; Coe, Lai, & Wójcik, 2014; MacKinnon, 2012). Global production networks rely on a firm–territory nexus (Dicken & Malmberg, 2001), in which the power of global lead firms is recognized through their position within a supply chain, and their ability to control or determine the nature of relationships that are 'downstream'. Taken together, this approach is focused on the reach of particular activities within relational context, in which the ability to scale and distribute information to extremities is enabled by characteristics of the product and services themselves.

In summary, then, the regional development literature has identified two key mechanisms for *why* organizations co-locate: (1) trustworthiness, which is aided by proximity; and (2) efficiency, which is aided by shared systems and processes. These two concepts are interrelated: trustworthiness reduces the transaction costs (i.e., efficiency) of risk-taking endeavours, and shared language (i.e., efficiency) enables evaluation of trustworthiness to occur more quickly. Whilst these mechanisms explain why organizations may cluster within particular regions, what is less well developed in this literature is why these cluster configurations may *change*: that is, why do regions come in and out of favour with specific organizations and in relation to specific functions? This is important because organizations constantly respond to evaluations of the macro-environment, forcing them to decouple and recouple with different strategic partners (Coe et al., 2014). Taylor, Catalana, and Walker (2004), for example, in their study of advanced producer service firms (including finance) within global cities found that these organizations continuously sought work that was 'strategic' and 'cutting edge' (i.e., had high status), yet gave limited account for the contingencies that explain the waxing and waning of relationships at the organization-regional interface over time.

HOW INFORMATIONAL CONTENT SHAPES THE REGION–ORGANIZATION INTERFACE

To explore this issue in the context of transnational banking, this article looks at the underlying content of the information being shared between bank actors and their strategic partners across space and time, and evaluates how the quality of this information may shape location decisions. By abstracting the analysis to the informational unit of analysis, it seeks to define it more broadly to include not just the financial transactions between banks, but the stickier, more strategic, less publicly displayed information that financial services actors (e.g., banks, their consultants, joint venture partners, financial technology start-ups, etc.) share with each other both inside and across organizational boundaries in order to secure organizational competitive advantage. Furthermore, in applying this analysis to regional development, this article examines the spatial dimensions of this information more broadly, rather than delimiting the theorizing to a regional or sub-regional scale.

A key departure point is Clark and O'Connor's (1997) key article on the global financial economy in which they linked the nature of information (or what they termed 'information content') to three types of densities: transparent, translucent and opaque. Transparent products were composed of information whose qualities and dimensions were well known, and therefore easy for market actors to interpret. For example, gold had functionally and spatially consistent informational content and could therefore be easily interpreted and transacted from different geographical standpoints. Equities, on the other hand, were translucent products because they contained information that involved institutional or organizational context. For example, asset managers might frame the risk–reward outcomes from a portfolio of equities differently based on proprietary methodologies. Finally, opaque products required specialist expertise to interpret 'private information' (p 10), such as unlisted, venture capital-funded investments that need detailed technology and management due diligence. This information was therefore hard to access and resulted in asymmetrical advantages to market actors 'in the know' (Bathelt & Glucker, 2011; Jones, 2002).

Clark and O'Connor (1997) linked these different types of financial products to different financial centres. They argued that transparent products were more easily traded across national boundaries and would therefore be dominated by international financial centres (e.g., London, New York). This was because these geographical agglomerations could reduce the transaction cost of trades: 'turnover efficiencies are only met in the larger global centres, so that the design and production of transparent products provides the apex of the world's financial system' (p. 12). By contrast, translucent and opaque products were better suited to national (e.g., Sydney, Hong Kong, Frankfurt) and sub-national (e.g., San Francisco, Boston) financial centres respectively, which could accommodate the advantages of proximate information (Clark & O'Connor, 1997; Knight & Sharma, 2016).

Clark and O'Connor (1997) provide one way for unpacking the relational dynamics shaping the spatial geography of information. However, their work is limited because it frames financial services activity in terms of financial transactions rather than in organizational terms. Indeed, many of the 'turnover efficiencies' they envisaged have *not* become a source of local competitive advantage as trading platform technologies have radically reduced the transaction costs of assets in diverse physical geographies. However, in subsequent work these has been a growing appreciation that *organizational actors*, or at least the nature of information shared between these actors (rather than the technology to effect transactions), is the real source of competitive advantage between cities, national and regional geographies. Clark and Thrift (2004), for example, subsequently argue that financial assets 'clustered in space and time, *even if* technology allows trading from anywhere at any time' (p. 238, emphasis added).

One literature that has focused on the nature of the informational content traded between organizational actors is the boundary-spanning literature. Organizational boundaries perform a central function in delimiting the social structures and processes of an organization from its external environment (Pfeffer & Salancik, 2003; Santos & Eisenhardt, 2005). Organizations incur a governance cost in managing information flow across organizational boundaries. These costs are caused by information problems (Williamson, 1985), as other actors (whether market participants or organizational actors in subsidiary units) incorrectly value product or service attributes in market exchange, leading to adverse selection and moral hazard (Santos & Eisenhardt, 2005). In order to minimize the cost of governing activities, boundary spanners help facilitate the exchange of information across boundaries in order to support efficient strategic coupling between organizations and/or their geographically dispersed subsidiaries.

The boundary-spanning literature recognizes that the practices of boundary spanning differ depending on the characteristics of the information being processed. Here two dimensions are relevant: (1) the degree of *perceived environmental uncertainty*; and (2) the *information need* in which the information arises. In relation to the degree of environmental uncertainty, the information-processing literature recognizes low and high degrees of *perceived environmental uncertainty*. Uncertainty refers to the extent to which organizational actors can discern informational cues with which to make decisions (Leifer & Delbecq, 1978; Leifer & Huber, 1977). High informational uncertainty arises when there is significant heterogeneity, variability and complexity in the information received from the external environment. On the other hand, low informational uncertainty arises when the information is relatively consistent (low variability), homogenous and simple. In the context of financial organizations, high environmental uncertainty may be present when, for example, unexpected or unanticipated issues appear in the environment. This might be based on radical changes to regulation, sudden shifts in technology, or catastrophic insolvencies which pose systemic and sudden risks to financial institutions. On the other hand, low perceived uncertainty will arise when the information is largely formalized, anticipated and easy to digest. This might include, for example, central bank updates or macroeconomic information, which is consistent with forecasts and macroeconomic trends. Elsewhere inside the organization this might include information about incremental changes in the competitor landscape, minor shifts in regulation or adjustments to internal corporate strategies.

The second dimension in information processing identified above is the *information need* in which information arises. This depends on whether information is anticipated and regular, and has an implication for the boundary-spanning activities conducted by organizational actors. Information is anticipated and regular when the provision of information is expected and formalized. This might be, for example, quarterly updates about financial results, or information provided as part of the annual strategic planning cycle. This dimension does not relate to *what* the information is, but rather *how* it is received. On the other hand, unanticipated and irregular information arises when the need for information is not known and it occurs in a one-off capacity. This might refer to, for example, surprise out-of-cycle earnings updates, market-sensitive deals that need to be disclosed as market-sensitive matters, or mergers-and-acquisition activities that unexpectedly change the competitor landscape.

SPATIAL DYNAMICS OF INFORMATION PROCESSING: WHY ORGANIZATIONAL ACTORS CHANGE THEIR REGIONAL PRESENCE

The boundary-spanning literature has been developed in organizational studies and strategic management to examine the personal traits (Mudambi & Swift, 2009; Schotter & Beamish, 2011) and competencies (Ancona & Caldwell, 1992; Mudambi & Navarra, 2004) that condition boundary spanners' ability to perform their spanning roles. However, the extension in this article is to link a boundary-spanning analysis back to its relational and geography context in order to understand how these relationships characterize the changing spatio-temporal distribution of transnational bank activities.

To do this, this article proposes linking the informational contingencies identified above to their spatial context, building on the relational mechanisms of 'trustworthiness' and 'efficiency'. In doing so, it extends prior literature on regional development by accounting for *how* and *why* organizations shift their position in the market as their informational needs change. It also adds spatial dynamics to boundary-spanning typologies, which are not envisaged in the aforementioned contributions.

These two dimensions identified above – low/high perceived environmental uncertainty; and low/high information need – are depicted in a two-by-two typology in Table 1. At the intersection of these two dimensions, boundary span-

Table 1 Spatial dynamics of boundary-spanning practices

Information need	Perceived environmental uncertainty	
	Low	High
Anticipated, regular	Scenario 1 Spatial dynamics: information managed at the periphery by frontline workers through standardized processes	Scenario 2 Spatial dynamics: centralized meta-routines emerge to manage bounded responses to information by senior managers in central and regional offices
Unanticipated, irregular	Scenario 3 Spatial dynamics: local partnerships and alliances enable the corporate centre to enact strategies regionally	Scenario 4 Spatial dynamics: strategic information needs proximity to the corporate headquarters for a timely response

Source: Adapted from Leifer and Delbeq (1978, p. 45).

ners triage information received and process it in order to make decisions. Each of the cells is characterized as a 'scenario' in which organizational actors adopt different boundary-spanning practices in order to make sense of the information. These situations need not be mutually exclusive (Aldrich & Herker, 1977). Instead, boundary spanners might find themselves more heavily weighted towards one scenario at any one time, and/or changing strategies over time as contexts change (Kunisch, Menz, & Ambos, 2015; Marrone, 2010).

In order to illustrate the distinctiveness of this approach in the context of transnational banking, this article now links examples of practices that boundary spanners adopt within each cell, and relate these to the spatial dynamics these impose. Each of these scenarios is guided by four overarching questions:

- *Where* does the information come from?
- *Where* are the boundary spanners located?
- How important is *proximity* of boundary spanners to the sources of information?
- How *centralized* is the collection of information in different types of boundary-spanning practices?

Scenario 1 (low uncertainty; anticipated/regular)

Informational content

In these situations, organizations have (1) low perceived environmental uncertainty about the information and (2) anticipated and regular information needs. As a result, this means that the way the information arrives is regulated, and the processing of information by boundary spanners follows a routine. An example of this in a financial context might be information about central bank announcements about interest rates. The timing of a central bank announcement may be widely anticipated and therefore have *low perceived uncertainty*. The information need of an organization is also *anticipated and regular*, because it feeds into established financial models for the cost of servicing debt across the different divisions of a bank.

Spatial dynamics

In these instances, the boundary-spanning activities can be geographically distributed and performed by non-strategic actors, such as front-line managers. This is because the low uncertainty associated with the information means that it can be easily accommodated by organizational routines and processes. These routines enable consistent responses to stimuli at dispersed geographical nodes. An example of this might be front-line managers' responses to lending rates following a change in central bank policy. Since these calculations are highly routinized, they can be enacted at the periphery and do not require proximity to the corporate centre.

Scenario 2 (high uncertainty; anticipated/regular)

Informational content

Organizations have (1) a high perceived environmental uncertainty about the information and (2) anticipated and regular information needs. An example of this might be an organization where monthly reports need to be developed, but where the environment changes rapidly, meaning that the sources of information can be difficult to identify. In these cases, even though boundary spanners have processes set up to search for information (anticipated, regular information need), the information itself has high perceived uncertainty.

Spatial dynamics

In these instances, the information is uncertain meaning that it requires judgement from more strategic actors, such as senior and middle managers in headquarters and regional offices. However, in order to create some flexibility for senior managers, responses are framed in terms of meta-routines that are condoned by the corporate centre. These meta-routines are defined as routines that formalize discretion levels. This might include centralized budget cycles that provide middle managers with (limited) budget discretion, and strategic planning workshops that formalize organizational strategy implementation at the periphery. This is likely to characterize the work of mid-office functions, such as senior managers, in which the bounded discretion is designed to cater for local contingencies and variations. An example of this might be a regional managers' discretion to open up new branch offices when the population density of a particular city reaches a particular level. This decision involves responsiveness to uncertainty (population levels in the city), but is formalized with an organizational routine (policy for branch openings).

Scenario 3 (low uncertainty; unanticipated/irregular)

Informational content

Organizations have (1) a low perceived environmental uncertainty and (2) unanticipated/irregular informational needs. An example of this might be how regional offices implement centrally agreed strategies through regional partnerships. In these cases, there is low uncertainty since the top management team has formulated the strategy of the organization. However, the implementation of this strategy is unanticipated and irregular as regional offices respond to opportunistic recruitment to address specific needs at any point in time, or pursue partnerships such as joint-venture relations, acquisitions or divestments. Since these are typically one-off events, they are irregular and the specific details are often unanticipated.

Spatial dynamics

In this case, the organizational strategy is likely to be established at the corporate centre, but implementation will take place in regional offices. These decisions will be implemented by regional senior managers, since they relate to change implementation so they have strategic content.

Scenario 4 (high uncertainty; non-regulated, non-routine)

Informational content

Organizations have (1) a high perceived environmental uncertainty and (2) unanticipated/irregular informational needs. Thus, the main difference from the previous scenario is that the new information is perceived as introducing high uncertainty. For example, the boundary spanners may have an urgent need to appraise a technology threat or opportunity for the financial organization based on a new venture opportunity. This means there is high perceived uncertainty about the significance of the information, and the information need is unanticipated and irregular. The boundary-spanning practices are *non-regulated*, since it is not anticipated or initiated within the organization's systems. Furthermore, because it is perceived as introducing high uncertainty, it triggers non-routine processes such as one-off strategic acquisitions, consulting projects or new investigations.

Spatial dynamics

This information involves highly strategic decisions, and therefore depends on boundary spanning at the corporate centre. These decisions are most dependent on proximity and centrality, since top managers need rich information as well as the ability to make decisions at short-notice (e.g., following the Brexit decision). These activities most closely reflect location decisions for corporate headquarters.

RELATING A BOUNDARY-SPANNING VIEW TO FINANCIAL GEOGRAPHY: A CASE STUDY OF HSBC

To illustrate how a geographically enriched boundary-spanning view expands one's understanding of how and why organizations shift the regional presence of particular service functions, this article draws on the case of HSBC and the spanning relationships that its organizational actors have formed with other organizations (e.g., business consulting, investors and government agencies). This article adopts an illustrative case study approach, drawing on interviews conducted with HSBC middle managers in Hong Kong and London, as well as the authors' long-term engagement in studying the commercial banking sector. This study is supplemented with secondary data, including company documents, newspaper articles covering interviews with key decision-makers, and other archival materials to compose a historical account of HSBC's corporate strategy in relation to regional presence and headquarters' location.

HSBC was started in 1865 when European and Chinese merchants founded an organization to finance trade between West and East. They originally considered Shanghai as the headquarters' location before settling on Hong Kong. Since that time, HSBC has either debated or moved its headquarters in 1941, 1946, 1981, 1986, 1990, 1993, 2008 and 2009 (*The Economist*, 2016a). Most recently, in 2016, it decided to retain its headquarters in London after 10 months of consideration. The study concentrates on HSBC's most recent history, focusing on particular episodes of change in the geographical location of HSBC's service functions, and accounting for these spatial changes.

Applying a boundary-spanning perspective, the case study of HSBC allows one to illustrate four instances of the organization's strategic coupling activities and their geographical consequences. The findings of the case study are summarized in Table 2. First, it is shown how spanning practices can take different forms based on the perceived environmental uncertainty and informational needs of organizational actors. This is represented by the four scenarios depicted, which illustrate distinct strategic issues facing the organization and functions performed. This is shown in the rows titled 'Service function' and 'Information process scenario'. It is important to note that these do not proceed serially (i.e., from one to four) because the article highlights the scenario that was at play during the time period in focus. Second and related, it is shown how these scenarios can co-exist or change over time. This is depicted in the four columns, which reflect four distinct periods in the organizational history of HSBC. Third, it is shown how strategic decisions made within each scenario can have geographical conse- quences. This is reflected in the second column titled 'Geographical focus'. Fourth, these consequences can be examined in multiple ways based on the different participants involved, as reflected in the row titled 'Participants involved'. This varies from the equity position of assets owned by HSBC around the world

Table 2 Summary of illustrative case: HSBC

	1993–2000	2010–14	Late 2014–15	Mid-2015–16
Information process scenario	Scenario 2	Scenario 3	Scenario 1	Scenario 4
Service function	Post-merger integration	Regional expansion and sales growth	Formalization, standardization, cost efficiencies	Strategic planning, investor relations
Geographical focus	America and Europe	Emerging– developed economies trade flows	Asia and Pearl River Delta	London
Participants involved	Acquired businesses	Divested businesses; consulting firms	In-house management expertise	Regulators; investor community

(and divestments over time) to the number of employees under management, inter-organizational relationships with financial and business service firms, and with regulators and investors. Taken together, this article now discusses the unfolding spanning activities taking place within HSBC over a 30-year period, and the consequences for the organization's geographical footprint and scope.

1993–2000: Becoming European and American (scenario 2)

Environmental uncertainty and informational need

In the 1980s HSBC was headquartered in Hong Kong. In 1993, the management team and board decided to move its headquarters to London. This coincided with two important informational uncertainties that were perceived in the macro-environment. First, HSBC had just fully acquired a leading British bank, Midland Bank. At the time, it was one of the largest banking acquisitions in history, and was part of the bank's strategic move to gain a foothold in Europe. The bank was diversifying into America and Europe, with Asia only accounting for a third of profits as late as 2004. In addition, Hong Kong was due to be handed back to China in 1997, and there were concerns that Beijing would impose heavy regulation on the bank. As the chairman at the time said, 'As night follows day . . . we would become a Chinese bank,' had the bank kept its domicile in Hong Kong after 1997 (*The Economist*, 2016a). Accelerating financial integration between the UK and the European Union from 1986 to the 1990s also meant the UK focus extended to a broader focus on Europe in general. A lesser focus on Asia was also influenced by the Asian financial crisis of 1997–98.

Spatial dynamics

The period immediately following large acquisitions (Midland Bank) and relocation decisions (London) was characterized by significant involvement from the bank's middle and senior managers. The post-merger integration still posed significant uncertainties in relation to how core banking and technology platforms would be integrated between Midland Bank and HSBC. In addition, there were also strategic issues that need attention with regulators, in relation to taxation and addressing systemic risk to the economy based by UK-based banks' total balance sheet compared to gross domestic product (GDP).

2010–Late 2014: Stuart Gulliver's arrival as CEO and focus on Asian trade flows (scenario 3)

Environmental uncertainty and informational need

Through the mid-to-late 2000s, however, the slowdown in Europe and the Americas following the global financial crisis instigated new questions about the bank's future, and highlighted the growing strategic importance of Asia to HSBC's organizational strategy. HSBC's focus on Asia, and building the business around trade finance flows between Europe and emerging economies, culminated in the appointment of Stuart Gulliver as chief executive officer (CEO) in 2010. Gulliver had worked in HSBC since the 1980s and had closely followed the failure of the bank to gain a foothold in America, especially after a succession of disastrous acquisitions stretching back to the Marine Midland business (in 1987) and leading up to Householder International, a sub-prime lender (acquired in 2003).

Gulliver's focus was on targeting markets where HSBC had a competitive advantage, and exiting those markets where it did not (e.g., HSBC left Poland and Georgia shortly after his appointment). This became the focus on the centrally agreed strategy. Gulliver described the nature of the bank's geographical footprint as follows: 'We have had a sprawl, as opposed to a set of cohesive, logically integrated businesses in a set of chosen countries. And because we've always been actually profitable there's never been the requirement to be disciplined about this' (*The Telegraph*, 2012). This reflected the need to concentrate highly strategic information close to the corporate centre, and reformulate how the strategy was implemented in regional offices.

The shift to focusing on trade flows between Europe and Asia, and China in particular, tapped into clear, long-term macroeconomic trends driven by China's rising middle class (i.e., low uncertainty). Whilst year-to-year variations constituted short-term informational uncertainty, the long-term environmental outlook was perceived as having relatively low uncertainty. China and Europe represented one of the world's largest trade corridors. Furthermore, the significant savings in China underwrote this decision. As Gulliver indicated in relation to the firm's commitment to doing more business in the Cantonese-speaking Pearl River Delta:

> Rising interest rates would boost lending margins mostly in Asia, which has a surplus of deposits, which need not be repriced as quickly as debt. HSBC is far more Asian than its Western rivals. *Not even a hard landing in China, a banking crisis there or a devaluation of the yuan would alter that.*
>
> (HSBC Holdings Plc, 2015, emphasis added)

In this respect, this phase was led by senior managers in regional offices since it involved strategy implementation rather than strategy formulation, thereby reducing the need for strong centralized control.

Spatial dynamics

Building the management team and expertise to deliver on emerging-developed market business required bespoke skills in the early stages of Gulliver's tenure. As part of this, HSBC aggressively tapped into a range of technology partnerships to access intellectual property in key regions that would spur its future business. For example, it worked with Accenture, an information technology consulting firm, to operate a 'Fintech lab' in regional locations (Hong Kong, New York and London) in order to access promising start-ups and on-board their technologies within the bank. This also guided its on-the-ground strategy to grow regional office presence in the Pearl River Delta, with access to high-tech, research-focused and digital businesses such as Tencent and Huawei, headquartered in Shenzhen. During this period as well, non-routine restructuring took place in line with reorienting the business towards Asia. Gulliver oversaw 78 businesses being sold across the HSBC group, almost halving the bank's exposure to the US time zone through North America and Brazil. Vast sums were also spent on compliance systems in order to support the bank's entry into developing countries, in particular where anti-money laundering and counter-terrorism checks are especially important. In this respect, the large-scale restructuring of the firm's headquarters' location and subsequent divestment decisions coincided with the need to centralize information flow to the corporate centre of control.

Late 2014–15: Formalizing Asian expertise in-house (scenario 1)

Environmental uncertainty and informational need

Gulliver's expansion into Asia was initially facilitated through close connections with the tacit network of professional service firms and advisers in London and the Pearl River Delta. However, as the strategy implementation matured, his focus became on strategy implementation at the local level through the opening of new regional offices, and organic expansion through Asia. This shift was important as it enabled information needs to be anticipated in a *regulated* manner, and for information search activities to be processed in a routine manner. The routine manner of these spanning activities was manifested in the fact that by being brought in-house, they were able to be formalized into the everyday practices of the organization. This also enabled these services to be distributed to regional offices in new markets.

Spatial dynamics

One example of this was the appointment of Andy Maguire, the former partner at the Boston Consulting Group leading the prior strategy engagement, to HSBC's Global Chief Operations Officer in London in late 2014. A key aspect of Maguire's role was to reduce the multiple management layers within the organization, and formalize the activities that frontline workers within the bank were doing. This led to a 10% reduction in the size of the workforce. Gulliver described the political tensions this created as follows: 'If you've had all this "country head is king" stuff, you end up with multiple head offices and within those, multiple layers of bureaucracy, and so we haven't been the nimblest firm, as bureaucracies are incredibly self-reinforcing' (*The Telegraph*, 2012). The process of formalizing internal processes enabled more effective decentralized management by reducing the amount of discretion senior managers had over asset allocation. This enabled the Gulliver, as Group CEO, and his senior executive team to pursue a group strategy in relation to Asia in a more consistent and distributed manner than under the bank's previously decentralized structure. This arguably also reduced the perceived uncertainty of environmental information (i.e., low uncertainty) as the bank was able to focus on executing against broad macro-trends rather than responding to local environmental issues as and when they arose.

Furthermore, HSBC moved to expand its employment footprint in the Pearl River Delta. In early 2015, for example, a plan to add 4000 new banking employees over three to five years was announced in addition to the existing 1500 (Reuters, 2016). In the case of HSBC, establishing new offices in this region was part of scenario 1, in which the bank had identified clear long-term trends (low uncertainty), and was ready to scale early initiatives in order to take advantage of the company's location strategy (unanticipated/ irregular).

Mid-2015–16: Headquarters' decision still to call London home (scenario 4)

Environmental uncertainty and informational need

The transition of the management side of the business around Asia resurfaced the decision of whether to move the corporate headquarters back to Hong Kong. Although there were a number of strategic issues for discussion, the decisive factors largely related to high levels of uncertainty around regulation and government policy more broadly. On the one hand, HSBC faced issues around the risk of Britain leaving the European Union. Directors reasoned that this would be an issue whether or not HSBC were headquartered in Hong Kong. There were also specific concerns around taxation. HSBC paid a US$1.4 billion levy cost in 2015, which was significantly more than its rivals due to its larger balance sheet. This charge was a 10% charge on profits from its global operations, and was in addition to other changes, such as ring-fencing its retail arm, capital surcharges, 'bail-in' bonds and liquidity buffers (*The Economist*, 2016b).

On the other hand, the more systemic issue facing HSBC was how it would negotiate with government authorities in the event of a financial crisis, especially given the ability of regulators to provide support in a financial crisis. As of 2016, the Hong Kong Market Authority had US$360 billion of foreign reserves, but it lacked the crisis tool kit of a central bank. Thus, HSBC would ultimately need to build relations with mainland China in a crisis; yet China's approach to finance was not considered transparent and fell outside the known expertise of senior management.

Spatial dynamics

The decision to leave its headquarters in London was framed as follows by HSBC's chairman: 'After considering all the relevant factors, the Board concluded that having our headquarters in the UK and our significant business in Asia Pacific led from Hong Kong, delivers the best of both worlds to our stakeholders' (HSBC Holdings Plc, 2015). Yet the decision of Britain to leave the European

Union triggered new revisions to this approach, including decisions about relocating some mid-office jobs to continental Europe.

Furthermore, HSBC had a more established base for managing investor relations in London, which was important for maintaining stability during periods of significant change (i.e., *non-routine* responses). London remained the source of price discovery for HSBC's share price, despite being listed in New York, London and Hong Kong (Wójcik, 2011). London also traded twice as many HSBC shares as Hong Kong, and seven times as many as New York. This infrastructure enabled HSBC to respond to unanticipated events effecting investor relations around the world.

CONCLUSIONS AND IMPLICATIONS

Geographers studying transnational banking services have largely focused on the city, country or regional units of analysis, whilst leaving the internal dynamics within organizations as a 'black box'. This article explores this issue by sensitizing future research agendas to three dimensions of spatial organization that come into focus through an organizational view: (1) the different types of service functions performed within transnational banks, (2) the spatial dynamics of the informational content comprising these functions and (3) how these functions respond to environmental conditions, including the inter-organizational partnerships. These three dimensions are highlighted in Figure 1. It illustrates an example of the constellation of organizations relating to HSBC through boundary-spanning activities. The organizations are represented by circles, and the spanning activities are represented by arrows. First, the labels in circles highlight an array of organizational types, including governments (Chinese and UK regulatory agencies), professional service providers (consulting firms, e.g., BCG and Accenture), as well as technology partners (Huawei). Second, the line type of the circles around the organization indicates the different types of informational needs these organizations service to HSBC. Anticipated and regular informational needs are depicted with a full line. These organizations have predictable routines in how information is shared, thereby enabling these functions to operate at considerable physical distance to the corporate centre. On the other hand, organizations depicted with a dotted line have an irregular (i.e., non-routinized) relationship with HSBC, and provide information when unanticipated information needs arise. This might include, for example, strategic advice that requires bespoke consulting. This is significant because spanning under these conditions requires close-at-hand relationships and proximity. Third, the dotted boxes show how the boundary-spanning relationships can operate under perceived conditions of environmental certainty and environmental uncertainty. This shows that professional service firm and government relationships are characterized by uncertainty, since there is significant variability and heterogeneity in the kinds of information shared in these relationships and the information is strategically important. On the other hand, in-house recruitment and joint-venture partnerships consolidate spanning activities under conditions of perceived environmental certainty. This reflects

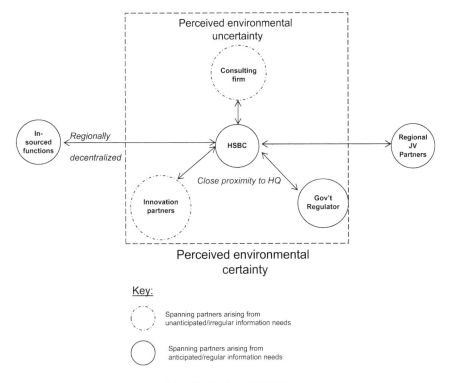

Figure 1 Summary of episodes identified in the HSBC illustrative case

greater degrees of trust and competence on behalf of HSBC spanners as they formalize these relationships, and can therefore operate through middle managers in regional offices.

Taken together, these three dimensions align with three contributions to the geography of transnational banking services. First, by depicting an array of organizations linked to a transnational bank, the model shows how the informational content of relationships can vary between organizations based on the strategic functions being performed. This in turn has spatial consequences, as the scenarios depict. This may offer qualifications to prior models that have either focused on a single organization or characterized the relationship between organizations based on industry or institutional factors. For example, Sassen argues that organizational actors in advanced producer service organizations act as the micro-network of the strategic decision-making process, based on face-to-face interactions supported by electronic communication (Sassen, 2001). However, by studying the types of *information* processed across these relationships and its spatial dynamics, this article offers a contingency model that reveals how certain types of spanning (and agglomerations) may be more important during certain periods of stress or environmental uncertainty, and for particular types of functions of services.

This leads to the second contribution, which is to highlight qualities within the informational content of boundary-spanning activities. The model seeks to 'theorize the arrows', looking at the kinds of information flow that become shared between organizations, the 'needs' that initiate these information processes, and their spatial consequences. This may offer a more dynamic and spatially nuanced view of *when* certain types of spanning functions become more or less in focus with certain types of organizations. Whereas prior studies in knowledge management in particular have highlighted the different scalar levels at which to position inter-organizational linkages, by focusing on information this article shows how an organization's presence may differ by organizational function. Thus, certain types of information exchange related to strategic issues may be co-located with corporate headquarters. By contrast, other types of information exchange can be conducted at the organizational periphery such as developing countries (e.g., outsourcing activities), and through automation (e.g., through technology). This is because of the highly predictable nature of the informational content involves in these spanning tasks. The model, therefore, offers a theoretical basis for explaining how these nested geographical dynamics emerge, and why transnational banks might shift particular types of activities to different regions over time.

Finally, this article makes a methodological contribution by suggesting new ways in which the activities of transnational banks can be measured and analysed. In the context of regional development in particular, the financial geography literature has tended to focus on transaction or stock price data (Wójcik, 2011), or the close financial relationships that emerge by 'being there' (Malmberg & Maskell, 2006) and having close-to-hand access to portfolio companies (Knight, 2012, 2013). Investment decisions and financial transactions clearly remain central to financial geography, but this article opens up a wider palate in terms of organizational actors' specific practices. This aligns with a burgeoning agenda in management geography that has called on the need to study the social practice of decision-makers more closely (Jones, 2014; Jones & Murphy, 2011).

A number of limitations are acknowledged as part of this study. First, the article has limited the discussion to transnational commercial banks that exhibit specific qualities as complex, multi-business organizations. Future studies in this area may consider whether these dynamics apply to other financial organizations that play a central role in finance, such as asset managers, sovereign wealth funds and investment banks. In addition, the analysis has been limited to an illustrative case study approach of a single organization. Future studies might consider developing finergrained approaches to studying *how* these decisions are made. For example, studies with a positivist focus might seek to consider cross-case comparisons between different types of transnational banks, which have specializations in different functions. Alternatively practice-based methodological approaches with a interpretive focus may seek to analyse the 'doings and sayings' of organizational actors through longitudinal case studies, highlighting their interpretive aspects (Schatzki, 2002). In these cases, studying strategy workshops and meetings through ethnographic techniques become important ways to identify and then examine micro-instantiations of larger decisions.

To conclude, the attention paid to industrial concentration and geographic distribution, as in the case of international economic and financial centres, has become increasingly important to geographers seeking to make sense of the changing landscape of international business and finance (Tickell & Peck, 1992). The Fordist era, in which the question of economic scale could be explained through the functioning of the stable, vertically integrated corporation seeking to standardize and reduce its cost of production, has given way to an age of flexible production. By examining the conceptual underpinnings of information processing and boundary-spanning activities between organizations, the intention here has been to enable finer-grained, dynamic views of how this flexibility is enacted in a regional scale in the case of financial organizations. This article not only seeks to encourage a research agenda that moves towards a more complex, multiscalar new of inter-organizational relationships in finance, but also one that attends to the conditions and limitations of geographical decisions as organizations decide on issues, such as headquarters' location, employee resource allocation, and investment/divestment decisions, by paying regard to their external environment and internal strategies.

ACKNOWLEDGEMENTS

All errors and omissions are the sole responsibility of the authors.

DISCLOSURE STATEMENT

No potential conflict of interest was reported by the authors.

FUNDING

This research was supported under the Australian Research Council's Discovery Projects funding scheme [project number DP160103855]. Dariusz Wójcik also received funding for this project from the European Research Council (ERC) under the European Union's Horizon 2020 research and innovation programme [grant agreement number 681337], and the Hong Kong Research Grants Council [grant number T31-717/12-R].

REFERENCES

Aldrich, H., & Herker, D. (1977). Boundary spanning roles and organization structure. *Academy of Management Review*, *2*, 217–230.

Ancona, D. G., & Caldwell, D. F. (1992). Bridging the boundary: External activity and performance in organizational teams. *Administrative Science Quarterly*, *37*, 634–665. doi:10.2307/2393475

Bathelt, H., & Glucker, J. (2011). *The relational economy: Geographies of knowing and learning*. Oxford: Oxford University Press.

Bathelt, H., & Li, P.-F. (2013). Global cluster networks – Foreign direct investment flows from Canada to China. *Journal of Economic Geography*, *1*, 31–56. doi:10.1093/jeg/lbt005.

Bathelt, H., Malmberg, A., & Maskell, P. (2004). Clusters and knowledge: Local buzz, global pipelines and the process of knowledge creation. *Progress in Human Geography*, *28*, 31–56. doi:10.1191/0309132504ph469oa

Beaverstock, J. V. (2004). 'Managing across borders': Knowledge management and expatriation in professional service legal firms. *Journal of Economic Geography*, *4*, 157–179. doi:10.1093/jeg/4.2.157

Boschma, R. (2004). Competitiveness of regions from an evolutionary perspective. *Regional Studies*, *38*, 1001–1014. doi:10.1080/0034340042000292601

Cassis, Y. (2006). *Capitals of capital: A history of international financial centres, 1780–2005*. Cambridge: Cambridge University Press.

Castells, M. (2010). *The rise of the network society*. Oxford: Blackwell.

Clark, G., & O'Connor, K. (1997). The informational content of financial products and the spatial structure of the global finance industry. In K. R. Cox (Ed.), *Spaces of globalization: Reasserting the power of the local* (pp. 89–114). New York: Guilford.

Clark, G. L., & Thrift, N. (2004). The return of bureaucracy: Managing dispersed knowledge in global finance. In K. Knorr Cetina, & A. Preda (Eds.), *The sociology of financial markets* (pp. 229–249). Oxford: Oxford University Press.

Coe, N., Lai, K. P., & Wójcik, D. (2014). Integrating finance into global production networks. *Networks, Regional Studies*, *48*, 761–777. doi:10.1080/00343404.2014.886772

Coe, N. M., Dicken, P., & Hess, M. (2008). Global production networks: Realizing the potential. *Journal of Economic Geography*, *8*, 271–295. doi:10.1093/jeg/lbn002

Dicken, P., & Malmberg, A. (2001). Firms in territories: A relational perspective. *Economic Geography*, *77*, 345–363. doi:10.2307/3594105

Faulconbridge, J. R. (2006). Stretching tacit knowledge beyond a local fix? Global spaces of learning in advertising professional service firms. *Journal of Economic Geography*, *6*, 517–540. doi:10.1093/jeg/lbi023

Faulconbridge, J. R. (2008). Managing the transnational law firm: A relational analysis of professional systems, embedded actors, and time–space-sensitive governance. *Economic Geography*, *84*, 185–210. doi:10.1111/j.1944-8287.2008.tb00403.x

Gertler, M. S. (2003). Tacit knowledge and the economic geography of context, or the undefinable tacitness of being (there). *Journal of Economic Geography*, *3*, 75–99. doi:10.1093/jeg/3.1.75

HSBC Holdings Plc. (2015). *Annual report and accounts 2015*. Retrieved from http://www.hsbc.com/investor-relations/events-and-presentations/quick-read

Jones, A. (2002). The global city misconceived: The myth of global management in transnational service firms. *Geoforum*, *33*, 335–350. doi:10.1016/S0016-7185(02)00010-6

Jones, A. (2014). Geographies of production I: Relationality revisited and the 'practice shift' in economic geography. *Progress in Human Geography*, *38*, 605–615. doi:10.1177/0309132513502151

Jones, A., & Murphy, J. T. (2011). Theorizing practice in economic geography: Foundations, challenges, and possibilities. *Progress in Human Geography*, *35*(3), 366–392. doi:10.1177/0309132510375585.

Knight, E. (2012). The economic geography of financing clean energy technologies. *Competition and Change*, *16*, 77–90. doi:10.1179/1024529412Z.0000000009

Knight, E. (2013). *Why we argue about climate change*. Melbourne: Black.

Knight, E., & Sharma, R. (2016). Infrastructure as a traded product: A relational approach to finance in practice. *Journal of Economic Geography, 16*, 897–916. doi:10.1093/jeg/lbv039

Kunisch, S., Menz, M., & Ambos, B. (2015). Changes at corporate headquarters: Review, integration and future research. *International Journal of Management Reviews, 17*, 356–381. doi:10.1111/ijmr.12044

Lawson, C., & Lorenz, E. (1999). Collective learning, tacit knowledge and regional innovative capacity. *Regional Studies, 33*, 305–317. doi:10.1080/713693555

Leifer, R., & Delbecq, A. (1978). Organizational/environmental interchange: A model of boundary spanning activity. *Academy of Management Review, 3*, 40–50.

Leifer, R., & Huber, G. P. (1977). Relations among perceived environmental uncertainty, organization structure, and boundary-spanning behavior. *Administrative Science Quarterly, 22*, 235–247. doi:10.2307/2391958

MacKinnon, D. (2012). Beyond strategic coupling: Reassessing the firm–region nexus in global production networks. *Journal of Economic Geography, 12*, 227–245. doi:10.1093/jeg/lbr009

Malmberg, A., & Maskell, P. (2006). Localized learning revisited. *Growth and Change, 37*, 1–18. doi:10.1111/j.1468-2257.2006.00302.x

Marrone, J. A. (2010). Team boundary spanning: A multilevel review of past research and proposals for the future. *Journal of Management, 36*, 911–940. doi:10.1177/0149206309353945

Maskell, P., & Malmberg, A. (1999). The competitiveness of firms and regions 'ubiquitification' and the importance of localized learning. *European Urban and Regional Studies, 6*, 9–25. doi:10. 1177/096977649900600102

Mudambi, R., & Navarra, P. (2004). Is knowledge power? Knowledge flows, subsidiary power and rent-seeking within MNCs. *Journal of International Business Studies, 35*, 385–406. doi:10.1057/palgrave.jibs.8400093

Mudambi, R., & Swift, T. (2009). Professional guilds, tension and knowledge management. *Research Policy, 38*, 736–745. doi:10.1016/j.respol.2009.01.009

Pfeffer, J., & Salancik, G. R. (2003). *The external control of organizations: A resource dependence perspective*. Stanford: Stanford University Press.

Reuters. (2016). HSBC renews push in China's Pearl River Delta with train sponsorship, *Reuters*, April 6.

Santos, F. M., & Eisenhardt, K. M. (2005). Organizational boundaries and theories of organization. *Organization Science, 16*, 491–508. doi:10.1287/orsc.1050.0152

Sassen, S. (2001). *The global city: New York, London, Tokyo*. Princeton: Princeton University Press.

Schatzki, T. R. (2002). *The site of the social: A philosophical account of the constitution of social life and change*. University Park: Penn State University Press.

Schotter, A., & Beamish, P. W. (2011). Performance effects of MNC headquarters–subsidiary conflict and the role of boundary spanners: The case of headquarter initiative rejection. *Journal of International Management, 17*, 243–259. doi:10.1016/j.intman.2011.05.006

Taylor, P. J., Catalana, G., & Walker, D. (2004). Multiple globalisations: Regional, hierarchical and sectoral articulations of global business services through world cities. *Service Industries Journal, 24*, 63–81.

The Economist. (2016a). HSBC: London v Hong Kong. East is Eden. *The Economist*, February 6. Retrieved from http://www.economist.com/news/finance-and-economics/21690101-bankings-longest-and-most-successful-identity-crisis-east-eden

The Economist. (2016b). HSBC's domicile dilemma: Asian dissuasion. *The Economist*, February 6. Retrieved from http://www. economist.com/news/leaders/21690032-despite-britains-bankbashing-mood-hsbc-should-stay-london-asian-dissuasion

The Telegraph. (2012). Gulliver's travels and the transformation of HSBC. The Telegraph, November 21. Retrieved from http://www.telegraph.co.uk/finance/newsbysector/bank-sandfinance/9120880/Gullivers-travels-and-the-transformation-of-HSBC.html

Tickell, A., & Peck, J. A. (1992). Accumulation, regulation and the geographies of post-Fordism: Missing links in regulationist research. *Progress in Human Geography*, *16*, 190–218. doi:10. 1177/030913259201600203

Wilhelm, W., & Downing, J. (2001). *Informational markets: What businesses can learn from financial innovation*. Cambridge, MA: Harvard Business School Press.

Williamson, O. E. (1985). *The economic institutions of capitalism*. New York: Simon & Schuster.

Wójcik, D. (2011). *The global stock market: Issuers, investors, and intermediaries in an uneven world*. Oxford: Oxford University Press.

The interregional migration of human capital and its regional consequences: a review

Alessandra Faggian, Isha Rajbhandari and Kathryn R. Dotzel

ABSTRACT

The interregional migration of human capital and its regional consequences: a review. *Regional Studies*. This paper reviews the literature on high human capital interregional migration with particular attention paid to the consequences of inflows and outflows on local economies. While other reviews focusing on the determinants of high-skilled interregional migration flows exist, this is the first attempt to organize and examine the extensive literature on the consequences of such flows on the economies of both receiving and sending regions as well as on the overall system. It is found that the majority of existing contributions focus on economic consequences for destination regions and highlight the strong need for future research that explores impacts on origin regions. In the critical assessment of the state-of-the-art, it is observed that lack of availability of suitable data on migration and migrant characteristics hinders the advancement of high-skilled migration research. The review also stresses the necessity of incorporating innovation, skill composition and gender in future analyses of impacts of high-skilled migration. It concludes with suggestions for novel avenues that researchers can exploit when pursuing future research on the consequences of high human capital interregional migration.

摘要

人力资本的跨区域迁徙及其区域性后果：文献回顾。*Regional Studies*. 本文回顾高级人力资本跨区域迁徙的文献，并特别关注流入与流出对于地方经济的影响。已有其他文献回顾聚焦高技术跨区域迁徙流动的决定因素，而本文则是初次尝试组织并检视这些潮流同时对于接收和送出区域的经济及总体系统的影响之大量文献。本文发现，大部份的既有文献，聚焦对目的区域的经济后果，并强调未来探讨该趋势对于起源区域的影响的研究之大量需求。本文在对于最先进的批判性评估中观察到，缺乏取得迁徙与迁徙特徵的合适数据之管道，将有碍高技术迁徙研究的推进。本回顾同时强调对于高技术迁徙的影响之未来研究，有纳入创新、技术组成与性别之需要。本文于结论中，提出研究者追求对于高级人力成本跨区迁徙的后果之未来研究时能够採用的崭新方向。

RÉSUMÉ

La migration interrégionale du capital humain et ses conséquencs pour les régions: une critique. *Regional Studies*. Cet article fait la critique de la documentation au sujet de la migration interrégionale du capital humain, prêtant une attention particulière aux conséquences des entrées et des sorties sur l'économie locale. Alors qu'il existe déjà des critiques consacrées aux déterminants des flux migratoires interrégionaux des personnes hautement qualifiées, ici on cherche pour la première fois à organiser et à examiner la riche documentation à propos des conséquences de tels flux sur les économies de la région d'accueil et de la région d'origine ainsi que sur le sytème global. Il s'avère que la plupart des contributions actuelles portent sur les conséquences économiques pour ce qui concerne les régions d'accueil et soulignent la nécessité de recherches futures qui étudient les conséquences pour les régions d'origine. Dans l'évaluation critique de l'état des choses, il est à noter que, faute de données adéquates sur les caractéristiques des flux migratoires et des migrants, la promotion de la recherche sur la migration des personnes hautement qualifiées est entravée. La critique met l'accent aussi sur la nécessité d'intégrer l'innovation, la composition des compétences et le sexe dans les analyses futures des conséquences de la migration des personnes hautement qualifiées. Pour conclure, on laisse supposer des pistes de recherche originales que les chercheurs peuvent exploiter à même de poursuivre des recherches sur les conséquences des taux élevés de la migration interrégionale du capital humain.

ZUSAMMENFASSUNG

Interregionale Migration von Humankapital und ihre regionalen Auswirkungen: eine Untersuchung. *Regional Studies*. In diesem Beitrag untersuchen wir die Literatur über die interregionale Migration von hohem Humankapital unter besonderer Berücksichtigung der Auswirkungen von Zu- und Abströmen auf lokale Ökonomien. Es gibt zwar auch andere Untersuchungen über die Determinanten von hochqualifizierten interregionalen Migrationsströmen, doch bei diesem Beitrag handelt es sich um den ersten Versuch, die umfangreiche Literatur über die Auswirkungen dieser Ströme auf die Ökonomien der Empfänger- und Senderegionen sowie auf das gesamte System zu ordnen und zu untersuchen. Wir stellen fest, dass sich die Mehrheit der bisherigen Beiträge auf die wirtschaftlichen Konsequenzen für die Zielregionen konzentriert und den starken Bedarf an weiteren Studien zur Untersuchung der Auswirkungen auf die Ursprungsregionen verdeutlicht. In einer kritischen Bewertung der aktuellen Lage wird festgestellt, dass Fortschritte in der Erforschung von hochqualifizierter Migration durch einen Mangel an verfügbaren geeigneten Daten über die Merkmale der Migration und Migranten behindert werden. Ebenso wird in der Untersuchung die Notwendigkeit einer Berücksichtigung der Innovation, der Zusammensetzung von Qualifikationen und des Geschlechts in künftigen Analysen der Auswirkungen von hochqualifizierter Migration betont. Wir schließen mit Vorschlägen für neue Methoden, die von Wissenschaftlern bei künftigen Studien über die Auswirkungen der interregionalen Migration von hohem Humankapital genutzt werden können.

RESUMEN

Migración interregional de capital humano y sus consecuencias regionales: una revisión. *Regional Studies*. En este artículo revisamos las publicaciones sobre la migración interregional de capital humano de alto nivel, prestando especial atención a las consecuencias de las entradas y salidas para las economías locales. Si bien existen otras revisiones que se centran en los determinantes de los flujos de migración interregional de personas altamente cualificadas, este artículo es el primer intento de organizar y examinar la amplia bibliografía sobre las consecuencias de tales flujos para las economías de las regiones emisoras y receptoras así como para el sistema en general. Constatamos que la mayoría de las contribuciones existentes se centran en las consecuencias económicas para las regiones de destino y subrayan la necesidad urgente de realizar futuros estudios en los que se analicen las repercusiones en las regiones de origen. En una valoración crítica de la situación actual, observamos que la falta de disponibilidad de datos adecuados sobre migración y las características de los migrantes demora el avance de la investigación sobre la migración de mano de obra altamente cualificada. En el análisis también hacemos hincapié en la necesidad de incorporar innovación, composición de habilidades y género en futuros análisis de los efectos de migración de mano de obra altamente cualificada. Concluimos con sugerencias para nuevos métodos que podrían aprovechar los investigadores en futuros estudios sobre las consecuencias de la migración interregional de capital humano de alto nivel.

INTRODUCTION

Human migration is a fascinating and complex topic that has been explored in a wide variety of disciplines. Wells and Stock (2012) underline how the ubiquity of human migration may be biological in nature, while Campbell and Barone (2012), in their study on the evolutionary basis of human migration, highlight how deeply rooted this process is by pointing out that 'recent finds in the fossil record make it clear that humans and their immediate ancestors have been migrating in one form or another since the origins of the genus *Homo*, almost 2 million years ago' (p. 45).

However, the nature of human migration has been changing over time. While humans have historically migrated in response to basic survival instincts, modern migration has stronger linkages to improving one's position in society ('voluntary migration') rather than simply ensuring one's survival ('forced migration'). Similarly, globalization has greatly increased the frequency, distance and length of migration. Technological advances in transportation have made international travel both faster and more accessible for the global populace. In 2013, the total number of migrants worldwide was estimated to be 232 million, most of which (93%) were voluntary migrants (United Nations, 2013).

Not only has migration become more voluntary over time, but also it has become more 'selective' of particular types of individuals. In fact, a key finding related to characteristics of recent migrants is that degree holders tend to be more mobile than their less educated counterparts. As noticed by Plane and Rogerson (1994), recent migration trends seems to display a degree of 'elitism', especially immigration to developed countries. The voluntary and selective nature of migration becomes even more evident if one focuses on interregional rather than international migration. Greenwood (1975), in his pioneering review of research on internal migration in the United States, clearly states that 'migration is selective of the younger, better-educated, and more highly productive workers' (p. 415). A more recent contribution by Molloy, Smith, and Wozniak (2011) shows how the average propensity to migrate internally in the United States increases with education. In fact, since the 1980s, college-educated individuals have consistently been more than twice as likely to migrate as individuals without a high-school diploma.

Given that internal migration is positively selective, it comes as no surprise that its effects on origin and destination economies can be substantial. However, to the best of our knowledge, no comprehensive review of studies on the consequences of internal migration of highly skilled individuals on regional economies exists. Although Greenwood (1975) reviews both determinants and consequences of internal migration, he only considers moves of the general populace and does not distinguish migrants by skill level. Likewise, Faggian, Corcoran, and Partridge (2015), while explicitly focusing on high-skilled internal migration, review the determinants but not the consequences of these flows. Nathan (2013) reviews the consequences of high-skilled migration, but with an emphasis on international movements between countries. Due to data availability, only in the past decade have empirical contributions specifically focusing on high-skilled internal migration become more ubiquitous in the literature (Corcoran & Faggian, 2017).

With this in mind, the main objective of this paper is twofold: first, to provide a review (and a classification) of the state of the art of the literature on the *consequences of high human capital interregional migration* flows on local economies; and second, to identify current gaps in the literature and possible extensions for the future.

The paper is organized as follows. The next section defines the scope of this review. The third section reviews the literature on the consequences of high-skilled migration classified by affected geographical areas (origins, destinations and the overall system). The fourth section discusses current gaps in the literature and possible avenues for future research. The fifth section concludes.

DEFINING THE SCOPE OF THIS REVIEW

A good review must begin with a clear description of its scope. Due to the complexity and wide range of studies published on migration – in many different disciplines – it would be impossible to summarize the entire literature in a single contribution. This section identifies the boundaries of this review by highlighting three key dichotomies commonly found in migration studies.

Voluntary versus forced migration

Most economic contributions on mobility focus specifically on voluntary rather than forced migration. There are several reasons for this. First, because economic considerations (i.e., labour market conditions at the origin and/or destination) motivate the majority of voluntary moves, this type of migration is of greatest interest to economists. Second, even as the recent refugee crisis in Europe has brought the devastating consequences and human price of mass forced migration into the limelight, the majority of migration, both international and internal, remains voluntary. Third, data on forced migration are scarce and unreliable, as forced migration more often than not includes a large number of illegal immigrants. As such, this review will focus exclusively on *voluntary* migration.[1]

International versus interregional migration

As Franklin and Plane (2006) argue, migration research is one of the 'core competencies' of regional scientists. However, in urban and regional studies the focus is on internal (or interregional) rather than international migration. Interregional migration, as the term indicates, deals with 'regions'. However, the definition of 'region' varies widely across studies. Goodall (1987) defines a region as 'any area of the earth's surface with distinct and internally consistent patterns of physical features or of human development which give it a meaningful unity and distinguish it from surrounding areas'. The interpretation of this definition is very subjective. In regional economics, the most appropriate definition of regional scale depends on the determinant or consequence under investigation. However, even when the phenomenon under investigation is the same across studies, there is still no consensus on what regional scale should be used or what defines a 'migration movement'. Aside from theoretical considerations, this is often also driven by practical issues, such as data availability, geography or laws governing mobility (e.g., movement between countries is relatively easier in the European Union compared with North America).

In the study of interregional migration, various definitions of 'region' have been used that differ not only in size but also in 'nature'. In fact, some studies use administrative regions, while others prefer more 'functional' definitions (e.g., travel-to-work areas, local labour markets). Therefore, when this paper refers to interregional migration, it will generally mean migration between sub-national areas, but variously defined. Table 1 summarizes the most common definitions of region used by the studies analyzed.

It is important to distinguish between international and interregional migration because they differ not only in distance of moves but also, sometimes, in more fundamental aspects, such as chosen destinations. Guinness (2002) points out that there is sometimes a contrast between the destinations of international and domestic migrants in a given country. Data from the 1990 US Census confirm this by showing that the most popular metropolitan areas among domestic migrants display relatively small gains from international immigration. 'Cultural avoidance' has been hypothesized as one of the possible reasons for this discrepancy (Faggian, Partridge, & Rickman, 2012). Although the emphasis of this review is on *interregional* migration, it also discusses some findings from the international migration literature that are highly relevant to interregional studies (Greenwood, 1975; Kanbur & Rapoport, 2005).

Low-versus high-skilled migration

Since the late 1980s, labour markets have become increasingly globalized, which has created new opportunities for mobility, especially of high-skilled workers. A report by the International Monetary Fund (IMF) (2007) concludes that 'the effective global labour force has risen fourfold over the past two decades' (p. 161). However, the higher migration propensity of highly educated, high-skilled migrants is not just restricted to those who migrate internationally. It is very well known in

Table 1 Definitions of regions in recent interregional migration studies

Definition of region	Countries	Examples of recent contributions
Administrative regions		
Large scale		
NUTS-1	European countries	Rodríguez-Pose and Vilalta-Bufí (2005)
	The Netherlands	Venhorst, Van Dijk, and Van Wissen (2010)
States	USA	Faggian and Franklin (2014); Dotzel (2016)
Medium scale		
NUTS-2	Great Britain	Faggian and McCann (2006, 2009a)
	17 Western European countries	Miguélez and Moreno (2013)
	Italy	Fratesi and Percoco (2014); Marinelli (2013)
Counties	USA	Waldorf and Yun (2015)
Smaller scale		
NUTS-3	Finland	Haapanen and Tervo (2012)
Functional regions		
Local labour markets	Sweden	Ahlin, Andersson, and Thulin (2016); Boschma et al. (2009)
	Germany	Granato, Haas, Hamann, and Niebuhr (2015)
	Denmark	Timmmermans and Boschma (2014)
	France	Combes, Duranton, and Gobillon (2008)
	USA	Zucker and Darby (2007)
Travel to work areas	UK	Nathan (2011)
Metropolitan statistical areas (MSAs)	USA	Rauch (1993); Moretti (2004)

regional science that the most educated individuals are also the most internally mobile and tend to relocate multiple times during their lifetimes. DaVanzo (1978) was the first to point out that the best-educated individuals can process information more efficiently, have job opportunities which are more national in scope and, therefore, have a higher probability of moving more than once during their lives. Faggian, McCann, and Sheppard (2007), when studying the interregional migration behaviour of British graduates, confirm that graduates who excelled in college are also more likely to become repeat migrants. In the last decade there has been a surge in the number of studies primarily focused on the migration behaviour of high-skilled individuals such as graduates, scientists and inventors (Faggian & McCann, 2006, 2009a; Miguélez & Moreno, 2013; Zucker & Darby, 2007). This increase in interest has been motivated by policy reasons and the advent of new data. On the policy side, different regions have become increasingly aware of the importance of highly educated individuals for their local economic growth and, thus, have implemented policies that allow them to compete more fiercely to attract and retain them. On the data side, large datasets containing information on highly educated individuals have recently become available in European countries (including the UK, the Netherlands and Sweden) and in Australia, allowing for detailed analyses of the interregional migration behaviour of their high-skilled populations. It is imperative that high-skilled migration be analyzed separately from general population migration because of its intrinsic peculiarities and differences. The authors recognize that migrants are self-selected, either positively or negatively, and based on that they could have varying impacts on the sending and receiving regions. However, by focusing only on the migration of high-skilled individuals, the regional consequences are being specifically analyzed due to positive selection on migrants (Kazakis & Faggian, 2016). This review will therefore focus specifically on the regional consequences of *high-skilled* migration.

REGIONAL CONSEQUENCES OF HIGH-SKILLED INTERREGIONAL MIGRATION

In the last decade the literature devoted to exploring the interregional migration behaviour of high-skilled individuals – including scientists, inventors, engineers and recent college graduates (Faggian & McCann, 2006, 2009a; Miguélez & Moreno, 2013; Zucker & Darby, 2007) – has grown rapidly. Although the majority of these contributions focus on the *determinants* of high-skilled internal migration, some also consider the *consequences* of these flows on regional economies. The latter contributions will be specifically reviewed here by being classified according to their region of focus, i.e., the destination, the origin or the overall system.

Consequences for the destinations

The majority of studies examining the consequences of high-skilled migration focus on the destination region and largely rely on a spatial correlation approach

(Borjas, 1999) 'where the effect of migration is identified from the spatial correlation between migrants' inflows and changes in the outcome variable within each geographical unit of analysis' (Gagliardi, 2015, p. 784). Although the majority of contributions on the consequences of high-skilled migration highlight the benefits for the destination regions, some authors point out that some costs might also exist. This section starts by reviewing the positive consequences on destinations identified in the literature; it then moves onto the possible negative ones.

Positive consequences

One of the ways in which high-skilled migration has been said to influence the destination region positively is by promoting *innovation* and creating *new knowledge*. Endogenous growth theory posits that economic growth and increased productivity result from the development of new knowledge, technologies and innovations by an enhanced human capital base (Jones, 2009; Lucas, 1988; Romer, 1986, 1987; Solow, 1957).

A number of studies in the endogenous growth literature have examined how local or *intra*regional labour mobility supports the development and diffusion of new knowledge and ideas (Eriksson, 2011; McCann & Simonen, 2005; Power & Lundmark, 2004), with some focusing specifically on moves of high-skilled migrants. Results suggest that impacts of such moves depend on how the migrant's skill set relates to the hiring firm's existing knowledge base. For example, Boschma, Eriksson, and Lindgren (2014) find that for Swedish regions intraregional labour mobility across different but related industries positively impacts regional productivity and employment growth and that moves between unrelated industries decreases regional unemployment. This suggests that industries benefit from hiring local employees that can grow their stock of knowledge through the introduction of novel – but somehow related – skills (Boschma et al., 2009). Only in the last decade have studies begun specifically to focus on the consequences of *inter*regional labour mobility of high-skilled workers for local growth. Timmermans and Boschma (2014) extend Boschma et al.'s (2014) analysis by comparing the effects of intra- and interregional labour inflows of highly skilled workers on plant performance, and ultimately determine that only interregional labour inflows positively impact labour productivity (McCann & Simonen, 2005). Using data on British graduates, Faggian and McCann (2009a) model the interrelationship between migration flows and regional innovation using a simultaneous equations framework, and their findings provide evidence that internal human capital in-migration is significantly related to regional patenting productivity in the UK, with the strongest results for high technology industries.

Some studies consider the possibility that high-skilled migration affects *specific types of innovation* in distinct ways. For example, Gagliardi (2015), using firm-level data from the Community Innovation Survey (CIS) for British travel-to-work areas, finds that skilled immigration has the largest positive effect on process innovation. Hunt and Gauthier-Loiselle (2009) link skilled migration to state-level patenting activity in the United States by finding that a 1% increase in a state's share of immigrant college graduates increases the state's patenting rate by 6%. This positive relationship between skilled immigration and patenting productivity is supported by other studies (Chellaraj, Maskus, & Mattoo, 2008; Le, 2008; Ozgen, Nijkamp, & Poot, 2011). Most recently, Bosetti, Cattaneo, and Verdolini (2015) separately examine the impact of high-skilled immigration to the European Union between 1995 and 2008 on patent applications and academic citations and find positive effects for both.

A share of the endogenous growth literature is specifically devoted to the impact of high-skilled migration on *wages* in the destination region. Behrens and Sato (2011) argue for the existence of two opposing effects. On the one hand, the influx of skilled workers directly influences the skill composition of a region's workforce by increasing the region's endowment of skills that the migrants possess. In response, wages of workers who share those skills decrease while wages of other workers increase. As noted by Schlitte (2010), 'if high[-]skilled workers are locally abundant, less skilled workers are relatively scarce, which brings them higher pay than identically skilled workers in a less skilled region' (p. 5). On the other hand, skilled migrants can bolster the productivity of the existing skilled workforce, thus increasing wages for this group and counteracting the negative endowment effect.

Evidence from the empirical literature is generally mixed as to whether the 'negative endowment effect' or 'positive externality effect' of high-skilled migration on wages ultimately dominates (Behrens & Sato, 2011). A number of studies (Moretti, 2004; Rauch, 1993) argue for the latter, concluding that high-skilled in-migration has a net positive effect on wages of high-skilled workers. For example, Dustmann, Fabbri, and Preston (2005) present evidence that inflows of college-educated immigrants positively impacts the wages of college-educated natives in the destination region. However, other studies suggest that low-skilled workers may benefit from inflows of high-skilled workers through higher wage levels. Borjas (2003) finds that a 10% increase in a region's college graduate population increases the wages of less skilled workers with equal years of experience by 1–3%.

In addition to considering potential *outcomes* of high-skilled migration such as innovation, technological development, and wage changes in destination regions, some studies specifically focus on the *channels* through which a larger high-skilled workforce may contribute to these outcomes. Nathan (2013, p. 6) emphasizes that skilled migrants 'can act as entrepreneurs and investors as well as workers' in host regions, potentially influencing regional outcomes through production- and consumption-side channels.

On the production side, Schlitte (2010) shows that firms with large shares of high-skilled workers are more likely to invest in new production technologies, which can in turn increase the productivity of both low- and high-skilled workers. In some cases, high-skilled migrants may contribute to innovation and technological development in the host region through the introduction of new skills that are complementary to those of the existing workforce (Dustmann, Glitz, & Frattini, 2008; Nathan, 2011, 2013; Ottaviano & Peri, 2006).

The consequences of knowledge and *skill complementarities* between the natives and high-skilled in-migrants on the local economy is a relevant issue for interregional migration. While one can expect internal migration to have some impact on innovations and technological developments at the destinations, the nature and magnitude of the impact depends on the skill composition of the natives relative to those introduced by the high-skilled in-migrants. The ambiguous relationship between high-skilled in-migration and its impact on the wages for both high- and low-skilled natives is likely influenced by the skill composition at the destination regions. Therefore, there is a strong need for further study to understand skill complementarities and their impacts on wages and regional economies in the context of interregional migration.

High-skilled migrants may exploit their *social and professional networks* to the benefit of hiring firm outcomes. Miguélez and Moreno's (2013) study of the interregional mobility of inventors in Western Europe and Scandinavia concludes that the prominent channel through which inventors enhance regional productivity is collaboration with inventors *outside* their region. Trippl's (2013) study on interregional and intraregional movements of 'star scientists' shows that they contribute to knowledge transfer between research systems through the 'follower phenomenon', meaning that the movement of star scientists encourages future movements of their students and colleagues.

On the consumption side, influxes of high-skilled migrants can potentially affect the *availability of regional amenities*. Most of the literature connecting migration to amenities focuses on amenities as a determinant of migration rather than a consequence. Early work by Graves (1979, 1980) uncovers a positive relationship between household preference for natural amenities and income level. Likewise, Carlino and Mills (1987) determine that mobile households prefer to locate to 'sunbelt' regions. More recent studies have explored how natural and built amenities influence the migration decisions of high-skilled internal migrants specifically (Dotzel, 2016; Fiore et al., 2015; Gottlieb & Joseph, 2006; Whisler, Waldorf, Mulligan, & Plane, 2008). In a study that considers amenities as a consequence of migration, Mazzolari and Neumark (2012) find that immigrants contribute to a more diverse restaurant sector but do not differentiate migrants by skill level. It is possible that high-skilled migrants could influence regional amenities in distinct ways. Following the publication of a number of studies focused on entrepreneurship of high-skilled immigrants (Anderson & Platzer, 2006; Drori, Honig, & Wright, 2009; Kerr, 2013; Saxenian, 2002; Wadhwa, Saxenian, & Siciliano, 2012), Alonso-Villar (2002, p. 572) shows that given low congestion costs and high inter-city transportation costs, 'the higher the human capital in a region, the higher the number of firms that can be supported there, but also the higher its ability to attract firms from other regions', suggesting that an increase in regional human capital stock may contribute to increased product variety.

Increased *ethnic and cultural diversity* resulting from high-skilled migration may be viewed as a positive amenity by the local workforce and ultimately attract additional high-skilled workers to a given region (Florida, 2002; Wang, De Graaff, & Nijkamp, 2016). According to Richard Florida (Florida, 2002, p. 55), 'the presence and concentration of bohemians in an area creates a . . . milieu that attracts other types of talented or high human capital individuals' and 'the presence of such human capital in turn attracts and generates innovative, technology-based industries'. A more diverse workforce could increase demand for 'hybridised' goods and services, increasing consumption opportunities for regional populations (Lee & Nathan, 2010; Nathan, 2015; Syrett & Sepulveda, 2011).

Interregional labour mobility can improve migrant outcomes by facilitating better job matches for high-skilled workers. Marinelli (2013), examining the interregional mobility of Italian graduates, finds that migrants who move to a region other than their home region following graduation are more likely to enter jobs that utilize the knowledge gained in college. Hensen, de Vries, and Cörvers (2009) similarly find lower rates of over-education for regionally mobile graduates in the Netherlands. Using US data, Waldorf and Yun (2015) determine that over-education probabilities for internal migrants who moved to a new county following graduation are lower than those for 'stayers' during periods of medium to high unemployment, suggesting that migration can act as an important coping strategy for young graduates during economic downturns.

Negative consequences

Although the negative consequences of high-skilled in-migration are less obvious than the positive ones, some authors point out that, if not the area as a whole, at least some groups of the population in the destination may lose from influxes of high-skilled migrants. For example, *prices of goods* characterized by inelastic supply – such as housing – could be positively affected by high-skilled in-migration, negatively affecting migrants and natives alike (Nathan, 2015; Ottaviano & Peri, 2006; Saiz, 2003).

Relying on data from the 1960–90 US censuses and the 1998–2001 Current Population Surveys (CPSs), Borjas (2003) finds that an increase in the supply of workers in a given skill and experience group decreases *wages* for that group of workers. This suggests that the 'negative endowment effect' (Behrens & Sato, 2011) associated with the in-migration of high-skilled workers (discussed above) may dominate any productivity gains and implies that native high-skilled workers lose from influxes of high-skilled immigrants. Suedekum (2006) determines that skill segregation between high- and low-skilled workers negatively affects low-skill employment growth and that concentration in given skill group negatively affects the employment prospects of that group, a result also found by Ciccone and Peri (2005) for high-skilled workers. Other studies (Ciccone & Peri, 2006; Islam & Fausten, 2008) find the effects of high-skilled migration on wages to be weak or insignificant.

Ramirez, Li, and Chen (2013) – in their study focused on Chinese science parks – find higher returns to intraregional labour mobility compared with interregional labour mobility, providing support for the view that local workers may possess tacit knowledge that makes them more productive than workers from other regions.

Findings by Rodríguez-Pose and Vilalta-Bufí (2005), based on data from the European Community Household Panel, suggest that factors such as job satisfaction may be more important for enhancing regional growth than the stock of educated workers. If high-skilled migration leads to an increase in regional diversity, this may result in *increased distrust and poorer communication* among workers, which could stifle productivity and innovative outcomes (Alesina & La Ferrara, 2005; Nathan, 2015). Lazear (1999) uncovers an inverse relationship between native language acquisition of immigrants and ethnic community size. In a later study, Florax, de Graaff, and Waldorf (2005) determine that the level of immigrant assimilation in the destination region is likely more important for native language acquisition than ethnic group size. It is important to note, however, that these findings may have less reverence in an interregional context in countries with ethnically homogenous populations, and for high-skilled migrants in particular, who are likely to be English proficient (Belot & Ederveen, 2012).

Consequences for the origins

Given that regional policy-makers increasingly implement policies to attract and retain highly skilled individuals, it has become essential to study how out-migration affects the economy at the origin. However, the number of studies that analyze the consequences of migration on origin regions is extremely limited. The main reason for this is that while migrants can originate from almost everywhere, they tend to target a select group of destinations, making it easier to collect data for the latter. Although this is more evident for international migration, where countries such as the United States, Australia and European countries attract the vast majority of migrants worldwide, it is also true for interregional migration where certain regions become 'hubs' for internal migrants. Faggian, Corcoran, and McCann (2013), looking at graduate migration directionality in the UK, show that this is also true when considering interregional moves by high-skilled individuals, with graduate migrants concentrating in a number of large cities. Haapanen and Tervo (2012) find a similar trend in the case of Finnish graduate migrants. Even though consequences of out-migration are mostly studied in the international setting, the theoretical and empirical analyses are equally applicable to the interregional migration context (Greenwood, 1975; Kanbur & Rapoport, 2005). This section will review the negative and positive consequences of migration on the origin regions.

Negative consequences

The few studies looking at the effects of migration on origins tend to focus on the *negative* (rather than positive) effects of out-migration on the source region, especially *reduced growth and brain drain*. These problems are especially severe for high-skilled out-migration where the migrants are positively selected, since the best individuals in the origin are also the most mobile. According to Carrington and Detragiache (1998), immigrants to the United States tend to have higher education than the average person in the origin and the proportion of individuals with higher education who migrate is particularly high (Kanbur & Rapoport, 2005).

In the literature, several mediums through which out-migration of highly skilled individuals could impact the origin economy have been identified. *Brain drain* is the most significant and widely studied consequence of out-migration. The term is generally used to designate transfer of human capital (i.e., people with tertiary education) from developing to more developed areas, with the idea that the current and future economic performances of an area are negatively influenced by the depletion of its stock of human capital (Kanbur & Rapoport, 2005). The majority of the brain-drain literature focuses on analyzing its impact in a theoretical context, with only few recent empirical contributions mainly focusing on international rather than regional brain drain. Bhagwati and Hamada (1974) and McCulloch and Yellen (1977), for example, in their seminal studies on international brain drain, explore the welfare implications of brain drain and emphasize the negative consequences of high-skilled emigration from developing to developed countries. Skilled emigration has been found to have a negative impact on employment (Bhagwati & Hamada, 1974) and growth (Beine, Docquier, & Rapoport, 2001) in the origin regions. Similarly, studies such as those by Miwagiwa (1991), Haque and Kim (1995), and Wong and Yip (1999), further highlight the negative consequences of brain drain within the framework of endogenous growth (Lucas, 1988). However, an important assumption in these contributions is that the pre-migration stock of human capital in the origin is exogenous to international migration, i.e., the incentives to invest in education domestically are not influenced by emigration (Docquier & Rapoport, 2012).

While the existing literature on brain drain focuses on international settings, the effect of human capital depletion is highly applicable to a regional context. Assuming that the pre-migration stock of human capital in the origin is exogenous to internal migration prospects, one expects negative consequences of out-migration of high-skilled individuals on the origin economy to be of a similar or even greater magnitude, as interregional migrants face lower barriers to migration relative to their international counterparts.

As Faggian and McCann (2009, p. 143) point out, 'heterogeneous human capital[2] migration flows can contribute to re-distributional effects between regions, in terms of their human capital stocks'. This, in turn, can influence their growth trajectories. However, regional brain drain requires more in-depth investigation, as the link between human capital and national economic development may not be the same as those between human capital and regional economic development. This is because the mechanism by which externalities spillover into a local region and the mechanisms which determine labour mobility are not necessarily congruent. When these two impacts coincide, regions will flourish, whereas if they do not, regions might struggle (depending on the relative magnitude of the two effects). Hence, further study is needed to analyze the pathways through which changes in barriers to migration influence regional growth in the origins.

Positive consequences

More recently published theoretical contributions on brain drain, argue that – under certain circumstances – high-skilled emigration could have *positive* impacts on the origin. In fact, it is possible that it could incentivise others in the origin *to invest* in their *education*, increasing their own human capital and promoting regional growth. A collection of studies, such as those by Beine et al. (2001, 2008), Beine, Docquier, and Oden-Defoort (2011), Stark (2004), Stark, Helmenstein, and Prskawetz (1997, 1998), Stark and Wang (2002), and Vidal (1998), argue that ex-ante migration prospects could foster investment in education in the origin, provided that origin–destination wage differentials exist. These studies assume that a region's pre-migration human capital stock is endogenous to the prospect and realization of migration. Thus, if migration prospects raise the expected return to human capital, it is likely that investment in education will increase in the origin (Docquier & Rapoport, 2012). This increase in educational attainment could foster growth in the economy in the origin through enhanced intergenerational transmission of skills and knowledge (Mountford, 1997; Vidal, 1998). The novelty of this literature is that it introduces uncertainty into the migration process, which allows the studies to assume that only a fraction of those who invest in education successfully migrate, thereby creating the possibility of productivity gains from brain drain in the origin (Kanbur & Rapoport, 2005).

With existing wage differentials across regions within a country, theoretical contributions on brain drain can be used to develop a framework to study the impact of high-skilled internal migration prospects on the source economy. However, unlike international migration, the barriers to internal migration are low, which could impact the migrants' incentives to invest in their education as a response to skilled migration prospects in distinct ways. To understand how human capital depletion impacts the investment in education and regional growth in the origin regions, it is imperative that one studies the consequences of brain drain in the context of interregional migration.

The growth in availability of migration data in recent years has given rise to evidence-based, empirical work on the effects of brain drain in the international migration literature. Overall, consistent with theoretical predictions, empirical studies find significant positive impacts of high-skilled emigration on investments in education and local growth. Beine et al.'s (2001) study is the first to attempt an empirical estimation using cross-sectional data for developing countries. The results show that migration prospects positively impact pre-migration human capital formation in the origin region. This is true especially for countries with low initial gross domestic product (GDP) per capita. However, due to limited data availability, the paper uses gross migration rates as a proxy for brain drain and hence is unable to measure accurately migration flows by level of education. Later contributions by Beine, Docquier, and Rapoport (2003, 2008) improve upon this initial estimation by dividing emigrants by education level and find a positive and significant impact of high-skilled emigration. Most recently, using a panel data estimation for 1975–2000, Beine et al. (2011) analyze the effect of high-skilled out-migration on incentives for education in the origin for rich, intermediate and poor countries separately. They find that skilled migration prospects foster human capital accumulation in the low-income countries, while the impact is negative for rich and intermediate countries. Additionally, some micro-level analyses such as those by Batista, Lacuesta, and Vicente (2012) and Gibson and McKenzie (2011) estimate a net positive effect of brain drain on human capital formation in Cape Verde, and Tonga and Papua New Guinea, respectively.

Even though the literature on interregional migration has not empirically examined the consequences of internal migration on education investment, it is possible that similar positive impacts of high-skilled interregional migration prospects on education investment and growth might occur in origin regions. However, relative to the stark differences between wages in developed and developing countries, wages across regions within a country are likely to be less varied. Additionally, lower barriers to internal migration may lead to fewer incentives for migrants to invest in their education to improve their migration prospects. Therefore, one can expect the magnitude of impacts of interregional out-migration on source economies to be smaller relative to international migration. Furthermore, depending on the level of rurality or urbanization of origin and destination regions, magnitudes of effects may vary significantly.

Other studies have identified additional sources of positive feedback on the origins such as *remittances, return migration* (after additional skills have been acquired in the host region), and the creation of *networks* that facilitate trade, capital flows and knowledge diffusion (Rapoport, 2004). Even though remittances are recognized as a means to offset some of the negative consequences of brain drain, studies examining the remittance behaviour of high-skilled out-migrants and its impact on the origin have been rather limited (Commander, Kangasniemi, & Winters, 2004). In an international setting, it is unclear whether high-skilled emigrants remit more or less compared with their low-skilled counterparts. Based on their cross-country analyses, Faini (2007) and Niimi, Ozden, and Schiff (2010) find that high-skilled migrants remit less. Although both studies show that increase in the proportion of high-skilled emigrants is associated with a decline in the amount remitted, they suffer from potential bias since they pair migration data for emigrants to Organisation for Economic Co-operation and Development (OECD) countries with remittance data that are not restricted to emigrants from these countries (Docquier & Rapoport, 2012). At the micro-level, Bollard, McKenzie, Morten, and Rapoport (2011) analyze the relationship between remittances and education outcomes, improving upon previous studies by using micro-data to link remittance decisions of migrants with their education levels. They ultimately judge the relationship between education and the likelihood of remitting to be ambiguous but, conditional on remittances being made, find a strong positive relationship between education and amount remitted. This explains the higher remittances of high-income migrants and suggests that remittance behaviour is accounted for primarily by income. However, their use of data from multiple surveys with different sampling methods and degrees of representatives could be problematic.

The ambiguity in the remittance behaviour of high-skilled migrants may be applicable at a regional level too. Similar to the case of emigrants depicted by Bollard et al. (2011), high-skilled internal out-migrants may remit more because they have higher income potential, and are more likely to have their education funded by family members (with remittances serving as repayment). Alternatively, high-skilled internal out-migrants may remit less because they are more likely to migrate with their immediate family, have lower propensity to return and are likely to be from richer households. The nature of the relationship between education and amount remitted, in the regional context, depends on which of the two scenarios dominate. To understand the distributional impact of remittance on economy at the origin, extensive study is needed.

Likewise, return migration is another channel through which internal out-migration may impact the economy at the origin. Because migrants self-select in their decision to return, return migration could induce either positive or negative feedback effect. Studies on international migration such as those by Borjas and Bratsberg (1996) and Cohen and Haberfeld (2001) characterize the return migration of foreign-born individuals from the United States as 'negative self-selection', which indicates that return migrants tend to be the least skilled emigrants. On the contrary, increase in wages and growth prospects at the origin tend to increase return migration rates among skilled professionals (Dustmann & Weiss, 2007; Kwok & Leland, 1982; Rosenzweig, 2008).

In the regional context, studies analyzing the impact of return migration of high-skilled individuals on the origin are rare. Zhao (2002) studies the consequences of return migration to rural areas in China and finds that return migrants invest more in farm machinery relative to non-migrants, thereby improving labour productivity in agriculture in the source region. While this study does not directly pertain to high-skilled migrants, it depicts a positive impact of return migration on regional economies. Nonetheless, return migration of high-skilled individuals could lead to an increase in the stock of human capital at the origin, thereby creating positive externalities for local labour market outcomes (Winters & Xu, 2014). The magnitude of the effect, to some extent, may be influenced by how relevant the migrant's skills are to the needs of the origin and whether they complement the existing skills of non-migrants at the origin regions. Additional potential for positive feedback in the origin could arise from the network linkages, financial resources and experiences brought by the high-skilled return migrants (Commander et al., 2004).

Consequences for the system overall

Aside from the negative and positive consequences of interregional migration on both destinations and origins, a fundamental question remains: Is migration good for the economic system overall? Should interregional migration be encouraged or discouraged? The answer ultimately depends on the system of beliefs being relied upon. In the neoclassical framework, migration is assumed to mitigate labour market imbalances across regions. As explained by Granato et al.

(2015, p. 515), '[i]n a neoclassical model setting where the labour market is flexible and competitive and mobility costs are not too high, workers tend to move from high to low unemployment regions in search of better labour market prospects'. This ultimately contributes to a decrease in unemployment disparities across regions in the long-run. However, most studies in the neoclassical literature do not consider that differences in migrant skill level may have crucial implications for the effects of labour mobility on labour market disparities across regions. In the case of 'selective migration' of individuals based on their skill level, some authors (Kanbur & Rapoport, 2005; Suedekum, 2004) suggest that high-skilled migration may actually *reinforce* differences in regional unemployment and wages, contrary to neoclassical assumptions. Arntz et al. (2014, p. 1734) conclude that selective migration is the product of employment disparities between regions in that 'the more unequal employment is spread across the regional workforce, the more a region attracts an increasingly skilled inflow of migrants'.

As seen above, Kanbur and Rapoport (2005) theorize that high-skilled migration affects human capital in two ways: directly, through moves of skilled workers to the destination and from the origin, and indirectly, by influencing incentives for acquiring education in the origin region. Thus, the ultimate determination of whether high-skilled migration leads to convergence or divergence of regional economic outcomes hinges on which of these two effects dominate.

Also of theoretical interest when considering spatial disparities that may result from interregional migration is Paul Krugman's (Krugman, 1991) 'New Economic Geography' model, which posits that given a number of assumptions (including monopolistic competition in one sector) agglomeration results from two key effects. As explained by Partridge (2010, pp. 515–516), (1) 'as more firms and workers locate in one region, additional firms move there to take advantage of serving a larger market with lower transportation costs', leading to a 'more than proportionate increase in production as home income rises'; and (2) as additional workers flock to a region, there will be greater product variety in the monopolistically competitive sector and, as a result, an increased willingness of workers to accept lower wages. Increasing competition creates a third mitigating effect whereby the associated decrease in output prices causes some firms to relocate to less populous regions.

Combes et al. (2008) conclude that spatial wage disparities largely result from differences in workforce skill sets across regions. A recent study of the impact of labour mobility on regional wage disparities that considers the dimension of skills is that by Granato et al. (2015), who provide support for the argument that when skills of migrants are not assumed to be homogenous, the neoclassical model of migration that predicts convergence of labour market conditions across regions does not hold. Looking at interregional migration flows in Germany, the authors find that the migration of college graduates increases labour market disparities between regions, while the migration of low- and medium-skilled workers confirms the neoclassical model prediction of regional convergence. They credit this result to complementarities between high- and low-skilled labour, arguing that inflows of skilled labour increase the marginal product of unskilled labour in the destination region, thereby increasing demand for unskilled labour and decreasing unemployment rates for this subset of workers. Skilled labour outflows have the opposite effect in the origin, decreasing the marginal productivity of unskilled labour and demand for these workers. Nonetheless, in the region of study, labour market consequences from the migration of low- and medium-skilled workers ultimately dominate the consequences due to the migration of high-skilled workers, although the authors argue that this may not be the case for all regions. Fratesi and Percoco (2014), when studying the case of high-skilled interregional migration in Italy, similarly conclude that interregional migration of high-skilled individuals results in regional divergence due its positive impact on GDP per capita in the destination region.

A subset of the high-skilled migration literature suggests that pre- and post-college moves by students may contribute to increased disparities between rural and urban labour markets. Some studies show that college students move to urban areas following graduation to take advantage of an urban wage premium (Glaeser & Maré, 2001; Wheeler, 2006; Yankow, 2006), implying that the moves of this group could further augment the disparities between rural and urban regions. Ahlin et al. (2016) provide evidence from Swedish regions that the likelihood of sorting into urban regions to attend college and following college graduation increases with student skill level. More specifically, a student with high-school grades that are 10% better than the average has a higher probability of attending college in an urban area and entering a career there.

Conversely, when separately examining moves of college graduates in the Netherlands by college major and achievement level, Venhorst et al. (2010) find that only in the field of economics do students who excelled in college display a propensity to move to the country's economic centre following graduation. Rural regions can benefit from the out-migration of college students and recent graduates in the long-term if return migrants apply skills and experience gained in urban labour markets to their rural home region (von Reichert, Cromartie, & Arthun, 2014).

Glaeser and Maré's (2001) finding that workers in cities earn 33% more than their counterparts with equivalent skills in rural regions suggests that the urban wage premium is not solely the result of high-skilled workers sorting themselves into cities, and that cities must additionally be associated with agglomeration effects that make urban workers more productive (Combes et al., 2008). When comparing returns to education in Sydney with other regions in New South Wales, Australia, Mallik, Basu, Hicks, and Sappey (2014) discover that postgraduate degree holders in Sydney are more likely to be employed and work longer hours than their more rural counterparts, but that postgraduate degrees command higher wages outside of Sydney, potentially due to a smaller pool of highly educated workers.

In developing countries, Fan and Stark (2008) theorize that unrestricted rural-to-urban migration of skilled workers results in decreased average income in both origin and destination regions, since the out-migration of skilled workers from origin regions decreases rural productivity and incentivises rural-to-urban migration for unskilled workers in greater numbers.

CONCLUSIONS AND FUTURE RESEARCH CHALLENGES

The study of migration has intrigued researchers from a wide array of academic disciplines for over a century. However, it is only in the last decade or so that greater attention has been paid to high-skilled migrants. Since the advent of endogenous growth models in the late 1980s, the role that individuals with high human capital play in fostering local economic development has been widely acknowledged.

This paper has offered an overview of the current state-of-the-art research on the economic consequences of migration of high-skilled individuals from a regional science perspective. It has classified the contributions through the lens of the geographical area considered, i.e., *origins*, *destinations* or the *overall system*. The authors have observed that although a selected number of studies look at how out-migration of high-skilled individuals affects the origin regions, the majority of the contribution focuses only on the economic consequences for the destinations. However, given that migration, especially of high-skilled individuals, plays a fundamental role in the economies of both destinations and origins, it is paramount to refine one's understanding of its consequences on both. One of the biggest challenges in analyzing the consequences of migration is the lack of availability of suitable data on migration and migrant characteristics at the national and international levels. In particular, the data on high-skilled migrants are scant. Therefore, there is a strong need to conduct interregional micro-surveys explicitly to capture the relationship between migration decisions of high-skilled individuals and the consequences of these decisions in origin and destination regions (Beine et al., 2011).

Moreover, the number of studies analyzing the determinants of migration outweighs those examining its consequences. This was observed by Greenwood (1975, 1997), but it is a trend that has remained unchanged in more recent years. Part of the issue is that it is very difficult to disentangle the effect of migration on regional economies, and this is more evident in the case of high-skilled interregional migration. There are clear self-selection (Sjaastad, 1962) and endogeneity[3] problems in studying the relationship between high-skilled migration and local economic growth.

The majority of studies examining the consequences of high-skilled migration rely on cross-sectional regressions. It is likely that these analyses suffer from misspecification biases, as it is impossible to capture fully the unobserved heterogeneity between areas (Beine et al., 2011). The lack of data that allow for consistent comparisons of mobility patterns across countries further complicates this process. National authorities have maintained inadequate databases on international mobility of high-skilled workers, with inconsistent definitions of skill and education categories and missing information on migrant attributes (Commander et al.,

2004). The GlobSci Survey, conducted by Franzoni, Scellato, and Stephan (2012), is a notable attempt at providing comparable cross-country data on the mobility of active researchers.

Increased access to detailed data on highly educated individuals has contributed to improved studies on interregional migration behaviour of high-skilled individuals in several Europeans countries. However, equivalent studies in the United States have been rather limited due to restricted availability of data. The United States has a few data sources with migration data at the national level such as the American Community Survey (ACS) and Current Population Survey (CPS). These annual sample datasets include information on migrants' geographical locations, education, and economic and demographic characteristics at the individual level and can be used to disentangle the effect of educated migrants on the regional economy (Winters & Xu, 2014). However, these datasets are not specific to high-skilled migrants. Furthermore, the annual estimates in the ACS are only available for areas with populations greater than 65,000, with only the three- and five-year estimates providing data at lower geographical levels.[4] Likewise, the CPS is a small sample dataset with reliable estimates only available at the state level.[5]

Overall, however, information on high-skilled migrants is limited, which makes it challenging to study their migration patterns and their impacts on the economy. Nevertheless, as a result of increasing availability of individual-level data, recently there has been an increase in the study of graduate (i.e., high-skilled) migration in the country. The Scientists and Engineers Statistical Data (SESTAT) system from the National Science Foundation (NSF) has longitudinal data on the education and employment of the college-educated science and engineering workforce in the United States.[6] However, the dataset only includes a relatively small sample of individuals in the science and engineering sector, with no information on graduates in social sciences and humanities. Likewise, the Integrated Postsecondary Education Data System (IPEDS), a database from the National Center for Education Statistics, includes data on postsecondary institutions.[7] However, IPEDS does support consecutive-year analysis of student migration since institutions are only required to provide data on state of residence of first-time students in every other year (Dotzel, 2016; Faggian & Franklin, 2014). Moreover, both datasets are at the state level, making it impossible to conduct the analysis at a smaller geographical level, such as counties, metropolitan areas or local labour markets.

Time horizon is also a limitation of most studies. Ottaviano and Peri (2008) and Behrens and Sato (2011) find that time horizon could be crucial to whether in-migration has a positive or a negative impact on the destination wage structure. In the case of interregional migration, it might be important to conduct both short- or long-run analyses to understand how in-migration of skilled workers would impact the wage structure in the destination region.

No studies have analyzed the remittances of high-skilled migrants and their propensity to return home in the regional context. One possible reason for this is the lack of good-quality data on remittances and return migration. So far, in an international context, macro- and micro-level studies have obtained contradictory results on whether or not high-skilled migrants remit more (Docquier & Rapoport, 2012), thus highlighting the need for better data and more in-depth analyses. The study of return migration, even more so than remittances, is especially important for sending regions and countries and there is a need for more analysis on this topic.

Docquier and Rapoport (2012) and Di Maria and Stryszowski (2009) briefly discuss 'migration[-]induced brain waste' in the origin. Due to differences in foreign and domestic needs of human capital, migration prospects could drive human capital investments away from domestically relevant sectors, in which case the origin may not benefit from the investments. However, little research has been done to analyze this negative impact in a regional context. Furthermore, migration of high-skilled individuals could influence regional skill and industry composition. It is unclear how change in skill composition and diversification could influence growth in the origin and destination. Moreover, there is a possibility that brain drain could induce severe occupational shortages in the origin. Beine et al.'s (2011) conclusion that when the emigration rate exceeds the threshold of 20–30%, human capital loss induced by the brain drain increases exponentially, has yet to be explored in the regional context. However, it is unclear how this threshold varies across regions and compares with the current rate of migration, which need to be studied in more detail.

When examining the local consequences of migration, increased innovation is often quoted. However, there is an overreliance on patent data as a metric of innovation. Carlino and Kerr (2014) argue that patents may be a poor measure of innovative activity since they represent only an initial step towards innovation and are not necessarily exploited in the region produced (Feldman, 1994). Furthermore, most highly skilled migrants end up working in advanced service sectors where patents heavily underestimate innovation (which is most common in the manufacturing sector). Also, even though the evidence points towards the presence of local knowledge spillovers of innovative industries, in many cases little is known about the extent to which highly innovative regions remain so because of the net inflow of human capital, or because these inflows are themselves a result of some regions being more dynamic and highly innovative (Faggian & McCann, 2009b). There are clear self-selection and endogeneity issues here that need to be fully addressed.

Lastly, the research on skilled migration focuses primarily on the experiences of male migrants. Data on heads of households, most often men, are more readily available when studying migration, especially in the case of interregional migration. For this reason, little work has been done on female migrants, including those who migrated as dependents of high-skilled males (Purkayastha, 2005). Although this is a common flaw of many studies in the labour-related literature, the role of female migrants must be addressed and studied in more detail.

DISCLOSURE STATEMENT

No potential conflict of interest was reported by the authors.

NOTES

1. It must be clarified that although the distinction between forced versus voluntary migration is common in the migration literature, this distinction is often not so clear-cut. Although migrants moving for employment reasons are traditionally classified as 'voluntary', the degree to which their movements are voluntary varies. A migration movement by a person with a good job wishing to improve his/her salary is obviously more voluntary than a migration movement by somebody who is unemployed and cannot find a job in his/her current city or area of experience. This subtle, but important, distinction is often completely overlooked in migration studies.
2. For a definition of what is intended here for human capital, see Faggian (2005) and Faggian, Partridge, and Malecki (2016).
3. Although, as Faggian and McCann (2009b) notice, the notion of endogeneity changes both subtly and fundamentally as one moves from a national aggregate to a regional context, as much of the regional growth stimulus is in the form of inflows of externally acquired human capital. The aspect of endogenous growth that is specifically internal to the host region is in the form of the local knowledge spillovers resulting from the interaction between the existing regional factors and the immigrant human capital. Conversely, for the origin region the process is in reverse, the aspect of endogenous growth which is specifically internal to the origin region is the process of cumulative decline due to localized negative externalities. The out-migration of local human capital is driven by external stimuli. This difference in terms of the definition of what is endogeneity, while appearing to be rather subtle, is in fact fundamental (pp. 143–144).
4. ACS: http://www.psc.isr.umich.edu/dis/acs/aggregator/.
5. CPS: https://www.census.gov/programs-surveys/cps/about.html/.
6. SESTAT: http://www.nsf.gov/statistics/sestat/.
7. IPEDS: http://nces.ed.gov/ipeds/.

REFERENCES

Ahlin, L., Andersson, M., & Thulin, P. (2016). *Human capital sorting – The 'when' and 'who' of sorting of talents to urban regions* (Working Paper No. 2016/10). Lund: Centre for Innovation, Research and Competence in the Learning Economy (CIRCLE), Lund University. Retrieved from CIRCLE website: http://wp.circle.lu.se/upload/CIRCLE/workingpapers/201610_Ahlin_et_al.pdf

Alesina, A., & La Ferrara, E. (2005). Ethnic diversity and economic performance. *Journal of Economic Literature, 43*(3), 762–800. doi:10.1257/002205105774431243

Alonso-Villar, O. (2002). Urban agglomeration: Knowledge spillovers and product diversity. *Annals of Regional Science, 36*(4), 551–573. doi:10.1007/s001680200090

Anderson, S., & Platzer, M. (2006). *The impact of immigrant entrepreneurs and professionals on U.S. competitiveness.* Retrieved from http://www.contentfirst.com/American-Made_study.pdf

Arntz, M., Gregory, T., & Lehmer, F. (2014). Can regional employment disparities explain the allocation of human capital across space? *Regional Studies, 48*(10), 1719–1738. doi:10.1080/00343404.2014.882500

Batista, C., Lacuesta, A., & Vicente, P. C. (2012). Testing the 'brain gain' hypothesis: Micro evidence from Cape Verde. *Journal of Development Economics, 97*(1), 32–45. doi:10.1016/j.jdeveco.2011.01.005

Behrens, K., & Sato, Y. (2011). Migration, skill formation, and the wage structure. *Journal of Regional Science, 51*(1), 5–30. doi:10. 1111/j.1467-9787.2010.00682.x

Beine, M., Docquier, F., & Oden-Defoort, C. (2011). A panel data analysis of the brain gain. *World Development, 39*(4), 523–532. doi:10.1016/j.worlddev.2010.03.009

Beine, M., Docquier, F., & Rapoport, H. (2001). Brain drain and economic growth: Theory and evidence. *Journal of Development Economics, 64*(1), 275–289. doi:10.1016/S0304-3878(00)00133-4

Beine, M., Docquier, F., & Rapoport, H. (2003). *Brain drain and LDCs' growth: Winners and losers* (Discussion Paper No. 819). Bonn: Institute for the Study of Labor (IZA).

Beine, M., Docquier, F., & Rapoport, H. (2008). Brain drain and human capital formation in developing countries: Winners and losers. *Economic Journal, 118*(528), 631–652. doi:10.1111/j.1468-0297.2008.02135.x

Belot, M., & Ederveen, S. (2012). Cultural barriers in migration between OECD countries. *Journal of Population Economics, 25*(3), 1077–1105. doi:10.1007/s00148-011-0356-x

Bhagwati, J., & Hamada, K. (1974). The brain drain, international integration of markets for professionals and unemployment: A theoretical analysis. *Journal of Development Economics, 1*(1), 19–42. doi:10.1016/0304-3878(74)90020-0

Bollard, A., McKenzie, D., Morten, M., & Rapoport, H. (2011). Remittances and the brain drain revisited: The microdata show that more educated migrants remit more. *World Bank Economic Review, 25*(1), 132–156. doi:10.1093/wber/lhr013

Borjas, G. J. (1999). The economic analysis of immigration. In O. Ashenfelter & D. Card (Eds.), *Handbook of labor economics* (pp. 1697–1760). Amsterdam: Elsevier.

Borjas, G. J. (2003). The labor demand curve is downward sloping: Reexamining the impact of immigration on the labor market. *Quarterly Journal of Economics, 118*(4), 1335–1374. doi:10.1162/003355303322552810

Borjas, G. J., & Bratsberg, B. (1996). Who leaves? The outmigration of the foreign-born. *Review of Economics and Statistics, 78*(1), 165–176. doi:10.2307/2109856

Boschma, R., Eriksson, R., & Lindgren, U. (2009). How does labour mobility affect the performance of plants? The importance of relatedness and geographical proximity. *Journal of Economic Geography, 9*(2), 169–190. doi:10.1093/jeg/lbn041

Boschma, R., Eriksson, R. H., & Lindgren, U. (2014). Labour market externalities and regional growth in Sweden: The importance of labour mobility between skill-related industries. *Regional Studies, 48*(10), 1669–1690. doi:10.1080/00343404.2013.867429

Bosetti, V., Cattaneo, C., & Verdolini, E. (2015). Migration of skilled workers and innovation: A European perspective. *Journal of International Economics, 96*(2), 311–322. doi:10.1016/j.jinteco.2015.04.002

Campbell, B. C., & Barone, L. (2012). Evolutionary basis of human migration. In B. C. Crawford & M. H. Campbell (Eds.), *Causes and consequences of human migration* (pp. 45–64). Cambridge: Cambridge University Press.

Carlino, G., & Kerr, W. (2014). *Agglomeration and innovation* (Working Paper No. 20367). Cambridge, MA: National Bureau of Economic Research (NBER). Retrieved from http://www.nber.org/papers/w20367

Carlino, G. A., & Mills, E. S. (1987). The determinants of county growth. *Journal of Regional Science, 27*(1), 39–54. doi:10.1111/j.1467-9787.1987.tb01143.x

Carrington, W. J., & Detragiache, E. (1998). *How big is the brain drain?* (Working Paper No. 98). Washington, DC: International Monetary Fund (IMF).

Chellaraj, G., Maskus, K. E., & Mattoo, A. (2008). The contribution of international graduate students to US innovation. *Review of International Economics, 16*(3), 444–462. doi:10.1111/j.1467-9396.2007.00714.x

Ciccone, A., & Peri, G. (2005). Long-run substitutability between more and less educated workers: Evidence from U.S. States 1950–1990. *Review of Economics and Statistics*, *87*(4), 652–663. doi:10.1162/003465305775098233

Ciccone, A., & Peri, G. (2006). Identifying human-capital externalities: Theory with applications. *Review of Economic Studies*, *73*(2), 381–412. doi:10.1111/j.1467-937X.2006.00380.x

Cohen, Y., & Haberfeld, Y. (2001). Self-selection and return migration: Israeli-born Jews returning home from the United States during the 1980s. *Population Studies*, *55*(1), 79–91. doi:10.1080/00324720127675

Combes, P.-P., Duranton, G., & Gobillon, L. (2008). Spatial wage disparities: Sorting matters! *Journal of Urban Economics*, *63*(2), 723–742. doi:10.1016/j.jue.2007.04.004

Commander, S., Kangasniemi,M.,& Winters, L. A. (2004). The brain drain: Curse or boom? A survey of the literature. In R. E. Baldwin & L. A. Winters (Eds.), *Challenges to globalization: Analyzing the economics* (pp. 235–272). Chicago: Chicago University Press.

Corcoran, J., & Faggian, A. (2017). Graduate migration and regional development: An international perspective. In J. Corcoran & A. Faggian (Eds.), *Graduate migration and regional development: An international perspective*. Cheltenham: Edward Elgar.

DaVanzo, J. (1978). Does unemployment affect migration? Evidence from micro data. *Review of Economics and Statistics*, *60*(4), 504–154 Retrieved from http://www.jstor.org/stable/1924242

Di Maria, C., & Stryszowski, P. (2009). Migration, human capital accumulation and economic development. *Journal of Development Economics*, *90*(2), 306–313. doi:10.1016/j.jdeveco.2008.06.008

Docquier, F., & Rapoport, H. (2012). Globalization, brain drain, and development. *Journal of Economic Literature*, *50*(3), 681–730. doi:10.1257/jel.50.3.681

Dotzel, K. R. (2016). Do natural amenities influence undergraduate student migration decisions? *Annals of Regional Science*. doi:10. 1007/s00168-016-0765-6

Drori, I., Honig, B., & Wright, M. (2009). Transnational entrepreneurship: An emergent field of study. *Entrepreneurship Theory and Practice*, *33*(5), 1001–1022. doi:10.1111/j.1540-6520.2009.00332.x

Dustmann, C., Fabbri, F., & Preston, I. (2005). The impact of immigration on the British labour market. *Economic Journal*, *115*(507), F324–F341. doi:10.1111/j.1468-0297.2005.01038.x

Dustmann, C., Glitz, A., & Frattini, T. (2008). The labour market impact of immigration. *Oxford Review of Economic Policy*, *24*(3), 477–494. doi:10.1093/oxrep/grn024

Dustmann, C., & Weiss, Y. (2007). Return migration: Theory and empirical evidence from the UK. *British Journal of Industrial Relations*, *45*(2), 236–256. doi:10.1111/j.1467-8543.2007.00613.x

Eriksson, R. H. (2011). Localized spillovers and knowledge flows: How does proximity influence the performance of plants? *Economic Geography*, *87*(2), 127–152. doi:10.1111/j.1944-8287.2011.01112.x

Faggian, A. (2005). Human capital. In R. Caves (Ed.), *Encyclopaedia of the city* (pp. 362–364). New York: Routledge.

Faggian, A., Corcoran, J., & McCann, P. (2013). Modelling geographical graduate job search using circular statistics. *Papers in Regional Science*, *92*(2), 329–343. doi:10.1111/pirs.12026

Faggian, A., Corcoran, J., & Partridge, M. (2015). Interregional migration analysis. In C. Karlsson, M. Andersson, & T. Norman (Eds.), *Handbook in the research of methods and applications in economic geography* (pp. 468–490). Cheltenham: Edward Elgar.

Faggian, A., & Franklin, R. S. (2014). Human capital redistribution in the USA: The migration of the college-bound. *Spatial Economic Analysis*, *9*(4), 376–395. doi:10.1080/1742 1772.2014.961536

Faggian, A., & McCann, P. (2006). Human capital flows and regional knowledge assets: A simultaneous equation approach. *Oxford Economic Papers*, *58*(3), 475–500. doi:10.1093/oep/gpl010

Faggian, A., & McCann, P. (2009a). Human capital, graduate migration and innovation in British regions. *Cambridge Journal of Economics*, *33*(2), 317–333. doi:10.1093/cje/ben042

Faggian, A., & McCann, P. (2009b). Human capital and regional development. In R. Capello & P. Nijkamp (Eds.), *Handbook of regional growth and development theories* (pp. 131–151). Cheltenham: Edward Elgar.

Faggian, A., McCann, P., & Sheppard, S. (2007). Some evidence that women are more mobile than men: Gender differences in UK graduate migration behavior. *Journal of Regional Science*, *47*(3), 517–539. doi:10.1111/j.1467-9787.2007.00518.x

Faggian, A., Partridge, M. D., & Malecki, E. (2016). *Creating an environment for economic growth: Creativity, entrepreneurship or human capital?* (MPRA Paper No. 71445). Munich: Munich Personal RePEc Archive (MPRA). https://mpra.ub.unimuenchen.de/71445/

Faggian, A., Partridge, M. D., & Rickman, D. (2012). Cultural avoidance and internal migration in the USA: Do the source countries matter? In J. Poot, M. Sahin, & P. Nijkamp (Eds.), *Migration impact analysis* (pp. 203–224). Cheltenham: Edward Elgar.

Faini, R. (2007). Remittances and the brain drain: Do more skilled migrants remit more? *World Bank Economic Review*, *21*(2), 177–191. doi:10.1093/wber/lhm006

Fan, C. S., & Stark, O. (2008). Rural-to-urban migration, human capital, and agglomeration. *Journal of Economic Behavior & Organization*, *68*(1), 234–247. doi:10.1016/j.jebo.2008.04.003

Feldman, M. (1994). *The geography of innovation*. Boston: Kluwer.

Fiore, A. M., Niehm, L. S., Hurst, J. L., Son, J., Sadachar, A., Russell, D. W.,. . .Seeger, C. (2015). Will they stay or will they go? Community features important in migration decisions of recent university graduates. *Economic Development Quarterly*, *29*(1), 23–37. doi:10.1177/0891242414559070

Florax, R. J. G. M., de Graaff, T., & Waldorf, B. S. (2005). A spatial economic perspective on language acquisition: Segregation, networking, and assimilation of immigrants. *Environment and Planning A*, *37*(10), 1877–1897. doi:10.1068/a3726

Florida, R. (2002). Bohemia and economic geography. *Journal of Economic Geography*, *2*(1), 55–71. doi:10.1093/jeg/2.1.55

Franklin, R., & Plane, D. (2006). Pandora's box: The potential and peril of migration data from the American community survey. *International Regional Science Review*, *29*, 231–246. doi:10.1177/0160017606289895

Franzoni, C., Scellato, G., & Stephan, P. (2012). Foreign-born scientists: Mobility patterns for 16 countries. *Careers and Recruitment*, *30*(12), 1250–1253. doi:10.3386/w18067

Fratesi, U., & Percoco, M. (2014). Selective migration, regional growth and convergence: Evidence from Italy. *Regional Studies*, *48*(10), 1650–1668. doi:10.1080/00343404.2013.843162

Gagliardi, L. (2015). Does skilled migration foster innovative performance? Evidence from British local areas. *Papers in Regional Science*, *94*(4), 773–794. doi:10.1111/pirs.12095

Gibson, J., & McKenzie, D. (2011). The microeconomic determinants of emigration and return migration of the best and brightest: Evidence from the pacific. *Journal of Development Economics*, *95*(1), 18–29.

Glaeser, E. L., & Maré, D. C. (2001). Cities and skills. *Journal of Labor Economics*, *19*(2), 316–342. doi:10.3386/w4728

Goodall, B. (1987). *The Penguin dictionary of human geography*. Harmondsworth: Penguin.

Gottlieb, P. D., & Joseph, G. (2006). College-to-work migration of technology graduates and holders of doctorates within the United States. *Journal of Regional Science*, *46*(4), 627–659. doi:10.1111/j.1467-9787.2006.00471.x

Granato, N., Haas, A., Hamann, S., & Niebuhr, A. (2015). The impact of skill-specific migration on regional unemployment disparities in Germany. *Journal of Regional Science*, *55*(4), 513–539. doi:10.1111/jors.12178

Graves, P. E. (1979). A life-cycle empirical analysis of migration and climate, by race. *Journal of Urban Economics*, *6*(2), 135–147. doi:10.1016/0094-1190(79)90001-9

Graves, P. E. (1980). Migration and climate. *Journal of Regional Science*, *20*(2), 227–237. doi:10.1111/j.1467-9787.1980.tb00641.x

Greenwood, M. J. (1975). Research on internal migration in the United States: A survey. *Journal of Economic Literature*, *13*(2), 397–433. Retrieved from http://www.jstor.org/stable/2722115

Greenwood, M. J. (1997). Internal migration in developed countries. In M. R. Rosenzweig & O. Stark (Eds.), *Handbook of population and family economics* (pp. 647–720). Amsterdam: Elsevier.

Guinness, P. (2002). *Migration.* London: Hodder Education.

Haapanen, M., & Tervo, H. (2012). Migration of the highly educated: Evidence from residence spells of university graduates. *Journal of Regional Science*, *52*(4), 587–605. doi:10.1111/j.1467-9787.2011.00745.x

Haque, N. U., & Kim, S. (1995). 'Human capital flight': impact of migration on income and growth. *Staff Papers – International Monetary Fund*, *42*(3), 577–607. doi:10.2307/3867533

Hensen, M. M., de Vries, M. R., & Cörvers, F. (2009). The role of geographic mobility in reducing education–job mismatches in the Netherlands. *Papers in Regional Science*, *88*(3), 667–682. doi:10.1111/j.1435-5957.2008.00189.x

Hunt, J., & Gauthier-Loiselle, M. (2009). How much does immigration boost innovation? (Discussion Paper No. 3921). Bonn: Institute for the Study of Labor (IZA).

International Monetary Fund (IMF). (2007). *World economic outlook (WEO): Globalization and inequality*. Washington, DC: IMF.

Islam, A., & Fausten, D. K. (2008). Skilled immigration and wages in Australia. *Economic Record*, *84*, S66–S82. doi:10.1111/j.1475-4932.2008.00485.x

Jones, B. F. (2009). The burden of knowledge and the 'Death of the renaissance man': Is innovation getting harder? *Review of Economic Studies*, *76*(1), 283–317. doi:10.1111/j.1467-937X.2008.00531.x

Kanbur, R., & Rapoport, H. (2005). Migration selectivity and the evolution of spatial inequality. *Journal of Economic Geography*, *5*(1), 43–57. doi:10.1093/jnlecg/lbh053

Kazakis, P., & Faggian, A. (2016). Mobility, education and labor market outcomes for U.S. Graduates: Is selectivity important? *Annals of Regional Science.* doi:10.1007/s00168-016-0773-6

Kerr, W. R. (2013). *U.S. high-skilled immigration, innovation, and entrepreneurship: Empirical approaches and evidence* (Working Paper No. 19377). Cambridge, MA: National Bureau of Economic Research (NBER). Retrieved from http://www.nber.org/papers/w19377

Krugman, P. (1991). Increasing returns and economic geography. *Journal of Political Economy*, *99*(3), 483–499. doi:10.1086/261763

Kwok, V., & Leland, H. (1982). An economic model of the brain drain. *American Economic Review, 72*(1), 91–100.

Lazear, E. P. (1999). Culture and language. *Journal of Political Economy, 107*(S6), S95–S126. doi:10.1086/250105

Le, T. (2008). 'Brain drain' or 'brain circulation': Evidence from OECD's international migration and R&D spillovers. *Scottish Journal of Political Economy, 55*(5), 618–636. doi:10.1111/j.1467-9485.2008.00468.x

Lee, N., & Nathan, M. (2010). Knowledge workers, cultural diversity and innovation: Evidence from London. *International Journal of Knowledge-Based Development, 1*(1/2), 53–78. doi:10.1504/JKBD.2010.032586

Lucas, R. E. (1988). On the mechanics of economic development. *Journal of Monetary Economics, 22*(1), 3–42.

Mallik, G., Basu, P. K., Hicks, J., & Sappey, R. (2014). Do the determinants of employability and earnings returns produce similar outcomes in metropolitan and regional labour markets? The case of New South Wales, Australia. *Regional Studies, 48*(10), 1706–1718. doi:10.1080/00343404.2013.812780

Marinelli, E. (2013). Sub-national graduate mobility and knowledge flows: An exploratory analysis of onward- and return-migrants in Italy. *Regional Studies, 47*(10), 1618–1633. doi:10.1080/00343404.2012.709608

Mazzolari, F., & Neumark, D. (2012). Immigration and product diversity. *Journal of Population Economics, 25*(3), 1107–1137. doi:10.1007/s00148-011-0355-y

McCann, P., & Simonen, J. (2005). Innovation, knowledge spillovers and local labour markets. *Papers in Regional Science, 84*(3), 465–485. doi:10.1111/j.1435-5957.2005.00036.x

McCulloch, R., & Yellen, J. L. (1977). Factor mobility, regional development, and the distribution of income. *Journal of Political Economy, 85*(1), 79–96. doi:10.1086/260546

Miguélez, E., & Moreno, R. (2013). Research networks and inventors' mobility as drivers of innovation: Evidence from Europe. *Regional Studies, 47*(10), 1668–1685. doi:10.1080/00343404.2011.618803

Miwagiwa, K. (1991). Scale economies in education and the brain drain problem. *International Economic Review, 32*(3), 743–759. doi:10.2307/2527117

Molloy, R., Smith, C. L., & Wozniak, A. (2011). Internal migration in the United States (Discussion Paper No. 5903). Bonn: Institute for the Study of Labor (IZA).

Moretti, E. (2004). Estimating the social return to higher education: Evidence from longitudinal and repeated cross-sectional data. *Journal of Econometrics, 121*(1–2), 175–212. doi:10.1016/j.jeconom.2003.10.015

Mountford, A. (1997). Can a brain drain be good for growth in the source economy? *Journal of Development Economics, 53*(2), 287–303. doi:10.1016/s0304-3878(97)00021-7

Nathan, M. (2011). *The long term impacts of migration in British cities: Diversity, wages, employment and prices* (Discussion Paper No. 67). Retrieved from http://www.spatialeconomics.ac.uk/textonly/SERC/publications/download/sercdp0067.pdf

Nathan, M. (2013). *The wider economic impacts of high-skilled migrants: A survey of the literature* (Discussion Paper No. 7653). Bonn: Institute for the Study of Labor (IZA). Retrieved from http://ftp.iza.org/dp7653

Nathan, M. (2015). After Florida: Towards an economics of diversity. *European Urban and Regional Studies, 22*(1), 3–19. doi:10.1177/0969776412463371

Niimi, Y., Ozden, C., & Schiff, M. (2010). Remittances and the brain drain: Skilled migrants do remit less. *Annals of Economics and Statistics* (97/98), 123–141. doi:10.2307/41219112

Ottaviano, G. I. P., & Peri, G. (2006). The economic value of cultural diversity: Evidence from US cities. *Journal of Economic Geography*, *6*(1), 9–44. doi:10.1093/jeg/lbi002

Ottaviano, G. I. P., & Peri, G. (2008). *Immigration and national wages: Clarifying the theory and the empirics* (Working Paper No. 14188). Cambridge, MA: National Bureau of Economic Research (NBER). Retrieved from http://www.nber.org/papers/w14188/.

Ozgen, C., Nijkamp, P., & Poot, J. (2011). *Immigration and innovation in European regions* (Discussion Paper No. 5676). Bonn: Institute for the Study of Labor (IZA). Retrieved from http://ftp.iza.org/dp5676

Partridge, M. D. (2010). The duelling models: NEG vs amenity migration in explaining US engines of growth. *Papers in Regional Science*, *89*(3), 513–536. doi:10.1111/j.1435-5957.2010.00315.x

Plane, D., & Rogerson, P. (1994). *The geographical analysis of population with applications to planning and business.* New York: Wiley.

Power, D., & Lundmark, M. (2004). Working through knowledge pools: Labour market dynamics, the transference of knowledge and ideas, and industrial clusters. *Urban Studies*, *41*(5–6), 1025–1044. doi:10.1080/00420980410001675850

Purkayastha, B. (2005). Skilled migration and cumulative disadvantage: The case of highly qualified Asian Indian immigrant women in the US. *Geoforum*, *36*(2), 181–196. doi:10.1016/j.geoforum.2003.11.006

Ramirez, M., Li, X., & Chen, W. (2013). Comparing the impact of intra- and inter-regional labour mobility on problem-solving in a Chinese science park. *Regional Studies*, *47*(10), 1734–1751. doi:10.1080/00343404.2011.632365

Rapoport, H. (2004). Who is afraid of the brain drain? Human capital flight and growth in developing countries. *Brussels Economic Review*, *47*(1), 89–101.

Rauch, J. E. (1993). Productivity gains from geographic concentration of human capital: Evidence from the cities. *Journal of Urban Economics*, *34*(3), 380–400. doi:10.1006/juec.1993.1042

Rodríguez-Pose, A., & Vilalta-Bufí, M. (2005). Education, migration, and job satisfaction: The regional returns of human capital in the EU. *Journal of Economic Geography*, *5*(5), 545–566. doi:10.1093/jeg/lbh067

Romer, P. M. (1986). Increasing returns and long-run growth. *Journal of Political Economy*, *94*(5), 1002–1037. doi:10.1086/261420

Romer, P. M. (1987). Growth based on increasing returns due to specialization. *American Economic Review*, *77*(2), 56–62.

Rosenzweig, M. R. (2008). Higher education and international migration in Asia: Brain circulation. In J. Y. Lin, & B. Pleskovic (Eds.), *Annual World Bank conference on development economics, regional 2008: Higher education and development* (pp. 59–84). Washington, DC: World Bank.

Saiz, A. (2003). Room in the kitchen for the melting pot: Immigration and rental prices. *Review of Economics and Statistics*, *85*(3), 502–521. doi:10.1162/003465303322369687

Saxenian, A. (2002). Silicon Valley's new immigrant high-growth entrepreneurs. *Economic Development Quarterly*, *16*(1), 20–31. doi:10.1177/0891242402016001003

Schlitte, F. (2010). *Local human capital, segregation by skill, and skillspecific employment growth* (Working Paper No. 1-32). Hamburg: Hamburg Institute of International Economics. Retrieved from http://www.hwwi.org/fileadmin/_migrated/tx_wilpubdb/HWWI_Research_Paper_1-32.pdf

Sjaastad, L. A. (1962). The costs and returns of human migration. *Journal of Political Economy Supplement*, *70*(5), 80–93. Retrieved from http://www.jstor.org/stable/1829105

Solow, R. M. (1957). Technical change and the aggregate production function. *Review of Economics and Statistics*, *39*(3), 312–320.

Stark, O. (2004). Rethinking the brain drain. *World Development*, *32*(1), 15–22. doi:10.1016/j.worlddev.2003.06.013

Stark, O., Helmenstein, C., & Prskawetz, A. (1997). A brain gain with a brain drain. *Economics Letters*, *55*(2), 227–234. doi:10.1016/S0165-1765(97)00085-2

Stark, O., Helmenstein, C., & Prskawetz, A. (1998). Human capital depletion, human capital formation, and migration: A blessing or a 'curse'? *Economics Letters*, *60*(3), 363–367. doi:10.1016/s0165-1765(98)00125-6

Stark, O., & Wang, Y. (2002). Inducing human capital formation: Migration as a substitute for subsidies. *Journal of Public Economics*, *86*(1), 29–46. doi:10.1016/s0047-2727(01)00104-9

Suedekum, J. (2004). Selective migration, union wage setting and unemployment disparities in West Germany. *International Economic Journal*, *18*(1), 33–48. doi:10.1080/1351161042000180629

Suedekum, J. (2006). *Human capital externalities and growth of hig-hand low-skilled jobs* (Discussion Paper No. 1969). Bonn: Institute for the Study of Labor (IZA).

Syrett, S., & Sepulveda, L. (2011). Realising the diversity dividend: Population diversity and urban economic development. *Environment and Planning A*, *43*(2), 487–504. doi:10.1068/a43185

Timmermans, B., & Boschma, R. (2014). The effect of intra- and inter-regional labour mobility on plant performance in Denmark: The significance of related labour inflows. *Journal of Economic Geography*, *14*(2), 289–311. doi:10.1093/jeg/lbs059

Trippl, M. (2013). Scientific mobility and knowledge transfer at the interregional and intraregional level. *Regional Studies*, *47*(10), 1653–1667. doi:10.1080/00343404.2010.549119

United Nations. (2013). *Population facts* (No. 2013/2). New York: United Nations. Retrieved from http://www.un.org/en/development/desa/population/publications/pdf/popfacts/PopFacts_2013-2_new.pdf

Venhorst, V., Van Dijk, J., & Van Wissen, L. (2010). Do the best graduates leave the peripheral areas of the Netherlands? *Tijdschrift voor Economische en Sociale Geografie*, *101*(5), 521–537. doi:10.1111/j.1467 9663.2010.00629.x

Vidal, J. (1998). The effect of emigration on human capital formation. *Journal of Population Economics*, *11*(4), 589–600. doi:10.1007/s001480050086

Von Reichert, C., Cromartie, J. B., & Arthun, R. O. (2014). Impacts of return migration on rural U.S. communities. *Rural Sociology*, *79*(2), 200–226. doi:10.1111/ruso.12024

Wadhwa, V., Saxenian, A., & Siciliano, F. D. (2012). *Then and now: America's new immigrant entrepreneurs, Part VII*. Kansas City: Ewing Marion Kauffman Foundation. Retrieved from http://www.kauffman.org/what-we-do/research/immigration-and-theamerican-economy/americas-new-immigrant-entrepreneursthen-and-now

Waldorf, B., & Yun, S. D. (2015). Labor migration and overeducation among young college graduates. *Review of Regional Research*, *3*(2), 99–119. doi:10.1007/s10037-015-0101-0

Wang, Z., De Graaff, T., & Nijkamp, P. (2016). Cultural diversity and cultural distance as choice determinants of migration destination. *Spatial Economic Analysis*, *11*(2), 176–200. doi:10.1080/17421772.2016.1102956

Wells, J. C. K., & Stock, J. T. (2012). The biology of human migration: The ape that won't commit? In B. C. Crawford & M. H. Campbell (Eds.), *Causes and consequences of human migration* (pp. 21–44). Cambridge: Cambridge University Press.

Wheeler, C. H. (2006). Cities and the growth of wages among young workers: Evidence from the NLSY. *Journal of Urban Economics*, *60*(2), 162–184. doi:10.1016/j.jue.2006.02.004

Whisler, R. L., Waldorf, B. S., Mulligan, G. F., & Plane, D. A. (2008). Quality of life and the migration of the college-educated: A life-course approach. *Growth and Change*, *39*(1), 58–94. doi:10.1111/j.1468-2257.2007.00405.x

Winters, J. V., & Xu, W. (2014). Geographic differences in the earnings of economics majors. *Journal of Economic Education*, *45*(3), 262–276. doi:10.1080/00220485.2014.9 17912

Wong, K.-Y., & Yip, C. K. (1999). Education, economic growth, and brain drain. *Journal of Economic Dynamics and Control*, *23*(5–6), 699–726. doi:10.1016/s0165-1889(98)00040-2

Yankow, J. J. (2006). Why do cities pay more? An empirical examination of some competing theories of the urban wage premium. *Journal of Urban Economics*, *60*(2), 139–161. doi:10.1016/j.jue.2006.03.004

Zhao, Y. (2002). Causes and consequences of return migration: Recent evidence from China. *Journal of Comparative Economics*, *30*(2), 376–394. doi:10.1006/jcec.2002.1781

Zucker, L. G., & Darby, M. R. (2007). *Star scientists, innovation and regional and national immigration* (Working Paper No. 13547). Cambridge, MA: National Bureau of Economic Research (NBER). http://nber.org/papers/w13547

Can transport infrastructure change regions' economic fortunes? Some evidence from Europe and China

Chia-Lin Chen and Roger Vickerman

ABSTRACT

Can transport infrastructure change regions' economic fortunes? Some evidence from Europe and China. *Regional Studies*. Claims and counterclaims about the likely impact of new transport infrastructure on a region's economic performance have existed for centuries going back to the early days of canals and railways. High-speed rail (HSR) as a new type of infrastructure has just over 50 years of existence. The persistent debate is questioning the power of HSR in reducing economic disparities between cities and effecting economic transformation. The paper goes beyond macro-modelling, looking to more disaggregated approaches of the structural changes. Two regions, one in Europe and one in China, are compared to gain insights for future research and practice.

摘要

交通基础建设能够改变区域的经济未来吗？来自欧洲与中国的若干证据。*Regional Studies*. 有关新的交通基础建设对于区域经济表现的可能影响之主张与反驳已存在数百年，并可追溯至早期的运河与铁路建设。高速铁路 (HSR) 是问世刚超过五十年的新形态基础建设。而持续的争论，则质疑 HSR 在减少城市之间的经济悬殊并影响经济变迁上的力量。本文超越巨观尺度的模式化，并有赖于更为分散的方法研究结构变迁。本文比较两个区域——一个在欧洲，另一个在中国——以取得未来研究及实践的洞见。

RÉSUMÉ

L'infrastructure de transport, peut-elle transformer l'avenir économique des régions? Des résultats à partir de l'Europe et de la Chine. *Regional Studies*. Il existe depuis des siècles, remontant jusqu'aux premières phases du développement des réseaux de canaux et de chemin de fer, des prétentions et des prétentions opposées à propos de l'impact éventuel de la nouvelle infrastructure de transport sur la performance économique d'une région. Le train à grande vitesse (high-speed rail; HSR) comme une nouvelle forme d'infrastructure existe depuis un peu plus de 50 années. Le débat continuel remet en cause si, oui ou non, HSR a la capacité de

257

réduire les écarts économiques entre les grandes villes et de déclencher une transformation économique. Cet article va au-delà de la modélisation macroéconomique, se tournant vers des approches plus désagrégées des changements structurels. On compare deux régions, l'une en Europe, l'autre en Chine, afin de s'informer sur les domaines de recherche et de pratique futurs.

ZUSAMMENFASSUNG
Kann die Verkehrsinfrastruktur die wirtschaftliche Zukunft von Regionen ändern? Belege aus Europa und China. *Regional Studies*. Thesen und Antithesen über die voraussichtlichen Auswirkungen von neuer Verkehrsinfrastruktur auf die Wirtschaftsleistung einer Region gab es bereits vor Jahrhunderten in den Tagen der ersten Kanäle und Eisenbahnen. Eisenbahn-Hochgeschwindigkeitsverkehr als neue Art der Infrastruktur gibt es hingegen erst seit etwas mehr als 50 Jahren. In einer anhaltenden Debatte wird das Potenzial von Hochgeschwindigkeitsstrecken zur Verringerung der wirtschaftlichen Disparitäten zwischen Städten sowie zur Erzielung von wirtschaftlichem Wandel infrage gestellt. In diesem Beitrag werden jenseits der Makromodelle stärker disaggregierte Ansätze der strukturellen Veränderung untersucht. Hierfür vergleichen wir zwei Regionen – eine in Europa und eine in China –, um Erkenntnisse für die künftige Forschung und Praxis zu gewinnen.

RESUMEN
¿Puede la infraestructura de transporte cambiar el futuro económico de las regiones? Algunas evidencias de Europa y China. *Regional Studies*. Los argumentos en pro y en contra sobre el posible impacto de nueva infraestructura de transporte en el desempeño económico de una región han existido durante siglos desde los primeros tiempos de canales y vías férreas. El ferrocarril de alta velocidad como un nuevo tipo de infraestructura tiene poco más de 50 años de existencia. En un largo debate se está cuestionando el poder del ferrocarril de alta velocidad para reducir las desigualdades económicas entre ciudades así como su efecto en la transformación económica. Este artículo va más allá del modelo macro y se centra en los enfoques más disgregados de los cambios estructurales. Comparamos dos regiones, una en Europa y otra en China, con el fin de adquirir conocimientos más profundos para la investigación y práctica futuras.

INTRODUCTION

How transport affects economic performance has been a recurring theme in discussions on transport appraisal. Traditional views were that a well-constituted cost–benefit analysis would include all such effects as part of the user benefits; to include any additional effects would involve double-counting. However, this depends on assuming that there is perfect competition in the rest of the economy. Where this does not occur there is scope for transport improvements to give rise to increased productivity and agglomeration effects that are cumulative. In this context transport infrastructure can have the potential to transform economies. The debate on these wider economic impacts of major infrastructure projects has developed considerably. This has been particularly the case in the UK over the last 10 years since the appraisal of Crossrail, which provided hard evidence of the scale of these potential impacts. The concern remains, however, that any such local effects may be essentially redistributional rather than having a net impact on economic performance overall. This is significant because it can provide the basis for an argument in support of the use of public funds in a project to ensure the capture of these wider impacts.

This paper looks at the specific case of high-speed rail (HSR) that has the potential to create step changes in accessibility. Can the development of such infrastructure have a transformational effect on economies? The paper first examines the theoretical arguments for the existence of wider economic impacts. It then looks at possible empirical methods to evaluate these before assembling some evidence from existing HSR projects in Europe and China to determine whether there is a case for their existence, and whether there are differences in these effects in the different geographical situations. In contrast to studies that have estimated aggregate impacts on national or regional economies (see Ansar, Flyvbjerg, Budzier, & Lunn, 2016, for a recent attempt to do this for China), the focus here is on the structural changes in city-regions and two have been chosen that experienced the arrival of HSR at around the same time. Although the Yangtze River Delta (YRD) in China and Kent in the UK are very different in scale, they both represent regions close to a major metropolitan area, Shanghai and London respectively. Finally, the paper suggests some ways forward in moving to a more robust and transparent way of assessing such impacts.

THE WIDER ECONOMIC IMPACTS DEBATE

Transport infrastructure has, for a long time, been the source of speculation concerning its impact on the economy; many studies have been published in this journal over that time. More than 50 years ago Fogel (1964) raised the question of the role of railways in the economic development of the United States, and the question of the 'social dividend' from historical transport developments such as canals and railways has continued to fascinate economic historians (Leunig, 2010). In the aggregate it is possible to identify a high degree of correlation between transport investment and economic performance; higher levels of investment are associated with higher levels of productivity and growth. Following the work of Aschauer (1989) there was quite an industry in demonstrating this at both national and regional levels. Aschauer tried to demonstrate that publically provided infrastructure could raise the level of private productivity and thus counter any fear that it crowded out private investments. But there is a much longer history going back to the works of von Thünen (1826), Christaller (1933) and Lösch (1940) that focused on the role of accessibility in determining the importance of central places.

Using the gravity model showing how the interactions between two locations depend on the economic mass of those places and the friction of the intervening distance between them, geographers showed how this economic potential of locations could be affected by improvements in infrastructure that reduced the access times between them (Clark, Wilson, & Bradley, 1969; Keeble, Owens, & Thompson, 1982a). Keeble, Owens, and Thompson (1982b) suggested that, assuming that the Channel Tunnel reduced journey times to those of the equivalent land distance, South East England would show an increase in potential of 10.05% and a 4.98% increase relative to the maximum potential in the European Community (given that the potential of all regions would increase if average accessibility increased).

The problem with these aggregate measures using the volume of investment or distance-based accessibility is that they do not distinguish differences in industrial structure or the potential of regions to take advantage of new opportunities. Often analyses of the impact of new infrastructure are taken from the perspective of the region promoting the scheme; the analysis shows how the improved accessibility will open up new markets for the region's industries, but ignores the fact that all such transport improvements work in both directions and open up the region's industries to more competition. It is very easy to jump to the conclusion from this that those regions that are already more advanced are more likely to suck economic activity out of the relatively poorer region. This is a revival of the problem identified by Hotelling (1929) that small cities would be better campaigning for more barriers to access than better access if they wished to avoid their markets being swamped by goods from larger cities.

Vickerman (1987) suggested that the Channel Tunnel would not have the impact suggested by Keeble et al. (1982b), at least on the regions lying between the major metropolitan areas. This idea that accessibility is not continuous is particularly relevant in the case of HSR as in order to benefit from the increase in speed it is necessary to restrict the number of stops on the network. Vickerman, Spiekermann, and Wegener (1999) demonstrated how these discontinuities would change the accessibility map of Europe with the adoption of the HSR lines defined in the Trans-European Transport Networks. Major centres would continue to benefit, but many intermediate areas would not, whilst more peripheral centres would also not gain a major redistribution of enhanced relative accessibility. But accessibility, however measured, cannot be interpreted as economic benefit; to understand this requires an understanding of how firms and industries (and indeed individuals) use transport and, in particular, how they use transport in imperfectly competitive markets. This leads one from the simple consideration of direct user benefits to that of wider impacts on the economy as a whole.

The more recent literature stems from the pioneering work of Krugman (1991). This has been developed more formally by Fujita, Krugman, and Venables (1999) and others, and a useful application to appraisal in the transport case is given by Venables (2007). The implications of this work have recently been summarized by Venables, Laird, and Overman (2014) for the Department for Transport in the UK. The essence of this so-called 'New Economic Geography' approach is that markets using transport are imperfectly competitive such that their response to falling transport costs is not necessarily an equivalent reduction in prices (see also Dodgson, 1973, 1974; Jara-Diaz, 1986). This implies that firms in larger cities will usually be more productive than firms in smaller cities due to agglomeration effects. Whereas conventional theory would argue that resources would then move towards the larger city until the cost differential was equalized, the new theory shows that a virtuous cycle can occur in which productivity continues to increase and the real wage to rise, confirming and reinforcing the advantage of the larger city over the smaller one. In this way transport improvements lead to divergence. But the new insight is that in some circumstances, depending on the initial level of transport costs between the two cities and the extent of the change, transport costs become less relevant for location choice and the smaller city can overcome the larger city's initial advantage. The key insight is that a given change in transport costs leads to an indeterminate change in the spatial distribution of the impact. Thus, one cannot say a priori that a new transport infrastructure will be centralizing or decentralizing. Whilst this can be shown theoretically and numerically, empirical testing is more difficult, but using the framework of Venables (2007), Graham (2007) related productivity change using firm level data to changes in the economic mass (effective employment density) of a location.

Graham developed the analysis initially on data for London to estimate the wider economic effects from the construction of a new urban railway, Crossrail, and the methodology has now been incorporated into the official guidance for transport analysis in the UK. What the work showed is that the elasticities of productivity with respect to a change in effective density were larger than most previous aggregate analyses of productivity and city size had suggested (Glaeser & Gottlieb, 2009), and that this was particularly true for employment in sectors such as business and financial services. Such sectors are more likely to use, and benefit from, HSR, and hence have the potential to change a region's economic structure, whereas highway improvements are likely to have a more neutral effect on structure as they increase accessibility and reduce transport costs more equally across all sectors.

Although clear evidence of wider economic benefits from transport investments exists for urban projects, these operate through impacts on clearly defined labour markets. Graham, Gibbons, and Martin (2010) showed that these effects are highly localized. Graham and Melo (2011) applied the same methodology to the case of the proposed HS2 HSR line in the UK and suggested that such agglomeration effects would be relatively small. Those seeking to identify transformational effects of major infrastructures have developed models of business and labour connectivity between cities for HS2 (KPMG, 2013), between countries for airport expansion (PwC, 2013a) or more detailed computable general equilibrium models (PwC, 2013b). These suggest much more significant overall impacts on gross domestic product (GDP) from such projects and, although these identify winners and losers from such developments, the net gain is significantly positive. Not surprisingly these estimates have been subject to a degree of criticism, as they appear to suggest impacts on the economy much larger than anything previously estimated (Overman, 2013).

On the negative side, Ansar et al. (2016) suggest that the assumption in the models discussed above, that lower transport costs translate into higher levels of productivity, which is beneficial to the economy, ignore the impact of typical underperformance relative to ex-ante forecasts. This, they suggest, leads to macroeconomic risks because of the financial costs from the ways that such projects are financed through debt or taxation. This is a return to the crowding-out hypothesis originally challenged by Aschauer (1989). The present authors find this attempt to use project-by-project data to assess overall macroeconomic performance less helpful in understanding the impact of new transport infrastructure than an approach that focuses on the real economic impact on the local economies affected.

ESTIMATING WIDER IMPACTS

The problem with the theoretical model from the new Economic Geography is that it does not have an analytical solution. Numerical simulations can show the range of possible outcomes, but this is less satisfactory as a decision-making model to build into an appraisal framework or to estimate impacts ex-post. Venables (2007) provided the link between the theoretical model and its potential use in an extended cost–benefit analysis framework. This was used in an empirical study by Graham (2007) and is the approach now adopted by the UK Department for Transport (2014) in its appraisal methodology WebTAG.

This model works well for large urban areas and was instrumental in the decision to proceed with the Crossrail project in London (Department for Transport, 2005) identifying wider impacts equal to more than 30% of the direct user benefits. These depend on relatively high elasticities associated with key employment sectors in the London metropolitan region such as financial and business services, when compared with the agglomeration elasticities traditionally found in urban size models that are heavily dominated by industrial sectors.

The model presents greater problems in dealing with larger scale inter-urban and inter-regional projects. Graham et al. (2010) have shown that the distance decay applicable to the effective density calculations is quite steep suggesting that benefits are confined to quite small areas around access points such as rail stations. Graham and Melo (2011) found relatively minor additional impacts when applying essentially the same model structure to the proposed HS2 HSR link between London, Birmingham and the North.

Venables (2013) has suggested that the clustering that lies at the heart of the agglomeration story may in fact apply, not at the sectoral level, but rather at the level of skills and occupations. Thus, in an inter-urban context it is activities that move and cluster, within sectors and even within firms, as the traditional Marshallian externalities operate more effectively at this level.

However, this attempt to extend the cost–benefit analysis framework to encompass wider impacts may not be the most appropriate way forward to understanding the overall impact on regional development from a major HSR project. Laird, Nash, and Mackie (2014) have attempted to map out the requirements of an extended cost–benefit analysis approach and contrast this with an alternative view that tries to go straight to the impact on output or gross value added (GVA). Models that try to do this have been around for many years in the form of land-use transport interaction (LUTI) models (Wegener, 2011). These have been supplemented in recent years by spatial computable equilibrium (SCGE) models (Bröcker & Mercenier, 2011).

The problem with these models is their dependence on imported data for calibration and the assumption of market clearing equilibrium. What is needed is an approach that allows for disaggregated behavioural responses to changing accessibility. One controversial approach is that developed by KPMG (2013) that attempts to estimate both labour market and business responses to changing accessibility to produce regional estimates of employment and output change. This has suggested that the potential impact of the HS2 network in the UK between London, Birmingham, Manchester and Leeds could be significantly greater than that suggested by conventional methods. The controversy has arisen over the assumptions made about modal elasticities from changing accessibility and the fact that very high, much higher than obtained from alternative methods, figures have been obtained for overall economic impact (House of Commons, 2013). In work related to the economic impacts of new airport runways in the UK, PwC (2013a) also explored connectivity between countries and subsequently developed a computable general equilibrium model for this purpose (PwC, 2013b).

In contrast to a much larger number of ex-ante HSR studies, ex-post HSR studies on wider impacts have been in scarcity. In the 1980s, early ex-post HSR impact studies largely focused on the Japanese and French experiences. These studies compiled a control group of places without HSR services, based on the comparison of economic performance (population, employment, property value etc.) before and after the introduction of the HSR services (Amano & Nakagawa, 1990; Hirota, 1984 Nakamura & Ueda, 1989; Sands, 1993) and tourism and service industries (Bonnafous, 1987). Since then, these descriptive statistical methods had been occasionally used to evaluate quite short-term effects of large-scale transport investment. The issue with these short-term evaluations lies in a short-term judgment on those supposed to be much longer-term impacts. Little wonder that the general picture is quite mixed (Givoni, 2006). Although some studies demonstrate faster growth rates of population and economic effects (i.e., employment and economic activity) for cities on HSR routes than those that are bypassed, some tend to be more reserved with insignificant findings (e.g., Preston & Wall, 2008). In recent years, a few ex-post studies attempted to examine wider HSR impacts at more disaggregated/multilevel, and long-term HSR impacts (e.g., Garmendia, Ureña, Ribalaygua, Leal, & Coronado, 2008; Ureña, Menerault, & Garmendia, 2009; Murakami & Cervero, 2010; Chen & Hall, 2011, 2012).

This paper takes a more detailed look at some ex-post evidence for the impact of HSR on two key variables: output or gross value added in the regions linked by HSR, and the change in employment in knowledge-related sectors. The authors feel that this approach helps one to understand the process of change better than the 'black box' inherent in the aggregate studies and a better transition to ex-post evaluation from the largely ex-ante studies discussed above. The focus here has been on output and employment-related data rather than the land-use approach used by Pugh and Fairburn (2008) for the reason suggested above that HSR has a more direct impact on certain sectors in specific locations than a highway improvement. Since HSR provides better links to those cities with stations than to wider regions, the focus here is on evidence at the most disaggregated spatial level. The choice of knowledge-related sectors reflects the fact that HSR does not fundamentally change the transport costs for more traditional manufacturing industries, but does provide better connectivity for those working in those sectors where knowledge exchange is paramount.

This more detailed look at the performance of cities where HSR has been introduced complements the evidence in Cheng, Loo, and Vickerman (2015) which showed how in city-regions with HSR there had been interesting changes in overall employment structure. In Europe, specifically relating to the Paris–Brussels–Cologne–Amsterdam–London network, the core city-regions had grown more alike in structure and their hinterlands had also converged. In China, in the Pearl River Delta region of Guangdong, there was less evidence of convergence. This suggests that, where HSR is introduced at an earlier stage of development it promotes divergence, but in more advanced economies it leads to convergence. This is entirely consistent with theories of economic development that suggest there is divergence in the earlier stages of development followed by convergence. It could be hypothesized that the introduction of HSR at a later stage serves to prevent fragmentation due to poor connectivity associated, for example, with congestion. Through this evidence it cannot be demonstrated that HSR is the cause of these changes, only that they are associated with the introduction of HSR.

THE EUROPEAN NETWORK CASE STUDY

In Europe, as in Japan, the early development of HSR was as often about creating new capacity on key routes as about reducing journey times. The potential for competition with airlines over medium distances of 400–600 km was also a key policy objective to reduce airport congestion and provide a more environmentally sustainable mode for transport between large cities (Vickerman et al., 1999). France led the way in the development of HSR in Europe. The network has developed to link the major cities of France and also to the neighbouring countries of Belgium, the UK, Spain and Germany. Particularly in the so-called PBKAL (Paris–Brussels–Cologne (Koln)–Amsterdam–London) network, the cities are ideally spaced at no more than 500 km (see Figure A1 in the supplemental data online), although national borders mean that there are lower levels of traffic (and hence frequencies) than would be expected if the cities were within a single country (Vickerman, 2015). That wider region was the focus of the research reported by Cheng et al. (2015). Chen and Hall (2012) have explored the impact of HSR on the Nord-Pas de Calais region (now part of the larger Hauts-de-France region) and especially the city of Lille.

This paper focuses on the UK region of Kent and Medway on the London branch of the PBKAL network (see Figure A2 in the supplemental data online). The line, known as HS1, was completed in 2007 to provide new high-speed infrastructure between the Channel Tunnel and London St Pancras for international services. The region has two HSR stations at Ashford and Ebbsfleet with services to Paris and Brussels. In 2009 frequent domestic high-speed services were introduced cutting the journey time from Ashford to London from around 80 to 37 minutes with the new station at Ebbsfleet just 17 minutes from London. HSR services also use the traditional network to serve a wider range of towns and cities in North and East Kent producing valuable reductions in journey times and improvements in reliability. As Vickerman (2015) has identified, the more limited international services from the Kent stations has restricted the potential for basing development on these links, a point made in the review of 10 years of operation of the Channel Tunnel by Hay, Meredith, and Vickerman (2004). However, the introduction of the domestic services not only enhances rail services to London but also, due to the siting of the London terminus, to much of the rest of the UK through the adjacency of St Pancras to Kings Cross and proximity to Euston.

IMPACTS OF HSR IN KENT

Figure 1 shows the rapid growth of traffic on domestic regional services using HS1 since its completion in 2009. The performance of the Kent economy since the opening of the Channel Tunnel is virtually indistinguishable from that of the South East or England as a whole (see Figure A3 in the supplemental data online). This implies that there was neither a strongly positive nor a negative impact of the Channel Tunnel on the growth of GVA because as expected Kent was now performing like the rest of the wider region.

However, at a district level (Figure 2) one can begin to discern some interesting differences. Clearly Dartford and Ashford, the locations of Ebbsfleet International and Ashford International rail stations, have grown much more strongly than Kent as a whole. Only Dartford, which as well as having the HSR station at Ebbsfleet is located on the M25 London Orbital Motorway at the major crossing of the River Thames, exceeded the average GVA/head for England or the South East. At the other extreme, Dover has fared much worse than the average, particularly since 2008. This was impacted by the subsequent closure of a major pharmaceutical research facility at Sandwich in the district. Figure 3 re-presents the data from Figure 2, but using the start of domestic HSR services as the base (2009 =

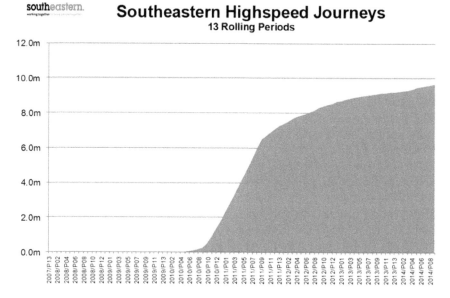

Figure 1 Regional services on HS1.
Source: Southeastern Railway.

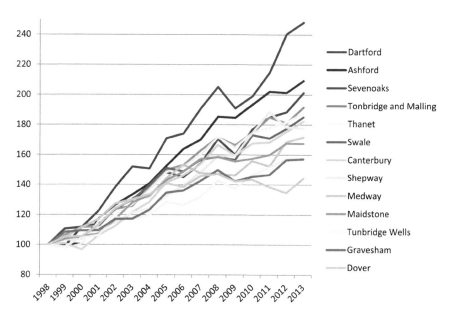

Figure 2 Growth in gross value added (GVA), Kent districts plus Medway, 1998–2013
(1998 = 100).
Source: Kent County Council.

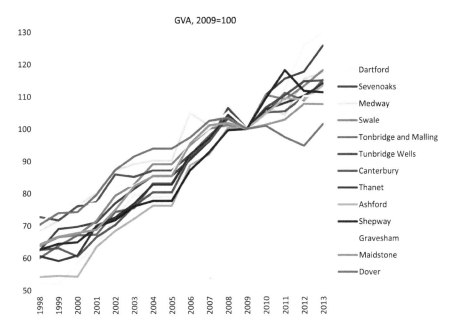

Figure 3 Growth in GVA, Kent districts plus Medway, 1998–2013 (2009 = 100).
Source: Kent County Council.

100). This shows that Ashford has not performed as well since the introduction of domestic services as it has over the longer period. Perhaps the Channel Tunnel effect was stronger than previously believed and the domestic services have served to support that growth but not change it fundamentally. The creation of opportunities at Ebbsfleet may, however, have had a stronger impact on Dartford.

Figure 4 shows the relative importance of jobs in the knowledge economy across Kent districts in comparison with the South East and Great Britain as a whole. Kent has a smaller proportion of such jobs than the economy as a whole although districts such as Canterbury, Tunbridge Wells and Sevenoaks were all above the national average and the first two above the South East average. The knowledge economy is defined using data from the Office of National Statistics (ONS) Business Register Employment Survey as 'a group of specific sectors within the economy that are knowledge intensive in their activity, that deal extensively with information/information technology and whose business is all about the distribution or exchange of the information that they hold'.

Figure 5 shows that in 1998–2008 Dartford had the largest increase in knowledge economy employment, but that Kent as a whole (excluding Medway) also showed faster growth than the rest of the country. Growth was also faster in the districts with relatively low levels of such jobs. After 2008 the picture changed somewhat. Kent continued to show faster growth in such jobs than the rest of the country, but the fastest growth was now in those with the higher concentrations,

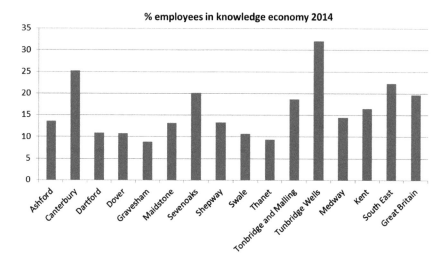

Figure 4 The knowledge economy, Kent districts, 2014.
Source: Kent County Council.

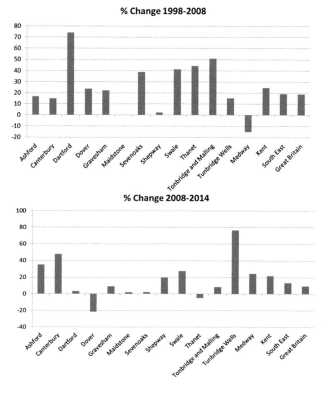

Figure 5 Changes in knowledge economy employment, 1998–2014.
Source: Kent County Council.

Canterbury and Tunbridge Wells, with Ashford also showing stronger growth in this period. It is not surprising to find that Canterbury, with three university institutions, has a high level of knowledge-economy employment, but the growth since 2008 suggests an HSR effect may be present. The locations in West Kent such as Tunbridge Wells and Dartford also benefit from their greater proximity to London, with or without HSR, although interestingly Dartford showed lower growth in the period after HS1 was completed. The closure of the research facility in Dover led to a dramatic fall of more than 20% of such jobs in this period.

For most districts in Kent, median earnings by workplace are lower than those measured by residence, suggesting that out-commuting is more important than in-commuting. This suggests that the benefit of HS1 has been to encourage new residents rather than new businesses. Median earnings by workplace in Ashford are significantly below the national median, whereas for residents they are close to the median. Moreover, Ashford earnings are below the Kent averages for both workplace and resident measures.

THE CHINESE NETWORK CASE STUDY

In comparison with Europe where rail infrastructure had been gradually modernized from the 1970s onwards, China did not do so until the 1990s by speed upgrading and its HSR network was not on the horizon until the early 2000s. The Intermediate and Long-Term Railway Network Plan (ILTRN) was first published in 2004 by the Ministry of Railways (MOR, abolished in 2013) and later revised with a grand investment plan in 2008 when the first HSR line of 120 km between Beijing and Tianjing arrived just prior to the Beijing Summer Olympic Games. The reaction to global financial crises was adopting a Keynesian economic approach by further infrastructure investment (including HSR and others) of 4 trillion yuan, which resulted in an even grander scale of HSR network expansion. In June 2016 the ILTRN plan was further revised and updated to reinforce the rail-led strategies of spatial development affirmed in the 13th National Plan (2016–20).

Improving accessibility for a size of country as large as China is critical. The aim is to make HSR connect all provincial capitals and cities of population over 500,000, which will allow the HSR network to serve 90% of the overall 1.2 billion population. The passenger-dedicated lines (PDLs) comprise two major HSR systems, i.e., crisscrossed PDLs across the country and inter-city PDLs around 10 city clusters that serve more economically advanced and densely populated areas (Chen, 2012; Yin, Bertolini, & Duan, 2015). The objectives manifested in the first HSR strategic plan of 2004 are far beyond accessibility to embrace rationales of modernization competitiveness through expanding network capacity for passengers and freight, rebalancing network inequality, extending international rail network, and fostering rail technological innovation and eventually exporting domestically developed technologies through international cooperation and competition. This last objective is akin to the way in which the French TGV has become one of the 10 favourite brands of France (Pepy & Leboeuf, 2005) and 'a symbol of modern society' (Arduin & Ni, 2005).

This paper chooses the Yangtze River Delta Area (YRDA)[1] as a suitable case for comparison with European situations because the YRDA, with merely 2% of Chinese territory that generates 20.23% of national GDP, is the most developed among three major mega-city-regions.[2] This sheer scale of territory and population makes YRDA larger than most European countries. Sixteen prefecture-level cities regarded as the core YRDA have more than 90 million registered residents and produced GDP per head more than double the national average (see Figure A4 in the supplemental data online). Most cities in the core YRDA have been served by new HSR lines in July 2010 (Figures 6 and 7). Prior to then, the major rail corridor in the YRDA was the conventional Beijing–Shanghai line that was upgraded to a maximum speed of 200 kph in 2004 and 250 kph in 2007. Current three of four non-HSR prefecture-level cities including Nantong, Taizhou and Yangzhou are located in 'Middle of Jiangsu' that are less developed than South of Jiangsu. The situation may change in the foreseeable future since these three cities are scheduled to be connected to Shanghai by improved rail services, while the fourth non-HSR city, Zhoushan, is an exception because of its offshore location.

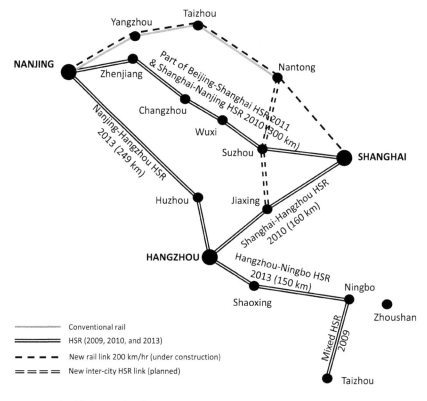

Figure 6 The high-speed rail (HSR) network in the core Yangtze River Delta Area (YRDA).

Source: Authors.

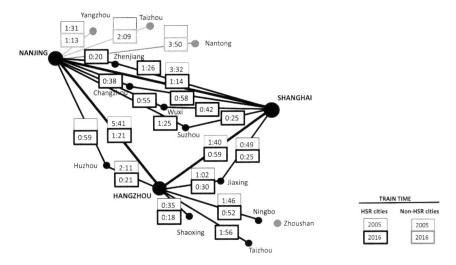

Figure 7 Changes in train time between the YRDA core cities (before and after HSR services).

Source: Authors.

IMPACTS OF HSR IN THE YANGTZE RIVER DELTA

Since a comprehensive dataset of rail passenger traffic is not publicly available, an alternative approach involves a combination of various sources to notice the popularity of new HSR services and how that might have impacts on existing rail services. Figure A5 in the supplemental data online shows a progressive rise from 2000 to 2008 and a dramatic drop of rail passengers from 2008 on the conventional Beijing–Shanghai line while there had been a general trend of an increase in rail passengers in these YRDA core cities over the years from 2000 to 2014. It can be argued that the popularity of new HSR services is reflected in the major shift from conventional rail to HSR services despite the early success of the upgraded HSR in attracting more rail passengers. The declining trend was reversed in 2012 when rail passenger volumes in many cities showed a steep rise, which can be regarded as the significant growth of rail passengers in general. By contrast, it is evident that non-HSR YRDA core cities presented in the bottom of the diagram show a stagnation in their rail passenger numbers over the years.

The arrival of upgraded HSR services in the core YRDA dated back to 2004 and the new HSR lines from 2010 onwards. In order to compare impacts among core YRDA cities, 2005 was selected as a time node because it was the earliest year when the statistical data were publicly available in different cities under study. Moreover, choosing three time-series (2005, 2009, 2014) allows a comparison of effects between upgraded HSR (2005–09) and new HSR (2009–14). Similar indicators to those adopted in the European case were drawn on to measure economic changes, including changes in economic output (GDP), population, employment and economic structure at both aggregate and disaggregate spatial levels. All the statistical data are sourced from statistical yearbooks with different levels of government in question.

Firstly, GDP is used as an indicator of economic performance because GVA figures are not available in China. In Figure A6 in the supplemental data online, two diagrams are juxtaposed to signify the varied impacts of HSR on economic performance on China, the YRDA and core YRDA. China, as a fast-growing emerging economy, demonstrated stronger economic growth than relatively developed regions (both YRDA and core YRDA). The difference between the two diagrams lies in the selection of the reference year. If GDP in 2005 is set as the index of 100, the arrival of HSR (either upgraded or newly built) did not seem to have transformative effects. Whereas a different picture is unveiled when 2010 (GDP = 100) is used as the reference year (see the bottom diagram). After the arrival of the Shanghai–Nanjing HSR line in 2010, the core YRDA had performed remarkably stronger than YRDA and national performance. The performance gap between core YRDA and YRDA as a whole appears to have widened. Such a finding critically highlights the importance of differentiating particular events in time in order to discern possible impacts. Moreover, the authors also take heed of a development pattern shown in fast-growing economies that the more developed an area is, the relatively lower economic growth rate it shows while being compared with other less developed areas. Therefore, when the core YRDA outperforms YRDA and China after the arrival of HSR, this could be regarded as a key structural force that overtakes the general trend.

A similar pattern that more developed places show a slower growth rate than less developed places is also found at the prefecture-city level. Figure A7 in the supplemental data online shows that all YRDA core cities had grown remarkably from 2005 to 2014 (GDP 2005 = 100) and that no apparent fluctuation of economic performance occurred as seen in Kent districts. The largest growth took place in three 'Middle of Jiangsu' cities (index 400 shown in Taizhou of Jiangsu) while Shanghai, the largest and most advanced city in the YRDA, had the relatively lowest growth (index 250). Likewise, the impacts of new HSR lines could be better identified when the economic base changes to 2010 (GDP = 100) (Figure 8). Again, all core cities in the YRDA showed considerable economic growth. The three non-HSR Middle of Jiangsu cities did not perform at the top of the league since 2010. Nanjing performed the most impressively (2014 GDP index nearly 170) better than the core YRDA average. Shanghai remained at the bottom of the league with nearly 140 (growth index) in 2014 against 100 in 2010.

Secondly, since China is undergoing rapid urbanization through rural–urban migration on the national scale, understanding population change is a useful indicator to perceive HSR impacts on job creation in places that can attract more residents whose registered residences are elsewhere. Two useful interrelated indicators are registered residence and permanent residence.[3] A place with more permanent residence than registered residence can be regarded as a more economically attractive place. Figure A8 in the supplemental data online clearly shows a

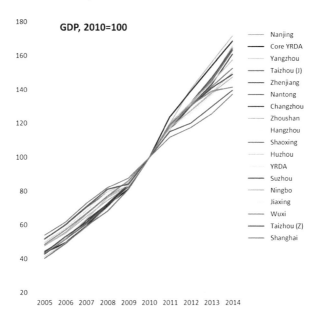

Figure 8 Growth in gross domestic product (GDP), YRDA core cities, 2005–14 (2010 = 100).

Source: Statistical yearbooks of various YRDA prefecture-level core cities, 2006–15.

generally higher permanent residence than registered residence in YRDA core cities except three non-HSR cities in Jiangsu province. Moreover, Figure 9 further displays that for all HSR cities, the growth in permanent residence was stronger after the HSR arrival than the earlier period of upgraded HSR service whereas three non-HSR cities appear to be more disadvantaged at losing permanent residence. However, employment change (Figure 10) presents a rather mixed picture. Although generally HSR cities show employment growth over time, the growth during 2005 and 2009 was stronger than during 2009 and 2014. Some HSR cities have shown decline in employment after 2010 such as Changzhou and Huzhou. Within three non-HSR cities, Yangzhou shows employment decline, whereas Nantong and Taizhou have very minor increase in jobs. More in-depth research is needed to explain what is the cause for employment changes in aforementioned HSR and non-HSR cities. Having said that, Suzhou and Shanghai have shown the largest growth in employment during 2009 and 2014. It implies that the arrival of HSR co-related with the enhancement of a few key cities in the core YRDA. It can be argued that the proximity of Suzhou to Shanghai by HSR is making Suzhou a much more attractive place for work and residence.

Thirdly, concerning changes in knowledge economies, similar approaches to the Kent case were adopted. Due to different contexts between post-industrial Europe and rapid industrialization in China, secondary industry is also analysed to perceive possible differentiations of HSR impacts between the two contexts. Figure 11 shows

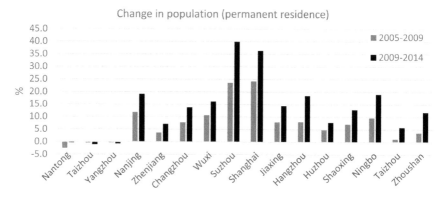

Figure 9 Change in permanent residence.
Source: Statistical yearbooks of various YRDA prefecture-level core cities, 2006–15.

the knowledge economy has higher presentations in Shanghai, Nanjing and Hangzhou in 2014. Except for these three cities as well as Zhoushan, which is an offshore prefecture-level city, all the rest of the core cities in YRDA had secondary industry accounting for more than 50% of employment structure. Examining the changes in the knowledge economy, Figure 12 shows that before the arrival of HSR (2005–09), the picture of economic structural change was rather mixed. Largest increases in the knowledge economy appeared in Changzhou and Shaoxing, two relatively small HSR cities in comparison with Shanghai and the provincial capitals Nanjing and Hangzhou. Even Shanghai had more growth in secondary industry than the knowledge economy. After the arrival of new HSR lines, growth in the knowledge economy appeared strongest in a few major cities such as Hangzhou, Shanghai, Nanjing, Suzhou and Ningbo, while Suzhou showed growth in secondary industry too. Two non-HSR cities, Nantong and Taizhou, in Jiangsu province had apparent growth in secondary industry in contrast to a decrease in the knowledge economy.

Suzhou has demonstrated its economic growth and strength in the rise of permanent residence and job creation after the arrival of HSR, meanwhile the growth is

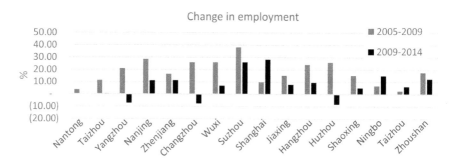

Figure 10 Change in employment.
Source: Statistical yearbooks of various YRDA prefecture-level core cities, 2006–15.

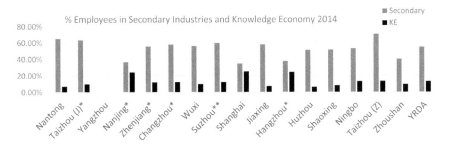

Figure 11 Secondary industry and knowledge economy, YRDA core cities, 2014.

Notes: The knowledge economy includes (1) information transmission, computer service and software industries, (2) finance, (3) real estate, (4) leasing and business service industries, (5) scientific research, technical service and geological prospecting, (6) education, (7) culture, sports and entertainment.

The secondary industry comprises mining, manufacturing, power, gas, water production and supply and construction.

In Taizhou (Z), the data collected are from urban units. In Taizhou (J), the latter two time-series are 2012 and 2014. Data in 2005 are not available.

*In Hangzhou, Nanjing, Taizhou (J), Zhenjiang, Changzhou and Nantong the employment data include individuals (whole municipality), private enterprises (whole municipality) and public enterprises (limited in units of township and town collectives and above).

**Data for Suzhou in 2014 are derived from *Suzhou Statistical Yearbook* (2015), tables 2–12 and 1–18/1–17.

Source: Statistical yearbooks of various YRDA prefecture-level core cities, 2015.

shown not only in the percentage of knowledge economy but also in secondary industry. The question then raised is whether benefits are spread into surrounding sub-regions or concentrated around the core sub-region. To answer this second question, Suzhou (city-region) is a good case for a more disaggregated analysis at the sub city-regional level – whether the benefits brought to Suzhou city-region could be redistributed and spread widely into a wider city-region.

Figure A9 in the supplemental data online shows the subdivision within Suzhou and the rail links within Suzhou city-region and Shanghai. Apart from Suzhou urban districts that are served by four HSR stations, Kunshan is the only county-level city with three stations served by HSR. Suzhou urban districts and Kunshan showed larger employment volumes and faster growth in both population and employment in contrast to an apparent fall in other non-HSR sub-regions (Table 1). Regarding economic restructuring, Figures 13 and 14 show varied impacts among sub-regions, which are indiscernible when Suzhou city-region as a whole is analysed. The most striking of all is Kunshan's strongest growth in secondary industry and least in the knowledge economy amidst the remarkable growth in population, GDP and employment. By comparison, non-HSR sub-region Taicang showed its growth in GDP and knowledge economy than the Suzhou city-regional average. Two points can be made here for preliminary explanations. First, Kunshan has been drawing on its locational proximity to Shanghai as a growth strategy in successfully attracting secondary industries

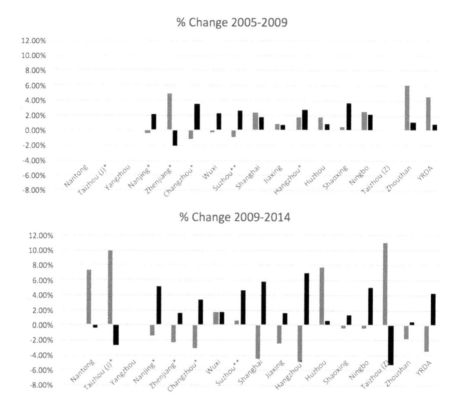

Figure 12 Changes in secondary industry and knowledge economy, YRDA core cities 2005–09 and 2009–14.

Source: Statistical yearbooks of various YRDA prefecture-level core cities, 2006–15.

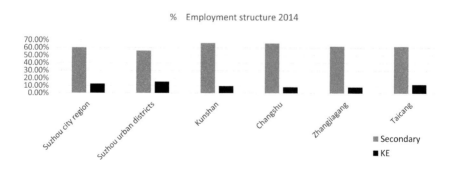

Figure 13 Secondary industry and knowledge economy, Suzhou sub-regions, 2014.

Source: *Suzhou Statistical Yearbook* (2015).

Table 1 Key socio-economic indicators within Suzhou (city-region).

	2014 Population (10,000 persons)	2014 Employment (10,000 persons)	Change in population (%)		Change in gross domestic product (GDP) (%)		Change in employment (%)	
			2005–09	2009–14	2005–09	2009–14	2005–09	2009–14
Suzhou (city-region)	661.08	693.4	4.28	4.39	5.59	8.59	38.13	26.07
Suzhou urban districts	337.51	348.29	5.62	5.71	3.25	7.71	49.20	26.71
Kunshan	76.97	116.34	6.06	9.96	13.93	13.99	35.65	54.65
Taicang	47.74	45.98	2.17	1.57	6.61	9.29	23.89	22.81
Changshu	106.88	105.1	1.90	−0.11	5.038	7.30	12.92	21.35
Zhangjiagang	91.98	77.69	2.29	2.19	7.56	8.13	47.06	2.44

Source: Suzhou Statistical Yearbook (2015).

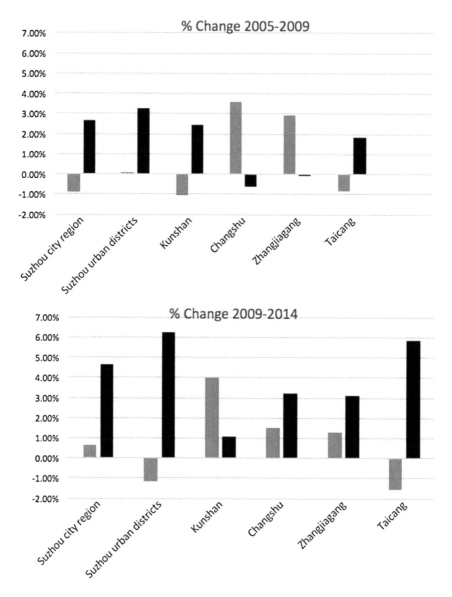

Figure 14 Changes in the secondary industry and knowledge economy, Suzhou sub-regions, 2005–09 and 2009–14.

Source: *Suzhou Statistical Yearbooks* (2006–15).

which could not be located in Shanghai (Chien, 2007). Secondly, both Kunshan and Taicang with their geographical advantages of being adjacent to Shanghai in recent years have further enhanced their transport connections with Shanghai (Wu, 2015). Active interventions in attracting industries and enhancing transport network seem to work well in generating spillover effects from Shanghai into neighbouring places. More research will be entailed for further in-depth analyses.

DISCUSSION

The main question posed at the outset was whether HSR, which dramatically enhances the accessibility between cities, will reduce or increase the economic disparities between them? Furthermore, can it effect a transformation in the economic structure of the regions connected or does it widen inequality? In both regions there is a mixed picture, but HSR appears to strengthen most HSR cities and not necessarily at the expense of non-HSR cities. This is seen most clearly in the growth in the knowledge economy.

However, the comparison of the two regions highlights that the role of HSR varies in different contexts. In particular there are distinctive economic trajectories e.g., YRDA, albeit the most advanced and quite diverse region in China, is still dominant in secondary industry in contrast to post-industrial Europe where secondary industry has largely moved out to industrializing countries. Since doubts have been cast on the mismatch between the strategic role of HSR in strengthening post-industrial Western Europe in its knowledge economies and the current economic trajectories in China (Chen, 2012), this new evidence is significant because it shows that in Europe, HSR mostly appears to assist the division of service labour between routine and knowledge-intensive activities whereas in China, in addition to this HSR potential for developing the knowledge economy, HSR has the potential to facilitate division of labour between manufacturing and the service sector. Most HSR cities are still dominant in secondary industry such as Suzhou (in particular its sub-region Kunshan) and Wuxi. With the arrival of HSR, manufacturing factories can be more easily decentralized for cheaper land and other costs whilst operations can be sustained by managers who take HSR for internal communication with parent companies and external activities among different firms. The high-frequency HSR services between various YRDA cities have begun to shape economic operations in this region and encourage more interaction between them. A HSR passenger survey (Wang, 2016) showed that about 61% of HSR trips were business-oriented, of which 34% were for internal communication within companies such as training and instruction activities and 66% for external contacts with other companies for deals, research and development, marketing and promotions. This difference echoes and illustrates further the argument of Cheng et al. (2015) on the convergence and divergence at different stages of economic development.

Non-HSR cities experienced much stronger economic growth in terms of overall GDP and a growth in secondary industry. This point is especially demonstrated by the lowest growth of GDP per head in Shanghai among all core YRDA cities. It is reasonable to argue that these places are still under rapid industrialization and many other investments contributed to the growth beyond HSR.

Moreover, with the disaggregated approach examining at the intra city-regional level, findings in Suzhou city-region present a more negative/unequal picture than districts in Kent County. Two factors can be involved for explaining this. Firstly, there is no administrative body and statutory planning power to consider the wider effects of HSR at the city-regional level. Rather, Suzhou city-region is vested with power to maximize fiscal extractions from surrounding sub-regions because Suzhou prefecture-level city that includes Suzhou urban districts and four sub-regions (county-level cities) reflects a 'city-leading-county' administrative system (Ma, 2005) through administrative restructuring and annexation that promotes 'inflated urbanisation' (Chung & Lam, 2004, p. 945). Likewise, there is an administrative fragmentation at the strategic level due to an overlap of regional development remits in YRDA designated to three central government departments (Wu, 2015). Although HSR is claimed to assist regional economic integration between cities, in reality, despite similar sounding strategies, many cities use it to promote competition more than collaboration. The Pearl River Delta Area has a similar situation. Xu (2008) argued that current practice can be understood as an important structural and strategic expression of locally and regionally articulated processes, which might be 'little more than a cosmetic makeover that hides the intensifying competition within major city-regions in China' (p. 157). Hence, it is difficult to address the inequality without a proper governance structure, an issue that is commonly shared by many other cities and regions in China. A similar lack of cooperation between the districts within Kent could also be argued to have had the effect of preventing full exploitation of the greater connectivity provided by HS1.

Secondly, apart from the lack of an administrative structure at more strategic levels that could somehow address intra-regional polarization, the distinct characters of the rail networks between the two regions also contribute to the widened intra-regional inequality in the Chinese example. In Kent and some other European regions, rail stations are mostly built with a reasonable size, located in the city centre with easy access from elsewhere. HSR and extensive conventional rail networks interoperate to serve the wider territory, which means that hinterlands can also benefit from HSR services in general although they might not have HSR stations. The arrival of HS1 in Kent in 2007 was followed by the introduction of domestic HS1 services in 2009 that are aimed to benefit Kent County more widely after the arrival of HS1. Whereas in YRDA and China in general, the territory is vast while the density of rail network is very thin in comparison with Europe. In addition, many HSR stations are generally large-scaled, located in the outskirts of cities, serving limited dimensions of rail flow despite vast volume, and lack sufficient connectivity with other levels of public transport systems (Chen, Hickman, & Saxena, 2014).

The distinct nature of rail network aforementioned further explains how differently HSR changes people's life in China and Europe. Over past 30 years, HSR services in Europe, in particular for a one-hour train time between two cities, tend to encourage daily commuting and economic development such as French TGV experiences (SNCF, 2011) and InterCity 125/225 in the UK (Chen & Hall, 2011). In this circumstance, the socio-economic geography as to where people live and where people work is more flexible and complex. In the case of Chinese HSR services, daily commuting is still unlikely to be a normal practice. As Wang (2016) shows in the HSR passenger survey in YRDA that the frequencies are mostly once a week or twice a week due to the large scale of cities and considerable amount of travel time spent on accessing and egressing enlarging urban transport systems due to urban expansion. For instance, the train time between Suzhou and Shanghai HSR stations is about 30 minutes. However, the travel time from an origin home in Suzhou to one of Suzhou HSR stations takes normally one hour by public transport and another one hour from Shanghai station to a destination in Shanghai. Altogether the train time is just one fifth of the overall journey unless the destination and origin are just next to the rail stations, which is rare. As a result, although there is the dramatic change in inter-city accessibility between HSR stations, there is a huge gap between HSR train time and the door-to-door journey time, which causes lots of serious issues in integration, interchanges and urban accessibility to and from the stations (Chen & Wei, 2013; Hickman, Chen, Chow, & Saxena, 2015).

Lastly, the authors also come to realize that researching differences in models of development following HSR arrival between Europe and China could allow one to explore more widely what kinds of transformational effects are most welcome, achievable and desirable, given the fact that in different regimes developmental imagination led to completely different outcomes so it is difficult to judge them comparatively. On the one hand, in Europe, at the appraisal stage, an investment as large as HSR will be debated and scrutinized by a series of feasibility and justification appraisals. For instance, the wider effects of HS2 in addressing north–south divide in the UK have triggered the great divide is the latest example of this situation (Hall, 2013). In the developmental process, in Kent, for many years no obvious development projects are taking place around the Ebbsfleet HSR station until more recently. On the other hand, in China, the development of HSR network is a key national transport policy and spatial strategy which also fits well with local urbanization and development strategy. Although current HSR stations in China tend to be located outside city centre, HSR is envisaged with a new modern central business district with high-rise office blocks. A new town concept is established optimistically with the HSR arrival, just in a couple of years, new buildings are built in the belief that once they are built, development will come (for more about the Chinese style of creating new cities, see Shepard, 2015). Suzhou North Station in the Xiangcheng district is a typical example. This development model is characterized and supported by government-led financing and land selling systems. Consequently, new physical transformation around the station seems to be achieved quickly but in reality, in most cases, tenants of these buildings still do not exist until later stages while incentives kick off to attract them. Many of these scenes are called 'ghost towns' since there are no other activities taking place except the stations' transport function. Once the boundary of a newly planned town is announced publicly, the landscape begins to enter a transitional stage because of uncertainty and speculation. Many traditional rural settlements are demolished for land sales and villagers are asked to move without the right to move back. A plethora of buildings are torn down and some still remain in pieces. As a result many social problems are derived from this development phenomenon (Wu, 2015). All these rapid practices in China actually create more questions than answers, namely how much time will be needed to allow transformational effects? Does it make sense to pursue physical or economic transformation while ignoring social justice and environmental issues? Through this comparative study of the two cases, there is a real danger to either underestimate or overestimate wider HSR impacts.

CONCLUSIONS AND IMPLICATIONS FOR THE FUTURE

This paper has attempted to go beyond the usual measurement of economic impact as GDP/GVA change and growth to consider how the transformational impact of new transport infrastructure, especially HSR, impacts on economic structure. This is also consistent with how the aggregate analysis has moved from simple definitions to more complex definitions of accessibility to a greater concern with connectivity. How businesses connect with each other, how businesses connect with labour and how individuals and families connect with each other are critical to the understanding of how HSR impacts on cities and regions. In this the authors have not only taken the understanding of the issue identified a step further, but also identified a number of challenges for future research.

By comparing two regions, some further light has been shed at the more localized level on the trends noted in Cheng et al. (2015). Regions at different stages of development respond to the introduction of HSR in different ways. The more advanced the regional economy the more HSR seems to promote convergence both between cities on the HSR network and between those on it and those off the network but dependent on those on it. In a less economically advanced region, the introduction of HSR may lead to greater sectoral specialization that may lead to convergence in aggregate performance but less convergence in economic structure. The authors have explored this in terms of employment in the knowledge economy, but further research into skill and occupational structure changes is needed, since it is at this level that connectivity is most significant.

In both cases there is evidence that regions and individual cities within them may not have gained the full advantage that a place on the network could have generated. Failure to understand the importance of connectivity between the HSR network and more local networks, failure to develop HSR stations fully within the urban infrastructure and failure to put in place complementary urban land use planning all diminish the potential impact of HSR. Moreover, this comparative study clearly indicates different local conditions, economic trajectories, and different national approaches play key roles in explaining transformational effects. A better understanding of how HSR will relate to the local economy and how it could help to transform it is key to whether HSR can in any sense be transformational.

This leaves the question of whether and how such potential effects can be included in any investment appraisal of new HSR lines. The analysis above suggests that there is no simple measure of wider economic impacts that is appropriate to interurban HSR projects of the type used in urban projects based on effective density or economic mass. A much more nuanced analysis looking in detail at economic structure and the effect on this of changes in connectivity is needed. The primary conclusion is that HSR can transform regional economies, but this transformation is not automatic or guaranteed and can take different forms in different circumstances.

ACKNOWLEDGEMENTS

The authors would like to express gratitude for valuable comments and suggestions given by two anonymous referees, Ivan Turok, Editor-in-Chief, and the editorial office on the revision.

DISCLOSURE STATEMENT

No potential conflict of interest was reported by the authors.

FUNDING

Chia-Lin Chen gratefully acknowledges financial support from the Research Development Fund of Xi'an Jiaotong-Liverpool University [grant number RDF 15-01-51].

SUPPLEMENTAL DATA

Supplemental data for this article can be accessed at http://dx.doi.org/10.1080/00 343404.2016.1262017.

NOTES

1. The boundary of the YRDA has been defined in different ways. The most widely accepted definition is to include Shanghai and two provinces, Jiangsu and Zhejiang. A wider YRDA tends to include Anhui province. If Anhui is further counted in, a wider YRD covers an overall area of 350,000 km^2.
2. Figures are sourced from China *Statistical Yearbooks*.
3. In China *Statistical Yearbooks*, a figure of 'permanent residence' in a place refers to the number of residents living in a place for more than six months and excluding residents who have not lived in a place for the most recent six months. Thus, permanent residence actually reflects a more updated pattern of development than registered residence. However, it is also true that the term 'permanent residence' given as an official English term by default in Chinese statistical datasets appears confusing.

REFERENCES

Amano, K., & Nakagawa, D. (1990). *Study on urbanization impacts by new stations of high-speed railway*. Paper presented at the conference of the Korean Transportation Association, Dejeon City, Korea.

Ansar, A., Flyvbjerg, B., Budzier, A., & Lunn, D. (2016). Does infrastructure investment lead to economic growth or economic fragility? Evidence from China. *Oxford Review of Economic Policy, 32*, 360–90.

Arduin, J.-P., & Ni, J. (2005). French TGV network development. *Japan Railway and Transport Review, 40*, 22–28.

Aschauer, D. (1989). Is public expenditure productive? *Journal of Monetary Economics, 23*, 177–200.

Bonnafous, A. (1987). The regional impact of the TGV. *Transportation, 14*, 127–137.

Bröcker, J., & Mercenier, J. (2011). General equilibrium models for transportation economics. In A. de Palma, R. Lindsey, E. Quinet, & R. Vickerman (Eds.), *A handbook of transport economics* (pp. 21–45). Cheltenham: Edward Elgar.

Chen, C.-L. (2012). Reshaping Chinese space–economy through high-speed trains: Opportunities and challenges. *Journal of Transport Geography, 22*, 312–316.

Chen, C.-L., & Hall, P. (2011). The impacts of high-speed trains on British economic geography: A study of the UK's InterCity 125/225 and its effects. *Journal of Transport Geography, 19*, 689–704.

Chen, C.-L., & Hall, P. (2012). The wider spatial–economic impacts of high-speed trains: A comparative case study of Manchester and Lille sub-regions. *Journal of Transport Geography, 24*, 89–110.

Chen, C.-L., Hickman, R., & Saxena, S. (2014). *Improving interchanges – Toward better multimodal railway hubs in the People Republic of China*. Manila: Asian Development Bank.

Chen, C.-L., & Wei, B. (2013). High-speed rail and urban transformation in China: The case of Hangzhou East rail station. *Built Environment, 39*(3), 385–398.

Cheng, Y.-S., Loo, B. P. Y., & Vickerman, R. W. (2015). Highspeed rail networks, economic integration and regional specialisation in China and Europe. *Travel Behaviour and Society, 2*, 1–14.

Chien, S.-S. (2007). Institutional innovations, asymmetric decentralization, and local economic development: A case study of Kunshan, in post-Mao China. *Environment and Planning C: Government and Policy, 25*, 269–290.

Christaller, W. (1933). *Die zentralen Orte in Süddeutschland*. Jena: Gustav Fischer.

Chung, J. H., & Lam, T.-C. (2004). China's 'city system=' in flux: Explaining post-Mao administrative changes. *China Quarterly, 180*, 945–964.

Clark, C., Wilson, F., & Bradley, J. (1969). Industrial location and economic potential in Western Europe. *Regional Studies, 3*, 197–212.

Department for Transport. (2005). *Transport, wider economic benefits, and impacts on GDP* (Technical Paper). London: Department for Transport.

Department for Transport. (2014). *Webtag: TAG unit A2-1 wider impacts*. London: Department for Transport. Retrieved from https://www.gov.uk/government/publications/webtag-tag-unita2-1-wider-impacts

Dodgson, J. S. (1973). External effects and secondary benefits in road investment appraisal. *Journal of Transport Economics and Policy, 7*, 169–185.

Dodgson, J. S. (1974). Motorway investment, industrial transport costs, and sub-regional growth: A case study of the M62. *Regional Studies, 8*, 75–91.

Fogel, R. M. (1964). *Railroads and American economic growth: Essays in economic history*. Baltimore: Johns Hopkins University Press.

Fujita, M., Krugman, P. R., & Venables, A. J. (1999). *The spatial economy: Cities, regions and international trade*. Cambridge, MA: MIT Press.

Garmendia, M., Ureña, J. M., Ribalaygua, C., Leal, J., & Coronado, J. M. (2008). Urban residential development in isolated small cities that are partially integrated in metropolitan areas by high speed train. *European Urban and Regional Studies, 15*(3), 249–264.

Givoni, M. (2006). Development and impact of the modern highspeed train: A review. *Transport Reviews, 26*(5), 593–611.

Glaeser, E. L., & Gottlieb, J. D. (2009). The wealth of cities: Agglomeration economies and spatial equilibrium in the United States. *Journal of Economic Literature, 47,* 983–1028.

Graham, D. J. (2007). Agglomeration, productivity and transport investment. *Journal of Transport Economics and Policy, 41,* 317–343.

Graham, D. J., Gibbons, S., & Martin, R. (2010). *The spatial decay of agglomeration economies: estimates for use in transport appraisal* (Report for the Department of Transport).

Graham, D. J., & Melo, P. C. (2011). Assessment of wider economic impacts of high-speed rail for Great Britain. *Transportation Research Record: Journal of the Transportation Research Board, 2261,* 15–24.

Hall, P. (2013). High Speed Two: The great divide. *Built Environment, 39*(3), 339–354.

Hay, A., Meredith, K., & Vickerman, R. W. (2004). *The impact of the Channel Tunnel on Kent and relationships with Nord-Pas de Calais* (Final Report to Eurotunnel and Kent County Council). Canterbury: University of Kent.

Hickman, R., Chen, C.-L., Chow, A., & Saxena, S. (2015). Improving interchanges in China: The experiential phenomenon. *Journal of Transport Geography, 42,* 175–186.

Hirota, R. (1984). *Present situation and effects of the Shinkansen.* Paris: International Seminar on High-Speed Trains.

Hotelling, H. (1929). Stability in competition. *Economic Journal, 39,* 41–57.

House of Commons Treasury Committee. (2013). *The economics of HS2, oral evidence* (November 5). Retrieved from http://data.parliament.uk/writtenevidence/committeeevidence.svc/evidencedocument/treasury-committee/the-economics-of-hs2/oral/3472.html

Jara-Diaz, S. R. (1986). On the relation between users' benefits and the economic effects of transportation activities. *Journal of Regional Science, 26,* 379–391.

Keeble, D., Owens, P. L., & Thompson, C. (1982a). Regional accessibility and economic potential in the European Community. *Regional Studies, 16,* 419–432.

Keeble, D., Owens, P. L., & Thompson, C. (1982b). Economic potential and the Channel Tunnel. *Area, 14,* 97–103.

KPMG. (2013). *HS2 regional economic impacts* (Ref. No. HS2/074). London: High Speed Two (HS2).

Krugman, P. (1991). Increasing returns and economic geography. *Journal of Political Economy, 99,* 483–499.

Laird, J., Nash, C., & Mackie, P. (2014). Transformational transport infrastructure: Cost–benefit analysis challenges. *Town Planning Review, 85,* 709–30.

Leunig, T. (2010). Social savings. *Journal of Economic Surveys, 24,* 775–800.

Lösch, A. (1940). *Die räumliche Ordnung der Wirtschaft.* Jena: Gustav Fischer.

Ma, L. J. C. (2005). Urban administrative restructuring, changing scale relations and local economic development in China. *Political Geography, 24*(4), 477–497.

Murakami, J., & Cervero, R. (2010). *California high-speed rail and economic development* (Station-Area Market Profiles and Public Policy Responses Symposium, December 2–3, 2010). Berkeley: University of California – Berkeley, The Centre for Environmental Public Policy.

Nakamura, H., & Ueda, T. (1989). *The impacts of the Shinkansen on regional development.* Paper presented at the 5thWorld Conference on Transport Research. Yokohama, Western Periodicals. III.

Overman, H. (2013). Oral evidence in House of Commons Treasury Committee. *The Economics of HS2,* November 5.

Pepy, G., & Leboeuf, M. (2005). Le TGV au XXIème siècle: Rompre sans dénaturer. *Revue Générale des Chemins de Fer,* May, 7–27.

Preston, J., & Wall, G. (2008). The *ex-ante* and *ex-post* economic and social impacts of the introduction of high-speed trains in South East England. *Planning Practice and Research, 23*(3), 403–422.

Pugh, G., & Fairburn, J. (2008). Evaluating the effects of the M6 Toll Road on industrial land development and employment. *Regional Studies, 42*, 977–990.

PwC. (2013a). *Econometric analysis to develop evidence on the links between aviation and the economy* (Final Report to the Airports Commission). Retrieved from https://www.gov.uk/government/publications/airports-commission-interim-report

PwC. (2013b). *Modelling airline sector linkages: A computable general equilibrium analysis* (Report to the Airports Commission). Retrieved from https://www.gov.uk/government/publications/airports-commission-interim-report

Sands, B. (1993).The development effects of high-speed rail stations and implications for California. *Built Environment, 19*(3/4), 257–284.

Shepard, W. (2015). *Ghost cities of China*. London: Zed.

SNCF. (2011). *Les infos hors-série, 30 ans de TGV 1981–2011. Trois décennies d'expériences à grande vitesse*. Paris: SNCF.

Ureña, J. M., Menerault, P., & Garmendia, M. (2009). The highspeed rail challenge for big intermediate cities: A national, regional and local perspective. *Cities, 26*(5), 266–279.

Venables, A. J. (2007). Evaluating urban transport improvement: Cost–benefit analysis in the presence of agglomeration and income taxation. *Journal of Transport Economics and Policy, 41*, 173–188.

Venables, A. J. (2013). Expanding cities and connecting cities: the wider benefits of better communications. Unpublished manuscript, Oxford.

Venables, A. J., Laird, J., & Overman, H. (2014). *Transport investment and economic performance: Implications for project appraisal* (Paper commissioned by UK Department for Transport).

Vickerman, R. W. (1987). The Channel Tunnel: Consequences for regional growth and development. *Regional Studies, 21*, 187–197.

Vickerman, R. W. (2015). High-speed rail and regional development: The case of intermediate stations. *Journal of Transport Geography, 42*, 157–65.

Vickerman, R. W., Spiekermann, K., & Wegener, M. (1999). Accessibility and economic development in Europe. *Regional Studies, 33*, 1–15.

Von Thünen, J. H. (1826). *Der Isolierte Staat in Beziehungauf Landwirtschaft und Nationalökonomie*. Hamburg: Perthes.

Wang, X. (2016). *High-speed rail new town planning and implementation in China – Experience from Beijing–Shanghai HSR line*. Guest lecture given on April 21, 2016. Suzhou: Department of Urban Planning and Design Xi'an Jiaotong Liverpool University.

Wegener, M. (2011). Transport in spatial models of economic development. In A. de Palma, R. Lindsey, E. Quinet, & R. Vickerman (Eds.), *A handbook of transport economics* (pp. 46–66). Cheltenham: Edward Elgar.

Wu, F. (2015). *Planning for growth: Urban and regional planning in China*. London: Routledge.

Xu, J. (2008). Governing city-regions in China: Theoretical issues and perspectives for regional strategic planning. *Town Planning Review, 79*(2–3), 157–186.

Yin, M., Bertolini, L., & Duan, J. (2015). The effects of the high-speed railway on urban development: International experience and potential implications for China. *Progress in Planning, 98*, 1–52.

Future green economies and regional development: a research agenda

David Gibbs and Kirstie O'Neill

ABSTRACT

Future green economies and regional development: a research agenda. *Regional Studies*. The past 30 years have seen an explosion of interest and concern over the detrimental impacts of economic and industrial development. Despite this, the environmental agenda has not featured substantially in the regional studies literature. This paper explores a range of options for regional futures from a 'clean-tech' economy and the promise of renewed accumulation through to more radical degrowth concepts focused on altering existing modes of production and consumption, ecological sustainability and social justice. In so doing, it investigates the potential role of regions as drivers of the new green economy, drawing on research into sustainability transitions.

摘要

未来的绿色经济和区域发展：一个研究议程。 *Regional Studies* 。对经济及产业发展的致命影响的兴趣与担忧，在过去三十年来有所激增。尽管如此，环境议程仍非区域研究文献中的重要特色。本文探讨区域未来的选项范围，从"乾淨科技" 经济以及恢復积累的承诺，到聚焦改变现有生产及消费模式、生态可持续性和社会正义这些更为激进的去成长之概念。以此，本文运用可持续性变迁的研究，探讨区域作为新兴绿色经济驱力的潜在角色。

RÉSUMÉ

Les économies vertes d'avenir et l'aménagement du territoire: un calendrier des recherches. *Regional Studies*. Les dernières 30 années ont vu se déclencher une explosion d'intérêt à l'égard des effets nuisibles du développement économique et industriel. Malgré cela, le calendrier environnemental n'a pas beaucoup figuré dans les études régionales. Ce présent article examine un éventail de possibilités pour ce qui est de l'avenir des régions, à partir d'une économie fondée sur des 'technologies propres' et la promesse de l'accumulation renouvelée jusqu'à des notions plus radicales de décroissance qui portent sur la transformation des modes de production et de consommation actuels, une écologie durable et la justice sociale. Ce faisant, on examine le rôle éventuel des régions comme forces motrices de la nouvelle économie verte, puisant dans des recherches sur le passage à la durabilité.

ZUSAMMENFASSUNG

Grüne Ökonomien und Regionalentwicklung der Zukunft: ein Forschungsprogramm. *Regional Studies*. In den letzten 30 Jahren hat das Interesse an den und die Besorgnis über die schädlichen Auswirkungen der Wirtschafts- und Industrieentwicklung rapide zugenommen. Dennoch spielen Umweltthemen in der Literatur der Regionalwissenschaften keine wesentliche Rolle. In diesem Beitrag untersuchen wir verschiedene Optionen der regionalen Zukunft: von einer Wirtschaft der 'sauberen Technik' und dem Versprechen erneuter Akkumulation bis hin zu radikaleren Konzepten der Wachstumsrücknahme, die sich auf eine Veränderung der vorhandenen Produktions- und Konsummethoden, ökologische Nachhaltigkeit und soziale Gerechtigkeit konzentrieren. Hierbei erforschen wir die potenzielle Rolle der Regionen als Motoren der neuen grünen Ökonomie, wofür wir uns auf die Forschung über Übergänge in die Nachhaltigkeit stützen.

RESUMEN

Economías verdes y desarrollo regional del futuro: un programa de investigación. *Regional Studies*. En los últimos 30 años se ha visto un crecimiento acelerado del interés y la preocupación por los impactos negativos del desarrollo económico e industrial. Pese a ello, el programa del medio ambiente ha sido ignorado en gran medida en la bibliografía de estudios regionales. En este artículo analizamos diferentes opciones del futuro regional, desde una economía de la 'tecnología limpia' y la promesa de una acumulación renovada hasta conceptos de decrecimiento más radicales que se centran en alterar los modos existentes de producción y consumo, sostenibilidad ecológica y justicia social. De este modo, investigamos el posible papel de las regiones como motores de la nueva economía ecológica, basándonos en el estudio de las transiciones hacia la sostenibilidad.

INTRODUCTION

A concern with the adverse environmental impacts of economic development has increasingly entered into the mainstream of economic policy-making and represents a key challenge for national, regional and local policy-makers in the 21st century (Piketty, 2014; Rockström et al., 2009). At one level it could be argued that there is nothing new about policy-makers' concerns over the environmental consequences of economic development – these date back (at least) to the Rio de Janeiro Earth Summit in 1992. However, despite the widespread adoption of the concept of sustainable development following Rio and some progress in combining economic, environmental and social aims, economic development strategies and policies have largely remained wedded to a high growth, carbon-based, consumer-led economy where success is measured by increasing gross value added (GVA) and higher levels of personal consumption (Jackson, 2009). More recently the emerging concept of a green economy has led to a policy focus upon the potential for change to existing socio-economic development pathways. A major component of this has involved low-carbon initiatives – attempts to reduce greenhouse gas emissions and so mitigate climate change – and the development of a low-carbon economy (e.g., Davies & Mullin, 2011; Smith, Voß, & Grin, 2010). This perspective is essentially one of ecological modernization, at the heart of which is a belief in technology, innovation and progress to solve environmental problems (Mol, 2002; Roberts & Colwell, 2001). While climate change may have been the initial driver behind low carbon policies and targets, policy-makers have increasingly come to recognize that the resultant shift to a greener future also offers the prospect of a more resilient and sustainable economy in future and/or alternative modes of economic development.

Much activity has been geared towards creating the basis for future growth and consumption, albeit that what is being consumed may be less environmentally damaging than before. However, as Jackson (2009, p. 8) comments:

> [while] most analyses assume that the ultimate aim is to re-stimulate the kind of consumption-driven growth that has dominated the last few decades ... this goal is in the long-term entirely unsustainable without significant changes in both macro-economic structure and the social dynamics of consumerism.

Indeed, Pàdranos (2013, p. 30) suggests that this form of a green economy amounts to 'trying to solve ecological problems with the same logic that causes and perpetuates them'. Thus, while the green economy is seen by some as a new source of capital accumulation and job creation, the associated policy measures have been criticized for failing to address the root cause of environmental crises and neglecting issues of social justice and equity (Kenis & Lievens, 2015). Critiques of this approach to the green economy offer alternative pathways for economic development based around ideas of degrowth and post-growth (e.g., Kallis, 2011; Latouche, 2006, 2010). According to the Research and Degrowth Association (2012), 'sustainable degrowth is a downscaling of production and consumption that increases human well-being and enhances ecological conditions and equity on the planet'. Degrowth proponents question the assumption that increased material prosperity leads to increased satisfaction. On the contrary, continuous growth does not lead to greater prosperity for all people, but rather to greater social injustice and an increase in individual dissatisfaction, health problems, social tensions and ecological crises (Bauhardt, 2014). Critically, degrowth advocates have a 'different vision of prosperity, one based on dramatically less material abundance and consumption' (Kallis, Kerschner, & Martinez-Alier, 2012, p. 174). In between the policy approaches which encompass low-carbon green economies and those who advocate degrowth are a range of other approaches which attempt to challenge Westernized high levels of consumption and environmental apathy, many more than can be explored in detail in this paper. However, the authors recognize the potential in approaches such as voluntary simplicity (Alexander, 2013), makerspaces (e.g., HackerLabs, FabLabs etc.), which experiment with new ways of producing and consuming at a more local level (Smith, Hielscher, Dickel, Söderberg, & van Oost, 2013), sharing economies (Grinevich, Huber, Baines, & Eder, 2015), social enterprises and grassroots sustainability innovations (Seyfang & Smith, 2007). These all represent interesting and challenging examples of alternatives to the neoliberal agenda of continued economic growth.

This paper examines visions for different futures and their implications for regional development research. In investigating these issues, it draws upon the theoretical perspective of socio-technical transitions research to provide a framework to conceptualize these shifts in performing economies. In doing so, it also identifies two shortcomings in transitions research that merit further attention. First, initial conceptualizations within transitions research neglected space, albeit this shortcoming has begun to be addressed (e.g., Murphy, 2015; Truffer, Murphy, & Raven, 2015). Second, while transitions research, by definition, envisages a transition towards sustainability, it is largely silent on the forms that sustainability and the green economy should take. Both these issues – the role of space and the form of future economies – are also key questions for regional development research in future.

The paper is structured as follows. The next section outlines the rise of interest in the range of approaches to green economies and indicates that it is comprised of multiple discourses. It then outlines the main tenets of sustainability transitions research. The following sections draw upon secondary research to explore contrasting examples of green economy strategies. The first of these is based around a technology-led, ecological modernization approach using the example of Styria in Austria as an illustration. Second, it explores a range of local and regional examples based around a degrowth approach. These two examples are not intended to be comparisons or indicative of the only responses to environmental and economic crises. The argument here is that these 'niche' experiments and philosophies are presenting examples that show how alternative futures may be possible. Following a discussion of the results from the case studies, the paper concludes by suggesting a research agenda for regional studies research around the green economy.

THE GREEN ECONOMY

Although the green economy has a legacy from Limits to Growth arguments and the Blueprint for a Green Economy (Pearce, Markandya, & Barbier, 1989), current mainstream iterations of the green economy entered policy discourse towards the end of the 2000s, notably at the Rio+20 conference (Bina, 2013; Borel-Saladin & Turok, 2013). For example, the United Nations Environment Programme (UNEP) (2011, p. 16) defined the green economy as

low carbon, resource efficient, and socially inclusive [where] growth in income and employment should be driven by public and private investments that reduce carbon emissions and pollution, enhance energy and resource efficiency, and prevent the loss of biodiversity and ecosystem services.

Such approaches combine environmental discourses with industrial and economic policy objectives 'in search of "win–win" solutions and virtuous cycles of progress and prosperity' (Bina, 2013, p. 1024). From a policy-maker's perspective, the green economy is increasingly seen as a source of new growth and jobs and the basis of a new round of capital accumulation. At the local scale, 'regions and cities see the challenge as an opportunity to take our societies out of the global economic crisis transformed into more sustainable, low carbon, less resource intensive and inclusive communities' (Bonsinetto & Falco, 2013, p. 126). Notwithstanding the use of a new discourse of green growth, few fundamental changes have been made to macroeconomic structures and policies after Rio+20 (Bulkeley, Jordan, Perkins, & Selin, 2013). As a result, the potential of developing green economies often emerges as a thinly veiled version of business as usual, rather than a radical shift to a more sustainable economy where social and environmental aspects have parity with economic aspects, epitomizing a process of paradigm *fixing* rather than paradigm *shifting* (Bina, 2013). Moreover, many of these debates and associated policy statements offer little for countries in the Global South and this has led to conflict at negotiations such as Rio+20 in 2012. Indeed, initiatives such as that of UNEP's green economy have been seen as promoting the continued expansion of extractivist economies to the detriment of Global Southern economies (Hollender, 2015). It is important that discussions on green economies do not elide the fundamental need for 'development' (whilst acknowledging the tensions within this term) in many countries, albeit not reproducing the problematic forms of economic development, which have contributed to significant environmental and social problems in many countries (Bell, 2016; Escobar, 2015).

Thus, while the green economy has rapidly become a focus for international and national policy documents (Bailey & Caprotti, 2014), the hegemonic discourse envisages incremental and reformist changes which do not challenge or undermine the dominance of neoliberal economic growth or consumption economies (Bina, 2013; Philips, 2013). Although there is recognition that the very premise of the green economy concedes that 'business as usual' has resulted in economic and ecological crises (Shear, 2014), the green economy frequently appears to be co-opted as a neoliberal project, proposing that it is the role of government to create new markets for capital investment, and to use markets to manage nature and climate change (Tienhaara, 2014). Such approaches have their roots in weak interpretations of sustainable development, the consequence of longstanding nature–society dualisms (Moore, 2015). Here, neoliberalism offers 'a range of "environmental fixes" to the endemic problem of sustained economic growth' (Castree, 2008, p. 146). This means 'environmental problems come to be framed as issues that are politically, economically and technologically solvable within the context of existing institutions and power structures and continued economic growth' (Bailey, Gouldson, & Newell, 2011, p. 683).

However, although these approaches predominate, they have been criticized about the extent to which current green economy policy measures will substantially address global environmental problems, such as global warming and rising greenhouse gas emissions (Borel-Saladin & Turok, 2013). Some authors, such as Caprotti (2012) and Gendron (2014), believe that the most likely scenarios involve mild reform along the lines of ecological modernization with limited environmental benefits. However, others, such as Davies (2013) and Shear (2014), suggest that such green economy developments can subsequently engender more substantive and radical change. Thus, while 'arguments about green jobs and growth through ecological modernisation are increasingly harnessed to elaborate positive expectations for many sustainability niches . . . alternative discourses concerning new sustainability politics and economics are also available and used' (Smith & Raven, 2012, p. 1033). Indeed, despite the hegemonic dominance of this particular discourse, one can identify a range of discursive approaches to the green economy. For example, Bina (2013) divides these into three categories: 'business-as-usual', 'greening' and 'all change', while Ferguson (2015) similarly has 'conventional pro-growth', 'selective growth' and 'limits to growth' (Table 1).

Different approaches to the green economy around

> post-growth, degrowth and décroissance all raise more fundamental questions concerning the relationship between material prosperity and individual and social well-being. This concept aims at developing forms of social and economic organization that reinterpret prosperity and quality of life, freeing these aspects from the dictate of economic growth
>
> (Bauhardt, 2014, p. 64)

Table 1 Discourses of the green economy

Frequently articulated in policy ↔ Rarely articulated in policy *Incremental change ↔ Transformative change* *Fit and conform ↔ Stretch and transform*		
Conventional pro-growth/almost business as usual	*Selective growth/greening the economy*	*Limits to growth/ socioeconomic transformation*
Greening as an investment opportunity	Resource efficiency	Steady-state economy
Restarting market economies	Low-carbon growth	Prosperity without growth
Green Keynesianism	Decoupling	Degrowth
Green job creation	Clean-technologies	Social well-being
Green New Deal policies	Ecological modernization Cleantech clusters Makerspaces	Alternative food networks Eco-housing developments

Sources: Adapted from Bina (2013) and Ferguson (2015).

whilst also lessening the environmental impacts of such organization. One criticism has been that these approaches also have little to offer the Global South as a result of fewer opportunities for commodity and manufactured exports and less availability of credits and donations (Kallis, Demaria, & D'Alisa, 2015). Conversely, there is an argument that degrowth strategies are closely related to, and overlap with, existing movements, especially in Latin America, such as post-extractivism, alternatives to development (A2D), solidarity economies and Living Well/Buen Vivir, all of which focus on issues such as livelihoods, environmental justice and land annexation (Hollender, 2015; Martínez-Alier, 2009). In this case, there may be common cause between the promoters of degrowth and such movements in the Global South. In total, as Table 1 indicates, there is a spectrum of interpretations of the green economy, from market-led, business-as-usual to proposals for more radical changes such as a steady-state economy and degrowth (Kenis & Lievens, 2015). Thus, rather than a clear or stable end point, the 'green economy remains a disaggregated and contested discourse' (Ferguson, 2015, p. 26) and an ongoing contest between different economic visions of the future (Bailey & Caprotti, 2014; Bailey & Wilson, 2009).

SUSTAINABILITY TRANSITIONS AND SPACE

A useful perspective from which to explore these issues is provided by research into sustainability transitions and, in particular, the multilevel perspective (MLP) of innovation (Geels, 2005; Smith, 2003). This approach has proved helpful in understanding the opportunities and constraints that a shift to a green economy may encounter. The MLP identifies three synergistic levels: (1) the socio-technical *landscape*, which encompasses the wider context, and that influences niche and regime dynamics, and includes spatial structures (e.g., urban infrastructures), political ideologies, societal values, beliefs, concerns, the media landscape and macro-economic trends (Geels, 2011); (2) a meso-level of socio-technical *regimes* (such as fossil fuel-based energy systems), which include interconnected systems of existing technologies, institutions, rules, norms and practices (Berkhout, Smith, & Stirling, 2003); and (3) a micro-level of protected *niches*, which act as test-beds for innovative ideas and technologies and the potential emergence of new socio-technical constellations that challenge the existing regime (Späth & Rohracher, 2010). These 'levels' refer to heterogeneous configurations of increasing stability, which can be seen as a nested hierarchy with regimes embedded within landscapes and niches existing inside or outside regimes (Geels, 2011). 'Utilising the analytical devices of transitional landscapes, regimes, and niches provides a useful toolkit for examining the causal agents and mechanisms through which individual green economy sectors, domains, and geographical spaces seek to influence or supersede existing regimes' (Bailey & Caprotti, 2014, p. 1804). In transitions research a key focus has been on experimentation with new ideas and technologies in niches (Smith, 2003). Niche developments are seen as the source of new socio-technical configurations that can grow, and perhaps eventually displace, incumbent unsustainable regimes (Berkhout et al., 2003). These tensions are a product of changing circumstances in the wider socio-technical landscape acting as a driver for regime transitions, where new imperatives, such as climate change, accelerated global warming and carbon-reduction targets, act as a challenge to existing techno-logical regimes (Smith et al., 2010), potentially providing a window of opportunity for niche experiments and ideas to migrate into the mainstream regime.

However, within the sustainability transitions literature 'the role of places and spatial scales in these transition processes has not been an explicit issue of concern' (Smith et al., 2010, p. 443). Much work has either explicitly or implicitly focused on national-scale transitions (Hodson & Marvin, 2010). Research that has investigated the role of space and place suggests that 'cities and regions can become powerful promoters of sustainability transitions when understood as rela-tionally embedded actors and providing crucial resources for successful innova-tion processes' (Truffer & Coenen, 2012, p. 15). Coenen, Raven, and Verbong (2010) suggest that niches are likely to be local-scale phenomena, which subse-quently play an important role in up-scaling these experiments to (implicitly) wider spatial scales, while Truffer (2008, p. 980) points out that 'a first nucleus of a new regime structure could emerge on a regional . . . level.' Truffer and Coenen (2012, p. 17) bring these arguments together by suggesting that 'the role of cities and regions may be to provide protected "spaces", where the usual selection pres-sures are somewhat modulated and therefore the construction of socio-technical configurations can take place'. Similar conclusions are reached by the European Observation Network for Territorial Development and Cohesion (ESPON) (2014) and Badinger et al. (2016) where European regions and cities are identified as key actors encouraging sustainability transitions. It will be important, given such circumstances, that those cities and regions that possess fewer endogenous resources and resourceful actors are not excluded from more sustainable econo-mies, improved environments and social justice.

Certainly, the likelihood of a specific transition may be unevenly distributed in space and will depend on the interplay of actors, networks and institutions avail-able in some places and not others. In this context, 'notions of niche and regime are potentially resourceful concepts in framing the possibilities and limitations for green-tech clusters to emerge and develop in particular regions' (Truffer & Coenen, 2012, p. 12). Some regions or places may offer greater opportunity both for strategic niches to develop and operate, and for the formation and develop-ment of green entrepreneurial activities. Although some of the factors at work in a region or area may not be specifically 'local', of importance is how actors adapt or adopt national and international factors and how these come to be configured locally (Truffer & Coenen, 2012). In MLP terms, while socio-technical land-scapes provide the broad context of opportunities and constraints for green devel-opments, they do not (despite sometimes being seen as 'external pressures') determine outcomes or mechanically impact niches and regimes (Hodson & Marvin, 2010). Actors within a locality need to perceive and translate these external landscape developments in order to have purchase (Geels & Schot, 2007). The role of purposive actors and institutions is therefore important in this process, not just within the local area, but also to help transcend the city and regional scale (Späth & Rohracher, 2010).

The following sections utilize secondary data and published research to illustrate these points, drawing on the spectrum of activity shown in Table 1. The first of these focuses on clean-tech, ecological modernization-type initiatives, reflecting an 'almost business-as-usual/selective growth approach' (Table 1) and use the example of Styria in Austria to represent these. Second, the paper turns to a more diverse group of initiatives representing more radical conceptualizations reflecting the 'limits to growth/socio-economic transformation' end of the spectrum in Table 1. The authors recognize the limitations of this approach, and this is not intended to be a direct comparison between clean-tech and degrowth, nor is this viewed as a binary divide. Rather these are stylized interpretations of the green economy that can help to orientate the debate and future research, as well as offering exploratory case studies to illustrate the diversity of initiatives that exist (Faccer, Nahman, & Audouin, 2014).

A CLEAN-TECH GREEN ECONOMY: ECO WORLD STYRIA

Styria's 'Green Tech Valley' has been developed in the Austrian province and is one of Europe's leading green economy locations with over 200 companies. Graz, the second largest city in Austria, is the administrative centre for the province of Styria and has won various European and international awards for its eco-city initiatives (Rohracher & Späth, 2014). The region had a history of experimentation with renewable energy technologies in the 1980s, especially in solar thermal and biomass technologies. In the case of the former, this was a product of bottom-up, self-build experiments, whereas biomass developments were more a product of established organizations, especially those related to agriculture and involving the Styrian chamber of agriculture (Schreuer, Katzmair, & Gulas, 2010). It has also been argued that the local population was mobilized in the 1980s to protest about air quality and pollution from 'dirty' industries such as steel and paper manufacturing plants, which led to a bottom-up sustainability agenda and the formation of 'niche thinking' (van Heyningen & Brent, 2012). The specific Green Tech Valley initiative has its origins in a project in 1998 and was formally established in 2005. It claims to be the 'world's highest concentration in the areas of bioenergy, solar energy, waste and resource management and green buildings' and 'the global hotspot for advanced energy and environmental technologies and proven growth through innovation' (Eco World, 2016, p. 6). This accords with a view that sees similar eco-clusters, defined as 'regional innovative networks with a focus on environmental friendly and sustainable technologies' (Pohl, 2015, p. 31), as a key source of green growth at the regional scale. Indeed, promotional material for Green Tech Valley claims that more than 1000 jobs have been created each year since 2005, with sales growth of 131% compared with 73% sales growth in green tech companies globally (for the period 2006–14). Eco World Styria is the specialized networking and support organization for the Green Tech Valley and is a provincial and city (Graz) government-supported initiative, but also involves a range of institutions in a triple helix research–industry–government approach (Schreuer et al., 2010). The organization provides information to firms, assists them in gaining new markets, engages in horizon scanning for new techno-logical developments and also provides regional support for research and devel-opment (R&D), training and apprenticeships. Styria conforms with Cooke's (2011) concept of 'transition regions' – defined as constituting sub-national administrative areas, with policies and support mechanisms in place to support green industries, clusters of related green industries and a platform of related variety sectors and subsectors.

Eco World uses the Green Tech Valley appellation and its designation as 'the worldwide No. 1 green tech cluster' by the US Clean Edge group in 2010 (Eco World, 2016, p. 6) to brand and position itself externally. Eco World is a member of a range of international green economy networks including the Green Tech Service Alliance, EcoCluP and the International Cleantech Network (ICN). These have promotional value, with Eco World staff giving presentations and study tours to representatives from overseas local and regional government staff. The development of the Green Tech Service Alliance, with partners in 10 countries (six in the European Union, plus Singapore, South Korea, Canada and the United States) also enables Styria's companies to access business opportunities in other green business clusters. Such international networking activities indicate the need to consider multi-scalarity in transitions research (Truffer et al., 2015) – these help to legitimize efforts to develop a green-tech cluster by emphasizing (1) Styria as an important global player in the green economy and (2) the potential gains to be derived locally through export opportunities and through potential inward invest-ment into Green Tech Valley. In this manner, networking activities transcend existing governance levels to create an additional source of pressure on incumbent regimes (Rohracher & Späth, 2014). Such networking activities in Styria also support Geels and Raven's (2006) argument that one needs to distinguish between 'local experiments' in local networks in specific geographical places and a 'global niche level' that is an emerging institutional environment of shared rules which transcends and connects particular places.

In terms of 'local experiments', while Eco World encourages firm location, new start-ups and innovation, it is not solely focused on economic development, with a major shift towards renewable energy use in the province and support for local, community and local energy initiatives. The drive towards renewable energy is assisted by a strong regime context, which encourages renewable energy use in the local market, and is supported by both federal and regional energy strat-egies. The regional government's Energy Strategy 2025 sends 'a clear signal of coordination and direction towards energy efficiency' (Miranda & Larcombe, 2012, p. 75). The city of Graz was an early mover in implementing demand-side energy management programmes and promoted the use of both district heating and solar thermal energy (Rohracher & Späth, 2014). Regional state policy also aims to integrate the development of eco-industries into regional development strategy (Pohl, 2015). However, in addition to encouraging transition at the local level (e.g., encouraging the adoption of renewable energy, specifying building regulations) Eco World's involvement with bodies such as EcoCluP, the ICN and the Global Cleantech Cluster Association involves creating a shared vision and dynamic across partners from different countries, representing an attempt to work at the 'global niche level' (Raven, Verbong, Schilpzand, & Witkamp, 2011).

From a sustainability transitions perspective, Styria indicates the important role of local visions to mobilize local actors (such as initial environmental protest) and the key role of intermediaries (such as Eco World) (Hansen & Coenen, 2015). For green economy firms, involvement in Eco World helps legitimize their activities and to counter competing industries and the dominant energy regime, as well as challenging institutionalized interest groups such as the Austrian federation of industries and the chamber of commerce (Schreuer et al., 2010). While the example of Styria does not indicate regime change, it can be taken to represent local 'regime variation' that is more sustainable than the dominant energy regime. International awards and branding have also played an important part, helping to alter regional self-perceptions. However, these may be less important in relation to actual imple-mentation than their role in creating a self-reinforcing process. Hence:

> the bases for such momentum building for sustainability transition were . . . not so much changes in the physical infrastructures or environmental policy outcomes, but rather the discursive dynamics and innovative concepts, interna-tional recognition and awards, and public appreciation of the eco-city identity.
> (Rohracher & Späth, 2014, p. 1421)

However, despite the promotion of Styria as a leading green economy region, the eco-cluster is only one sector amongst others that are being supported locally through Styria's Economic Strategy 2020 – these include health-tech and mobility sectors, as well as the much less environmentally friendly automotive and steel industries (Perkonigg, 2013). Although presented as a new form of economic development, it could be argued that Styria's green economy represents the incumbent capitalist–consumerist economy, albeit with a green hue. Thus, while Styria's green industries might 'constitute new socio-technical configurations with potential for larger long-term impacts' and its 'programmes and projects are typical socio-technical niches for nurturing and experimenting with emerging technologies', to date local outcomes represent 'gradual improvements rather than disruptive transformation' (Rohracher & Späth, 2014, pp. 1421–1422), This aligns with Smith and Raven's (2012) 'fit and conform' perspective where niche innovations are readily aligned and competitive within existing contexts and are hence incremental in terms of their broader socio-technical implications.

'DISRUPTIVE TRANSFORMATION': EMERGING DEGROWTH HOTSPOTS

This section now considers alternative forms of economies at the niche level that may challenge incumbent regimes. At this level initiatives enact a 'stretch and transform' perspective, whereby niches are empowered to change radically the socio-technical context and incumbent regime (Smith & Raven, 2012). These initiatives and projects may be geographically disparate, but share principles and ideals connected to sustainability, social justice, post-consumerism and so on under the various rubrics of degrowth, steady-state economies, solidarity econo-mies, 'transition towns', slow cities etc. This section highlights how cities and regions, as well as dispersed networks of committed activists, are driving forward these agendas. Although such initiatives may currently be small-scale, they can represent hotspots of 'disruptive transformation' (Rohracher & Späth, 2014) and, even if not scaled up in their current format, can illustrate the possibilities and encourage broader debates about the extent to which the status quo needs trans-forming. Initiatives such as degrowth, and other visions of alternative economies, represent an agenda that policy-makers, businesses and communities find harder to visualize and enact as it radically challenges the incumbent way of life (Purcell, 2014). Reconfiguring (or reorganizing) discourse in this manner can open up new possibilities for climate action (Swyngedouw, 1992) and performing economies and societies differently (Gibson-Graham, 2008). Given their fragmented nature, it is more difficult to pinpoint whole regions that are adopting such an approach compared with clean-tech examples.[1] The section now considers a number of empirical examples to illustrate the range of initiatives that challenge incumbent regime practices and discourses.

Longhurst (2015) examines how an alternative milieu in a particular place can encourage (or, conversely, discourage) the development of niche experiments, drawing on evidence from Totnes in Devon in the UK. He argues that the presence of an alternative milieu – a localized density of countercultural institutions, networks, groups and practices – creates a particular form of geographical niche protection for the emergence of sustainability experiments. Within Totnes, Long-hurst (2015; see also Longhurst, 2012) identifies a range of different experiments – from organic agriculture and permaculture, to a local exchange trading scheme (LETS). He shows how these initiatives are interlinked in nature, with connec-tions between the permaculture philosophy, a green community office that supported the LETS scheme, the Transition Towns movement (Hopkins, 2008) and the Landmatters low-impact community, the members of which are attempting to develop viable self-sufficient lifestyles. One might, therefore, reasonably expect places with an existing 'alternative milieu' to develop such initiatives in advance of other places.

In addition to this example of initiatives for degrowth societies (Whitehead, 2013), other examples exist such as localized currencies (Longhurst, 2015; North, 2014; Seyfang, 2003), voluntary simplicity (Alexander, 2013), diverse economies (Gibson-Graham, 2008; Roelvink, St Martin, & Gibson-Graham, 2015), solidarity purchasing groups, solidarity economy districts, Slow Food (Grasseni, 2014) and Slow Cities (Mayer & Knox, 2008). Slow Cities, for instance, imply the practice of a Slow movement philosophy in all aspects of city life. The goal is to preserve the quality of life of their residents and the biodiversity that shapes their cultural traditions by reducing noise, pollution and stress, plus investment in community, public spaces, cooking and gardening, or healthy habits like walking and cycling (Pàdranos, 2013). Similarly, the solidarity economy draws on various projects and initiatives that focus on the everyday practices of alternative ways of living, producing and consuming. This includes cooperative housing and urban gardening projects, barter clubs, self-governed businesses and eco-villages. Each underlines particular aspects and represents a vision for the reinvention of society through a radical rethinking of the economy and the ecology of capitalist consumption (Grasseni, 2014). While degrowth may ultimately require a sharp break with capitalism at a macro-sociological level, in terms of everyday life this transition may involve a series of improvisational triggers in and through which small-scale changes can lead to the emergence of alternative socio-ecological trajectories (Boonstra & Joosse, 2013). Put differently, such initiatives may be part of a series of steps towards more transformational actions which 'stretch and transform', whereby niches are empowered to change the socio-technical context and incumbent regime (Smith & Raven, 2012).

Schindler (2016) illustrates how even cities once at the heart of globalized, capitalist networks can turn to degrowth principles as a result of economic crisis. Drawing on Detroit as an example, Schindler argues that the 2008 global financial crisis hit some cities (and regions) harder than others – Detroit was declared bankrupt in July 2013, and suffered from a mass exodus of residents leading to abandonment of large swathes of the city. The resultant available land resources are now seen as a resource that can be leveraged to create a new green and sustainable city through the Detroit Future City plan. Detroit's bankruptcy has not resulted in straightforward 'austerity urbanism', and bankruptcy has allowed city and state governments to defy the demands of extra-local bondholders (Walsh, 2014a, 2014b). Howsoever reached, these means of defiance offer a foothold for new ways of doing things. While many of the proposals to revitalize Detroit do draw on conventional urban entrepreneurial approaches to regeneration (such as sports stadia, entertainment and retail districts etc.), there are also plans that draw on degrowth principles, based on the realization that conventional economic growth is unlikely in the short-term and would not be adequate to deal with the severity of issues experienced there. In contrast to other so-called green cities being developed (e.g., Masdar City; Cugurullo, 2013), in Detroit it is proposed that neighbourhoods will be redeveloped to produce a 'stronger, greener, and more socially and economically vital Detroit, where neighbourhoods feature a wide variety of residential styles from apartments to houses, and where residents are connected to jobs and services by many transportation options' (Schindler, 2016, p. 827), and where cycling is promoted. While the elements of Detroit's future described by Schindler (2016) do not all necessarily align to degrowth as such, and there are overlaps with ecological modernization ideas of 'smart growth' (Gibbs & Krueger, 2012), they are, as Schindler notes, exceptional given Detroit's past as the centre of the motor industry.

The example of Detroit illustrates the degrowth argument that it is 'better to start adapting to . . . de-growth, in order to find a prosperous way down' (Martínez-Alier, Pascual, Vivien, & Zaccai, 2010, p. 1745), rather than deal with the harsh realities of collapse (Tomlinson, Six Silberman, Patterson, Pan, & Blevis, 2012). However, definitions of 'prosperous' in this context are qualitatively different to contemporaneous understandings, and might involve valuing time to grow one's own food, or spending time with family and friends, rather than having the newest car or a foreign holiday (Kallis et al., 2012). These examples are drawn from a developed world perspective, but there are overlaps between degrowth and similar initiatives in the Global South such as the adoption of Buen Vivir as government policy in Bolivia and Ecuador, Ubuntu in South Africa, and ecological Swaraj in India, all of which have an emphasis on self-reliance, mutuality, harmony with nature and environmental justice (Hollender, 2015; Kothari, Demaria, & Acosta, 2015). There is thus a great diversity of practices and ideas that characterize degrowth-type initiatives, but rather than seeing such internal diversity as a weakness, proponents suggest that the multiplicity within the degrowth movement is key to its long-term ability to have global widespread appeal (Demaria, Schneider, Sekulova, & Martinez-Alier, 2013).

TRANSITIONS, ECOLOGICAL MODERNIZATION AND DEGROWTH

In terms of transitions research, both ecological modernization approaches to the green economy, such as in Styria, and degrowth initiatives can be viewed as niche developments that offer a challenge to the dominant regime. However, the potential to gain acceptance and articulation varies – green economy developments such as those in Styria are much more readily aligned with the dominant regime and/or can be incorporated by it ('fit and conform'). Shifting landscape imperatives around climate change and reducing carbon emissions provide legitimacy to the niche. By contrast, in the case of degrowth, such landscape shifts (challenging the fundamental basis of capitalist economies) have barely registered outside of a small group of proponents and legitimacy is lacking – 'stretch and transform' is far more problematic (Smith & Raven, 2012). Thus

> niche innovations must be compatible with elements in the incumbent regimes, or with the wider landscape context such that an alternative socio-technical regime might emerge. Such alignments enable niche innovations to be translated, articulated, and/or anchored within dominant or alternative socio-technical regimes.
>
> (Murphy, 2015, p. 79)

In both examples there have been attempts to move beyond 'local experiments' to construct a 'global niche' of an emerging institutional environment of shared rules which transcends scale and particular places. In the case of Styria this has taken on a fairly conventional form of participating in, and helping to build, international networks of similar green economy developments (often funded through the European Union) such as the International Cleantech Network. Such networking initiatives help to legitimize the activities of their members (such as Eco World, Styria), but also serve as a means to promote increased exports, sales and investment, and read as traditional versions of neoliberal capitalism albeit with different 'products'. Degrowth initiatives are also linked through international networks, although these are rarely as focused and are often more informal (Demaria et al., 2013) – for example, the Research and Degrowth Association is an informal network that 'strives to bring scientists, civil society, practitioners, and activists together to think, imagine, discuss, and create proposals for sustainable degrowth'.[2] Other networks are more substantial. For example, the Transition Network lists 479 separate initiatives; Cittàslow has 213 member towns and cities; and Slow Food has 2000 food communities – but their activities remain largely marginal in their impact upon the dominant regime. As such, degrowth interpretations of the green economy may remain niche developments, with little potential to offer a challenge to the mainstream economy.

Moreover, the limited evidence to date suggests that they may only offer a 'temporary niche solution' or 'short term sustainability fix' in those cities and regions where there has been a substantial breakdown in the capitalist economy, such as in Detroit, Southern Europe and parts of Latin America, until economic growth as usual can be reinstated. The official adoption of Buen Vivir in Bolivia and Ecuador has also been criticized as masking a continued focus on the extractive economy by national governments (Hollender, 2015). However, such examples are important in making such other worlds possible and further work is needed to expose how degrowth is being adopted in practice and how it interlinks with, and challenges, neoliberal, capitalist economic development in different places globally. Empirical examples can help bring theoretical discussions to life, and illustrate to policy-makers and others the vibrancy and difference that is possible and desirable. Such examples help to move economic development debates beyond the limited concept of sustainable development to consider new forms of regional development where social, economic and environmental considerations are on an equal footing rather than regularly being superseded by economic imperatives.

CONCLUSIONS: MOVING FORWARD – A REGIONAL STUDIES RESEARCH AGENDA

This paper has focused on the need to address environmental degradation and global change associated with economic development, with the intention of encouraging the regional studies community to address sustainability transitions more wholeheartedly. In particular the authors have been concerned with investigating policy responses that aim to develop a green economy and address key environmental problems. While there is general agreement that 'something needs to be done' to address these, especially climate change, there is little consensus on the types of policies and programmes that need to be adopted and implemented. Although international agreements, such as the Paris Agreement on climate change, and nation states' policies are of key importance, there is also evidence that cities and regions can play an important role in driving forward change through experimentation and as locations for niche developments. However, to date, regional development research has had relatively little engagement with issues of the environment and sustainability. Truffer and Coenen (2012), in a review of past work published in *Regional Studies*, indicate three main strands based around ecological modernization, industrial ecosystems and frameworks to analyse the policy process. Conversely, research from a sustainability transitions perspective has, by definition, engaged with environmental change and sustainability, but has largely lacked any consideration of the role that space plays in influencing transitions. There is, therefore, a key research agenda that needs to be developed further to explore the role of cities and regions in sustainability transitions building on the work of Truffer and Coenen (2012), Coenen et al. (2010), Smith et al. (2010), Hodson and Marvin (2010) and Murphy (2015), with the potential for fruitful cross-fertilization between regional studies and transitions scholars.

Both strands of research, on regional development and sustainability transitions, also lack any detailed consideration of what the outcomes of a shift to a more sustainable future or a green economy would entail. In both cases, there is often an explicit or implicit assumption that this would rely heavily on technological solutions and approaches drawn from ecological modernization. This paper has shown that, in reality, the green economy is a contested concept – while the hegemonic discourse may currently be around clean-tech, low-carbon developments, there is a spectrum of green economy discourses available. The paper has illustrated some of these differences by drawing on examples from both ecological modernization and degrowth discourses and it explored how transitions research can help one to understand the potential for change towards a more sustainable economy in both cases. Future research therefore needs a focus on 'the spatial contexts in which sustainability transitions evolve and take place' and 'an understanding of transition spaces, that is, a synthesis of locally embedded contexts of events, objects and actions coupled with the wider socio-political, institutional and cultural context' (Truffer & Coenen, 2012, p. 11). The aim for research in regional studies should be to investigate the socio-spatial embedding of conditions in particular locations that encourage and support new technologies, new policies and sustainability transitions (Truffer et al., 2015). Future research needs an 'analysis of the particular settings (places) in which transitions are embedded and evolve, while at the same time paying attention to the geographical connections and interactions (i.e., the spatial relations) within and between that place and other places' (Hansen & Coenen, 2015, p. 95). Drawing on the analysis here of the green economy spectrum, one can add to this the need for an analysis of the particular forms of the green economy that are being developed and promoted, as well as *where* these are being developed, as well as a means of evaluating their 'sustainability'.

In transition terms, Truffer and Coenen (2012, p. 14) argue that both green-tech cluster initiatives and more alternative forms, such as transition town movements, can be seen as representative of the kinds of 'protected "spaces" . . . where the construction of socio-technical configurations can take place'. As for hegemonic discourses of the green economy, therefore, a useful line of research is to explore how certain cities or regions provide protected 'spaces' for the emergence of degrowth experiments. This may be the case in parts of Latin America where A2D initiatives 'offer potential spaces to advance innovative regional policy frameworks' (Hollender, 2015, p. 97). While degrowth may not be relevant as a counter to the excesses of over-growth in parts of the Global South, such initiatives may indeed offer a route to more sustainable economies and societies. For cities and regions in the Global North, such as Detroit and those in Southern Europe, degrowth has been an unavoidable consequence of the 2008 financial crisis rather than a deliberate policy choice (Schindler, 2016). A key question is whether degrowth will only be adopted or have traction in cities and regions that perceive themselves as having no viable alternative, such as bankrupt Detroit and parts of Greece and Spain. In these instances, the 'decision' to pursue degrowth strategies may reflect the lack of more conventional options and, perhaps, may be short-lived if conventional growth patterns return in future. In these cases the niche will remain an area for experimentation, with little impact on the broader regime.

Degrowth and other related initiatives can, thus, arise for a variety of reasons and from various stimuli. There are significant differences between managed decline and active degrowth approaches that do not just envisage financial shrinkage, but radically new and different forms of 'economic' development and social vibrancy. A number of research questions arise from this: Can these initiatives dovetail with green economy regions, such as the example from Styria, as well as mainstream economies, given that changes will not happen overnight? Will such sustainable initiatives remain marginal and limited in their impact on the mainstream (unsustainable) regime? What support will be necessary to ensure that these degrowth examples can flourish and offer hope, rather than being excluded in favour of further economic growth and ecological decline? Are such initiatives only focused on those unable to participate in the conventional economy? Future research needs to explore these questions in more depth through detailed case study work that can deepen one's understanding of alternative futures for urban and regional transitions. Here the authors concur with Hodson, Burrai, and Barlow (2016, p. 145) that this calls 'for more work on better understanding the range of alternatives and an examination of the interconnections and possible interconnections between alternative initiatives and formal priorities'.

In focusing on different forms of new green economies, it has been highlighted here how different places are adopting and adapting new forms of economies and societies, and how sustainability can be differently interpreted. Sustainability transitions research offers a powerful tool to emphasize the conflicts and power structures in transitions in particular places and to 'reveal novel insights into the power relations and political processes underlying transition processes, and thus enable transition researchers to better account for the relationalities and context-specific forces determining the pace, scale, and direction of socio-technical change' (Murphy, 2015, p. 83). Whilst it might seem that the two 'case studies' of different forms of the green economy are incongruous, this is an important distinction. As Hansen and Coenen (2015) make clear, struggles and conflicts need to be investigated, given that transitions are not all about consensus and alignment of actors. Difficult changes that challenge long-ingrained ideals and widely held views about economic growth, for instance, are unlikely to result in consensus but rather in fierce debates and disagreements about the best approach – this is not to say that such debates should not take place, but that they represent important milestones in progressing towards more sustainable futures. Given the potential severity of the impacts of climate change, especially in some parts of the world, it is unlikely that such changes would be easy or uncontested. However, the status quo is not tenable either.

ACKNOWLEDGEMENTS

The authors are grateful to the two anonymous referees and Ivan Turok for their helpful comments on an earlier draft of this paper.

DISCLOSURE STATEMENT

No potential conflict of interest was reported by the authors.

FUNDING

David Gibbs acknowledges the support of a Regional Studies Association Fellowship Research Grant.

NOTES

1. Thus, while the previous section focused on Styria, it could equally have chosen as exemplars Copenhagen, Boston or Stockholm city-regions. Outside a Western context, both South Korea and China have developed similar green industry initiatives (Bell, 2016; Quitzow, 2015).
2. See http://www.degrowth.org/description. Retrieved May 13, 2016.

REFERENCES

Alexander, S. (2013). Voluntary simplicity and the social reconstruction of law: De-growth from the grassroots up. *Environmental Values*, *22*(2), 287–308. doi:10.3197/096327 113X13581561725356
Badinger, H., Bailey, D., De Propris, L., Huber, P., Janger, J., Kratena, K., Pitlik, H., Sauer, T., Thillaye, R., & van den Bergh, J. (2016). *New dynamics for Europe: Reaping the benefits of socio-ecological transition, Part II model and area chapters* (WWWforEurope Synthesis Report, Final Version). Vienna and Brussels: WWWforEurope.

Bailey, I., & Caprotti, F. (2014). The green economy: Functional domains and theoretical directions of enquiry. *Environment and Planning A, 46*, 1797–1813. doi:10.1068/a130102p

Bailey, I., Gouldson, A., & Newell, P. (2011). Ecological modernisation and the governance of carbon: A critical analysis. *Antipode, 43*(3), 682–703. doi:10.1111/j.1467-8330.2011.00880.x

Bailey, I., & Wilson, G. (2009). Theorising transitional pathways in response to climate change: Technocentrism, ecocentrism, and the carbon economy. *Environment and Planning A, 41*, 2324–2341. doi:10.1068/a40342

Bauhardt, C. (2014). Solutions to the crisis? The green new deal, degrowth and the solidarity economy: Alternatives to the capitalist growth economy from an ecofeminist economics perspective. *Ecological Economics, 102*, 60–68. doi:10.1016/j.ecolecon.2014.03.015

Bell, K. (2016). Green economy or living well? Assessing divergent paradigms for equitable eco-social transition in South Korea and Bolivia. *Journal of Political Ecology, 23*, 71–92.

Berkhout, F., Smith, A., & Stirling, A. (2003). *Socio-technological regimes and transition contexts*. Brighton: Science and Policy Research Unit (SPRU), University of Sussex.

Bina, O. (2013). The green economy and sustainable development: An uneasy balance? *Environment and Planning C: Government and Policy, 31*, 1023–1047. doi:10.1068/c1310j

Bonsinetto, F., & Falco, E. (2013). Analysing Italian regional patterns in green economy and climate change. Can Italy leverage on Europe 2020 strategy to face sustainable growth challenges? *Journal of Urban and Regional Analysis, 2*, 123–142.

Boonstra W. J., & Joosse, S. (2013). How degrowth can develop from within capitalism. *Environmental Values, 22*(2), 171–189. doi:10. 3197/096327113X13581561725158

Borel-Saladin, J. M., & Turok, I. N. (2013). The green economy: Incremental change or transformation. *Environmental Policy and Governance, 23*, 209–220. doi:10.1002/eet.1614

Bulkeley, H., Jordan, A., Perkins, R., & Selin, H. (2013). Governing sustainability: Rio+20 and the road beyond. *Environment and Planning C: Government and Policy, 31*, 958–970. doi:10.1068/c3106ed

Caprotti, F. (2012). The cultural economy of cleantech: Environmental discourse and the emergence of a new technology sector. *Transactions of the Institute of British Geographers, 37*(3), 370–385. doi:10.1111/j.1475-5661.2011.00485.x

Castree, N. (2008). Neoliberalising nature: The logics of deregulation and reregulation. *Environment and Planning A, 40*, 131–152. doi:10.1068/a3999

Coenen, L., Raven, R., & Verbong, G. (2010). Local niche experimentation in energy transitions: A theoretical and empirical exploration of proximity advantages and disadvantages. *Technology in Society, 32*, 295–302. doi:10.1016/j.techsoc.2010. 10.006

Cooke, P. (2011). Transition regions: Regional–national eco-innovation systems and strategies. *Progress in Planning, 76*, 105–146. doi:10.1016/j.progress.2011.08.002

Cugurullo, F. (2013). How to build a sandcastle: An analysis of the genesis and development of Masdar City. *Journal of Urban Technology, 20*(1), 23–37. doi:10.1080/10630732.2012.735105

Davies, A., & Mullin, S. (2011). Greening the economy: Interrogating sustainability innovations beyond the mainstream. *Journal of Economic Geography, 11*(5), 793–816. doi:10.1093/jeg/lbq050

Davies, A. R. (2013). Cleantech clusters: Transformational assemblages for a just, green economy or just business as usual? *Global Environmental Change, 23*(5), 1285–1295. doi:10.1016/j.gloenvcha.2013.07.010

Demaria, F., Schneider, F., Sekulova, F., & Martinez-Alier, J. (2013). What is degrowth? From an activist slogan to a social movement. *Environmental Values*, *22*(2), 191–215. doi:10. 3197/096327113X13581561725194

Eco World. (2016). *Green Tech Valley guide*. Retrieved May 17, 2016, from www.eco.at/ news/docs/31991_Green%20Tech%20Valley %20Guide.pdf/.

Escobar, A. (2015). Degrowth, postdevelopment, and transitions: A preliminary conversation. *Sustainability Science*, *10*, 451–462. doi:10.1007/s11625-015-0297-5

European Observation Network for Territorial Development and Cohesion (ESPON). (2014). *GREECO: Territorial potentials for a greener economy* (Final Report). Luxembourg: ESPON/Tecnalia.

Faccer, F., Nahman, A., & Audouin, M. (2014). Interpreting the green economy: Emerging discourses and their considerations for the global south. *Development Southern Africa*, *31*(5), 642–657. doi:10.1080/0376835X.2014.933700

Ferguson, P. (2015). The green economy agenda: Business as usual or transformational discourse? *Environmental Politics*, *24*(1), 17–37. doi:10.1080/09644016.2014.919748

Geels, F., & Raven, R. (2006). Non-linearity and expectations in niche-development trajectories: Ups and downs in Dutch biogas development (1973–2003). *Technology Analysis and Strategic Management*, *18*(3/4), 375–392. doi:10.1080/09537320600777143

Geels, F., & Schot, J. (2007). Typology of socio-technical transition pathways. *Research Policy*, *36*, 399–417. doi:10.1016/j.respol. 2007.01.003

Geels, F. W. (2005). *Technological transitions and system innovations: A co-evolutionary and socio-technical analysis*. Cheltenham: Edward Elgar.

Geels, F. W. (2011). The multi-level perspective on sustainability transitions: Responses to seven criticisms. *Environmental Innovation and Societal Transitions*, *1*, 24–40. doi:10.1016/j.eist.2011.02.002

Gendron, C. (2014). Beyond environmental and ecological economics: Proposal for an economic sociology of the environment. *Ecological Economics*, *105*, 240–253. doi:10.1016/j.ecolecon.2014.06.012

Gibbs, D., & Krueger, R. (2012). Fractures in meta-narratives of development: An interpretive institutionalist account of land Use development in the Boston city-region. *International Journal of Urban and Regional Research*, *36*(2), 363–380. doi:10.1111/j.1468-2427.2011.01061.x

Gibson-Graham, J. K. (2008). Diverse economies: Performative practices for 'other worlds'. *Progress in Human Geography*, *32*(5), 613–632. doi:10.1177/ 0309132508090821

Grasseni, C. (2014). Seeds of trust. Italy's gruppi di acquisto solidale (solidarity purchase groups). *Journal of Political Ecology 21*, 127–221.

Grinevich, V., Huber, F., Baines, L.,& Eder, M. (2015). *Upscaling in the sharing economy: Insights from the UK* (Research Report) Southampton: University of Southampton and Seekirchen am Wallersee: University Seeburg Castle.

Hansen, T., & Coenen, L. (2015). The geography of sustainability transitions: Review, synthesis and reflections on an emergent research field. *Environmental Innovation and Societal Transitions*, *17*, 92–109. doi:10.1016/j.eist.2014.11.001

Hodson, M., Burrai, E., & Barlow, C. (2016). Remaking the material fabric of the city: 'Alternative' low carbon spaces of transformation or continuity? *Environmental Innovation and Societal Transitions*, *18*, 128–146. doi:10.1016/j.eist.2015.06.001

Hodson, M., & Marvin, S. (2010). Can cities shape socio-technical transitions and how would we know if they were? *Research Policy*, *39*, 477–485. doi:10.1016/j. respol.2010.01.020

Hollender, R. (2015). Post-growth in the global south: The emergence of alternatives to development in Latin America. *Socialism and Democracy*, *29*(1), 73–101. doi:10.1080/08854300.2014.998472

Hopkins, R. (2008). *The transition handbook*. Totnes: Green Books.

Jackson, T. (2009). *Prosperity without growth?* London: Sustainable Development Commission.

Kallis, G. (2011). In defence of degrowth. *Ecological Economics*, *70*, 873–880. doi:10.1016/j.ecolecon.2010.12.007

Kallis, G., Demaria, F., & D'Alisa, G. (2015). Introduction: Degrowth. In D'Alisa, G., Demaria, F., & Kallis, G. (Eds.), *Degrowth: A vocabulary for a new era* (pp. 1–17). London: Routledge.

Kallis, G., Kerschner, C., & Martinez-Alier, J. (2012). The economics of degrowth. *Ecological Economics*, *84*, 172–180. doi:10. 1016/j.ecolecon.2012.08.017

Kenis, A., & Lievens, M. (2015). *The limits of the green economy: From reinventing capitalism to repoliticising the present*. London: Routledge.

Kothari, A., Demaria, F., & Acosta, A. (2015). Buen Vivir, degrowth and ecological Swaraj: Alternatives to sustainable development and the green economy. *Development*, *57*(3–4), 362–375.

Latouche, S. (2006). *Le pari de la décroissance*. Paris: Fayard.

Latouche, S. (2010). De-growth. *Journal of Cleaner Production*, *18*(6), 519–522. doi:10.1016/j.jclepro.2010.02.003

Longhurst, N. (2012). The Totnes pound: A grassroots technological niche. In Davies, A. (Ed.), *Enterprising communities: Grassroots sustainability innovations* (pp. 163–188). Bingley: Emerald.

Longhurst, N. (2015). Towards an 'alternative' geography of innovation: Alternative milieu, socio-cognitive protection and sustainability experimentation. *Environmental Innovation and Societal Transitions*, *17*, 183–198. doi:10.1016/j.eist.2014.12.001

Martínez-Alier, J. (2009). Socially sustainable economic de-growth. *Development and Change*, *40*(6), 1099–1119. doi:10.1111/j.1467-7660.2009.01618.x

Martínez-Alier, J., Pascual, U., Vivien, F. D., & Zaccai, E. (2010). Sustainable de-growth: Mapping the context, criticisms and future prospects of an emergent paradigm. *Ecological Economics*, *69*, 1741–1747. doi:10.1016/j.ecolecon.2010.04.017

Mayer, H., & Knox, P. (2008). Slow cities: Sustainable places in a fast world. *Journal of Urban Affairs*, *28*(4), 321–334. doi:10.1111/j.1467-9906.2006.00298.x

Miranda, G., & Larcombe, G. (2012). *Enabling local green growth: Addressing climate change effects on employment and local development* (OECD LEED Working Paper No. 2012/01). Paris: Organisation for Economic Co-operation and Development (OECD) Publ.

Mol, A. P. J. (2002). Ecological modernisation and the global economy. *Global Environmental Politics*, *2*(2), 92–115. doi:10.1162/15263800260047844

Moore, J. W. (2015). *Capitalism in the web of life: Ecology and the accumulation of capital*. London: Verso.

Murphy, J. (2015). Human geography and socio-technical transition studies: Promising intersections. *Environmental Innovation and Societal Transitions*, *17*, 73–91. doi:10.1016/j.eist.2015.03.002

North, P. (2014). Ten square miles surrounded by reality? Materialising alternative economies using local currencies. *Antipode*, *46*(1), 246–265. doi:10.1111/anti.12039

Pàdranos, L. I. (2013). Toward a euro-Mediterranean socio-environmental perspective: The case for a Spanish ecocriticism. *Ecozon*, *4*(2), 30–48.

Pearce, D., Markandya, A., & Barbier, E. (1989). *Blueprint for a green economy*. London: Earthscan.

Perkonigg, P. (2013). *Financing innovative projects in Styria* (National Report). PROFIS. Retrieved from http://www.profisproject.eu/.

Philips, M. (2013). On being green and being enterprising: Narrative and the ecopreneurial self. *Organization, 20*(6), 794–817. doi:10.1177/1350508412455084

Piketty, T. (2014). *Capital in the twenty-first century*. Cambridge, MA: Harvard University Press.

Pohl, A. (2015). *Eco-clusters as driving force for greening regional economic policy* (Policy Paper No. 27). WWWforEurope. Retrieved from www.foreurope.eu/.

Purcell, M. (2014). Possible worlds: Henri Lefebvre and the right to the city. *Journal of Urban Affairs, 36*(1), 141–154. doi:10.1111/juaf.12034

Quitzow, R. (2015). Dynamics of a policy-driven market: The coevolution of technological innovation systems for solar photovoltaics in China and Germany. *Environmental Innovation and Societal Transitions, 17*, 126–148. doi:10.1016/j.eist.2014.12.002

Raven, R., Verbong, G., Schilpzand, W., & Witkamp, M. (2011) Translation mechanisms in socio-technical niches: A case study of Dutch river management. *Technology Analysis and Strategic Management, 23*(10), 1063–1078. doi:10.1080/09537325.2011.621305

Research and Degrowth Association. (2012). Retrieved May 16, 2016, from http://www.degrowth.org/definition-2/.

Roberts, P., & Colwell, A. (2001). Moving the environment to centre stage: A new approach to planning and development at European and regional levels. *Local Environment, 6*(4), 421–37. doi:10. 1080/13549830120091716

Rockström, J., Steffen, W., Noone, K., Persson, A., Chapin, F. S., Lambin, E. F., & Foley, J. A. (2009). A safe operating space for humanity. *Nature, 461*(7263), 472–475. doi:10.1038/461472a

Roelvink, G., St Martin, K., & Gibson-Graham, J. K. (2015). *Making other worlds possible: Performing diverse economies*. Minnesota: University of Minnesota Press.

Rohracher, H., & Späth, P. (2014). The interplay of urban energy policy and socio-technical transitions: The eco-cities of Graz and Freiburg in retrospect. *Urban Studies, 51*(7), 1415–1431. doi:10.1177/0042098013500360

Schindler, S. (2016). Detroit after bankruptcy: A case of degrowth machine politics. *Urban Studies, 53*(4), 818–836. doi:10.1177/0042098014563485

Schreuer, A., Katzmair, H., & Gulas, C. (2010). Analysing the regional innovation system of renewable energy technologies in Styria: Actor constellations and innovation system functions. Paper presented at the Knowledge Collaboration and Learning for Sustainable Innovation ERSCP-EMSU conference, Delft, the Netherlands, October 25–29, 2010.

Seyfang G. (2003). Growing cohesive communities one favour at a time: Social exclusion, active citizenship, and time banks. *International Journal of Urban and Regional Research, 27*, 699–706. doi:10.1111/1468-2427.00475

Seyfang, G., & Smith, A. (2007). Grassroots innovations for sustainable development: Towards a new research and policy agenda. *Environmental Politics, 16*(4), 584–603. doi:10.1080/09644010701419121

Shear, B. W. (2014). Making the green economy: Politics, desire, and economic possibility. *Journal of Political Ecology, 21*, 193–209.

Smith, A. (2003). Transforming technological regimes for sustainable development: A role for alternative technology niches? *Science and Public Policy, 30*(2), 127–135. doi:10.3152/147154303781780623

Smith, A., Hielscher, S., Dickel, S., Söderberg, J., & van Oost, E. (2013). *Grassroots digital fabrication and makerspaces: Reconfiguring, relocating and recalibrating innovation?* (SPRU Working Paper Series No.   2013–02). Brighton: Science and Policy Research Unit (SPRU), University of Sussex.

Smith, A., & Raven, R. (2012). What is protective space? Reconsidering niches in transitions to sustainability. *Research Policy, 41*, 1025–1036. doi:10.1016/j.respol.2011.12.012

Smith, A., Voß, J.-P., & Grin, J. (2010). Innovation studies and sustainability transitions: The allure of the multi-level perspective and its challenges. *Research Policy, 39*, 435–448. doi:10.1016/j.respol.2010.01.023

Späth, P., & Rohracher, H. (2010). 'Energy regions': The transformative power of regional discourses on socio-technical futures. *Research Policy, 39*, 449–458. doi:10.1016/j.respol.2010.01.017

Swyngedouw, E. A. (1992). Territorial organization and the space/technology nexus. *Transactions of the Institute of British Geographers, 17*(4), 417–433. doi:10.2307/622708

Tienhaara, K. (2014). Varieties of green capitalism: Economy and environment in the wake of the global financial crisis. *Environmental Politics, 23*(2), 187–204. doi:10.1080/09644016.2013.821828

Tomlinson, B., Six Silberman, M., Patterson, D., Pan, Y., & Blevis, E. (2012). Collapse informatics: Augmenting the sustainability & ICT4D discourse in HCI. In Proceedings of the SIGCHI conference on Human Factors in Computing Systems, pp. 655–664.

Truffer, B. (2008). Society, technology, and region: Contributions from the social study of technology to economic geography. *Environment and Planning A, 40*, 966–985. doi:10.1068/a39170

Truffer, B., & Coenen, L. (2012). Environmental innovation and sustainability transitions in regional studies. *Regional Studies, 46*(1), 1–21. doi:10.1080/00343404.2012.646164

Truffer, B., Murphy, J. T., & Raven, R. (2015). The geography of sustainability transitions: Contours of an emerging theme. *Environmental Innovation and Societal Transitions, 17*, 63–72. doi:10.1016/j.eist.2015.07.004

United Nations Environment Programme (UNEP). (2011). *Towards a green economy: Pathways to sustainable development and poverty eradication – A synthesis for policy makers*. Retrieved from www.unep.org/greeneconomy/.

Van Heyningen, J. P., & Brent, A. (2012). Assessing the emergence of sustainability-oriented innovation systems and the transition towards sustainability in Styria, Austria. Paper presented at the 23rd ISPIM conference Action for Innovation: Innovating from Experience, Barcelona, Spain, June 17–20, 2012.

Walsh, M. W. (2014a). Detroit turns bankruptcy into challenge of banks. *New York Times*, February 3. Retrieved May 16, 2016, from http://dealbook.nytimes.com/2014/02/03/detroit-turnsbankruptcy-into-challenge-of-banks/.

Walsh, M. W. (2014b). Judge disallows plan by Detroit to pay off banks. *New York Times*, January 16. Retrieved May 16, 2016, from http://dealbook.nytimes.com/2014/01/16/judge-rejectsdetroits-deal-to-exit-swap-contracts/?_r=0/.

Whitehead, M. (2013). Degrowth or regrowth? *Editorial, Environmental Issues, 22*(2), 141–145.

Analysing the regional geography of poverty, austerity and inequality in Europe: a human cartographic perspective

Dimitris Ballas, Danny Dorling and Benjamin Hennig

ABSTRACT

Analysing the regional geography of poverty, austerity and inequality in Europe: a human cartographic perspective. *Regional Studies*. This paper presents a human cartographic approach to the analysis of the impact of austerity and the economic crisis across Europe's regions. It reflects on past insights and debates on the analysis and mapping of poverty and wealth, and of the effects of austerity in particular. It then presents a wide range of cartograms highlighting social and spatial inequalities across Europe. Finally, the paper highlights the increasingly important role of the field of regional studies in current debates about the future of the European project and of the possibility of a Europe of regions rather than a Europe of nation-states.

摘要

分析欧洲的贫穷，财政紧缩和不均的区域地理：人类製图的观点。 Regional Studies. 本文呈现一个分析欧洲各区域财政紧缩及经济危机之影响的人类製图方法。本文反思过往对于分析并绘製贫穷与富裕地图，特别是财政紧缩的影响之洞见与辩论。本文接着呈现一系列强调欧洲各地社会与空间不均的比较统计地图。本文最后强调区域研究领域在当前有关欧洲计画的未来，以及由区域组成欧洲，而非由民族国家组成欧洲的可能性之辩论中的重要角色。

RÉSUMÉ

Analyser la géographie régionale de la pauvreté, de l'austérité et de l'inégalité en Europe: du point de vue de la cartographie humaine. *Regional Studies*. Cet article présente une approche fondée sur la cartographie humaine pour analyser l'impact de l'austérité et de la crise économique à travers les régions européennes. Il réfléchit aux aperçus et aux débats antérieurs à propos de l'analyse et de la cartographie de la pauvreté et de la richesse, et notamment des effets de l'austérité. Dans un deuxième temps l'article présente une série importante de cartogrammes qui soulignent les inégalités sociales et spatiales à travers l'Europe. Pour terminer, l'article met l'accent sur le rôle de plus en plus important que joue le domaine des études régionales au sein des débats actuels sur l'avenir du projet européen et du développement éventuel d'une Europe des régions plutôt que d'une Europe des états-nations.

ZUSAMMENFASSUNG

Analyse der regionalen Geografie von Armut, Sparmaßnahmen und Ungleichheit in Europa: eine human kartografische Perspektive. *Regional Studies*. In diesem Beitrag wird ein human kartografischer Ansatz zur Analyse der Auswirkungen der Sparmaßnahmen und Wirtschaftskrise auf die Regionen Europas vorgestellt. Wir untersuchen frühere Erkenntnisse und Debatten über die Analyse und Kartierung von Armut und Reichtum sowie insbesondere von den Auswirkungen von Sparmaßnahmen. Anschließend stellen wir ein breites Spektrum von Kartogrammen zur Verdeutlichung der sozialen und räumlichen Ungleichheiten in Europa vor. Abschließend verdeutlichen wir die zunehmend wichtige Rolle des Gebiets der Regionalstudien in den aktuellen Debatten über die Zukunft des europäischen Projekts und über die Möglichkeit eines Europas der Regionen statt der Nationalstaaten.

RESUMEN

Análisis de la geografía regional de la pobreza, la austeridad y las desigualdades en Europa: una perspectiva cartográfica humana. *Regional Studies*. En este artículo presentamos un enfoque cartográfico humano para analizar el impacto de la austeridad y la crisis económica en todas las regiones europeas. Examinamos perspectivas y debates anteriores sobre el análisis y la cartografía de la pobreza y riqueza, y especialmente los efectos de la austeridad. Luego presentamos una amplia gama de cartogramas en los que se destacan las desigualdades sociales y espaciales en Europa. Para terminar, ponemos de relieve el creciente papel importante del campo de los estudios regionales en los debates actuales sobre el futuro del proyecto europeo y la posibilidad de una Europa de las regiones más que una Europa de los Estados nacionales.

INTRODUCTION

Europe is currently suffering a deep political and economic crisis following years of turmoil and austerity measures that have disproportionately and brutally hit the most disadvantaged regions and citizens across most of the continent. At the same time, there has been a revival of nationalisms and divisions in this part of the world that, a decade ago, seemed to be united in diversity and moving towards ever-closer union. Concentrated poverty near to riches and profound spatial inequality have long been persistent features of all European countries, with disparities often being most stark within the most affluent cities and regions, such as London. In other parts of Europe levels of inequality and poverty have been reducing and are often much lower. However, the severe economic crisis and austerity measures have led, in many cases, to an enhancement of existing disparities.

There is a long and successful history of theoretical and empirical work in the field of regional studies aimed at analysing social and spatial disparities in Europe. This paper aims to build on this work and to offer new insights into the analysis of austerity in Europe with the use of innovative geovisualizations that can be used to present more information in more useful ways than has been possible before and which enhance more subtle understanding of key issues. The work presented here draws on and builds on recent and ongoing relevant work (Ballas, Dorling, & Hennig, 2014, 2017; Hennig, Ballas, & Dorling, 2015), which considers and visualizes Europe and its economy, culture, history and human and physical geography in terms of a single large land mass. In particular, this paper uses images created for a social atlas of Europe using state-of-the-art geographical information systems (GIS) and new cartography techniques in order to offer an alternative way of visualizing the continent and its people in a more fluid way, in many cases plotting aspects of the lives of Europeans without imposing artificial national boundaries on those patterns.

This paper uses a human cartographic approach to illustrate the impact of austerity and the economic crisis across Europe's regions, highlighting particular areas and types of regions. First, it reflects on past insights and debates on the analysis and mapping of poverty and wealth and of recent austerities in particular. It then presents and discusses examples of human cartograms highlighting social and spatial inequalities and also illustrating that the real social divides within Europe are more often within states rather than between them. Finally, it highlights the increasingly important role of geographers and of the field of regional studies in the debates about the future of the European project. The paper is accompanied by Appendix A in the supplemental data online which has additional maps that could not be included in this paper.

REGIONAL STUDIES OF POVERTY AND WEALTH

There is a long tradition of regional studies of poverty and wealth and of uneven development between cities and regions at various levels and in different contexts. These studies can be distinguished between efforts to provide an evidence base and highlight spatial disparities in income and wealth as well as studies that focus on geographical divisions of labour and capital, and studies that attempt to theorize, analyse and understand the mechanisms that lead to social and spatial inequalities. Such inequalities can be viewed either as a process or as an outcome of a process. As Doreen Massey put it in her seminal paper 'In what sense a regional problem?' (published in this journal when the current authors were all children):

> The word [inequality] tends to get used indiscriminately in the literature in two rather different ways. First, there is inequality in the degree of

attractiveness of a particular area to the dominant form of economic activity; secondly, there is inequality in terms of various indicators of social well-being (rate of unemployment, per capita income, degree of external control of production, for example). The two are evidently not necessarily the same. In a crude sense, one is a cause and the other an effect.

(Massey, 1979, p. 234)

Examples of studies that explore causes and mechanisms include the above work (and much follow up work, such as Massey, 1995), as well as the seminal work of Gunnar Myrdal on cumulative causation (Myrdal, 1957). There has been further and significant progress to that direction over the years (e.g., Amin & Thrift, 1992; Dicken, 2015; Dorling, 2015; Fujita, Venables, & Krugman, 1999; Harvey, 2011; Hudson, 2007; Krugman, 1991; Martin, 2011; McCann & Sheppard, 2003; Peck, 1996; Pike, Rodrigues-Pose, & Tomaney, 2007). There has also been a considerable amount of relevant work focusing on the current post-2007 crisis (Hadjimichalis, 2011; Hadjimichalis & Hudson, 2014; Martin, 2011; Rae, 2011; Smith, 2013).

For instance, Hadjimichalis (2011) highlighted the significant role and contribution of what he describes as neoliberal urban and regional development discourses in the context of the economic and financial crisis in Europe to the downplaying of socio-spatial justice issues. Rae (2011) focused on the impact of the crisis upon the Central and Eastern European countries that became part of the European Union (EU) as part of its 2004 and 2007 enlargement and argued that their peripheral status within the EU made them vulnerable to the financial crisis and helped to further enhance the historical East–West divide in Europe. However, he also pointed out that the EU membership status of these countries resulted in them benefiting from the introduction of counter-measures that have partly offset these disparities. Another example of a relevant study is the work of Smith (2013), who highlighted the geopolitical and geoeconomic manifestations of the crisis across Europe's interdependent regions and beyond.

It is interesting to note that one of the key arguments made in relation to the causes and impacts of the crisis is that the creation of the euro was not based on criteria that are thought to be prerequisites for a successful monetary union, which include 'a degree of economic and productive similarity' between countries and regions, 'high rates of geographical mobility, not only for capital but also for labour', 'similar propensities to inflation' and an automatic fiscal mechanism that through a centrally organized tax and benefit system compensates for different national and regional shocks and growth rates (Hadjimihalis & Hudson, 2014, p. 211; Martin, 2001). Also of relevance here is the work of Midelfart, Overman, and Venables (2003) who considered the degree to which the economic geography of Europe may matter for the success of the euro as well as the possible impacts of the adoption of the euro upon the economic geography of the continent, including how it may affect the location of different economic activities, social and spatial inequalities and population mobility.

It is also important to recognize the long tradition of regional studies of poverty and wealth aimed at measurement and analysis of key indicators. Amongst the key proponents of such work was Peter Townsend, whose seminal book entitled *Poverty in the United Kingdom* (1979) provided a theoretical and conceptual basis for the estimation and mapping of deprivation, poverty and social exclusion and for subsequent relevant studies (e.g., Carstairs, 1995; Smith et al., 2015; Townsend, 1987), including extensions that aimed at measuring both poverty and wealth (Dorling et al., 2007). There has also been considerable work aimed at providing estimates of income, wealth and other related socio-economic indicators at regional and local levels using a wide range of methods including statistical approaches (Bramley & Smart, 1996; Hamnett, 1997) and labour market accounts (Bailey & Turok, 2000). There are also many examples of regional studies that present and use evidence to map and analyse the impact of the current post-2007 crisis (e.g., Kitson, Martin, & Tyler, 2011).

Another important aspect that relates to the second type of studies described above is that of mapping and visualization. Again, there has been considerable progress in the development of mapping methods for the visualization of social structure and social and spatial inequalities across cities and regions (e.g., Dorling, 1995; Dorling & Thomas, 2016; Hennig & Calzada, 2015).

However, despite some exceptions, most of the regional studies of poverty and wealth tend to focus on geographical data and patterns within countries and regions rather than exploring potential interregional linkages and patterns between regions from different countries. Amongst the notable exceptions has been the work of organizations such as the European Commission (2015) that aimed at systematically considering all regions of the EU in one set of analysis and mapping (also see Annoni & Dijkstra, 2013). The remainder of this paper builds on this work by using new geovisualization methods to highlight regional disparities in Europe, while at the same time engaging with issues raised in relevant theoretical and empirical studies such as those briefly reviewed above.

A HUMAN CARTOGRAPHIC APPROACH TO MAPPING A EUROPE OF REGIONS

we must *re-create the European family in a regional structure*, called, it may be, the United States of Europe
> (Winston Churchill, speech given at The Churchill Society,
> Zurich, Switzerland, 19 September 1946; added emphasis)

It may sound inconceivable today (and especially given the 2016 UK referendum result on the membership of the EU) that a statement such as the above could be made by a British prime minister and even more so by the leader of the Conservative Party. Yet, this is an extract from a speech delivered by Churchill calling for a more united Europe. The idea of a Europe of Regions and of a European People instead of a Europe of nation-states has long been at the heart of the thinking and efforts that have gradually led to the creation of the EU. Nevertheless, the recent ascendancy of extremist and populist groups (e.g., see Doxiadis & Matsaganis,

2012; Fieschi, 2016; Zonderop, 2012) has contributed to a painting of a picture of Europe where Euroscepticism is becoming a dominant trend and where the revival of old nationalisms and divisions is, apparently, inevitable. The 2016 Brexit referendum result in the UK further enhances this picture and adds strength to such a view. In addition, the nationalist populist trends seem to be more dominant in countries that were most badly hit by the 2008 financial crisis and austerity measures and especially where the political scapegoating of the EU has been most prevalent (Halikiopoulou & Vasilopoulou, 2014) and where the social safety net protecting the most vulnerable is weakest (Halikiopoulou & Vlandas, 2016).

Growing social divisions following austerity is also the case in Britain, where the massive austerity measures imposed by domestic political parties since 2010 had a devastating impact upon the most disadvantaged people and regions,[1] while at the same time there have been attempts to put the blame on immigration rather than the systematic underfunding of public services and the increasing tolerance of unaffordable housing and poverty (Dorling, 2016). However, despite this climate, there is still evidence of widespread expressions of feelings of solidarity and common European transnational belonging across the continent (Friedman & Thiel, 2016), including from within the UK and even after the Brexit referendum result there have been reports for a surge of support for the EU in big European countries (Rose, 2016) as well as many very recent manifestations of support for the EU within Britain such as the *#marchforeurope* events in September 2016 (Stone, 2016).

This paper engages with the idea of a Europe of Regions from a human cartographic and human geography perspective, with a focus on regional inequalities in poverty and wealth. The work presented here has many antecedents, but draws especially on an ongoing mapping project of European countries, cities and regions (Ballas et al., 2014, 2017) which aims to highlight the notion of Europe as a single entity by looking at its physical and population geography simultaneously in new ways, using up-to-date statistics, state of the art GIS and novel human cartography techniques.

People are used to conventional maps of their regions and countries. Conventional maps appear on television and especially in weather reports showing geographical regions as they appear from space. However, looking at a city, region or country from space is not the best way to see its human geography. Often details within urban areas with large populations (but small area size) are virtually invisible to the viewer. It has long been argued, admittedly initially by a relatively small group of scholars, that there is a need for human-scaled visualizations to address these issues (Dorling, 2007; Dorling & Fairbairn, 1997; Dorling & Thomas, 2004; Ballas & Dorling, 2011; Hennig, 2013).

The mapping approach adopted here involves the redrawing of geographical regions on the basis that the area of each should be proportional to the number of people who live in each small neighbourhood, rather than land mass. Such maps are known as cartograms (Tobler, 2004) and it can be argued that they are also part of recent trends in geography that see a revival and further advancement of spatial analysis and visualization techniques in the set of methods used in the discipline (Turner, 2006). This kind of visualization differs from traditional maps and rebalances the emphasis on treating all experiences as equally important, rather than greatly highlighting what occurs in the most sparsely populated rural regions (Rittschof, Stock, Kulhavy, Verdi, & Johnson, 1996). In particular, the cartographic technique used here applies the density-equalizing approach proposed by two physicists, Michael Gastner and Mark Newman. Using the diffusion of gas analogy in physics, these two physicists developed a cartogram approach that moved the borders of territories with the 'flow' of people, until density is equal everywhere (Gastner & Newman, 2004).

The population cartogram technique is a more appropriate way to visualize geographical data in the social sciences if you are interested in mapping people rather than land, especially if you do not wish to concentrate on over-emphasizing empty land in the map image. What the technique does is to iteratively alter the original map so that areas of high density expand and areas of low density shrink in such a way that eventually all areas are of, say, equal population density. This method has been used extensively for the mapping of countries using state-level data (Dorling, 2006; Dorling, Newman, & Barford, 2008), but as yet there are relatively limited applications for mapping at regional and sub-regional levels.

The maps presented in this paper are created with a method that takes the approach outlined above a step further and is more suitable for the mapping of cities and regions across an entire continent. In particular, the maps were created using the gridded-population cartogram approach (Hennig, 2013). Its creation builds on the same density-equalizing approach described above, but it is implemented in order to create a gridded-population cartogram, meaning that the underlying projection onto which the map has been transformed is one where people are equally distributed on a grid stretched so that each grid cell has an area proportional to the population within that cell. In particular, this involves dividing the whole territory to be mapped into a grid of cells of equal size and estimating the population distribution accordingly. The next step is to apply the density equalizing method to resize each cell proportionally to the number of people living within it. This process results in a contiguous gridded-population cartogram, meaning that each new grid cell has an area proportional to the number of people that live there, but still touches only its original eight neighbouring cells. The edges of each cell become curved lines. The size of each of the grid cells therefore reflects the number of people living in this area; the projection means that the base map itself reflects the real population distribution on a coherent geographical reference (and not the population based on artificial administrative units like nation states). Figure 1 illustrates how the method works with a hypothetical example of four areas (Hennig, 2013). The sizes of the areas (and borders) are changed until the space between the people in each area is the same everywhere (and therefore the population density in all areas is the same). The cartogram is created by 'diffusing' the people resulting in a final visualization with an even spatial spread of population. As people diffuse, borders are moved with them until all spatial units have equal population density.

As noted above, the approach adopted here aims to highlight the notion of Europe as a single entity by looking at its physical and population geography

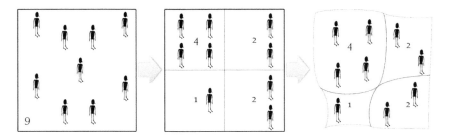

Figure 1 Illustration of applying the Gastner and Newman diffusion-based method for creating gridded population cartograms.

Source: After Hennig (2013).

simultaneously in new ways. To that end, the authors have included all states that (at the time of creating the cartograms presented in this paper) have demonstrated a commitment to a common European future by being closely associated with the EU, either as current members or as official candidate states (or official potential candidates for EU accession) and/or states which are signed up to any of the following agreements: European Economic Area, the Schengen Zone, the European Monetary Union. Figure 2 shows a gridded population cartogram of these European countries using a rainbow colour scheme denoting the year of association with the EU and also signposting some of the major city-regions (with the capital cities underlined).

Figure 2 has been produced as the result of the application of the method described in Figure 1 in order to redraw the spatial extent of each geographical area on the basis of fine-level spatial information about where people live rather land mass. The map highlights clearly where most people are concentrated – in many cases in cities, but also giving the more rural populations especially in Eastern Europe a fair representation. For instance, Madrid, Paris, Istanbul and London are huge, while the whole of Scandinavia is small. Countries and regions that are more densely populated (e.g., most of the UK, Italy, Poland and Romania) are more visible on the map whereas the large rural areas in the north of Europe appear considerably smaller. The Rhine-Ruhr metropolitan region in Western Europe, including stretching from Cologne in the west to Dortmund as its eastern edge and other urban areas that appear to be expanding towards the Netherlands, is much more prominent on this projection than it is on a conventional map.

These cartograms differ from conventional approaches to mapping socio-economic data, such as those approaches that use choropleth maps of population data which typically shade regions with boundaries defined on the basis of their area size in proportion to the measurement of a variable of interest and which make concentrations appear where they are not and tend to dissolve existing patterns. In contrast, the human cartographic approach adopted in this paper addresses such issues much more effectively and it is particularly suitable for the analysis of social and spatial inequalities as it places the focus on where most

Year of joining the EU or implementing Schengen (if not an EU member state)

1952
1973
1981
1986
1995
2001
2004
2007
2008
2011

Acceding country
Candidate countries
Potential candidates

Figure 2 Gridded-population cartogram of Europe.

people are, and then on how they most differ from each other, offering new insights into the geographical manifestations of poverty and wealth.

MAPPING AND ANALYSING REGIONAL GEOGRAPHIES OF POVERTY, AUSTERITY AND INEQUALITY IN EUROPE

This section adopts the regional geovisualization approach described above to highlight the geographical dimension of social inequalities, poverty and wealth in Europe. It first considers inequality as the degree of attractiveness of a particular area to the dominant form of economic activity, following Massey's (1979) definition, discussed above. In particular, it uses the traditional measure of gross domestic product (GDP). The authors use the latest data from EUROSTAT on GDP by NUTS-2 region,[2] with each area being compared with the EU average in order to paint the current picture of the geography of wealth and purchasing power in Europe. The map shown in Figure 3 is drawn with small areas resized in proportion of the population living within them (see Figure 2 for city labels). The total GDP per capita by region is then used to shade and classify areas. In this map it is becoming evident that some of the most affluent city-regions have more in common with other wealthy regions across Europe than the rest of the country within which these regions lie and this relates to the discussion of some of the conditions that are widely accepted as prerequisites for a successful monetary union.

The values mapped show GDP per capita in purchasing power standards (PPS) in relation to the EU average set to equal 100. If the index of a region is higher than 100 then this region's level of GDP per head is higher than the EU average and vice versa. The cartogram reveals an East–West divide (and to some extent a North–South divide) across Europe. But there are also considerable disparities within countries. It should be noted that if regional data for the Western Balkan countries and Turkey had been available, then the regions within them would almost certainly have also been at the bottom of the league the cartogram reveals. It is also interesting to note the disparity in the GDP of Madrid compared with most of the rest of Spain and that of Rome and Milan at the possible expense of Naples and much of the rest of Italy. Paris takes even more in comparison to almost all the rest of France. However, it is the city-region of London which has by far the highest GDP per capita (index 325 compared with EU-28 = 100), followed by the city-regions of Luxembourg (index of 257.7), Brussels (207.2), Hamburg (207.2) and Groningen (187.2). Looking at the least affluent areas in Europe, the city-region of Severozapanden in north-west Bulgaria is the poorest in Europe (with an index of 30.1) together with most other regions in the country as well as in neighbouring Romania but also in Hungary and Poland.

It is also interesting to consider these patterns in relation to the earlier discussion regarding the need to meet the criteria for a successful monetary union and the arguments that failure to do so has been a contributing factor to the 2008 crisis. For instance, London has much more in common with the other very affluent (in

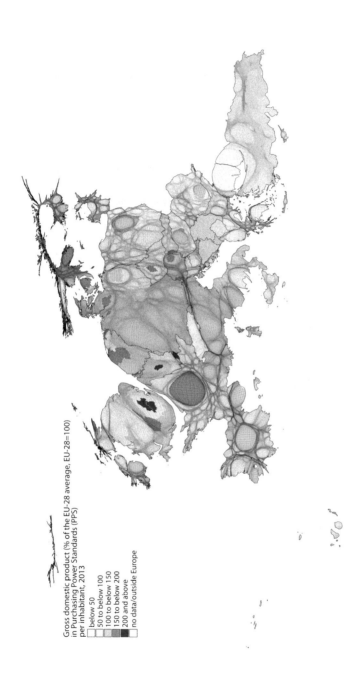

Gross domestic product (% of the EU-28 average, EU-28=100)
in Purchasing Power Standards (PPS)
per inhabitant, 2013

below 50
50 to below 100
100 to below 150
150 to below 200
200 and above
no data/outside Europe

Figure 3 Gross domestic product (percentage of the EU-28 average, EU-28 = 100) in purchasing power standards (PPS) per inhabitant, NUTS-2 regions, 2013.

Source: Data from EUROSTAT.

terms of GDP) regions highlighted above, at least from an economic and productive similarity point of view. In addition, there are high rates of geographical mobility to these regions (not just of capital but also labour). On the other hand, it is interesting to note that regions in northern England and Scotland are more similar in terms of GDP with regions elsewhere in Europe compared with regions within the British sterling monetary area they belong to in the South and South East England. The regions of South Yorkshire (index 75.9 compared with EU-28 = 100), Lincolnshire (index = 75.7) and Cornwall and the Isles of Scilly (70.3) are more similar to the Southern Aegean island region of Greece (index = 76.2), the Portuguese Madeiras islands (74.3) and the region of Lower Silesia (75.5) in south-west Poland, rather than the British south.

It should also be noted that some of the city-regions highlighted above are linked through extensive commuting networks to a larger hinterland and that the inhabitants of that hinterland contribute to the GDP produced within the cities but are usually not counted in indicators per head, such as the one mapped here. Therefore, some of these regions (and perhaps most notably London, Brussels and Hamburg) may emerge as having an exaggeratedly high GDP per inhabitant simply because so many of their workers reside outside their boundaries. In order to obtain a more accurate picture of the income and living conditions of the people actually residing within the regional borders it is more appropriate to draw on indicators pertaining to the second type of Massey's definition of inequality, that of social well-being. An example of such an indicator is shown in Figure 4, which depicts the regional distribution of Europeans who are in poverty or are considered to be at risk of poverty. These are persons who live in a household with an equivalized (to control for household size) disposable income below the risk-of-poverty threshold, set at 60% of the national median equivalized disposable income (after social transfers).

The cartogram shown in Figure 4 is drawn with small areas resized in proportion of the population living within them and then shaded to show the numbers of people across European regions who live on an income that is less than that of the 60% of the national median income. High rates of poverty have been a persistent stark feature of the most affluent cities within the most economically unequal regions of Europe. The most characteristic example is the city-region of London which has a very high poverty rate (32%) and at the same time, as seen in Figure 3, has by far the highest level of GDP per capita in Europe. Similarly, the city-region of Brussels which has the third highest GDP per capita in Europe also has a very high poverty rate (33.7%). Nevertheless, it is also interesting to note that other large European capitals such as Berlin, Paris, Madrid and Rome do not tolerate such extreme poverty. However, the severe economic crisis and austerity measures have led in many cases to an enhancement of poverty in Southern and Eastern Europe. There are 40 European regions that have extremely high poverty rates (of over 25% of their populations being poor) and all these are shaded in deep blue, as well as Turkey, which is mapped as a single region here due to the lack of data for smaller areas within Turkey. These 40 regions are mostly in Southern and Eastern Europe and in particular in Bulgaria, Greece (all Greek

Figure 4 At risk of poverty, NUTS-2 regions, 2014.
Source: Data from EUROSTAT.

regions except the capital city-region of Athens), Southern Italy and Spain (including the Canary Islands).

Figure A1 in the supplemental data online shows the regional distribution of another relevant variable: the average annual net household disposable income (for a detailed definition, see in the supplemental data online). Most of the regions with very high average household income are found in Germany, especially in the west of Germany, and in France, Austria, northern Italy and a small slither of the south of England and now the very centre of London. On the other hand, the regions in the lowest household income category are all in Eastern Europe and in particular in Bulgaria, Czechia, Estonia, Hungary, Latvia, Poland, Romania and Slovakia. It should be noted that, as it was the case with the regional maps of GDP, there were no data for regions of Turkey and Western Balkan countries that have some of the poorest regions in Europe. It is even more important to note that these are arithmetic mean averages. Most households will be living on less than these amounts in all regions (as shown in the following maps) and very many where income inequalities are the highest in Europe, such as in Southern England. Most people are not well off in richer regions.

Amongst the key determinants of poverty are low pay, social exclusion and unemployment. Following the economic crisis of 2008, some countries and regions of Europe have been sinking into a protracted period of mass unemployment reminiscent of the pre-Second World War. The unemployment rate in the EU rose from 7% in 2008 to 11% in 2013, by when there was an estimated total of 32 million unemployed people. Of these, an estimated 7 million were aged

15–24. The overall youth unemployment rate in the entire EU by 2013 was 25.8% with very little signs of this improving recently. However, there are huge variations between countries and regions as well as within regions and cities, with the highest unemployment rates mostly found in austerity-stricken Greece, Italy and Spain. The next two cartograms give an impression of these geographical disparities in work and in having no work, showing how much a few areas have suffered while others have seen very little rise in unemployment at all since 2008.

Figure 5 depicts the geographical distribution of unemployment rates for the most recent year for which data were available at regional level. The highest unemployment rates are mostly found in the austerity-stricken regions of Greece, Italy and Spain. The Spanish region of Andalusia has the highest unemployment rate in Europe (34.8%). In addition, there were a total of 30 regions with unemployment rates of over 20%. These include all of the 13 Greek regions as well as 13 regions in Spain and four in Italy. In contrast, the lowest observed regional unemployment rate in Europe in 2014 was 2.5% and is observed in two regions: the capital city-region of Prague in Czechia and the German region of Upper Bavaria (which includes the city of Munich).

Overall, the regions with very low unemployment rates in that year (less than 5%) were mostly found in Central and Northern Europe and in particular, Germany, Austria, Switzerland, the Scandinavian countries, but also in Romania and the UK. It is also worth noting that unemployment is now often highest in areas where more women have moved away compared with the number of men who have emigrated from those areas. The patterns in Figure 5 also suggest that unemployment rates are lower in major cities than in the areas around them, as people are drawn into the cities for work and cannot afford to live there if they do not have work in most, but not all, cases. Rates are also a little higher in places where benefits are less punitive and where sanctions are not applied to force people to take work they would rather not do because it is often dangerous, dirty, undignified and very lowly paid.

The next cartogram considers change in unemployment rates during a period of severe recession and austerity affecting many parts of Europe. The cartogram shown in Figure 6 shows the geographical distribution of changes in unemployment rates across European regions between 2008–14. The regions with the highest increases (over 10%) are all in the south of Europe, in countries very badly hit by the economic crisis. In particular, these regions include most of Spain, all of Greece and Cyprus, the region of Calabria in Southern Italy and the Portuguese island region of the Azores. On the other hand, there have been 83 regions across Europe where the unemployment rate in 2014 was lower than that of 2008. Most of these regions are in Germany and Turkey, but also in Eastern Europe and the UK. Nevertheless, as noted above, unemployment rates fell in many parts of the UK because in recent years up to a million people a year have been 'sanctioned' if they do not take any job and so many take what are called zero-hours jobs (which can involve no work in particular weeks) or pretend they are self-employed while receiving handouts from relatives.

Figures A2 and A3 in the supplemental data online show snapshots of changes related to the earlier stages of crisis and austerity. In particular, they show how

Figure 5 Unemployment rate by NUTS-2 region, 2014.
Source: Data from EUROSTAT.

Figure 6 Unemployment rates by NUTS-2 region: change between 2008 and 2014.
Source: Data from EUROSTAT.

the changes in household incomes and the GDP index respectively, following the beginning of the financial crisis and recession in Europe in 2007–08 through to 2011 which was the most recent consistent regional data at the time of writing this article. The largest falls in household disposable income (Figure A2) are seen in Greece. The highest decline in income recorded across the whole of Europe during these four years was in the Athens capital city-region of Attiki. However very considerable falls in average income were also experienced in some regions of Italy, Spain and the UK (including London where bankers' bonuses were cut for a few years). Conversely, most of the regions where average household incomes increased are generally found in Central and Eastern Europe and this picture may be consistent, to some extent, with the conclusions of Rae (2011) that were briefly discussed above. The map of regional GDP (Figure A3) change also reveals similar patterns, showing that a very large number of the regions experiencing a decrease in GDP per inhabitant were in the south of Europe, but they can also be seen in the periphery of some central and northern European countries. In great contrast to those areas, there were 22 regions experiencing an increase of more than 2% in their GDP per capita. Of these, 13 are in Poland, seven in Germany (mostly in the east) and the remaining two are the French island region of Corsica and the Slovakian capital city-region of Bratislava.

It is also worth noting that many of the regions that are most heavily affected by the recent recession and austerity also have the highest rates of highly qualified human resources and University graduates (especially in Greece and Spain; see Figure A4 in the supplemental data online). Furthermore it is also worth noting that the highly qualified professionals in the regions hit the hardest by the recession and massive government cuts have been migrating over the past five years to areas with lower unemployment (Barnato, 2012), mostly into the north and into countries like Germany. It can be argued that such movements of population help some regions and countries to overcome their skill shortages. These developments are also very relevant to the 'successful monetary union' prerequisite of 'high rates of geographical mobility, not only for capital but also for labour' that was briefly discussed above.

However, recent population movements can also be seen as a brain-drain for the originating regions (Anastasiadou, 2016; Labrianidis & Vogiatzis, 2013) with further negative economic and social implications. In any case, it is very important to point out that the cost of educating highly qualified professionals was typically not covered by the receiving country, but rather by the taxpayers of those sending countries, like Greece, Italy, Spain and Portugal, which made huge investments in their higher education systems in past decades. The same argument can also be made over the initial costs of education of many of the migrants from Syria that have arrived in such large numbers in Europe in recent years (Ballas, 2016). In particular, the investments in higher education made by these countries in the past decades (and which have contributed to their high overall levels of government debt) are now benefiting the EU as a whole via the migration of highly skilled groups of individuals (Ballas, 2014).

CONCLUSIONS AND DIRECTIONS FOR FURTHER RESEARCH

This paper has offered a human cartographic approach to conceptualizing Europe as one place and of mapping its regional geography to that end, with a particular focus on themes that are timely and relevant to current debates about the need for pan-European solidarity as a prerequisite for pan-European policy responses to offset and reverse the impact of austerity in regions that suffered the most.

The maps presented here highlight very important and sometimes extreme social and spatial disparities, including revealing many economic inequalities that call strongly for socially and environmentally sustainable action. They also reveal that the real differences in the quality of life and the types of challenges and problems faced by Europe's populations are not found across national borders but between regions within countries, between villages and cities or between rich and poor quarters of a town. And the rich quarters of Europe are all more similar to each other than to the poorer areas that are nearer to them.

There have been considerable efforts expended over the past couple of decades aimed at putting in place and implementing cohesion policies at the European level and at correcting imbalances and ameliorating geographical inequalities. Examples of such policies include the European Social Fund, the European Regional Development Fund and the Cohesion Fund. The more recent initiative is the European Commission 'Investment Plan for Europe' aimed at mobilizing investment of at least €315 billion and kick-starting the real economy (European Commission, 2016) and which has been described as a new Marshall plan for the EU (Bell, 2015). The human cartographic approach presented in this paper can be used to offer insights into which regions are most in need for different types of economic support and which areas are more likely to benefit from such initiatives, providing the basis for further analysis.

Overall, the themes mapped and discussed in this paper can be used to inform debates about the role that geographers and regional studies researchers can play in contributing to and informing as well as shaping debates about the possible revival of the idea of full employment, better employment and social progress as a key European goal, freedom and ideal. There is a need, apart from the political and economic argument, to enhance the feelings of social cohesion and solidarity amongst the people of Europe if political progress is to be made. The work presented in this paper could be used to achieve this by highlighting important disparities and inequalities and, at the same time, reminding Europeans how much they have in common, how they live in one continent with great similarities across its space, and the potential for what can be achieved if there is a move away from a 'nation state mentality', thinking instead about Europe as a continent of cities and regions rather than states.

ACKNOWLEDGEMENTS

The authors are grateful to the editor and three anonymous referees for their very constructive comments.

DISCLOSURE STATEMENT

No potential conflict of interest was reported by the authors.

TRANSITIONS IN REGIONAL ECONOMIC DEVELOPMENT

SUPPLEMENTAL DATA

Supplemental data for this article can be accessed at http://dx.doi.org/10.1080/00343404.2016.1262019

NOTES

1. Movingly illustrated in the film *I, Daniel Blake*, winner of the Cannes Palme d'Or 2016 top filmmaking prize.
2. NUTS – omenclature of Territorial Units for Statistics; see http://ec.europa.eu/eurostat/web/nuts/overview/.

REFERENCES

Anastasiadou, S. (2016). Economic crisis in Greece and the consequential 'brain drain'. In A. Karasavvoglou, Z. Aranđelović, S. Marinković, & P. Polychronidou (Eds.), *The first decade of living with the global crisis* (pp. 113–120). Cham: Springer.

Annoni, P., & Dijkstra, L. (2013). *EU regional competitiveness index 2013* (European Commission EUR 26060). Luxembourg: Publication Office of the European Union. Retrieved May 17, 2016, from http://ec.europa.eu/regional_policy/sources/docgener/studies/pdf/6th_report/rci_2013_report_final.pdf

Amin, A., & Thrift, N. (1992). Neo-Marshallian nodes in global networks. *International Journal of Urban and Regional Research, 16*, 571–587.

Bailey, N., & Turok, I. (2000). Adjustment to job loss in Britain's major cities. *Regional Studies, 34*, 631–653. doi:10.1080/00343400050178438

Ballas, D. (2014). The political economy of 'a country called Europe'. *speri.comment: The political economy blog*. Retrieved from http://speri.dept.shef.ac.uk/2014/11/27/political-economy-a-countrycalled-europe/

Ballas, D. (2016). A letter from Lesvos. *speri.comment: The political economy blog*. Retrieved from http://speri.dept.shef.ac.uk/2016/01/06/a-letter-from-lesvos/

Ballas, D., & Dorling, D. (2011). Human scaled visualisations and society. In T. Nyerges, H. Couclelis, & R. McMaster (Eds.), *Handbook of GIS & society research* (pp. 177–201). London: Sage.

Ballas, D., Dorling, D., & Hennig, B. (2014). *The social atlas of Europe*. Bristol: Policy Press.

Ballas, D., Dorling, D., & Hennig, B. (2017). *The human atlas of Europe: A continent united in diversity*. Bristol: Policy Press.

Barnato, K. (2012). Emigrating Greeks prove the EU is working. *CNBC*, June 18. Retrieved from http://www.cnbc.com/id/47828618

Bell, C. (2015). The European investment plan – A new Marshall plan for the EU? *Parliament Magazine*. Retrieved from https://www.theparliamentmagazine.eu/articles/special-report/european-investment-plan-new-marshall-plan-eu

Bramley, G., & Smart, G. (1996). Modelling local income distributions in Britain. *Regional Studies, 30*(3), 239–255. doi:10. 1080/00343409612331349608

Carstairs, V. (1995). Deprivation indices: Their interpretation and use in relation to health. *Journal of Epidemiology and Community Health, 49*, S3–S8. doi:10.1136/jech.49.Suppl_2.S3

Dicken, P. (2015). *Global shift: Mapping the changing contours of the world economy.* London: Sage.

Dorling, D. (1995). *A new social atlas of Britain.* Chichester: Wiley.

Dorling, D. (2006). New maps of the world, its people and their lives. *Society of Cartographers Bulletin, 39*(1–2), 35–40.

Dorling, D. (2007). Worldmapper: The human anatomy of a small planet. *PLoS Medicine, 4*(1), 13–18.

Dorling, D. (2015). *Injustice: Why social inequality still persists.* Bristol: Policy Press.

Dorling, D. (2016). Brexit: The decision of a divided country. *British Medical Journal, 354, i369.* Retrieved from http://www.bmj.com/content/354/bmj.i3697/.

Dorling, D., & Fairbairn, D. (1997). *Mapping: Ways of representing the world.* Harlow: Longman.

Dorling, D., Newman, M., & Barford, A. (2008). *The atlas of the real world.* London: Thames & Hudson.

Dorling, D., Rigby, J., Wheeler, B., Ballas, D., Thomas, B., Fahmy, E., Gordon, D., & Lupton, R. (2007). *Poverty, wealth and place in Britain, 1968 to 2005.* Bristol: Policy Press.

Dorling, D., & Thomas, B. (2004). *People and places: A census atlas of the UK.* Bristol: Policy Press.

Dorling, D., & Thomas, B. (2016). *People and places: A 21st century atlas of the UK.* Bristol: Policy Press.

Doxiadis, A., & Matsaganis, M. (2012). *National populism and Xenophobia in Greece.* Counterpoint UK, Creative Commons. Retrieved October 28, 2016, from http://counterpoint.uk.com/wp-content/uploads/2013/01/507_CP_RRadical_Greece_web-1.pdf

European Commission. (2015). *EUROSTAT regional yearbook 2015. EUROSTAT statistical books.* Luxemburg: Publication Office of the European Union. Retrieved May 17, 2016, from http://ec.europa.eu/eurostat/documents/3217494/7018888/KS-HA-15-001-EN-N.pdf

European Commission. (2016). *Investment plan for Europe.* Retrieved from http://ec.europa.eu/priorities/jobs-growth-and-investment/investment-plan_en

Fieschi, C. (2016). Populism and the sad revolution of ordinariness. *Counterpoint UK.* Retrieved October 28, 2016, from: http://counterpoint.uk.com/publications/populism-and-the-sad-revolution-of-ordinariness/.

Friedman, R., & Thiel, M. (Eds.). (2016). *European identity and culture: Narratives of transnational belonging.* Abingdon: Routledge.

Fujita, M., Venables, A. J., & Krugman, P. (1999). *The spatial economy: Cities, regions, and international trade.* Cambridge, MA: MIT Press.

Gastner, M. T., & Newman, M. E. J. (2004). From the cover: Diffusion-based method for producing density-equalizing maps. *Proceedings of the National Academy of Sciences, USA, 101,* 7499–7504. doi:10.1073/pnas.0400280101

Hadjimichalis, C. (2011). Uneven geographical development and socio-spatial justice and solidarity: European regions after the 2009 financial crisis. *European Urban and Regional Studies, 18*(3), 254–274. doi:10.1177/0969776411404873

Hadjimichalis, C., & Hudson, R. (2014). Contemporary crisis across Europe and the crisis of regional development theories. *Regional Studies, 48,* 208–218. doi:10.1080/00343404.2013.834044

Halikiopoulou, D., & Vasilopoulou, S. (2014). Scapegoating Europe? How discontent with domestic politics determined the EU vote. *Open Democracy.* Retrieved from https://www.opendemocracy.net/can-europe-make-it/daphne-halikiopoulou-sofia-vasilopoulou/scapegoating-europe-how-discontent-with-d

Halikiopoulou, D., & Vlandas, T. (2016). Risks, costs and labour markets: Explaining cross-national patterns of far right party success in European Parliament elections. *Journal of Common Market Studies*, *54*(3), 636–655. doi:10.1111/jcms.12310

Hamnett, C. (1997). A stroke of the Chancellor's pen: The social and regional impact of the Conservative's 1988 higher rate tax cuts. *Environment and Planning A*, *29*, 129–147. doi:10.1068/a290129

Harvey, D. (2011). Roepke Lecture in Economic Geography: Crises, geographic disruptions and the uneven development of political responses. *Economic Geography*, *87*(1), 1–22. doi:10.1111/j. 1944-8287.2010.01105.x

Hennig, B. (2013). *Rediscovering the world. Map transformations of human and physical space*. Heidelberg: Springer.

Hennig, B. D., Ballas, D., & Dorling, D. (2015). Europe's uneven development. *Political Insight*, *6*(3), 20–21. doi:10.1111/2041-9066.12109

Hennig, B. D., & Calzada, I. (2015). In focus: Regions between recentralisation and Independence. *Political Insight*, *6*(1), 20–21. doi:10.1111/2041-9066.12083

Hudson, R. (2007). Regions and regional uneven development forever? Some reflective comments upon theory and practice. *Regional Studies*, *41*(9), 1149–1160. doi:10.1080/00343400701291617

Kitson, M., Martin, R., & Tyler, P. (2011). The geographies of austerity. *Cambridge Journal of Regions, Economy and Society*, *4*, 289–302. doi:10.1093/cjres/rsr030

Krugman, P. (1991). *Geography and trade*. Cambridge, MA: MIT Press.

Labrianidis, L., & Vogiatzis, N. (2013). Highly skilled migration: What differentiates the 'brains' who are drained from those who return in the case of Greece? *Population, Space and Place*, *19*, 472–486. doi:10.1002/psp.1726

Martin, R. (2011). The local geographies of the financial crisis: From the housing bubble to economic recession and beyond. *Journal of Economic Geography*, *11*, 587–618. doi:10.1093/jeg/lbq024

Martin, R. (2001). EMU versus the regions? Regional convergence and divergence in Euroland. *Journal of Economic Geography*, *1*, 51–80. doi:10.1093/jeg/1.1.51

Massey, D. B. (1979). In what sense a regional problem? *Regional Studies*, *13*, 233–243. doi:10.1080/09595237900185191

Massey, D. (1995). *Spatial divisions of labour: Social structures and the geography of production* (2nd ed.). London: Macmillan.

McCann, P., & Sheppard, S. (2003). The rise, fall and rise again of industrial location theory. *Regional Studies*, *37*, 649–663. doi:10.1080/0034340032000108741

Midelfart, K. H., Overman, H., & Venables, A. (2003). Monetary union and the economic geography of Europe. *Journal of Common Market Studies*, *41*(5), 847–868. doi:10.1111/j.1468-5965.2003.00466.x

Myrdal, G. (1957). *Economic theory and under-developed regions*. London: Methuen.

Peck, J. (1996). *Work-place: The social regulation of labor markets*. New York: Guilford.

Pike, A., Rodrigues-Pose, A., & Tomaney, J. (2007). What kind of regional development and for whom? *Regional Studies*, *41*, 1253–1269. doi:10.1080/00343400701543355

Rae, G. (2011). On the periphery: the uneven development of the European Union and the effects of the economic crisis on Central–Eastern Europe. *Global Society*, *25*(2), 249–266. doi:10.1080/13600826.2010.548057

Rittschof, K. A., Stock, W. A., Kulhavy, R. W., Verdi, M. P., & Johnson, J. T. (1996). Learning from cartograms: The effects of region familiarity. *Journal of Geography*, *95*(2), 50–58. doi:10. 1080/00221349608978925

Rose, M. (2016, July 20). EU support surges in big European countries after Brexit vote. Reuters. Retrieved from http://uk.reuters.com/article/uk-britain-eu-poll-idUKKCN1002A0

Smith, A. (2013). Europe and an inter-dependent world: Uneven geo-economic and geo-political developments. *European Urban and Regional Studies, 20*(1), 3–13. doi:10.1177/0969776412463309

Smith, T., Noble, M., Noble, S., Wright, G., McLennan, D., & Plunkett, E. (2015). *The English indices of deprivation 2015: Research report.* London: Department for Communities and Local Government. Retrieved from https://www.gov.uk/government/publications/english-indices-of-deprivation-2015-research-report

Stone, J. (2016). March for Europe: Thousands take to streets in cities across Britain in support of EU membership. *The Independent, September 3.* Retrieved from http://www.independent.co.uk/news/uk/politics/march-for-europe-eu-protest-london-edinburgh-birmingham-oxford-cambridge-september-saturday-a7224186.html

The Churchill Society. (1946). Mr Winston Churchill speaking in Zurich 19 September 1946. Retrieved from http://www.churchill-society-london.org.uk/astonish.html

Townsend, P. (1979). *Poverty in the United Kingdom: A survey of household resources and standards of living.* London: Penguin/Allen Lane.

Townsend, P. (1987). Deprivation. *Journal of Social Policy, 16,* 125–46. doi:10.1017/S0047279400020341

Turner, A. J. (2006). *Introduction to neogeography.* Sebastopol: O'Reilly Media.

Tobler, W. R. (2004). Thirty-five years of computer cartograms. *Annals of the Association of American Geographers, 94*(1), 58–73. doi:10.1111/j.1467-8306.2004.09401004.x

Zonderop, Y. (2012). *The roots of contemporary populism in the Netherlands.* Counterpoint UK, Creative Commons. Retrieved October 28, 2016, from http://counterpoint.uk.com/wp-content/uploads/2013/01/507_CP_RRadical_Dutch English_web.pdf

Index

Entries in **bold** denote tables; entries in *italics* denote figures.

INDEX

Great Divergence 129, 134, 145
Great Recession 84, 91, 94–5
Greece: FDI in 188; impact of financial crisis on 198n10; *see also* Athens
green economy 10–11, 289–93, 295–7, 300–4; discourses of **292**
greenhouse gas emissions 289, 292
green-tech clusters 294, 296–7, 302
Green Tech Valley 295–6
green-washing 11
Gulliver, Stuart 216–18
GVA (gross value added) 88, 263–5, *266–7*, 272, 289
GVCs *see* global value chains

HDI (Human Development Index) 87–8
heterogeneity 107, 174, 195, 210, 220, 245
high-skilled migration: data on 245–6; impact on destination 233–8; impact on origins 238–42 (*see also* brain drain; remittances); literature on 230, 233; overall consequences of 244–7
historical development, stages theories of 126
Hong Kong: democracy movement in 118; HSBC headquarters in 215–16, 219; as national financial centre 209; Umbrella Revolution 118; urbanization in 133
housing prices 105, 315
HS1 line 265, *266*, 269, 280
HS2 network 261–2, 281
HSBC: boundary spanning activities of **215**, 216–20, *221*; headquarters location of 205–6, 214–15; organizations relating to 220
HSR (high-speed rail): beneficiaries of 9–10; in China 9, 144, 259, 269–79, *270–1*; economic impact of 262–4, 279–83; in Europe 260–1, 264–9 (*see also* HS1; HS2)
human capital: and agglomeration 90; attracting 8–9; and economic development 4, 245; innovation and entrepreneurship 158–9; and interregional migration 230, 236–7, 239–41, 243, 247, 248n3
human cartography approach 312, 314–15, 317, 325–6
human flourishing 88, 93
human geography 315
humanistic geography 39, 43
human migration *see* migration
hybridised goods and services 237
hysteresis 157

ICN (International Cleantech Network) 296–7, 300
ICT (information and communications technologies) 10, 69, 175
identity regionalism 18, 22
ILTRN (Intermediate and Long-Term Railway Network Plan) 269
incubation spaces 65
industrial clusters 94–5
industrial districts 91, 156
industrial divides *132*
industrial ecosystems 302
industrialization: geography of 125, 128–31, 136–7; state role in 143–4
Industrial Revolution 129, 134
industry life cycles 155, 157
inequality: 20th century trends in 146–7n1; and capitalism 125, 139–40; in Europe 311–12, 315, 319–22, 326; geography of *see* territorial inequality; use of term 312–13
informal institutions 6, 59
informational content, spatial dynamics of 207–14, 220–2
information exchange 3, 210, 218, 222
information processing 210–12, 223
information society 207
infrastructure: and regional development 9–10, 94; and urbanization 109; *see also* transport infrastructure
innovation: bricolage mode of 57–8, 61; broader view of 164; geography of 6–7, 91, 155–7, 165; global networks of *see* GINs; lifetime of 155; and migration 234, 247; MLP of 293–4; and niches 11, 65; normal and grand-challenges 73–4; radical 6, 156, 164
innovation processes: recombinative 195; resource-scarce 61; social-constructivist understanding of 63; spatial structure for 63–4
innovation systems: and spatial fetishism 44; technological 63
institutional entrepreneurship 58, 60, 62, 65, 70–3
institutionalization of regions 19, 40
institutional quality 6, 90
institutional turn 92, 97
institutional work 64, 68, 70, 72–3
institutions: and development 92–3, 97; local and regional *see* regional institutions
integrative regionalism 18–19, 22, 26
interdependence, global 174, 176, 196

335

interdependencies, untraded 20, 91
internationalization: bi-directional 179;
    propensity for 195; spatialization of 182
international migration 230–1, 238–42
international relations 16, 125–8
interregional migration: and brain drain
    240–1, 325; of highly-skilled individuals
    230, 232–4, 236 (*see also* brain drain;
    high-skilled migration); hubs for 238;
    and international migration 231; overall
    impact of 242–4
inventors, interregional mobility of 233, 236
investment: differentiated 137–8; global
    flows of 85, 174–82; state-directed 143;
    see also FDI
investment incentives, regional 94
IPEDS (Integrated Postsecondary
    Education Data System) 246
IPF (institutional possibilities frontier) *112,*
    113–5, *114*
Italy: northern separatism in 24; regional
    government in 28

Jacobs, Jane 6, 153, 159–61, 165
Japan: economic growth in 125, 131, 133, 139;
    HSR in 264; industrialization of 128–9,
    140–1, 143; influence on Asia of 142
justice: environmental 293, 300; social 89,
    282, 289, 294, 298; territorial 21

Kent, HSR in 259, 265–9, *266–8*, 280–1
Keynesianism, spatial 18, 93–4
keywords, spatial 37–8
knowledge: codifiable 155; and corporate
    dynamic capabilities 179; and
    innovation 195; non-excludable
    properties of 156–7; tacit 20, 207, 237;
    see also new knowledge
knowledge diffusion 145, 178, 195, 241
knowledge economy: and HSR 267, *268,*
    274, *275–6, 278,* 282; place in 159
knowledge hubs 3, 164
knowledge production 6–7, 178
knowledge sources, internal and external
    176–7, 180
knowledge spillovers: and agglomeration
    economies 89–90, 156–7, 161; and
    innovation 138; from MNEs 177–8
Kunshan 275, 278–9

labour force, regional 158
labour markets: and activation policies 22;
    regional differences in 89–90; regulation
    of 1; urban 106, 244

labour mobility 178, 234, 237, 239, 243–4;
    see also migration
labour productivity: in NEG 261; and
    U&CD 128, 135–9, 242
language acquisition 238
large firms: incumbent 70; and regionalism
    27
Latin America: democracy in 106, 117–18;
    sustainability in 293, 301, 303
lead firms 208
learning, networks of 206
learning regions 36, 208; and fetishism 44;
    institutions in 92
Lee Kwan Yew 113
Lega Nord (Northern League) 24
legitimacy: as resource 61, 64; of state
    intervention 25
LETS (local exchange trading scheme)
    298
Linz/Moreno Question 24
Little Divergence 129, 134, 145
local development *see* regional
    development
lock-in 57–8, 63, 74n1, 91–2, 157
London: GDP per capita 319, 321; HSBC
    offices in 205–6, 215–16, 219–20; as
    international financial centre 209; urban
    rail in 261–2
low-carbon economy 10, 289
LUTI (land-use transport interaction)
    263

Maguire, Andy 218
mapping methods 314–15; *see also*
    cartograms; human cartography
    approach
MAR (Marshall-Arrow-Romer theory)
    156–7
markets, institutional and cultural
    frameworks of 92–3
Marshall, Alfred 7, 20, 106, 156
Marx, Karl 152, 154
Marxism: and fetishism 42–3; and
    regionalism 39; *see also* Trotsky, Leon
mayors, strong 92
M-C-M' circuit 137, 139
mega-regions 36
meso-regions 17, 26
metageography 36
meta-routines 213
Miami 162
Midland Bank 216
migrants: assimilation of 238; creative
    163; integrating 3

For Product Safety Concerns and Information please contact
our EU representative GPSR@taylorandfrancis.com Taylor & Francis
Verlag GmbH, Kaufingerstraße 24, 80331 München, Germany